John H. Walsh

The Dogs Of The British Islands

being a series of articles on the points of their various breeds, and the treatment of

the diseases to which they are subject. Third Edition

John H. Walsh

The Dogs Of The British Islands
being a series of articles on the points of their various breeds, and the treatment of the diseases to which they are subject. Third Edition

ISBN/EAN: 9783337829551

Printed in Europe, USA, Canada, Australia, Japan

Cover: Foto ©Andreas Hilbeck / pixelio.de

More available books at **www.hansebooks.com**

THE

Dogs of the British Islands,

BEING

A SERIES OF ARTICLES

ON

THE POINTS OF THEIR VARIOUS BREEDS,

AND

THE TREATMENT OF THE DISEASES TO WHICH THEY ARE SUBJECT.

REPRINTED FROM "THE FIELD" NEWSPAPER.

By J. H. WALSH
("STONEHENGE").
Editor of "The Field"
(WITH THE AID OF SEVERAL EXPERIENCED BREEDERS).

THIRD EDITION.

LONDON
"THE FIELD" OFFICE, 346, STRAND, W.C.
1878.

LONDON :
PRINTED BY HORACE COX, 346, STRAND, W.C.

PREFACE TO THE THIRD EDITION.

WENTY YEARS have nearly elapsed since I first undertook for Messrs. Longman the task of revising the book on the natural history of the dog published by them for Mr. Youatt. As far as foreign varieties are concerned, that careful observer possessed very great advantages in having access to the collection of dogs which belonged to the Zoological Society soon after its institution, but which, owing to disease, was very soon abandoned. Our native breeds, however, were not so well described or illustrated by him, and his book did not meet the demands of the public, whose attention was just then (1859) specially drawn to them by the contemplated establishment of dog shows, which, in the same year, were instituted at Newcastle and Birmingham. By great good fortune I was enabled to obtain much reliable information upon most of our breeds; and many of the illustrations which were then given in the volume on "The Dog in Health and Disease" (notably Mr. Lukey's "Wallace," Mr. Stockdale's bulldog "Top," Mr. Morrison's pug and English terrier, Mr. Govan's Italian greyhound, Mr. George's Sussex spaniels, and the specimens of the Dandie Dinmont) are nearly, if not quite, equal in fidelity to those which Mr. Baker has recently drawn with so much accuracy and spirit. In spite, however, of all the efforts I could make, it was found impossible to settle many of the points in dispute, and the several descriptions given were too loose in detail to serve as guides to young breeders or incipient judges. For this reason I commenced, in 1865, a series of articles in the *Field*, beginning with that on the pointer, in which I made the attempt not only to describe in detail all his points, but to settle their numerical value, on the basis just laid down by the National Dog Club, by means of a committee instituted by myself, and embracing most of the prominent breeders and judges of the day. Having thus started the subject, motives of delicacy to the publishers of the above-named volume caused me to leave the continuance of the series chiefly to "Idstone" and one or two other well-known breeders, confining myself to the articles on the Skye and Dandie Dinmont terriers, the mastiff, and the greyhound. The publication of most of these articles in the *Field* led to a very interesting correspondence, by which the views of the various judges were elicited on disputed points; and thus it has come to pass that from the crude descriptions first published by me in 1859, and further improved on in 1865-6 under my supervision, we have now arrived at a definite agreement on all points.

This state of things almost necessitated the publication of a book on *The Dog* embodying these settled opinions, and the Messrs. Longman having set me at liberty by declining to do more than allow me to partially revise my early efforts made in 1859, I determined to throw all my energies into the task, with the aid of my numerous friends. Under these favourable conditions I have been enabled to publish article after article in the year just past, describing every point in detail, and giving its numerical value, without eliciting any objections, except on very minor points, and these from two or three gentlemen who fancy themselves so much that they cannot allow the slightest deviation from their *dicta*, and who may, on that account, be dismissed from all consideration. I may, therefore, practically allege that these articles have been published *nemine contradicente*, and I flatter myself that my labours in this direction are now over. I may here state, that when I have not been fully acquainted with any breed I have committed the task of describing it to others, and that Mr. Hugh Dalziel is entirely responsible for the Bedlington, Yorkshire, and English terriers; while to "Wildfowler" I am equally indebted for the description of the poodle, and to Mr. R. G. Ridgway for the Irish terrier. To Mr. J. C. Macdona, Mr. J. H. Murchison, Mr. W. Lort, Mr. Vero Shaw, Mr. W. W. Boulton, and Mr. W. Hickman, I have also to return my thanks for the assistance they have given me in describing the several breeds with which they are most familiar.

With regard to the specimens selected for illustration, they have chiefly been chosen from among the prize winners at our best shows. In some few instances I have not hesitated to depart from this rule, as in the case of

Mr. Macdona's Irish setter "Rover," Mr. Vero Shaw's bulldog "Smasher," Mr. Boulton's spaniel "Brush," Mrs. Skinner's colley "Vero," and Mr. Ray's bloodhound "Harold." In nearly every case, however, the subsequent success of my selections has given me a "bill of indemnity;" and I believe all the examples selected by me in the past year, as illustrations of the various breeds, have subsequently been prize winners, with the exception of Mr. Ray's dog, whose legs are too much deformed to permit any judge to give him a prize, *malgré* his magnificent head—in which he is unrivalled. To Mr. Baker, I think, are due the thanks of all lovers of the dog, for the care with which he has rendered every detail, while at the same time producing a pleasing drawing of the animal on which he has been engaged. As far as my knowledge goes, no such reliable animal portraits have hitherto appeared in this or any other country.

In conclusion I would remark, that it is only after a constant study, for nearly half a century, of the dog in all his varieties as met with in this country, and with unequalled opportunities for this task which have been afforded me as Editor of the *Field*, that I have ventured to define his points in the following pages with a dogmatic minuteness which nothing else would justify.

" STONEHENGE."

Putney, *March*, 1878.

TABLE OF CONTENTS.

PART I.
GENERAL MANAGEMENT.

BOOK I.
MANAGEMENT OF DOGS IN HEALTH.

BOOK II.
DRUGS COMMONLY USED FOR THE DISEASES OF DOGS, AND THEIR MODES OF ADMINISTRATION.

BOOK III.
THE ORDINARY DISEASES OF THE DOG AND THEIR TREATMENT.

BOOK IV.
JUDGING AT DOG SHOWS AND FIELD TRIALS.

PART III

NON-SPORTING DOGS.

BOOK I.

WATCH DOGS.

CHAPTER I.

CHAPTER II.

BOOK II.

SHEEP AND CATTLE DOGS.

CHAPTER I.

CHAPTER II.

BOOK III.

TERRIERS
(OTHER THAN FOX AND TOY).

CHAPTER I.

CHAPTER II.—SPECIAL BREEDS OF ROUGH TERRIERS.

CHAPTER III.—SMOOTH TERRIERS (OTHER THAN TOYS).

BOOK IV.

TOY DOGS.

CHAPTER I.—ROUGH-COATED TOY DOGS.

CHAPTER II.—SMOOTH TOY DOGS.

APPENDIX

LIST OF ILLUSTRATIONS.

—◦◦◦◦◦◦—

INDEX TO PART I.

THE DOGS

<small>OF THE</small>

BRITISH ISLANDS.

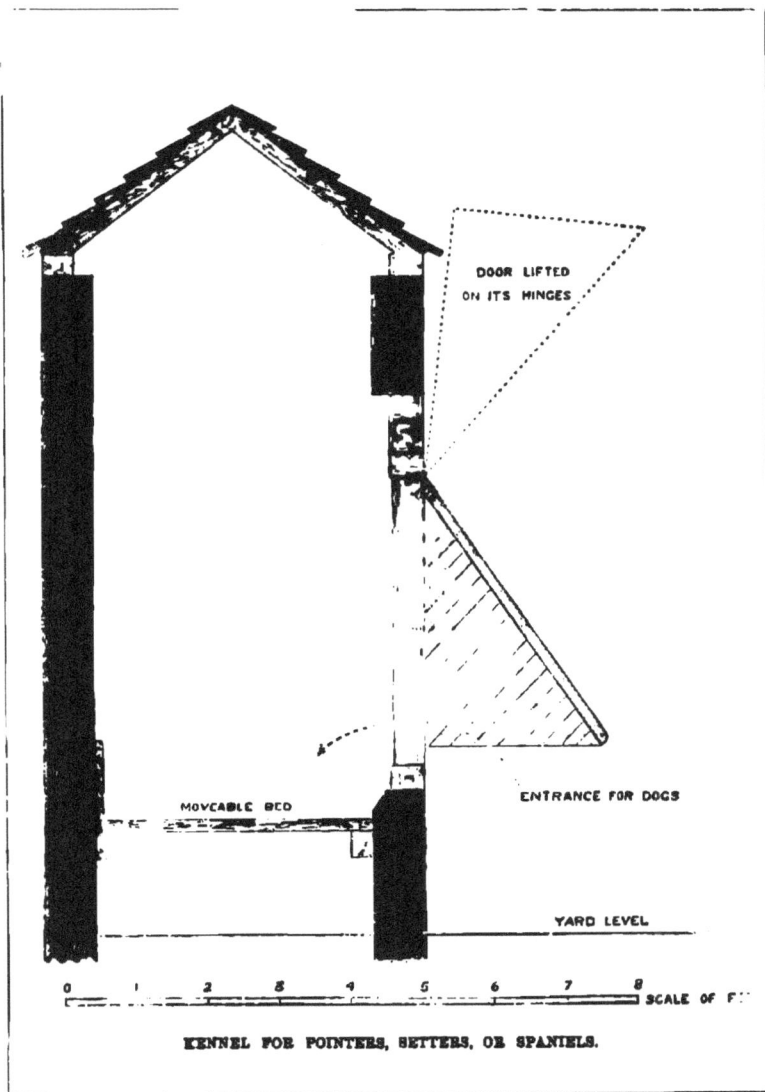

DOOR LIFTED ON ITS HINGES

MOVEABLE BED

ENTRANCE FOR DOGS

YARD LEVEL

0 1 2 3 4 5 6 7 8 SCALE OF F

KENNEL FOR POINTERS, SETTERS, OR SPANIELS.

PART I.

BOOK I.
MANAGEMENT OF DOGS IN HEALTH.

CHAPTER I.
KENNEL MANAGEMENT OF LARGE DOGS.

THE kennel management of greyhounds, foxhounds, harriers, and other sporting dogs varies almost with each kind. Thus, greyhounds are most carefully protected from the weather by a roof to their yard as well as by body clothing, which is worn when in severe training. Next to these come hounds, and then pointers, setters, spaniels, and retrievers, all of which last are allowed a run into an open yard at discretion. In many cases this leads to colds and rheumatism, against which the best precaution is a sloping door for the opening into the sleeping chamber, hinged at the top, and made up at the sides with a ∧ shaped piece of wood, but not at the bottom. This, when in its place, allows the dogs to jump up on to their beds, while it protects them from wind and rain when there, and can at any time be lifted completely up so as to allow of the kennel man entering and making all clean. The accompanying engraving shows a plan of such a door, with the dimensions suitable for the purpose, and from it any carpenter will easily be able to construct one. The advantage is too obvious to need dilating on it. In the summer time a wooden bench, if protected in this way, and guarded from the wall by planking, needs no straw, which only harbours fleas; but in the winter it, or deal shavings, which do not harbour fleas, must be provided, and, whichever is used, it should be changed twice a week. The floor of the yard should be of glazed tiles, cement, or asphalte, and all the woodwork should be either painted or dressed with best gas tar, the latter being the better material of the two. If the look of the tar is objected to, it may be coated with lime-wash, which, however, requires a renewal at least once a year.

Sporting dogs are all better fed only once a day, and for those whose noses are of the utmost importance, viz., pointers and setters, the food should be almost entirely of meal, either made into biscuit or well boiled and converted into pudding. In either case, a *very weak* broth must be made of flesh or greaves, which is then used to boil the meal in or to soak the biscuits. Spratt's and other biscuits have lately been introduced into general use, by which all this trouble is avoided—dried flesh, imported from abroad, being mixed with the meal before it is baked. I have tried those of Spratt and Co. with great advantage on pointers and setters, when containing not more than ten per cent. of meat; but a larger proportion I have found much too heating, causing loss of nose, and a tendency to eruption. They should be given whole and dry, not soaked, the dogs breaking them up easily with their teeth; and they appear to agree much better in this way than when soaked. Two or three times a week, whatever may be the kind of meal or biscuit used, some green vegetables, well boiled, should be given in addition, by which means the blood is kept cool, the coat blooming, and the nose cool and moist. Messrs. Spratt and Co. add a certain quantity of dates to their biscuits for the same purposes, but they are not sufficient for any length of time to supersede the necessity for green food in the case of kennelled dogs, who cannot get at grass, which instinct prompts those at liberty to bite off and swallow. The number of biscuits required for a pointer or setter daily averages from 3 to 3½, but some gross feeders are sufficiently nourished with 2½, and others demand as many as 4½ or even 5.

For large dogs, Calvert's carbolic acid wash, diluted with thirty or forty times its bulk of water, and used as a wash, forms the best application for fleas and ticks, and it is also useful as a vermin-destroying wash for the kennel walls and fittings, followed by lime-wash when dry. If preferred, the application described for pet dogs may be employed, or a small quantity of benzine collas may be rubbed in along the back.

CHAPTER II.
HOUSE MANAGEMENT OF PET DOGS.

ET DOGS require a different treatment, to understand which it will be better to begin at the beginning. We will suppose that a puppy six weeks old, and of a breed not exceeding 15lb. weight, is presented to one of our readers—What is to be done? First of all, if the weather is not decidedly warm, let it be provided with a warm basket lined with some woollen material, which must be kept scrupulously clean. The little animal must on no account be permitted to have the opportunity of lying upon a stone floor, which is a fertile source of disease; bare wood, however, is better than carpet, and oilcloth superior to either on the score of cleanliness. In the winter season the apartment should have a fire, but it is not desirable that the puppy should lie basking close to it, though this is far better than the other extreme. Even in the severest cold a gleam of sunshine does young creatures good, and the puppy should, if possible, be allowed to obtain it through a window in the winter, or without that protection in the summer. It will take exercise enough in playing with a ball of worsted or other material indoors until it is ten weeks old, but after that time a daily run in the garden or paddock will be of great service, extending to an hour or an hour and a half, but not so as to overtax its limbs. After this age, two or three hours a day, divided into periods of not more than an hour each, will be of service; but it is very seldom that young pet dogs can reckon upon this amount of exercise, and, indeed, it is not by any means necessary to their healthy growth. Until after the tenth week, cow's milk is almost essential to the health of the puppy. It should be boiled and thickened at first with fine wheat flour, and, after the eighth week, with the mixture of coarse wheat flour and oatmeal. The flour should be gradually increased in quantity, at first making the milk of the thickness of cream, and, towards the last adding meal in quantity sufficient to make a spoon stand up in it. If the bowels are relaxed the oatmeal should be diminished, or if confined increased. This food, varied with broth made from the scraps of the table, and thickened in the same way, will suffice up to the tenth or twelfth week, after which a little meat, with bread, potatoes, and some green vegetable, may be mixed together and gradually introduced as the regular and staple food. The quantity per day will of course vary according to the size of the puppy; but, as an approximation to the proper weight required, it may be laid down that, for each pound the puppy weighs, an ounce of moderately solid food will be sufficient. From the time of weaning up to the tenth week it should be fed four times a day; then up to four months, three times; and afterwards twice until full grown, when a single feed will, in our opinion, conduce to its health, though many prefer going on with the morning and evening supply. When the puppy is full grown, meat, bread, and vegetables (either potatoes, carrots, cabbage, cauliflower, or parsnips), in equal proportions, will form the proper diet, care being taken to avoid bread made with much alum in it. Dog biscuits, if sound, answer well for pet dogs; but the quantity required is so small that in most houses the scraps of the bread basket and plates are quite sufficient. Bones should be supplied daily, for without them not only are the teeth liable to become covered with tartar, but the digestion is impaired for want of a sufficient secretion of saliva.

If the above quality and quantity of food and exercise are given, in combination with the protection from cold recommended, the pet puppy will seldom require any medical treatment. Sometimes, in spite of the most careful management, it will be attacked by distemper contracted from some passing dog infected with it; but with this exception, which will not often occur, it may be anticipated that the properly treated pet dog will pass through life without submitting to the attacks of this disease, which is dire in its effects upon this division of the canine race. If care is taken to add oatmeal and green vegetables to the food in quantity sufficient to keep the bowels from being confined, no aperient will ever be required; but

sometimes this precaution is neglected, and then recourse must be had either to
castor oil or the compound rhubarb pill—the dose being one drop of the former or
half a grain of the latter to each pound the puppy weighs. If the oil is stirred up
with some milk the puppy will take it readily enough, and no drenching is required;
but care should be taken that the quality is good, and that the oil is not the rank
stuff sometimes used in the kennels of sporting dogs. The compound rhubarb pill
may be given by opening the mouth with the left hand, and then dropping in the
pill. It must be boldly pushed well down the throat as far as the finger will reach,
no danger being risked in effecting this simple process. If the liver is not acting
(which may be known by the absence of the natural gingerbread colour of the
evacuations), from half a grain to a grain of blue pill may be added to either dose,
and repeated, if necessary, every day or every other day till the desired effect is
produced; or from one-sixth to one-third of a grain of podophyllin, which has a
similar effect on the liver. Very young puppies should not be washed even in the
summer season, as they are very liable to chill. After they are three months old,
however, a bath of warm water, with or without soap, will do good rather than
harm, provided that care be taken to dry them well afterwards. For white dogs,
white soap is required to give full effect to this operation; and it may be either
"curd" or white soft soap, whichever is preferred, the latter being most effective in
cleaning the coat. Long-haired dogs, such as spaniels, the Maltese and Skye terriers,
require combing and brushing until they are dry, which should be done in the
winter before a fire; and in the latter breeds the coat should be parted down the
back with the comb in the most regular manner. If the hair has become matted,
a long soaking will be necessary, the comb being used while the part of the dog
submitted to its teeth is kept under water, which will greatly facilitate the unrolling
of the tangled fibres. After the coat is dry, where great brilliancy is demanded, a
very slight dressing of hair-oil may be allowed occasionally; but the brush is the
best polisher, and when "elbow-grease" is not spared, a better effect will be produced
than by bear's grease at half-a-crown a pot.

With the exception of fleas, pet dogs ought never to be infected with any
vermin. Sometimes, however, they catch from others either lice or the ticks which
infest the canine race. The appearance of the first two parasites is well known to
everyone; but the tick is not among the things commonly presented to the eye, and
we may therefore mention that it may be known by its spider-like shape and by its
close adhesion to the skin by means of its legs, with which it digs into the surface.
In size it varies from that of the head of a small pin to the magnitude of a small
grain of wheat, but not being so long in proportion to its width. The colour
changes with that of the dog and with the quantity of blood imbibed, which always
gives a greater or less tint of bluish-red; but in very young ticks the colour is a
pearly grey. In destroying fleas the best remedy is the insect-destroying powder
sold by Butler and M'Culloch, of Covent Garden, by Keating, of St. Paul's Church-
yard, and most chemists, which may be well rubbed in without fear of consequences.
Lice and ticks require a stronger drug to destroy them, and this should be used
with more care, as, being a mercurial preparation, it is liable to be absorbed if the

skin is wetted, and then produces serious mischief, accompanied by salivation; or, if the dog is allowed to lick himself, this effect is still more likely to follow. The dog should therefore be kept carefully from all wet for at least twelve hours, and during the application of the remedy it should either be carefully watched and prevented by the hand from licking itself, or it should be muzzled. The remedy is white precipitate, in powder, well rubbed into the roots of the hair over the whole body, and left on for six hours, after which it should be brushed out. At the expiration of the week the application should be repeated, and possibly it may be required a third time; but this is seldom needed.

BOOK II.

DRUGS COMMONLY USED FOR THE DISEASES OF DOGS,

AND THEIR MODES OF ADMINISTRATION.

[*It is to be constantly borne in mind that the doses given below are those suited to the dog of average size and strength. Where, therefore, the patient is a toy dog, the dose must be reduced to one-third or even one-fourth of that given. The same rule applies to puppies.*]

————◦◦◦◦◦————

CHAPTER I.

THE ACTION OF MEDICINES, AND THE FORMS IN WHICH THEY ARE GENERALLY PRESCRIBED.

————◦◦◦◦◦————

ALTERATIVES.

ALTERATIVES are intended to produce a fresh and healthy action, instead of the previous disordered function. The precise mode of action is not well understood, and it is only by the results that the utility of these medicines is recognised.

1. Æthiops mineral, 2 to 5 grains; powdered ginger, ½ to 1 grain; powdered rhubarb, 1 to 3 grains. Mix, and form into a pill with syrup, to be given every evening.

2. Plummer's pill, 2 to 5 grains; extract of hemlock, 2 to 3 grains. Mix, and give every night.

3. Stinking hellebore, 5 to 8 grains; powdered rhubarb, 2 to 4 grains. Mix, and form into a pill, to be given every night.

4. Liquor Arsenicalis—of which the dose is 7 drops to an average sized dog—this is specially serviceable to dogs rendered gross by over feeding and no work.

5. Podophyllin, ½ grain; compound rhubarb pill, 3 grains. Mix, and give once or twice a week until the liver acts freely.

6. Cod liver oil, from a teaspoonful to a table spoonful, with one or two drops of wine of iron, twice a day.

ANODYNES.

Anodyne medicines are given either to soothe the general nervous system, or to stop diarrhœa; or sometimes to relieve spasm, as in colic or tetanus. Opium is the chief anodyne used in canine veterinary medicine, and it may be employed in very large doses.

ANODYNE PRESCRIPTIONS.

1. FOR SLIGHT PURGING.—Prepared chalk, 2 drachms; aromatic confection, 1 drachm; tincture of opium, 5 to 8 drachms; rice water, 7 ounces. Mix; dose, two tablespoonfuls after every loose motion.

2. FOR LONG-CONTINUED PURGING. — Diluted sulphuric acid, 3 drachms; tincture of opium, 2 drachms; compound tincture of bark, 1 ounce; water, 6½ ounces. Mix; two tablespoonfuls every four hours.

3. Castor-oil, 2 ounces; tincture of opium, 1 ounce. Mix by shaking; a tablespoonful night and morning while the bowels are loose.

4. Powdered opium, ¼ to 2 grains; prepared chalk, 5 to 10 grains; catechu, 5 grains; powdered ginger, and powdered caraways, of each 1 to 3 grains. Mix, and form it into a pill with syrup, and give every three hours.

ANTISPASMODICS.

Antispasmodics, as their name implies, are medicines which are intended to counteract excessive muscular action, called *spasm*, or, in the limbs, *cramp*.

1. ANTISPASMODIC MIXTURE.—Laudanum, and sulphuric æther, of each, ½ to 1 drachm; camphor mixture, 1 ounce. Mix, and give every two hours till the spasm ceases.

2. ANTISPASMODIC INJECTION.—Laudanum, sulphuric æther, and spirit of turpentine, of each 1 to 2 drachms; gruel, 3 to 6 ounces. Mix.

APERIENTS.

APERIENTS, or purges, are those medicines which quicken or increase the evacuations from the bowels, varying, however, a good deal in their mode of operation. Some act merely by exciting the muscular coat of the bowels to contract; others cause an immense watery discharge, which, as it were, washes out the bowels; whilst a third set combine the action of the two. The various purges also act upon different parts of the canal, some stimulating the small intestines, whilst others pass through them without affecting them, and only act upon the large bowels; and others, again, act upon the whole canal. There is a third point of difference in purges, depending upon their influencing the liver in addition, which mercurial purgatives certainly do, as well as rhubarb and some others, and which effect is partly due to their absorption into the circulation, so that they may be made to act by injecting into the veins, as strongly as by actual swallowing and their subsequent passage into the bowels. Purgatives are likewise classed, according

c

to the *degree* of their effect, into laxatives acting mildly, and drastic purges acting very severely.

1. STRONG APERIENT BOLUS.—Calomel, 4 grains; jalap, 14 to 20 grains. Linseed meal and water, enough to make one or two boluses, according to size.

2. A GOOD APERIENT BOLUS.—Blue pill, ½ scruple; compound extract of colocynth, 1 scruple; powdered rhubarb, 5 grains; oil of aniseed, 2 drops. Mix, and give to a large dog, or divide into two or three for medium-sized or smaller ones.

3. CASTOR OIL MIXTURE.—Castor oil, ½ pint; laudanum, ½ ounce; oil of aniseed, 1 drachm; olive oil, 2 ounces. Mix, and give one, two, or three tablespoonfuls, according to the size of the dog.

4. PURGATIVE INJECTION. — Castor oil, ½ ounce; spirit of turpentine, 2 drachms; gruel, 6 to 8 ounces. Mix.

ASTRINGENTS

Cause contraction in those living tissues with which they come in contact, whether in the interior or exterior of the body; and whether immediately applied or by absorption into the circulation. They are divided into astringents administered by the mouth, and those applied locally to external ulcerated or wounded surfaces.

1. ASTRINGENT BOLUS USEFUL IN DIABETES OR HEMORRHAGE.—Powdered opium, 2 to 3 grains; gallic acid, 4 to 6 grains; alum, 5 to 10 grains; powdered bark, 10 grains; linseed meal, enough to form a bolus, to be given to a large dog (or divided for a small one) two or three times a day.

2. ASTRINGENT WASHES FOR THE EYES.—Sulphate of zinc, 5 to 8 grains; water, 2 ounces. Mix.

Or, goulard extract, 1 drachm; water, 1 ounce. Mix.

Or, nitrate of silver, 2 to 8 grains; water, 1 ounce. Mix, and drop into the eyes with a quill; or wine of opium to be dropped into the eye.

3. WASH FOR THE PENIS.—Sulphate of zinc, 6 to 10 grains; water, 1 ounce. Mix.

Or, chloride of zinc, ½ to 1½ grains; water, 1 ounce. Mix.

4. ASTRINGENT OINTMENT FOR PILES.—Gallic acid, 10 grains; goulard extract, 15 drops; lard, 1 ounce. Mix.

BLISTERS

Require great care in their application to the skin of the dog, and should never be used without a muzzle, which may only be removed during feeding time. Before applying them, cut off the hair with scissors from the part to be blistered.

1. ORDINARY BLISTER FOR PURPOSES OF COUNTER-IRRITATION.—Powdered cantharides, ½ ounce; Venice turpentine, 6 drachms; lard, 3 ounces. Mix, and rub in with the hand.

2. SWEATING APPLICATION FOR ENLARGED GROWTHS.—Red iodide of mercury,

1 drachm; lard, 1 ounce. Mix; rub in a little every day till a watery discharge is produced, then desist for a day or two, and repeat as often as necessary.

3. Tincture of iodine, 1 ounce. Paint on some of the tincture every day till a sufficient effect is produced.

CAUSTICS

Are substances which burn away the living tissues of the body, by the decomposition of their elements. They are of two kinds, viz., first, the actual cautery, consisting in the application of the burning iron, and called firing; and, secondly, the potential cautery, by means of the powers of mineral caustics, such as potash, lunar-caustic, corrosive sublimate, &c.

Firing is seldom practised on the dog, but sometimes it may be had recourse to with advantage, when a very thin iron must be used. The red-hot iron is also sometimes needed to stop bleeding from warts in the mouth removed by the knife; or in a similar way for piles.

STRONG SOLID CAUSTICS are as follows:—

1. FUSED POTASS.—Difficult to manage, because it runs about in all directions, and little used in veterinary medicine.

2. LUNAR CAUSTIC, OR NITRATE OF SILVER.—Very valuable to the veterinary surgeon. It should always be kept at hand in the portable wooden case made specially for it.

3. BLUE STONE, OR SULPHATE OF COPPER.—May be handled safely, and no case therefore is required. When used, it should be freely rubbed in to the part affected. It is valuable for unhealthy sores, &c.

4. CORROSIVE SUBLIMATE is only required to remove warts, but can seldom be trusted to any but a practised surgeon.

CORDIALS

Are medicines which act as warm temporary stimulants, augmenting the strength and spirits when depressed, and often relieving an animal from the ill-effects of over-exertion.

1. CORDIAL BALLS.—Powdered caraway seeds, ½ to 1½ drachms; ginger, 20 to 40 grains; oil of cloves, 3 to 8 drops. Mix, and give 10 grains for a dose.

2. CORDIAL DRENCH.—Tincture of cardamoms, ½ to 1 drachm; sal volatile, 15 to 30 drops; infusion of gentian, ½ to 1 drachm; camphor mixture, 1 ounce. Mix.

DIURETICS

Are medicines which promote the secretion and discharge of urine, the effect being produced in a different manner by different medicines; some acting directly upon the kidneys by sympathy with the stomach, while others are taken up by the blood-vessels, and in their elimination from the blood cause an extra secretion of the urine. In either case their effect is to diminish the watery part of the blood, and thus promote the absorption of fluid effused into any of the cavities, or into the cellular membrane, in the various forms of dropsy.

1. DIURETIC BOLUS.—Nitre, 6 grains; digitalis, ½ to 1 grain; ginger, 4 grains. Linseed meal and water to form a bolus, which is to be given night and morning.

2. DIURETIC AND ALTERATIVE.—Iodide of potassium, 3 grains; nitre, 4 grains; digitalis, ½ grain; extract of gentian, 5 grains. Mix, and give twice a day.

EMETICS

Are sometimes required for the dog, though not so often as is commonly supposed. Vomiting is a natural process in that animal, and seldom wants provoking; indeed, if emetics are often had recourse to, his stomach becomes so irritable that neither medicine nor food will remain on it; hence their administration should be carefully kept within the bounds of absolute necessity.

1. STRONG EMETIC.—Tartar emetic, ½ to 1 grain; powdered ipecacuanha, 4 to 5 grains. Mix, and dissolve in a little water, to be given as a drench; and to be followed by half a pint of lukewarm water in a quarter of an hour.

2. COMMON SALT EMETIC.—A teaspoonful of salt and half this quantity of mustard are to be dissolved in half a pint of warm water, and given as a drench.

EXPECTORANTS

Excite or promote a discharge of mucus from the lining membrane of the bronchial tubes, thereby relieving inflammation and allaying cough.

1. EXPECTORANT BOLUS.—Ipecacuanha powder, 1 to 1½ grains; powdered rhubarb, 1 to 3 grains; compound squill pill, 1 to 2 grains; powdered opium, ½ to 1 grain. Linseed meal and water, enough to make a bolus, to be given night and morning.

2. Ipecacuanha powder, and powdered opium, of each a grain. Confection enough to make a pill, to be given every six hours.

3. AN EXPECTORANT MIXTURE FOR CHRONIC COUGH.—Friar's balsam, 10 to 15 drops; syrup of poppies, 1 drachm; diluted sulphuric acid, 5 to 10 drops; mucilage, ½ ounce; water, ½ ounce. Mix, and give two or three times a day.

4. AN EXPECTORANT IN RECENT COUGH.—Tincture of lobelia, 10 to 15 drops; almond emulsion, 1 ounce; extract of conium, 2 to 3 grains; ipecacuanha wine, 5 to 10 drops. Mix, and give two or three times a day.

LINIMENTS OR EMBROCATIONS

Are applied to the skin for the purpose of producing counter-irritation, and are specially useful in chronic rheumatism, colic, &c. The most generally useful is the following:—

Laudanum, liquid ammonia (strong), spirit of turpentine, soap liniment, of each ½ ounce. Mix.

FEBRIFUGES.

Fever medicines are given to allay fever, which they do by increasing the secretions of urine and sweat, and also by reducing the action of the heart.

1. FEBRIFUGE PILL.—Calomel, 1 to 3 grains; digitalis, ½ grain; nitre, 3 to 5 grains. Confection to form a pill, to be given every night.

Or, 2. Nitre, 3 to 5 grains; tartar emetic, ¼ grain. Confection to form a pill, to be given night and morning.

3. FEVER MIXTURE.—Nitre, 1 drachm; sweet spirits of nitre, 3 drachms; mindererus spirit, 1 ounce; camphor mixture, 6½ ounces. Mix, and give two tablespoonfuls every six hours.

OINTMENTS

Are greasy applications, by means of which certain substances are brought into contact with the vessels of the skin.

1. MANGE OINTMENT.—Green iodide of mercury, 1 drachm; lard, 1 ounce. Mix, and rub in a small quantity every other day to the parts affected.

N.B.—Not more than a quarter of the body should ever be dressed at one time. Care should be taken to avoid leaving any superfluous ointment on the surface of the body.

2. DIGESTIVE OINTMENT.—Red precipitate, 1 ounce; Venice turpentine, 1½ ounces; bees' wax, ¾ ounce; lard, 2 ounces. Mix.

STOMACHICS

Are given to increase the tone of the stomach in particular.

1. STOMACHIC PILL.—Extract of gentian, 5 grains; powdered rhubarb, 2 grains. Mix, and give twice a day.

2. STOMACHIC DRAUGHT.—Tincture of cardamoms, ½ drachm; compound infusion of gentian, 1 ounce; tincture of ginger, 5 drops. Mix, and give twice a day.

STYPTICS.

Styptics are remedies which have a tendency to stop the flow of blood either from internal or external surfaces. They are used either by the mouth, or to the part itself in the shape of lotions, &c.; or the actual cautery, which is always the best in external bleeding.

1. INTERNAL STYPTICS—FOR BLOODY URINE, OR BLEEDING FROM THE LUNGS. —Superacetate of lead, 12 to 24 grains; tincture of matico, ½ to 1 ounce; vinegar, 2 drachms; water, 7 to 7½ ounces. Mix, and give two tablespoonfuls two or three times a day to a full-sized dog.

TONICS

Augment the vigour of the whole body permanently, whilst stimulants only act for a short time. They are chiefly useful after low fever.

1. TONIC PILLS.—Disulphate of quinine, 1 to 3 grains; ginger, 2 to 3 grains. Extract of gentian, enough to form a bolus, to be given twice a day.

2. TONIC MIXTURE.—Compound tincture of bark, 1 ounce; decoction of yellow bark, 7 ounces. Mix, and give two tablespoonfuls twice or thrice a day.

3. DISTEMPER TONIC.—Aromatic spirit of ammonia, 1 drachm; decoction of yellow bark, 1 ounce; compound tincture of bark, 1 drachm. Mix.

WASHES OR LOTIONS.

1. MANGE WASH.—Calvert's carbolic wash diluted with twenty times its bulk of water, and rubbed into the roots of the hair in red mange.

2. BISHOP's MANGE LOTION is a preparation of lime, &c., which is said by good judges to be extremely successful in curing mange, and especially red mange. It is at all events not likely to be injurious.

WORM MEDICINES.

1. Areca nut powdered, of which 2 grains for every pound the dog weighs, is the dose, for worms generally.

2. Santonine is the remedy for round worm. Dose for the average dog, 3 grains in a pill.

3. Spirit of turpentine, 1 to 4 drachms, to be tied up in a piece of bladder and given as a bolus in obstinate cases of tape worms.

4. MALE FERN.—Root, 1 to 3 drachms; oil, 10 to 30 drops, in tape worm.

CHAPTER II.
ADMINISTRATION OF REMEDIES.

WITHOUT some little patience and a knowledge of the temper of the dog, it is often very difficult to administer physic in any shape. A large powerful animal, of a savage temper, is scarcely to be controlled even by his keeper; but any dog of less than 40lbs. or 50lbs. weight is within the power of a resolute man, especially with his hands properly guarded by gloves.

In giving a pill or bolus to a small dog, he should be gently taken into the lap of the operator, or left in that of his attendant, then laying hold of the space between the canine teeth and the molars on each side with the thumb and forefinger of the left hand, the mouth is forced open, and the pill dropped into the throat by the other hand, following it rapidly with the forefinger and pushing it down as far as the finger will reach. The mouth is then kept shut for a second or two until the pill has had time to reach the stomach.

A large dog must be backed into a corner, then stride over him, and put a thick cloth into his mouth. The ends of this should be brought together over his nose, and held with the left hand. An assistant then lays hold of the lower jaw with the aid, if necessary, of another cloth, and wrenches the jaws apart, the right hand of the operator pushes the pill or bolus down the throat, taking care, as

before, to keep the head up *with the jaws closed* for a short time. The mode of drenching is either to pour the fluid down, using the cheek as a funnel, as shown in the engraving, or to open the mouth as for a bolus, and pour it down the throat by means of a small sauce ladle, or a soda-water bottle. The mouth must be shut directly the fluid is received, to enable the dog to swallow it.

BOOK III.
THE ORDINARY DISEASES OF THE DOG AND THEIR TREATMENT.

—•◦❉◦•—

CHAPTER I.
FEVERS.

—━━━━━━━—

SIMPLE EPHEMERAL FEVER.

IN the Dog, simple fever is merely a condition in which there is first a chilliness, accompanied by actual increase of surface heat, and quick respiration and pulse; then loss of appetite and diminished secretion of urine, with frequently costive bowels; and, finally, a tendency to congestion in the mucous membrane of the lungs or nostrils, or of some other internal organ, but generally of the lungs and nose, producing cough and running at the nose and eyes. The febrile symptoms usually run a short course, seldom going beyond three days, but the congestion of the mucous membrane often remains much longer.

In the first place, complete rest should be accorded; next, a dose of aperient medicine, with calomel, in the following shape, will generally be advisable, as it will clear away any sources of irritation which may exist: Calomel, 2 to 4 grains; jalap in powder, 10 to 15 grains; ginger, 1 grain—mix. The dose will be in proportion to the size and strength of the dog, giving one half or a quarter to a small one, or to a young puppy. When this has operated, with the assistance of some gruel, very little more will be necessary under ordinary circumstances, and in a few days the dog will be well.

SIMPLE EPIDEMIC FEVER, OR INFLUENZA.

This species of fever is closely allied to the preceding variety in everything but the cause, which, instead of being exposure to cold, is some peculiar condition of the air, to which the name epidemic is given, in order to conceal our ignorance, for it is really only giving a name and nothing else. The term influenza is precisely similar, both only signifying the peculiar and general prevalence of the complaint, and not defining its nature or its cause. The latter term is, however, applied more especially to epidemic catarrh, which is the form we are now considering. As the symptoms are very closely similar to those of simple cold, or ephemeral fever, it is unnecessary to repeat them; nor is the treatment in the first stage at all different. But as the cough and running seldom disappear without some extra care and attention, it does not always do to trust to nature here for a cure. Lowering medicines and diet after the first few days are not at all successful; and, on the other hand, warm expectorants, with tolerably good and nourishing slops, will be found to answer the best. The expectorant bolus, No. 1, may be given night and morning with advantage. As soon as the cough and running at the nose have somewhat subsided, and before exercise is allowed, the bark mixture (Tonic No. 2) may be given; and only when the strength and spirits are so recruited as to warrant the supposition that the health is greatly restored is the dog to be allowed exercise, and then only at first with great caution. It is often the case that a premature exposure to air and excitement brings on a relapse, and especially when the lungs are at all implicated either in their substance or mucous membrane. A human patient can be taken out in a carriage, but dogs, unless they are great pets, are seldom allowed that indulgence; and hence the necessity for the above precaution.

DISTEMPER.

Distemper may be defined as a feverish disease, always marked by rapid loss of strength and flesh, in proportion to the severity of the attack. It may occur at any period of life, and even more than once in the same individual; it is, however, generally met with in the puppy, and in most cases the dog is afterwards exempt. The essence of the disease appears to consist in a poisoned state of the blood, which may be either produced by contagion or by putrid emanations from filthy and overcrowded kennels; and it is from the efforts of nature to throw off this poison that the various symptoms are produced by which we know the disease. These symptoms differ according to the peculiar constitution of each dog, and to the state of the air and other causes which produce them. Hence it is usual to speak of distemper as either simple or attended with certain complications in the head, chest, belly, &c. But, although they are all essentially the same disease, these variations may be conveniently described as—1st, Mild Distemper; 2nd, Head Distemper; 3rd, Chest Distemper; 4th, Belly Distemper; and 5th, Malignant Distemper.

In Mild Distemper there are in almost all cases the following symptoms, which also show themselves in the other kinds, with the additional symptoms peculiar to each. The first thing noticeable is a general dullness (particularly shown in the eyes), accompanied by a dislike to play or take any kind of exercise, and by a want of appetite. Soon there appears a short cough, attended by a disposition to sneeze; and the dog often seems as if he hardly knew which of these acts to do first. The cough and sneezing are seldom heard while the dog is quiet, but when he is brought out of his kennel into the air, and particularly after he begins to play or run about, the mucous membrane is irritated and the coughing is set up, either by itself or alternately with sneezing. There is some slight thirst, a warm dry nose generally (but not invariably), a disordered state of the bowels, which may be either confined or relaxed, and a scanty secretion of high-coloured urine. In a few days the dog loses flesh and strength to a great extent, but then gradually recovers.

Head Distemper commences in the same way as the mild form, but the cough or sneezing is very slight, and sometimes there is not a vestige. On separating the eyelids, the whites are seen to be covered with blood-vessels loaded with dark blood, and a strong light seems to give pain. This kind of distemper is often indicated, soon after its commencement, by a fit, lasting a short time, and leaving a state of torpor from which the dog can with difficulty be aroused. If the brain is not relieved, the fits recur at short intervals, and the stupor increases, until the dog becomes quite insensible, and dies in a violent convulsion.

Chest Distemper appears to be an extension downwards into the chest of the irritation which produces the cough. It there generally sets up the kind of inflammation known as *bronchitis*, together with which, however, there is often inflammation of the substance of the lungs (*pneumonia*), or even of the external surface (*pleurisy*).

Distemper of the Belly is too often the result of mismanagement, produced either by the abuse of violent drugs or by neglect of attention to the secretions for some time previously. In the former case the bowels become very relaxed at the end of a week or ten days from the first commencement of a case of *mild distemper*, and then there is a constant diarrhœa, soon followed by the passage of large quantities of blood. This may be quite black and pitchy when it comes from the small intestines, or red and florid where the lower bowels are affected. Sometimes these symptoms appear of themselves, but generally they result from calomel or other violent medicines. When there has been neglect, and the bowels have been allowed to become confined, while at the same time the secretion of bile has been checked, a most dangerous symptom, known as "the yellows," shows itself, the name being given in consequence of the skin and white of the eyes being stained of a yellow colour, from the presence of bile. This may occur without distemper, and then it is not so fatal; but when it comes on during an attack of this disease it is almost invariably followed by death.

Malignant Distemper may come on at first, the dog attacked being as it were at once knocked down by the severity of the poison; or it may show itself at the end of a week or ten days from the first commencement. It may follow either of the four kinds already described, being marked by an aggravated form of the symptoms peculiar to each; but there are some additional evidences of the poisoned state of the blood, which show themselves in the four stages into which the disease, when well marked, divides itself. These stages are—1st, *incubation*, during which the disease is, as it were, hatching or brewing; 2nd, *reaction*, when nature is working herself up to throw off the poison; 3rd, *prostration*, following these efforts; and 4th, *convalescence*, wherein the constitution recovers its usual powers. In a well-marked case of malignant distemper these four stages average about a week or ten days each; and it is important to ascertain their existence, inasmuch as the treatment proper to each varies very considerably. The period of *incubation* is known by the symptoms described as common to mild distemper, as well as to the other kinds;

but, in the malignant form, the strength is lost much more rapidly, while the appetite is almost entirely absent, and the secretions are very much disordered. During the *reaction*, the pulse becomes quick and hard, the breathing is much hurried, and *is often much quicker than the pulse, without the existence of any inflammation*. This is very important to notice, as, when such is the case, any lowering measures are highly improper; but, on the other hand, the pulse may be very high and strong, and the breathing laboured, which, together with other unmistakable evidences afforded to the practised ear, prove the existence of inflammation, and require energetic and lowering treatment. At this time, also, are developed those dangerous affections of the brain, bowels, or liver, to which I have before alluded. When the stage of *prostration* sets in the whole system is thoroughly reduced, the dog is so weak that he is unable to stand, his appetite is often entirely gone—so that he must be drenched if he is to be kept alive; his gums, tongue, and teeth are coated with a black fur, and his breath is highly offensive. At this time an eruption of the skin generally shows itself, sometimes consisting in mere purple spots, in others of small bladders filled with yellow matter, but most frequently of bladders varying in size from a pea to half a hen's egg, and containing matter more or less stained with purple blood, or occasionally blood alone. This eruption is thickest on the skin of the belly and inside of the thighs, but sometimes it extends to the whole body. It is a favourable sign, taken by itself, though it generally attends upon severe cases. In the *convalescence* from malignant distemper, health gradually returns; but without the greatest care in all respects a relapse is very apt to occur, and is then generally fatal.

To distinguish these several forms of distemper from the diseases which most nearly resemble them, it is chiefly necessary to bear in mind that the peculiarity of distemper, especially in its malignant form, is the rapid tendency to loss of strength and flesh which accompanies it. Thus a common cold with cough is attended with slight feverishness, languor, loss of appetite, &c., but it may go on for several days without the dog losing *much* flesh, and with a very partial loss of strength. So, also, with ordinary diarrhœa; it is astonishing how severe an attack is required to reduce a dog in anything like the same degree which a few days' distemper will effect. In diarrhœa the dog gets thin, it is true, but he does not become the living skeleton which distemper produces; nor does he lie exhausted in his kennel, utterly unable to rise from his bed, and obliged to be supported in order to relieve himself. The same may apply to *simple* inflammation of the lungs, which may be treated most energetically by bleeding and lowering medicine with good effect, and without knocking the dog off his legs; while in chest distemper, even though the local symptoms are apparently as severe, a treatment one-half as energetic will be fatal from the exhaustion following upon it.

The sequels of distemper should also be alluded to, as consisting of *chorea*, commonly called "the twitch," and a kind of *palsy*, known as "the trembles." Both are produced by some obscure mischief done to the brain or spinal marrow in the course of the disease, and they generally follow the kind which I have described as head distemper. *Chorea* may be known by a peculiar and idiotic-looking drop in one fore-quarter when the dog begins to move, so that he bobs his head in a very helpless way. Sometimes the twitch is slight and partial, at others it is almost universal; but it always goes off during sleep. *Shaking palsy* affects the whole body, and is far more rare than *chorea*, which is fortunate, as I believe it to be incapable of cure.

The treatment of the several forms and sequels of distemper must always be conducted upon the acknowledged principle that this is a most debilitating disease, and that any very lowering measure must be avoided, if possible. On the other hand, inflammation is always to be feared attacking either the brain, lungs, or bowels; and as bleeding and other remedies of a similar tendency form the most active means for getting rid of inflammation, there is often left to the person in charge only a choice between two dangers. Two things, therefore, are to be attended to in the general treatment. 1st. Not only to avoid lowering the system, but also in bad cases to support it by good diet, as far as is consistent with the avoidance of encouragement to inflammation. 2nd. To take especial care that inflammation does not go far enough to destroy life, or to leave such organic change in the brain or lungs as shall render the dog useless for the purposes to which he is designed. This requires some experience in practice, though in theory it is simple enough; and, indeed, one is sometimes obliged to blow hot and cold at the same time, lowering the dog with one hand and propping him with the other. It must always be remembered, also, that this is a disease which has a natural tendency to recovery, its essence being an effort of the powers of the system to throw off a poison in the blood. Hence nature requires to be aided, not opposed; and that man will succeed the best in the long run who interferes the least with her operations. With these preliminary observations I shall proceed to give special directions for the treatment of each form.

1. GENERAL TREATMENT.—In the early stage give a mild dose of aperient medicine, such as castor oil and syrup of poppies in equal proportions; or, if the liver is not acting, calomel and jalap. It is always better, however, to avoid giving calomel if there is plenty of bile in the evacuations. After the early stage is gone by, give nothing in the shape of medicine, but keep the kennel dry, clean, and airy, but warm. Change the litter frequently, and avoid exercise till the cough and running at the eyes have entirely ceased. For several days the diet should consist of nourishing broths, thickened, when there is diarrhœa, with flour, rice, or arrow-root; or, if the bowels are confined, with oatmeal. If there is little water passed, give every night (as a drench) five or six grains of nitre, with half a teaspoonful of sweet spirits of nitre.

2. HEAD DISTEMPER requires very energetic local treatment in addition to that recommended above. From four to eight leeches may be applied to the inside of the ears, washing the part well with milk and water first. Then put in a seton to the back part of the neck, first smearing the tape with blistering ointment. If the head is very much affected apply cold water to it by means of a wet cloth, or, if that is not allowed, by the watering-pot. Calomel and jalap must be given to act on the liver and bowels, and a pill (consisting of half a grain to one grain of tartar

emetic) two or three times a day. As soon as the urgent symptoms have disappeared, the dog often requires supporting with beef tea and tonics, as described in No. 5.

3. CHEST DISTEMPER must be met with bleeding if there is evidence of inflammation; but if not, it is better to avoid such a lowering measure, and trust to antimony or ipecacuanha. Mix one grain of either of these with half a grain of opium, and give two or three times daily. If there is long-continued mischief, apply a blister to the chest, or rub in mustard mixed with vinegar. When the breathing is more rapid than the pulse, stimulants will be required, such as the bark and ammonia mixture in No. 5.

4. DISTEMPER OF THE BELLY, attended with purging, requires the immediate use of astringents, of which opium is the best. There is nothing better than the following mixture. Take of prepared chalk 2dr., mucilage of acacia 1oz., laudanum 1oz., tincture of ginger 2dr., water 5½oz. Of this give from a dessert-spoonful to a tablespoonful every time the bowels are relaxed. The diet should be almost entirely of boiled rice, flavoured with milk or broth, and if there is much thirst rice-water only should be allowed. On the other hand, where there is a confined state of the bowels, which is generally attended with "the yellows," calomel, rhubarb, and aloes are the only remedies to be relied on. Take of calomel 3gr. to 5gr.; rhubarb and aloes of each 5gr. to 10gr.; mix, and form into a bolus with water, and give twice a day till it acts freely. A turpentine enema may also be administered, but this requires some practical skill to carry out. Should bile begin to flow, there is still great care required to avoid checking the diarrhœa on the one hand, while on the other the exhaustion caused by it is often frightfully great. Strong broths thickened with flour or rice must often be given by force, as the appetite is generally much reduced in this disease. Where there is great exhaustion from diarrhœa, arrow-root with port wine will be of use.

5. MALIGNANT DISTEMPER is less difficult to manage than that of the head, and far less than the "yellows," when complicated with the ordinary attack. The great thing is to avoid reducing the system in the early stage, and to give at that time only such remedies as are imperatively required. A mild dose of oil, as described under No. 1, will be of service, after which the less done the better till the usual weakness shows itself. In the interval it may be necessary to treat the case as one affecting the head, chest, or belly, as described under Nos. 2, 3, or 4; but so soon as the excessive exhaustion shows itself, there is no chance of recovery without resorting to strong tonics and good food. For this purpose there is no remedy like port wine, or bark and ammonia—the former of which may be given, mixed with an equal part of water, and with the addition of a little spice, such as nutmeg or ginger. For the latter, take of decoction of bark 1oz., aromatic spirit of ammonia 1dr., compound tincture of bark 1dr. Mix and give twice a day to a large dog, or half the quantity to a small one. The greatest care here is required to support the strength by drenching the dog, if needful, with beef tea; and, if the bowels are at all relaxed, give the dog the astringent mixture ordered under No. 4. Clean straw, a warm dry kennel, and absolute rest, are also essential to recovery.

6. CHOREA or PALSY may be treated by a change to country air if the puppy has been in the town, and by giving from 3gr. to 5gr. of sulphate of zinc in a pill every day. The eyes are best left to themselves ; and, however bad they may appear, they will generally recover their brilliancy as the strength is restored. If not, apply a wash composed of 2gr. or 3gr. of nitrate of silver dissolved in 1oz. of distilled water, or the same proportions of the sulphate of zinc and water.

N.B.—The above doses are calculated for a full-sized dog. For their reduction see the directions at the head of list of drugs at page 8.

RHEUMATIC FEVER,

Or Acute Rheumatism, is a very common disease in the dog, though not very generally attended to or described by writers on their complaints. It arises from exposure to cold, when the dog has been overfed, and rendered unfit to bear its attacks upon a system full of inflammatory matter. The pampered pet is the most liable ; but greyhounds and pointers which are highly fed, and sometimes not sufficiently exercised, are also very liable to its approaches. In the dog rheumatism is either confined to the muscular system or to the coverings of the spinal marrow, which sometimes take on the rheumatic inflammation to such an extent as to cause paralysis of the hind-legs. General rheumatic fever, or acute rheumatism, is characterised by intense soreness of the surface, so that the dog shrinks on the approach of the hand from fear of being touched. He will almost always retire to some corner, and refuse to leave it on being called by his owner; and if brought out by force, he will stand and snarl at every hand; and this is one of the best methods of diagnosis with which we are acquainted. The treatment should be as follows: First give a smart purge (1) or (2) in the list of aperients. After this has acted give the following pill, or half of it, according to the size of the dog, three times a day until the pain has abated : Calomel and powdered opium, of each 1 grain; colchicum powder, 2 grains; syrup to form a pill. When the pain is gone, if the bowels are not very relaxed, give a dose of castor oil; and during the whole continuance of the pain use a warm anodyne embrocation, composed of laudanum, spirit of camphor, and liq. ammoniæ in equal proportions. This will act still better if the dog is first put into a hot bath at 100 degrees of Fahrenheit, then dried well by a good fire, and afterwards the liniment rubbed into the parts which are most full of pain. For the more chronic forms, called kennel-lameness and paralysis of the hind-quarter, the warm bath and liniment may be used with the aperients, as above; but instead of the calomel and opium, give one or two tablespoonfuls of the following mixture twice a day : Iodide of potassium, 1 drachm; sweet spirits of nitre, 3 drachms; nitre, 1½ drachm ; camphor mixture, 6 ounces. Mix. The diet in each case should be low, all animal food should be taken away, and the dog fed upon meal or rice, according to the state of the bowels. It is a disease in great measure the result of too stimulating a food, and a withdrawal of meat will go far towards a cure, which, however, is seldom of long continuance when the disease has become chronic.

CHRONIC RHEUMATISM.

This generally receives a specific name according to the part attacked. Thus, if it seizes on the muscles of the chest or shoulders, it is called

KENNEL LAMENESS, or CHEST-FOUNDER, which is the great bugbear of the foxhound kennel, and is produced in those animals from cold, after the extraordinary fatigues which they undergo. When a hound is worn down by long-continued exhaustion, and is then placed to lie in a damp or cold kennel, he is almost sure to contract rheumatism, especially if he is fed upon stimulating food, which most hounds are, in order to enable them to bear their labours. Thus, over-work and no work at all alike engender the disease, but in a very opposite state; the former producing an active fever of a rheumatic character, whilst the latter brings on a more chronic and low kind, attended with great muscular stiffness, but not with high fever.

PARALYSIS, or loss of power in the hinder extremities (improperly so called), is another result of the low kind of rheumatic fever which comes on from long-continued high feeding followed by cold; and it is exactly of the same character as chest-founder, but confined to the hinder limbs instead of the shoulders. I have said that it is improperly called paralysis, and my reason for this is, that it is not at all analogous to other forms of paralysis, though there is temporary loss of power; but so there is in all rheumatic conditions; yet who would say that the poor rheumatic subject, who can neither move hand nor foot, is suffering from paralysis? Assuredly no one who understands the nomenclature of disease, because the essence of paralysis is considered to be loss of power *from disease in the nervous system*; hence, when the loss is dependent upon want of tone in the muscles affected, it is clearly a misnomer to apply the term *paralysis*.

The treatment of these local affections is often attended with little or no advantage, but the following somewhat empirical remedy has been found to be successful in many cases. At all events, I know no more reliable remedy. It is called the red herring recipe, and is as follows: Score a red herring with a knife and well rub in two drachms of nitre; give every morning on an empty stomach, and keep the dog without food for two hours after; at night give a drachm of camphor made into a ball. The herring may be mixed with a little broth and meal if he will not eat it otherwise. Trimethylamine, which is obtained from a similar source, has been recommended by Dr. Richardson as superior to the red herring. The dose is from 10 to 15 drops given in milk.

CHAPTER II.

INFLAMMATIONS.

RABIES.

(IMPROPERLY CALLED HYDROPHOBIA.)

OST MORTEM examination has not revealed with certainty the exact seat of this disease, but there is little doubt that it is confined to the spinal cord and base of the brain. It is admitted by the medical profession throughout Europe and America that no cure has yet been discovered for this terrible disease, and therefore it will only be needful here to describe the symptoms, so that proper precautions may at once be taken, when they appear, to prevent the dog from communicating the disease by his saliva, or, if he has already bitten man or animal, to stamp it out in the latter case, or in the former to prevent the inoculation from taking effect by absorption.

The Hon. Grantley Berkeley has taken on himself of late years, with very little experience of rabies, to resuscitate the long exploded fallacy that the rabid dog may be distinguished from the animal whose brain is only attacked in an ordinary way, by the fear of water which the former, as he alleges, always displays. Every modern authority is against him, yet he fearlessly recommends owners of dogs which are attacked by madness in any form to run all sorts of risks so long as they show no fear of water. He says they may handle such patients with perfect impunity; and as his name stands high with the multitude because of his position in the world of sport, he is likely to mislead a good many into taking his advice. My own experience is not much greater than his in true rabies, having only seen three cases of it; but, as far as it goes, it is dead against him, there being no fear of water in either of the cases seen by me, but, on the contrary, a strong desire and craving for it. In each case the disease was propagated from, and in two of them both from and to, others; so that there could be no doubt of its being true rabies. Still, I should lay little stress on so limited a number, and prefer to rest the question on the general opinion of the medical profession, which, as I said before, is unanimous on this point, and I shall therefore dismiss it as settled without further discussion.

The symptoms of canine madness are very much the same in all cases, though varying somewhat in their manifestations. The first and most marked is a change of disposition and temper, so that the naturally good tempered dog becomes morose and snappish, and those which are usually fondling in their manners are shy and retiring. Sometimes the change is even so great that the usually shy dog becomes bold; but this is not nearly so common as the opposite extreme. Generally the rabid dog shows a warning of his coming disease by this change of manner for several days before it breaks out with severity; though I have seen one well-marked attack which began and ended in death within forty-eight hours. This was in a Newfoundland dog, which I bought in perfect health to all appearance, and shut up in order to accustom him to his new master for a week or ten days, feeding him myself at the end of the first twenty-four hours, and observing no change from the usual habits of a strange dog. On the evening of the tenth day, however, after he had appeared in very good spirits, and eaten his dinner from my hand in the morning, he began to show signs of bad temper, and exhibited that peculiar snapping at imaginary objects well described by Mr. Youatt. On the next day he was in a highly rabid state, and died in the night after. When these premonitory symptoms have lasted an uncertain time, varying from twenty-four hours to three or four days, the dog begins to attack imaginary objects, and if real ones are presented to him he will tear them savagely to pieces. He is now exceedingly irritable, and wanders restlessly from place to place, having apparently a strong desire to do something, but not caring what that is, so that he is not quiet. If he is confined by a chain he will try and gnaw it to pieces; and if restrained by a door within narrow bounds he vents his fury upon that. In this state he knows not the sensation of ordinary pain, but will bite a red-hot poker presented to him exactly as if it were a cold one. As the disease advances water is eagerly swallowed, but in his hurry the dog will generally upset his stock of that fluid; and hence he is often thought to be unable to swallow, whilst all the time he is burnt up with thirst, and will constantly imbibe it, if he can do so without knocking over the vessel containing it in his haste. The howls and groans are generally peculiarly deep and melancholy, and by them a mad dog *in confinement* may often be recognised, though sometimes the patient is quite silent, and in that state is said, in common language, to be "dumb mad." When at large, however, no warning noise is made, and the dog seems only determined on a straightforward trot. If he is interfered with in any way, and more especially if he is struck, he will wreak his vengeance on the offender; but he seldom goes out of his way to do a mischief, and will often pass through crowds of people without biting them; even if pursued and annoyed by cries and hootings, he takes no notice until he is injured, and then more frequently endeavours to escape into solitude, than turn upon his assailants. This desire to wander appears to me an instinctive attempt to get rid of the disease by muscular action, and if indulged in quietly, I am inclined to think that there might be some chance of a recovery; but as it would not be wise to run the risk, the experiment can never be tried. The disease is evidently caused by some poison, and, as in other cases, poisons are got rid of by some extraordinary secretion, so I am led to believe that the wearing down of the muscular, and with it the nervous system by long-continued fatigue, is the natural cure of the disease.

PREVENTIVE MEASURES are the only ones of service in this complaint, which, if fully established, has hitherto been uniformly fatal in all animals attacked by it, including man himself. When a bite has taken place, the best plan is to destroy

the animal at once : for though excision may most probably prevent the occurrence
of the disease, no risk should be run. In man, immediate excision, followed by
caustic, should always be had recourse to, previously taking care to suck the wound,
with a mouth free from ulcers, to discover which put a little salt in the mouth,
when it will by its smarting show their existence, if there are any. It is supposed
that confinement is the cause of the disease ; and I am strongly inclined to believe
that such is the case, as in those countries where dogs are suffered to be at large,
rabies is an unknown disease. A wooden caustic case, containing a pointed piece
of lunar caustic, is sold by all chemists, and should be carried in the pocket by
those who run any risk of a bite from a rabid dog.

The average time elapsing between innoculation and the appearance of the
disease is about two or three months. It has been known to break out in less than
three weeks ; and, on the other hand, not till fully six months after the reputed
bite.

TETANUS

Is a disease very similar in its nature to rabies, but manifesting itself in spasms
of the muscles, rather than in general irritability of them. I have, however, only
seen one case in the dog, which was the result of a severe injury, and it is said to
be very rare indeed. No remedy seems to exert any power over it any more than
over rabies itself. Chloroform, by inhalation, might be tried ; but I can scarcely
expect any good result in the dog, when its effects on the human being are so far
from satisfactory.

TURNSIDE

Appears to be an inflammation of one side of the brain only, producing a tendency to turn round in a circle, like "the gidd" of sheep. It is rather a rare
disease, and is easily recognised by the above characteristic sign. There is no
apparent constitutional disturbance, and the dog eats much as usual ; but the
moment he attempts to walk he begins to turn round. In a case which I saw some
years ago, the dog recovered by the use of a seton, with purgatives, followed by
nitrate of silver, given three times a day in a pill, as follows :—

Nitrate of silver, carefully powdered, 2 grains ; crumb of bread, enough to
make eight pills.

INFLAMMATIONS OF THE EYE.

The Eye is the seat of various inflammations, coming on from causes totally
distinct from one another. Thus, in distemper, there is generally an inflammation,
with discharge, and sometimes the inexperienced attendant will fear that the eye
will be lost ; but if the dog recovers his strength, the eye, in almost all cases, is
restored also, and especially if it is not interfered with. If, on the other hand, an
attempt is made to apply remedies, with the intention of saving the sight, the effect
is the reverse of good, and the disease is aggravated so far as often to cause the
ulceration to extend through the cornea, and destroy the eye. In *ordinary
ophthalmia*, arising from cold, there is considerable injection of the vessels of the

white of the eye, which become red and swollen. In this kind, if an ulcer appears, it will often eat through the cornea, and the eye will be lost by a discharge of its contents. Sometimes, again, in a weakly young dog, there is a low kind of inflammation, with great intolerance of light, and a discharge of watery fluid instead of thick pus. This is strumous ophthalmia, and requires a very different treatment. A third kind of ophthalmia, the rheumatic, is unattended by discharge; the vessels are deeply gorged, and the pain great. This, however, is a disease peculiar to old dogs, and from that cause may generally be distinguished from the strumous, and from the ordinary ophthalmia, by the absence of discharge. There is also an inflammation, the result of accident, which sometimes destroys the eye rapidly, and requires energetic treatment. *The treatment* of ordinary ophthalmia should depend upon its severity, which, if great, will demand bleeding and strong purgatives, followed by a grain of calomel and opium two or three times a day. When an ulcer appears, a wash should be used daily, consisting of the nitrate of silver in solution, or the sulphate of zinc, according to the formulæ given under Eye-washes. In the strumous kind tonics are necessary, consisting of 1 grain of quinine and 3 of hemlock, in a pill, three times a day. When the rheumatic form shows itself, a brisk purge must first be given, and then the iodide of potassium should be administered according to the formula at page 12. If this does not succeed, a seton may be inserted in the neck.

CATARACT consists in an opacity of the crystalline lens, for which nothing can be done; for although it might be removed by operation, the dog would still be unable to see for want of the glasses which, in the human subject, supply its place. It may easily be recognised by the clear white pupil, which takes the place of the ordinary dark centre of the organ.

DROPSY of the eye is only the result of chronic inflammation, and little can be done to alleviate it, as the eye is almost always destroyed before the disease proceeds so far as to cause dropsy.

AMAUROSIS, or paralysis of the nerve, is generally a sign of disease of the brain, either produced by injury or from overfeeding. The dog is more or less blind without the eye showing any change in form, and even at first being preternaturally bright. But if the dog is watched, he is seen to be blind by his striking his head against objects in his way, and by his timid mode of moving about. If the disease is recent, the dog may possibly be cured by smart purgatives and a seton; but, in most cases, very little benefit is experienced from these remedies.

INFLAMMATIONS OF THE EAR.

DEAFNESS often arises from severe cold, and may then be expected to disappear as the dog recovers, but it is sometimes congenital, and when such is the case, no remedies are of any avail. If it comes on after distemper, it will generally disappear, or if it occurs from ordinary cold. Whenever it is obstinately persistent for more than a fortnight, a seton in the neck is the best remedy, kept in for some weeks.

CANKER of the ear is an eruption attacking the ear passage or external ear, as the case may be, rather than a disease of the ear itself. According to its seat, as above mentioned, it is termed external or internal, and then requires very different treatment. Internal canker may be suspected when the dog is seen to shake his head constantly without having any eruption on the external ear to account for this habit. On looking into the ear passage, it will generally be found to be full of yellow matter, but sometimes the membrane lining is thickened, red, and dry. In either case it is inflamed, and requires local as well as general treatment. A solution of nitrate of silver should be dropped into the passage every other day, alternating its use with the green iodide of mercury, which should be blown in without admixture with lard. The dog should be physicked with a mild aperient, his diet should be reduced in quantity and quality, and some boiled green vegetables should be added to it every other day. These remedies generally effect a cure in a fortnight, unless the disease has extended beyond the drum of the ear into the delicate structures of the interior, in which case it is often incurable.

EXTERNAL CANKER attacks the tips of the ears, producing a scabby sore, on one or both, which is greatly aggravated by the dog continually shaking his head. Hence it often requires a canvas cap to be tied on, so as to confine the ears, without which, in bad cases, no remedy is effectual. The general treatment is the same as for internal cankers, but the sores require touching with bluestone after rubbing off the scales, and afterwards applying the ointment of green iodide of mercury.

In very bad cases of either kind, when the system is in a very gross state, 6 or 8 drops of liquor arsenicalis should be added to the food twice a day, proportioning the dose to small dogs accordingly. It should be continued for weeks or even months, until it produces a redness of the white of the eye.

INFLAMMATION OF THE MOUTH.

The MOUTH is liable to inflammation from decayed teeth, or from the collection of tartar about them. The only remedy is the removal of these causes of irritation.

WARTS sometimes infest the mouth to a very troublesome extent. They must be removed with scissors, and the bases should then be touched with a small red-hot iron, or with lunar caustic, the former being simpler, and giving less pain, if properly applied.

INFLAMMATION OF THE NOSE (OZENA).

The NOSE is sometimes attacked by inflammation of its lining membrane, producing a stinking discharge, which the dog is constantly dropping about. A solution of chloride of zinc (2 grains to the ounce of water) may be thrown up with a syringe daily.

INFLAMMATION OF THE SKIN.

MANGE is the kennel term for several inflammations of the skin, whether acute or chronic, the chief popular distinction from surfeit or blotch being, that it is communicable from one to the other by contact—that is to say, that it is "catching." Hence, the sporting public exclude surfeit, blotch, &c., from this definition, and only include under the term mange those chronic eruptions which are capable of being taken by one dog from another. There are, however, several distinct varieties, which are not sufficiently described; and every now and then I see a fresh and perfectly new form, so that I cannot give a complete epitome of them. Every sportsman must know that when his dog has an eruption, the first question asked is the following, namely, "Is it mange, or not?" and to this it is not always easy to give a satisfactory reply. The following are, however, the forms of mange which I have met with; but, as I said before, I am constantly meeting with a new variety.

1. VIRULENT MANGE, in its more ordinary form, occurs most commonly in utterly-neglected and large kennels, where dogs are suffered to remain in large numbers together, in all their filth, and without exercise. It is seldom met with elsewhere, but it is highly contagious. The skin is bare of hair in large patches, but these are not in regular forms, being gradually shaded off into the hairy parts, as if from scratching, and are nowhere quite free from hairs. It is dry and rough, with a few oozing scabs here and there, and with inflamed creases, extending wherever there is a fold. The eruption is generally confined to the back, bosom, and inside of the thighs. The health is not much affected, but from the loss of sleep, and constant irritation caused by the itching, there is sometimes some little fever. An insect (acarus) is the cause of this form of mange, but my readers will be none the wiser for reading its scientific name. The *treatment* consists in a gentle dose or two of aperient medicine internally, and externally of the application of the ointment of green iodide of mercury, which should not be rubbed in at one time over more than one quarter of the body, for fear of absorption. In such virulent cases, therefore, as extend to more than this extent of surface, a part should be first anointed sparingly, taking care to leave no superfluous ointment on the coat, but rubbing it till it has nearly or quite disappeared. With this precaution no danger is to be apprehended from licking, as a small quantity does no harm to a dog of average strength. By repeating the application every second or third day, the most severe cases are soon cured, no remedy within my knowledge being so certain in its operation. In case of failure, carbolic acid may be applied, using Calvert's carbolic acid wash, diluted with forty times its bulk of water.

2. MANGE, WITH THICKENING OF THE SKIN, appears to be more dependent on constitutional disorder than the first variety, and for it the arsenical solution is no doubt very valuable. In this disease the discharge is very offensive; the skin is thick, and pouring out an irritating ichor, which occasions a constant and violent itching; the hair falls off, and the dog is continually scratching himself.

The REMEDY for this state is a cooling diet, without any animal food of any kind, and composed chiefly of potatoes and other vegetables. A smart purge may be first given, and then the liquor arsenicalis in doses of from two to ten drops three times a day, *mixed with the food,* according to the size of the dog. If this dose makes the eyes red, or stops the appetite, or occasions vomiting, it may be diminished one-half; but the best plan in all cases is to begin with a full dose at first, and when the desired effect is produced, gradually to diminish it. Less than two or three months will seldom effect a cure, and green iodide ointment will often be required to complete it.

3. RED MANGE is the most easily detected of all the varieties, because it always shows itself by altering the colour of the hair, whether the dog is white or not. If white, the hair becomes pink; and if brown or red, it is of a brighter shade; while if black, it becomes reddish brown. It does not, however fall off, except from the constant scratching which takes place. There is no eruption visible, but the skin is more red than natural.

The REMEDY is either the ointment of green iodide of mercury, which, however, sometimes fails, or the carbolic acid wash above mentioned applied to the roots of the hair with a stiff brush every other night. Liquor arsenicalis should also be given as above described. Mr. E. Bishop, of Ogwell, Newton Abbot, Devon, has lately brought out a wash which is said to be very efficacious in red mange.

BLOTCH OR SURFEIT is one of those skin diseases which is dependent upon too gross a diet, and is not of a specific nature, that is to say, it is not caused by contagion, nor by a parasitic insect. It begins with an irritation of the skin, which causes the dog to be constantly scratching. On examination, there is a matted mass of loose hair, as if some starch had been dropped on the coat; and when this comes off, the skin underneath is red, and deprived of its cuticle, discharging also a thin watery fluid. These patches occur chiefly on the back and the inside of the thighs, and also on the scrotum, where they are very commonly met with.

The TREATMENT consists in giving cooling and laxative medicines, with starvation and plenty of exercise. This will almost always effect a cure. Locally, a piece of bluestone may be rubbed upon the sores, but they will not heal until the constitutional foulness of blood has been relieved, after effecting which local measures are seldom needed.

An ERUPTION between the toes is also constantly occurring in sporting dogs; and it is precisely similar in its nature and cause, and also in the treatment. Bluestone is almost invariably successful, if combined with purgation and starvation. It generally requires to be well rubbed into the roots of the nails, and also to the clefts between the toes.

INFLAMMATION OF THE ORGANS OF RESPIRATION.

The LARYNX, situated at the top of the windpipe, is not so often the seat of acute inflammation as in man and the horse, but chronic laryngitis is by no means unfrequent in the dog. Both are recognised by the hoarseness of the cough and bark, and by a rough sound in breathing, sometimes very audible at a short distance; and accompanied by a certain degree of increased quickness in respiration, varying according to the intensity of the attack.

The TREATMENT will vary according to the acuteness and severity of the disease; and if this is urgent, bleeding and emetics will be necessary, followed by small doses of calomel, digitalis, and nitre, as prescribed at page 13. If, on the other hand, the more common form of chronic laryngitis is developed, remedies of a different nature must be adopted. A seton should be inserted in the throat, and a good discharge from it promoted by the application of blistering ointment to the tape. Iodide of potassium may generally be given in one, two, or three grain doses, with five or six drops of ipecacuanha wine, and five grains of nitre three times a day, mixed in a little water. When this has been given for a short time without benefit, any of the warm expectorants given at page 12 may be tried; and sometimes one, and sometimes another, will be of service. The dog, during the continuance of the disease, must be kept rather low than otherwise, but not rigidly starved, as is necessary in some inflammations of the respiratory organs, and should have a fair allowance of walking exercise.

PNEUMONIA, or inflammation of the substance of the lungs, must be distinguished from pleurisy (inflammation of the pleura) and bronchitis, which, when simple, is confined to the lining membrane; but very commonly there is a combination of two out of three in the same attack.

All are characterised by fever, with quickened respiration and pulse; generally there is cough, but not always; and in all cases there is great anxiety depicted in the countenance. The following series of symptoms mark the difference between the three forms of inflammation, whether acute or chronic:

SYMPTOMS OF ACUTE PLEURISY

COMMENCE with shivering, with slight spasms and sweats. Inspiration short, unequal, and interrupted, as from pain; expiration full; air expired not hotter than usual. Slight cough only, and without expectoration. Pulse quick, small, and wiry.

The STETHOSCOPE gives the usual respiratory murmur, accompanied with a rubbing sound in the parts attached.

PERCUSSION elicits at first little or no deviation from the natural sound; after effusion has taken place there is a dull sound.

DISEASE TERMINATES in a gradual disappearance of the symptoms, or in the effusion of fluid (pus or lymph).

SYMPTOMS OF CHRONIC PLEURISY.

INSPIRATION always deep; expiration short. Cough dry, sometimes with expectoration; frequently changing from dry to moist cough.

STETHOSCOPE indicates an absence of respiratory murmur in the lower parts of the chest, and sometimes a gurgling noise.   Strong respiratory murmur in the superior portion of the lung, very often of one side only.

TERMINATES either by cure or by effusion and infiltration of the whole of the cellular membrane of the chest and belly, and sometimes of the scrotum and thighs: at last the serum in the thorax presses upon the lungs till it causes suffocation.

SYMPTOMS OF ACUTE PNEUMONIA

COMMENCES with shivering, without spasms.   Inspiration full; expiration short; air expired hot.   Nostrils red in the interior.   Cough generally violent, with expectoration of rusty mucus, not very profuse.   Pulse quick, full, and soft.

The STETHOSCOPE gives a crackling sound in the early stage, followed by increased dulness, and, finally, by crepitating wheezing.

PERCUSSION gives after the first stage a dull return to the finger.

DISEASE TERMINATES in resolution, with cessation of the bad symptoms; or in solidification, called hepatization; or sometimes in abscess of the lung.

SYMPTOMS OF CHRONIC PNEUMONIA.

INSPIRATION and expiration both difficult and interrupted.   Cough present, but not frequent, and evidently avoided and suppressed.   Expectoration rarely profuse; sometimes absent.

STETHOSCOPE indicates hepatization, from the entire absence of murmur.

PERCUSSION also gives a very dull return to the fingers.   Sometimes there is a mucous rattle.

TERMINATES sometimes in resolution; or, if fatal, in a discharge from the nostrils of purulent matter, coloured with blood, and often very fetid.   The animal never lies down at length, but sits up on his hind legs.

SYMPTOMS OF ACUTE BRONCHITIS

COMMENCES also with shivering, followed by constant hard cough.   Air expired warm, but not so hot as in pneumonia.   Inspiration and expiration both full.   Cough after a time attended with expectoration of mucus, at first sticky, soon becoming frothy, and, finally, profuse and frothy.   Pulse full and hard.

The STETHOSCOPE gives a soap-bubble kind of sound, with wheezing.

PERCUSSION elicits nothing of consequence.

DISEASE TERMINATES either by resolution, or by extension to the cellular membrane, constituting pneumonia in combination with bronchitis.

SYMPTOMS OF CHRONIC BRONCHITIS.

RESPIRATION free, but quicker than natural.   Cough constant and intense, evidently not restrained by fear of pain: sometimes to such an extent as to cause soreness of the muscles of the belly.

STETHOSCOPE gives a rattling sound, as of soap-bubbles, with a great deal of wheezing.

PERCUSSION gives no result different from a state of health.

TERMINATES in resolution; or, if fatal, in an accumulation of mucus, and consequent suffocation. Until very near suffocation the dog will almost always lie down; whereas the contrary is the case in pneumonia.

The TREATMENT will a good deal depend upon which of the above three conditions is present, though not to such an extent as to be of very great consequence. In pleurisy and pneumonia, bleeding will almost always be required in the early stage, but not in bronchitis, which seldom is benefitted by loss of blood. Blisters, again, relieve pneumonia and bronchitis, but are actually prejudicial in pleurisy, where the close relation between the vessels of the pleura lining the chest, and the skin covering it, often causes the irritation of the latter to extend to the former, and thus increase the mischief it was intended to relieve. With regard to internal medicines, they are, fortunately, much the same in all three. Calomel and opium, with or without digitalis and tartar emetic, will generally be useful; and in bronchitis, rhubarb, opium, and ipecacuanha, as follows:—

Calomel and opium in powder, of each ¼ to 1 grain; tartar emetic, ¼ to ½ grain; digitalis, ½ grain.

Confection enough to form a pill, to be given three times a day. Or,

Rhubarb powder, 2 grains; ipecacuanha powder, ½ to 1 grain; extract of opium, ½ to 1 grain; compound tincture of benzoin, 2 drops.

Mix, and form a pill, to be given three times a day.

When these remedies have had the desired effect of relieving the inflammation, as evidenced by the breathing and pulse becoming slower, and by the dog being able to lie down, if the pneumonia has been present, some one of the cough mixtures or pills given in the chapter on drugs, under the head of Expectorants, will be found beneficial; but it is generally difficult to say which of them will best suit any particular case. A trial may be made of one for two or three days, and if that fails, another should be substituted for it. The diet should be very low at first, and afterwards only a milk and farinaceous one, with vegetables, should be allowed for some weeks. When dropsy of the chest supervenes upon pleurisy, tapping has occasionally been had recourse to; but for sporting dogs it is wholly useless, because the animal never recovers sufficient bodily powers to be of real service in the field; and it is only in pets whose lives are valued by their masters or mistresses that this operation should ever be had recourse to.

CHRONIC BRONCHITIS, WITH SPASM, usually known as spasmodic asthma, is very common among ladies' pets, who become overfed in consequence of the kindness of their mistresses, and their blood vessels gorged with foul blood, when spasm comes on with congestion of the mucous membrane of the large air-tubes, causing that frightful panting for breath which is so distressing in the human subject, and which even in the dog is by no means calculated to afford pleasure to the spectator. A fat, pursy, and asthmatic old dog is a miserable object of pity, and had far better be destroyed than suffered to live on in misery. The nose

F

is dry and hot, the animal spirits are flagging; there is a distressing cough, and exercise is followed by an aggravation of the symptoms.

The TREATMENT should be by giving nauseating doses of tartar emetic, camphor, and henbane; or of ipecacuanha with the two last, as follows:—

Ipecacuanha, ½ to 1½ grains; camphor, 1 to 2 grains; extract of henbane, 1½ to 3 grains. Make into a pill, and give three times a day.

A blister or seton may be applied to the side, and low diet in small bulk should be given; but there is little chance of doing more than to relieve a dog labouring under this complaint.

CONSUMPTION, OR PHTHISIS, is a disease of the lungs, in which a peculiar condition, called tubercle, is developed in them; and when aggravated by cold, or often by the natural constitution of the dog, they become inflamed, are converted into abscesses, and cause the death of the animal by constitutional fever (hectic), and by the suffocation produced either by a vessel giving way, or by the quantity of matter discharged into the air-passages. The symptoms are very insidious, and many dogs have them developed to a great extent before their owners take any notice of their condition. Very little good can be effected by treatment, but sometimes cod-liver oil, with steel, will be of temporary service. In sporting dogs, however, it is seldom that it is desirable to prolong life with this condition of the system; and it is never right to breed from dogs or bitches suffering under this disease, it being decidedly hereditary.

INFLAMMATION OF THE HEART is another of the diseased conditions which attack the dog, generally from over-exertion in an unprepared state. There is usually a very rapid action of the heart, with a strong bounding pulse, and laborious breathing, unaccompanied by cough.

The TREATMENT is to be conducted upon lowering principles, with digitalis and nitre, and blistering or a seton in the side.

INFLAMMATION OF THE ORGANS OF NUTRITION.

GASTRITIS, or inflammation of the stomach, is either acute or chronic. *Acute gastritis* is generally caused by poison administered wilfully, or by some similar accidental circumstance, such as highly-seasoned food, &c. There is constant violent retching, with intense thirst, and apparently great pain. The nose is dry, and the breathing quick; no kind of food is retained on the stomach; and the poor wretch lies extended on the cold earth with his belly applied closely to it. There is a constant desire to lick cold marble or iron, so as to cool the tongue, and cold water is eagerly sought after.

The TREATMENT chiefly consists in removing the sickness, which is best accomplished by calomel and opium, 1 grain of each in a pill twice a day.

HEPATITIS, or INFLAMMATION OF THE LIVER, is one of the most common of all diseases to which the dog is subject. In the acute form it is the disease which is characterised by the yellow skin and eyes, commonly called "the yellows," which in sporting dogs is very commonly fatal. Acute hepatitis comes on from exposure to cold and wet, one or two days after which the dog is shivering and feverish, with a small, hard, and wiry pulse, and a dry nose; there is generally obstinate costiveness, and when the bowels are moved, the motions are white or slate-coloured and entirely devoid of bile. If these symptoms are not soon alleviated, the inflammation goes on to destroy the substance of the liver, and the dog dies rapidly from constitutional disturbance, arising chiefly from the want of depurating power of the liver. To remove the inflammation, bleeding is sometimes necessary in the early stage, but as it reduces the strength greatly, and as this is required to be kept up during convalescence, it is always attended with danger. Calomel, with or without opium, is the only medicine to be relied on in extreme cases, but when there is time enough, podophyllin may be substituted for it. If there is no diarrhœa produced by these drugs, opium may be omitted, but it must be added to counteract that effect in sufficient doses. If the bowels are confined, a dose of rhubarb and castor-oil may be given, mixing 10 grains of rhubarb with a tablespoonful of oil and a teaspoonful of syrup of poppies for a full-sized dog, and less, in proportion, for a smaller one. Sometimes a blister must be applied to the side when the inflammation runs very high; and, in all cases, the mercury must be continued until the motions acquire a natural colour, when the stomachic No. 2 may be given and the mercury discontinued. Chronic hepatitis is a very different disease, and is more frequently the result of bad general management than of cold. Want of exercise is the usual cause, which has given the liver the work of the lungs. The symptoms of chronic hepatitis are multiform, and no one can be depended upon except the absence of bile in the fæces, which is an invariable sign, for no gland in a state of chronic inflammation will be able to secrete good bile.

The TREATMENT is to be conducted by rubbing into the region of the liver on both sides the ointment of biniodide of mercury, together with castor oil and rhubarb internally, in sufficient doses to keep the bowels gently moved. If the mercurial ointment does not soon cause the bile to flow, it may be assisted by small doses of blue pill or Plummer's pill, added to the rhubarb and oil, and the stomachic draught, No. 2, should be regularly administered in addition. If these means are perseveringly continued, and the dog is regularly but gently exercised, with plain farinaceous food, mixed with weak broth, the disease, unless very inveterate, will generally subside, and if a free flow of bile is obtained little doubt need be felt of the ultimate recovery.

INFLAMMATION OF THE INTESTINES

May be said to be divided into four varieties, though one of them is more of a spasmodic than of an inflammatory nature; these are—first, peritoneal inflammation; secondly, colic, or inflammation and spasm of the muscular coat; thirdly, diarrhœa, or acute inflammation of the mucous coat; and, fourthly, constipation, from chronic inflammation of the same membrane.

1. PERITONITIS and ENTERITIS are merely different parts of the same membrane inflamed; the former comprehending the peritoneum lining the abdominal

walls, whilst the latter embraces the peritoneum covering the intestines. In practice, there is very little difference between them, and the symptoms and treatment are the same. It is a frightful disease, and soon runs its course to a fatal termination; beginning with shivering, cold legs, ears, and nose; breath hot; pulse hard, quick, and small; the expression is an anxious one, with a staring eye; the tail is pressed firmly against the anus, and there is intense tenderness of the belly; bowels generally costive, and urine scanty; tongue dry and rough; with thirst and loss of appetite. As the disease advances all these symptoms become aggravated, and very soon the dog dies, worn out with irritation and pain.

The TREATMENT consists in full bleeding, with calomel and opium, of each a grain every four hours. Blisters, or stimulating applications to the belly, and a warm bath, will be beneficial in some few cases; but whatever is done must be done quickly, as the disease soon passes on to a fatal termination, if unchecked by remedies.

2. COLIC is very common in all kinds of dogs, and is partly of a spasmodic, partly of an inflammatory nature. There is intense pain, coming on in paroxysms, during which the dog howls with agony. Very often the attack is quite sudden, and comes on after a full meal which has been eaten much as usual; suddenly the dog starts up, with something between a moan and a groan, and then lies down again; soon after there is another groan, and a shifting of the position, and then, after an interval of rest, and perhaps sleep, there comes on a regular paroxysm of pain, with violent howls, which soon, however, cease, only to be repeated at intervals, varying in length according to the severity of the attack. The nose is not dry or hot, the tongue is clean and moist, and the appetite even is not affected; pulse full and soft, and not much quicker than natural. There is no tenderness of the belly, and pressure seems to alleviate the pain, rather than to increase it.

The TREATMENT consists of giving ether and laudanum internally, in doses of from thirty to sixty drops of each, and a clyster of turpentine and laudanum, one teaspoonful of each in half a pint of gruel. The stimulating embrocation, page 12, should be well rubbed into the bowels; and in bad cases a very hot bath may be administered. When the colic comes on in young dogs, the injection of turpentine with laudanum and a little ether will generally suffice without any internal medicine; but a dose of castor oil will almost always be necessary to carry off the offending matter.

Sometimes colic is followed or attended by INTUSSUSCEPTION, in which one contracted part of the bowel is driven into the expanded part below it. It cannot be distinguished from colic, and the animal is sure to die, unless an operation is performed to liberate the bowel; which might be easily done if the disease could be discovered with certainty; but, unfortunately, this is not the case.

3. DIARRHŒA, or DYSENTERY, comes on either from epidemic causes, or from some irritating and improper food, or from too violent aperient medicine. Unless there is an epidemic raging at the time, or the diarrhœa is clearly connected with distemper, the treatment should generally commence with a dose of castor oil, having with it a few drops of laudanum. If this is not enough to stop the purging,

the anodyne mixture, No. 1, may be tried, and failing that, No. 2, adding more laudanum to each dose, if necessary, up to any extent, for this medicine is well borne by the dog in full doses. Rice-water is to be the only drink allowed; and arrowroot or rice the only food, flavoured with milk or weak mutton-broth. If the dysentery is very bad, an injection of laudanum and starch may be tried; but it is seldom retained, even for a minute or two, and unless mechanical pressure is kept upon the anus by means of a towel, it is quite useless.

4. COSTIVENESS is generally the result of chronic inflammation of the bowels, or of the liver, by which their functions are impaired; and when the former is torpid, the healthy stimulus of the bile is not afforded. Dogs which are regularly exercised are not very liable to costiveness, but those which are confined to the house or to their kennels, are often terribly tormented by it, and suffer severely from the consequences, including that painful affection, piles, to which the dog is much subject. Very often the dog suffers very severe pain from the obstruction afforded by pent-up fæces, and is utterly unable to pass them until Nature has set up an inflammation of the rectum, by which mucus is poured out, and the mass comes away with much straining. The dog thus affected is almost mad with pain ; he runs to and fro, rushes into odd corners, and shakes his head in the most odd manner, and in this stage may very easily be mistaken for a "mad dog;" but the suddenness of the attack, and the mass of hardened fæces easily felt in the flank mark the difference between the two cases.

The TREATMENT of costiveness should be by diet if possible, and the substitution of oatmeal, with or without the addition of boiled green vegetables, will generally effect this. If not sufficient, give a pill of rhubarb and ipecacuanha—5 grains or more of the former, with ½ grain of the latter—*at the time of feeding*, every day.

INFLAMMATION OF THE KIDNEY AND BLADDER.

INFLAMMATION OF THE KIDNEY is not very common in the dog, but it sometimes occurs from the use of turpentine as a vermifuge. Very rarely there is met with in the kidney a formation of stone, called *Renal Calculus*, but no means can be used to remove it, nor are there any symptoms which indicate its presence during life.

INFLAMMATION OF THE BLADDER AND URETHRA is very usual in the dog, and is marked by a discharge of yellow mucus from the end of the penis. This is the result of high feeding generally, though sometimes it comes on from mechanical irritation.

The TREATMENT is to be conducted by giving saline aperients: sulphate of magnesia, ½ to 1 ounce; nitre, 10 to 15 grains; water enough to dissolve. Mix, and give twice a week.

Balsam of copaiba may be given in obstinate cases, in doses varying from 4 to 15 drops, in a little mucilage; but it seldom is retained on the stomach, and the best chance is to give one or two of the capsules now commonly sold, which may be pushed down the throat. When the discharge is clearly in the sheath, a wash of the sulphate of zinc, as here prescribed, may be used. Sulphate of zinc, 10 to 15 grains; rose water, 1 ounce. Mix.

CHOREA AND SHAKING PALSY.

The former is almost always a sequel of distemper, and may be known by the peculiar nodding of the head, or twitch of the fore-leg, which all dog owners must have seen. Shaking palsy is a general agitation of the body, without the twitching so characteristic of chorea. Chorea generally occurs as a sequel of distemper (see page 19); but sometimes it appears without that combination. Little can be done in either case; but nitrate of silver, in doses of $\frac{1}{4}$th of a grain, has sometimes effected a cure of chorea. When the disease first comes on, a general tonic treatment should be tried, the first principle being to improve the general health by good food and fresh air, aided by stomachic medicines; and secondly, to give such strengthening and tonic medicines as are likely to improve the tone of the nervous system. Fresh country air is of the utmost consequence, and this alone will often dispel the attacks of chorea; but when united to a liberal diet it is doubly likely to be successful. The puppy should have plenty of good milk, or, if that cannot be obtained, beef tea or mutton broth, with oatmeal or wheaten flour added in proportion to the looseness of the bowels. If these are confined, they must be acted on by castor oil or rhubarb and aloes, or some of the aperients which merely act without producing much loss of strength. When the strength is somewhat improved by diet and stomachics, sulphate of zinc, in doses varying from 2 to 4 grains three times a day, may be given; or a grain or two of quinine, with 2 or 3 grains of extract of hemlock in a pill, will be likely to be serviceable, but either must be used regularly for some weeks in order to have a fair chance of success. By these means many bad cases may be relieved, or perhaps nearly cured; but with sporting dogs, if the attack is really severe, it is seldom that sufficient improvement is effected to make the dog as efficient as before. Hence, in these instance it is perhaps better to destroy him, than to persist in patching him up in a way which will only render him a burden and disgrace to his master. Shaking palsy, I have already remarked, is wholly incurable.

EPILEPSY

May be distinguished from the fits of puppyhood by the great champing of the jaws and struggling of the limbs during the fit, and also by the frothing at the mouth, which is generally an accompaniment of it. It comes on without notice, and in the setter and pointer is peculiarly annoying, because it generally shows itself at the time when their services are most wanted, namely, during the middle of a day's shooting. Very often this happens during the excitement of the "point," but the fit is scarcely remarked till the birds are sprung, when the dog generally falls, and is seized with struggles and foaming at the mouth. Generally this lasts for a few minutes, extending sometimes to half an hour, after which he recovers himself, and will even continue his work without loss of nose. With regard to the causes of epilepsy nothing is known, but its attacks are aggravated by improper food, and by the addition of flesh without due preparation, as is often heedlessly done just before the shooting season.

The TREATMENT consists in attention to the general health, which is all that can be done, as in confirmed epilepsy a cure is out of the question. Aperients, or even emetics, will be more likely to do good than any other medicine, and the use of the former is by far the most likely palliative measure.

By FITS may be understood those which occur to the puppy during dentition or from distemper, both of which indicate either disease of the brain, or great disturbance of the digestive apparatus in consequence of worms. These fits are accompanied by slight convulsions, but no foaming at the mouth, and the dog is not speedily recovered from them, but lies exhausted after he recovers his consciousness. They are very fatal in distemper, being symptoms of great mischief in the brain; but they are not invariably fatal, because the severity of the fit does not always indicate a corresponding degree of internal mischief.

In their TREATMENT Mr. Mayhew recommended injections of ether and laudanum; but I can scarcely assign to this remedy the credit which he claims for it, knowing that many epileptic fits are recovered from without any aid at all, and finding that he classes all under the one head of "fits." In the kind I am now considering, there is generally some exciting cause present, as distemper, or the irritation of worms, or of teething; and if these are removed, the fits will generally subside, and, consequently, the whole attention should be directed to this object. These fits seldom recur many times in succession, being either speedily fatal, or else ending in a complete cure; and in this respect they are unlike epilepsy, as well as in their symptoms and treatment.

GENERAL DROPSY.

ANASARCA, or general dropsy in the dog, is not a very uncommon disease among old kennelled dogs, owing to the improper way in which they are fed and kept without exercise. It consists of an infiltration of serum from the blood vessels into the cellular membrane, caused by the kidneys refusing to act, as a consequence generally of inflammation; and the disease, therefore, is merely a symptom of inflammation of the kidneys, for which reason I might have classed it among the inflammatory diseases, but that it sometimes occurs from a different condition of that organ, owing to a want of tone in the general system. Its most frequent cause is either improper stimulants—in the case of the stallion greyhound, a very frequent cause—or a gross kind of food, or sometimes from simple over-crowding of the dogs in a small kennel, occasioning a breaking down of the system, and an exudation of serum as a consequence. Among over-stimulated pets, which are not allowed any exercise, it is a very common disease, and often carries them off in a very disgustingly loathsome condition. When the liver is in fault, by throwing too much work upon the kidneys, as is sometimes the case, the urine is *yellow*, but in the usual way it is highly charged with salts, and dark *brown*, not yellow.

THE TREATMENT consists in acting in accordance with the cause—that is to say, in treating the case so as to relieve the dropsy, and not upon any fixed principles; thus, supposing the kidneys are inflamed, blood must be taken, and calomel and digitalis given in grain doses of each, without any violent diuretics, which will only aggravate the disease. If the dropsy is merely a symptom of a breaking down of the system, this must be propped by bark and steel, with perhaps ammonia in addition. When the urine is mixed with blood, in a broken down constitution, the following mixture may be given, on the authority of Mr. Mayhew, and I have my doubts of its success:—Tincture of cantharides, 3 drops; water, 2 ounces. To be given twice a day.

If the dropsy is from the kidneys refusing to act, 6 or 8 grains of nitre may be given two or three times a day, in the diuretic mixture, No. 2, but the great principle is to make out the cause and act accordingly.

WORMS.

The PRESENCE OF WORMS in the intestinal canal is one of the greatest annoyances to the proprietors of dogs of all classes. In the greyhound they are a constant source of mischief, and in the other varieties of sporting dogs they are equally common. In the puppy they are particularly injurious, cutting off his supplies of food, and also irritating his nervous system, to a degree which can scarcely be credited without actual experience. Whenever a puppy is seen to look rough and unhealthy in his coat (mere roughness is no indication), and when he is also thinner than he ought to be, with a ravenous appetite, and the constant passing of small quantities of faeces, the first part of which is solid, while the latter part is loose and frothy; when he also is more dull than natural, with a hot dry nose, and offensive breath, it may generally be concluded that he has some kind of intestinal worm, and the only thing is to find out which species is present, and then to exhibit the appropriate remedy. For this purpose the areca nut is a very useful medicine, given in proportion to the age and size, from a whole nut powdered, which is the dose for a full grown dog of 40lb. or 50lb., down to a quarter of a nut for a little dog of 10lb. weight. This should be given, and followed in a few hours by a mild dose of castor oil, when some of the worms present will most likely make their appearance, and according to their nature must the remedy be.

The VARIETIES OF WORMS are as follows:

1. The COMMON MAW-WORM.—This is a short white worm, about an inch long, with a pointed head, and a flat broad tail, the intervening part being nearly oval. These worms exist chiefly in the large intestines, where they are often in great numbers, and they are generally supposed not to interfere much with the health of the dog; but as it appears, according to Dr. Cobbold, that they are joints of the tape worm, it may, I suppose, be considered that this idea is not correct.

2. The LONG ROUND-WORM (*Ascaris lumbricoides*).—A pink or red worm, resembling the garden worm in appearance, but somewhat less in size, and not so red in colour. They chiefly inhabit the small intestines, and are very injurious to

the health, interfering with the digestion in every way, since they take up the chyle for their own use, and also irritate the mucous membrane by their presence.

3. The TAPE-WORM (*Tænia solium and Tænia lata*).—This worm is found in two or three species, but for our purpose it is sufficient to describe its general appearance, which is that of a long flat worm, *divided into joints*, and often coming away in portions, but leaving the head behind. It is, when suffered to remain long enough, from six to eight feet long, and the dog may often be seen running about with a foot or two hanging from his anus, or curled round his tail, to his great annoyance and disgust. The tape-worm inhabits the small intestines, and is much worse even than the round worm in its effects upon the health of the animal. Its expulsion should therefore be effected with great care, and its head, which is larger considerably than the diameter of the rest of the body, should be diligently sought for, for until this is found it cannot be asserted with positive certainty that the vermifuge has been successful.

The GENERAL PRINCIPLES of treatment consist in starving the dog for from twelve to twenty-four hours, and then administering the appropriate vermifuge followed by a mild dose of aperient medicine, to carry off the worms from the intestines. The following is a complete list of vermifuges suited to the various conditions and kinds of worms; but it will be necessary to repeat here what are the best for each kind, and their respective advantages and disadvantages, for, unfortunately, all are more or less injurious to the dog, and their use is only to be encouraged as a less evil than the continued existence of worms.

The REMEDIES FOR ROUND-WORM are as follows :—

> Wormwood (*Artemisia absinthium*).
> Garlic (*Allium sativum*).
> Cowhage (*Mucuna pruriens*).
> Santonine, or the active principle of worm-seed (*Artemisia contra*).
> Indian Pink (*Spigelia Marylandica*).
> Areca nut (*Nux areca*).
> Stinking hellebore (*Helleborus fœtidus*).
> Powdered tin and glass.
> Calomel (*Hydrargyri chloridum*).

For TAPE-WORM and MAW-WORM the following may be used with advantage :

> Areca nut (*Nux areca*).
> Kousso (*Brayera anthelmintica*).
> Barbadoes tar (*Petroleum Barbadense*).
> Pomegranate bark (*Punica granatum*).
> Male fern (*Filix mas*).
> Spirit of turpentine (*Spiritus terebinthinæ*).

Of these wormwood, garlic, and cowhage are nearly inert; santonine is useful for round worms, as also are Indian pink and hellebore; calomel is unsafe in the highest degree, and powdered tin and glass nearly useless. With the exception of Barbadoes tar, all the remedies enumerated for tapeworm are efficacious, but more or less injurious when the constitution is at all weakly.

Areca nut is the remedy upon which reliance is now chiefly placed, its careful and repeated exhibition being almost always sufficient to procure the expulsion of the worms; the dose of the freshly grated nut is 2 grains for each pound the dog weighs, and this should be given freshly mixed in broth, or, if the dog refuses it, mixed into a pill with a little jam or treacle; it should be repeated every four or five days for about four or five doses, when it may reasonably be hoped that a cure is effected, but, if not, a second course will almost always succeed. For round worm santonine is the most efficacious remedy, the full dose being 3grs.

RICKETS AND ENLARGED JOINTS.

When a puppy is unable to stand strongly on his legs, which are more or less twisted and the joints enlarged, the condition is known by the name rickets, and if the case is a bad one, he had better be destroyed. The disease is often produced by bad management, but sometimes it is the result of breeding "in and in," or of diseased parents. Phosphate of lime is the main agent in stiffening the skeleton, and if food containing this salt is not afforded in sufficient quantity the bones are of a gelatinous character, easily bending under the dog's weight, and consequently rendered by nature too bulky for his future well-being as an animal fitted for the chase. Many breeders like to see a puppy show larger joints than usual, and consider them an indication of strength; but I am strongly of opinion that the reverse is the case, and that the puppy which has them is not nearly so strong as one whose limbs are grown more like those of an old dog. This, however, is a disputed point, and I would never advise the rejection of a puppy because his joints were *all* enlarged; but if one is much larger than the others, it is a sign of worse disease than rickets, and more nearly allied to what, in human pathology, is called *scrofula*. Sometimes the swellings disappear, and the disease is cured, but generally these joints become more and more inflamed, and finally go on to form matter, and to make the dog entirely lame. Little can be done for this in the way of treatment, and the destruction of the puppy is the best plan of proceeding. In rickets, however, a great change sometimes takes place, and the bending of the limbs or the enlargement of the joints gradually disappears, leaving only some slight indication of what has existed. Too often, however, the bone is weak and liable to fracture; and at the time when the dog is wanted for the sport to which it is dedicated, the bone gives way, and the time and trouble occupied in its rearing are found to have been totally thrown away; hence the necessity for good feeding in the rearing of all young dogs, and too much care can scarcely be bestowed upon them.

CANCER AND FUNGUS HÆMATODES.

These malignant diseases usually attack the bitch either in the uterus or teats. Cancer, in the early stage, is known by its peculiar hardness, while fungus is distinguished by its comparatively soft and elastic feel, and by its general tendency to bleed. Both are incurable, and the only chance is to remove the tumours with the knife if they occur in the teats, but the disease generally returns.

ENCYSTED TUMOURS

Are very common in the dog, and consist of small soft bags lying close under the skin, of a circular form, and devoid of pain or inflammation. They vary in size from that of a pea to the volume of a small orange. The only remedy is the knife, which may be used with perfect safety by any one accustomed to it. The skin must be saved and dissected back, and the tumour, when exposed, may readily be lifted out of its bed without much dissection; after which the parts may be suffered to heal of themselves.

DISEASES OF PARTURITION.

In HEALTHY PARTURITION the bitch seldom suffers much; but sometimes in a small bitch, when the sire is of much larger size, the disproportion between the whelps and the mother is so great as to occasion great difficulty and danger. This sometimes also happens without any apparent reason.

In order to ascertain whether or not the bitch is in pup, a careful external examination will generally be necessary; when, on pressing the fingers deeply into the flank, several small round or oval bodies may be felt, in number according to the future litter. Between the fourth and seventh weeks the whelps cannot so easily be felt; but, though they are said to be lost, a careful examination by a practised hand will always detect nearly all of them lying close against the spine. After the seventh week they appear very plainly, and the belly rapidly swells till it attains the size which it presents at whelping time; about three or four days before which the teats begin to swell, and on the day before generally are full of milk—a pretty sure indication of the near approach of labour.

In the PROCESS OF PARTURITION, the bitch should be left to herself as much as possible; and if of good size and healthy, she will nearly always pass through it without trouble. Sometimes, however, her pelvis is too small to allow of the passage of the whelp, and then either she must die, or man must afford his aid by mechanical means; but this operation is too difficult for any but a practised hand, and therefore I should recommend the aid of a skilful veterinarian to be in all cases called in. If a part of the whelp is born, and the remainder does not come

away for some time—owing apparently to the exhausted condition of the bitch—
it is quite safe to give a little brandy and gruel by the mouth, and then steadily to
draw away the whelp, by laying hold of the part presenting with a piece of tape
round it, or a strip of calico.

As soon as all the whelps are born, the bitch may be allowed to rest for a short
time, unless she is very much exhausted, when the brandy and gruel may be
given, as directed in the last paragraph. After an hour, a little lukewarm gruel
may generally be allowed; and in the course of four hours another quantity
of the same. No meat of any kind should be given for three days, during which
time the state of the bowels should be regulated, if necessary, by castor oil; and milk
thickened with oatmeal or wheat-flour, or broth with the same thickening, or with
arrowroot, if diarrhœa is present, should be the only food. Sometimes, after the
first week, the whole litter is too great a draw upon the system, and part must
be removed from the bitch, and brought up by hand, if it is wished to preserve
them, feeding them from a common baby's bottle, with the India-rubber nipple now
so commonly in use; but a very thick and stout one should be selected, or the puppy
will compress it too much with its tongue. When the bitch is much reduced by her
suckling, she sometimes is subject to fits, for which the only remedy is the removal
of her whelps, and the exhibition of strong beef tea, with bark, and ammonia in
addition; together with port wine and arrowroot, if the bowels are relaxed. After
the first week, and, indeed, gradually during the fourth, fifth, and sixth days, meat
must be added to the other food, or earlier even if the bitch has had much animal
food before whelping.

If the bitch is inclined to devour her young, she should be allowed to remain
very quiet, and very little animal food should be given her. A dose of oil should
always be given a short time before her whelping time; and if she should, nevertheless, devour them, another dose should follow, so as to carry off the effects of so
heating a meal.

If a foster-mother is determined upon, all that is necessary is to muzzle her until
the strange whelps have sucked her, and lain for some time with her own; she will
then fail to distinguish between them, and her own offspring may be removed with
safety, leaving the foster-whelps to her care, which she will exercise just as fully
towards them as if they were really hers.

If the bitch has been "put by," as it is called, and is not in whelp at the end of
nine weeks from her "heat," she will be fat and indolent, with her teats full of milk.
At this time it is better to take a little blood from her, and to give her a smart purge
once or twice, together with vegetable food; after which she will generally
recover her health and spirits, and become much as usual at the expiration of
another month or five weeks. This ought to be fully considered in the case of all
sporting dogs.

CUTS, TEARS, AND BITES

Are easily treated in the dog, because his skin is very readily healed, though
not so speedily or in the same manner as that of man. In man a clean cut, if

properly treated, heals as if by magic; and in three days large surfaces of many inches in extent will often be firmly healed by a kind of glue thrown out from the cut surfaces, which afterwards becomes organised. In the dog and horse, however, no such glue is thrown out, and the oozing is always of a watery nature; so that apposition must always be maintained by stitches, and even they are only of use in preventing extreme displacement while they remain inserted. In slight cuts, tears, and bites, therefore, it is better to leave them alone to the healing powers of the dog's tongue; but in those cases where a large flap is torn down, as in the legs, for instance, a stitch or two should always be inserted, over which a bandage should be fixed, and the dog kept muzzled until union takes place. Without the last precaution stitches and bandages are of no use, since the dog will always manage to remove them, and will tear out any stitches which may be inserted, however carefully they may be tied. The first thing to be done is to wash the parts, if dirty, and then with a common needle and thread to put in several stitches, according to the extent of the wound; but only fixing it so as to keep it nearly in position, for an exact adaptation is of no use whatever. In putting in the stitches, the following is the plan to be adopted: take the needle and thread and insert it in the outside of the skin, on one side of the wound, and bring it out on the inside; then pass it from the inside towards the out of the opposite part of the corresponding flap on the other side, and tie the ends so as to close the wound. Repeat this as often as necessary, and cover all up with the bandage as already directed. After four or five days the threads may be cut and removed, because they are no longer serviceable, and only serve to irritate the skin; and from this time the whole dependence must be placed upon the bandage in keeping the parts together. In some parts—as, for instance, the flank, a bandage can scarcely be applied; but even there it is wonderful how nature fills up an apparently irremediable gap. I have often seen a flap torn down by a spike, which has hung down from the flank for five or six inches, but at the end of a month scarcely any scar can be seen. The owner therefore need never despair as long as the skin only is the seat of the accident; but when the abdominal muscles also are torn the bowels are apt to protrude, and the parts, if left to themselves, will never regain their original condition. Here a circular stitch must be practised, so as to pucker up the parts like the mouth of an old-fashioned purse, and if the walls are thick enough the plan may be practised with success; but in the thin tendinous expansions covering the middle of the belly there is great difficulty in carrying out this plan of rectifying the injury. The mode by which nature heals all the wounds of the dog is by *granulation*, in which small red bladders are thrown out by both surfaces, which, after they are in contact for some hours or days, coalesce and form a bond of union; but if they are allowed to rub against each other this union cannot take place, and the growth is confined to the angle of the wound only. Hence the use and necessity of a bandage, which keeps the two surfaces in close contact, and hastens the cure in a remarkable manner; effecting in ten days what would often require ten weeks if left

to the dog's tongue alone. When the granulations rise above the level of
the surrounding skin, a piece of bluestone may be rubbed over them daily;
and if the whole sore is too red, and the granulations large and smooth, a
little friar's balsam may be brushed over it ; or, what is far better, a solution
of nitrate of silver, of the strength of from three to eight grains to an ounce
of *distilled* water.

FRACTURES

May easily be treated in the dog by any person possessed of ordinary
mechanical ingenuity. The bones most commonly fractured are those of the
extremities; but almost all throughout the body are at times subject to this
accident.

FRACTURES OF THE RIBS are very common from the kick of a horse, or
from the thick boot of a man, who sometimes in his rage, at the attack of a
dog, administers a blow with his iron-shod toe which is sufficient to destroy
life, or, at all events, to break one or more ribs. When from any cause they
are fractured, the best plan is to apply a horse-girth round the whole chest, by
buckling it smoothly twice round, or, if the size of the dog will not admit of
this, the girth may be adapted to one circle only. This may be buckled so
tightly as to prevent the dog using his ribs in breathing, and to confine him
to the use of his diaphragm for that purpose, by which means the ribs are kept
quite still, and nature in about three weeks unites the broken ends. For a
broken shoulder-blade, or true arm, there is little to be done, nor in the case
of a fractured pelvis or upper thigh-bone can much good be effected by interference. Nature will in all cases work a cure so far as to enable a new joint
to be formed; but the animal is rendered useless for sporting purposes, and
can only be kept for his or her breed.

In FRACTURES OF THE LIMBS, splints or strips of deal should be neatly
applied round the limb and encircled with tapes to keep them in position. The
first thing to be done is to adapt the splints to the leg, so that the parts shall
be kept in a tolerably correct position while the inflammation is being subdued ;
for if the fracture has been the result of much violence there will be considerable
swelling of the soft parts, and the tapes require constant attention to prevent
undue pressure. Some experience in such matters is, however, required, and a
surgeon should always be called in when the animal is of sufficient importance.

DISLOCATIONS

Consist in a displacement of the end of a bone from its connexion with the one
above it ; and they may occur at the hip, stifle, shoulder-joint, or knee, as well as the
joints of the toes. The hock is seldom dislocated without fracture, but such an
accident has been known to occur, and great trouble would be experienced in its

reduction, on account of the shape and nature of the joint. Dislocation of the stifle-joint is not very common, it being very strongly guarded by ligaments, and broad also in the surface of the bones of which it is composed. The hip-joint is very often the seat of dislocation, and is one of the most intractable of all to manage. The socket projects in a prominent manner from the body of the pelvis, and when the head of the thigh bone is thrown out of its cup it sinks at once deeply by the side of it, and can scarcely be drawn out of its bed by any force which can be applied. In the anterior extremity, the knee is the chief seat of this kind of accident, and it is dislocated quite as frequently as the hip, but its reduction is ten times as easy, because both bones can easily be grasped, and extension being made, they are speedily brought into a proper relative position. But though they are readily reduced, they are as easily thrown out again; and, therefore, great care is required to prevent this unhappy result. The elbow and the point of the shoulder are seldom put out, because these joints are so securely guarded, that the bones of which they are composed are more inclined to break than to leave their sockets. In both the hind and fore-legs the toes are often put out; and, besides this accident, the tendons are apt to give way, causing the accident which is called "the letting down of the toes."

The TREATMENT of all dislocations consists in putting the displaced bone back again into its socket as speedily as possible, for if allowed to remain long out of its proper situation it contracts fresh adhesions, and can scarcely be drawn away from them by any practicable force. The dislocated knee is reduced simply by pulling steadily the two bones away from one another; an assistant seizing the arm, and the operator making extension by laying hold of the foot and pastern. After it is reduced, a piece of list should be crossed in the form of a figure of eight behind the joint, so as to prevent it from being straightened, and thus again displaced; and this position must be maintained for some time, in order that the torn ligaments may have time to unite. In the dislocated hip, unless very recently done, chloroform should be used, because the muscles of that joint are very powerful, and it will require great force to overcome their action without its assistance. The dog is first placed on a table, with a firm cushion under it; chloroform is then administered, by placing a sponge dipped in it in the end of a leather muzzle, such as is used for the greyhound. The holes at the side should be stopped, by pasting strong paper over them, so as to make a complete cone, one end of which is adapted to the jaws, and the other is closed by the sponge; so that the dog, when it is put on, can only breathe through the sponge. After a short time he snores, and breathes heavily, and then the sponge may be withdrawn for a time, and the attempt made to lift the bone into its socket. I have, however, lately failed, even with the aid of this agent, in reducing a hip dislocated only for about ten days; and I am not aware of any case of more than a few hours' duration where a hip has been replaced. Nevertheless, in a valuable dog, such as that in which I made the attempt, which was a highly-prized puppy, presented to me, and of a very scarce breed, the attempt is worth making, especially as it occasions no pain.

OPERATIONS.

In Operating on the Dog, either a regular muzzle should be put, or ordinary tape or cord should be applied to the mouth, as indicated in the annexed engraving,

binding it firmly round the jaws two or three times, and carrying it back to encircle the neck so as to prevent the dog pulling it off.

BOOK IV.

JUDGING AT DOG SHOWS AND FIELD TRIALS.

— ·•◦◆◦•· —

CHAPTER I.

JUDGING AT SHOWS.

— ·•◦◆◦•· —

HATEVER difference of opinion may exist as to the utility of dog shows in improving the breeds of this animal, there can be no doubt of their popularity, or that they have become permanent institutions. Large sums of money are annually spent in rearing and feeding dogs with the express purpose of exhibiting them; and it may, therefore, be admitted without argument that it is desirable to conduct these shows in the way most likely to give satisfaction to their supporters.

From their institution at Newcastle in 1858 there has been a growing feeling of dissatisfaction with the awards of the judges. Animals which have been successful under one set of judges in obtaining a first prize, have been altogether overlooked by another, not even obtaining a commendation, though in equally good condition at both places, and often with the same or nearly the same competitors. That these have been exceptional cases is true enough, but nothing has been more common than that the position of first and second prizeholders should be reversed within the same month—remarkable examples of which might be adduced, but the instances are so well known that it is needless to specify them. I have repeatedly drawn attention to these facts, and attempted to demonstrate that for the cause of this fickleness we must look to the absence of any recognised standard by which to measure the particular breed which is being judged. Among cattle and sheep-breeders it is generally admitted that certain leading qualities shall be considered all-important, such as the propensity to carry flesh of good quality on the parts most valuable to the butcher, early maturity, and, in the sheep, quantity and quality of wool. But in horses and dogs, and more especially in the varieties of the latter, there is not the same unanimity, even in leading principles; and in matters of detail, as may naturally be supposed, the difference of opinion is very great.

At the present time (1877) Dog Shows have reached such a pitch of general interest, that the question of judging demands a very careful consideration, and very recently in the *Field* I inserted the following article with that view:—

"ON JUDGING AT DOG SHOWS."

" It is needless for us to return to the much-vexed questions relating to the discrepancies between the decisions given on the merits of competing dogs at the various exhibitions of those animals which are now so common as to occupy our columns largely with their reports from week to week throughout the year. That they exist is admitted by all who are in the slightest degree acquainted with the facts, and that they are much to be lamented is equally to be taken for granted. The subject for our present consideration is how this lamentable state of things is to be avoided or reduced within reasonable limits; for no one can expect absolute uniformity in any machinery composed of fallible human beings.

" In regard to this selection of prize winners, there are now five open questions under general consideration : First, shall the judges be public or private? secondly, shall there be one, two, or three judges? thirdly, shall the judge or judges select the prize winner at random, or be guided by any written law? fourthly, shall he or they be compelled to draw up a numerical estimate of each of the prize winners, founded on a standard of points furnished for the purpose; and if so, shall it be published? and fifthly, how shall the judges be elected? Each of these subjects we now propose to discuss seriatim.

" In reference to public v. private judging, the general verdict is certainly in favour of the former whenever it can be managed, and all the clubs devoted to any particular breed have, we believe, adopted it. The only large show whose managers hold out against it is that held at Birmingham, where the want of space is a sufficient reason to forbid it ; and the choice lies between the abandonment of Curzon Hall, with all its counterbalancing advantages, and the continuance of the old system of judging in private. The Birmingham Show being the oldest annual exhibition of dogs, and having always been well managed on the whole, has obtained a strong hold on the public, and, in spite of the above-mentioned drawback, it seems likely to continue its career with success. Nevertheless, it is quite clear that public judging is now established, and will be adopted at all other large shows.

" The next question is not so easily settled, and it is only recently that it has been fairly tried. One thing has, however, been fully shown by experience, viz., that when more than one judge is appointed, they should possess equal knowledge of the breed or breeds placed before them. Nothing is so liable to lead to dissatisfaction as the importation of a judge specially acquainted with a particular breed, and the coupling of him with a 'gentleman of position.' Wherever this has been done some *fiasco* has occurred, and at length the plan has been abandoned. Our own opinion, founded on a long experience in every department of dog shows, is that ultimately single judging will be found to act most beneficially; but it requires some length of education to develop firmness of purpose sufficient to carry good principles into fair practice, and there are many men possessed of sufficient knowledge, who have yet such a deficiency of moral courage as to make them require a coadjutor to share the onerous responsibility of condemning to the ranks the dogs of their friends. On the other hand, if, as we allege, it is necessary that both the judges of a class should be possessed of equal knowledge, it reduces its amount to a much lower level if double or treble the number of individuals are required, since we all know that the managers of our shows have not a very large circle from which the choice can be made. The question is, however, now fairly submitted to the test of experience, and we need not, therefore, discuss it more at length.

"But now we have to examine the most vexed of the five questions before us, and yet it seems to us so clear as to be incapable of two opinions about it. In examining it, we must remember that the judicial bench is not composed of the same individuals at the various shows, and that many of them are known to have proclivities as regards types, &c., which render it possible for a clever exhibitor to 'place' successfully under different judges, the various members of his kennel, all of which could scarcely have a chance of a prize under any one judge possessed of reasonable consistency and fairness. It is quite true that it is impossible entirely to avoid this, and that, even with all the much-vaunted integrity of the judges in our higher courts of law, well deserved as it no doubt is, suitors and their solicitors are very apt to have a preference, founded upon well-known proclivities. But without statute laws, and precedents equally binding in our common law, our courts would resemble a lottery office still more than they now do, and we think no one but a madman would desire to wash out the written and unwritten code which guides us in all our transactions. Why, then, should we leave our canine judges to a 'rule of thumb,' when in our more important relations of life we adopt a different plan? To this question we know no answer, and we confess that this judicial blindness of the world of 'doggy' men is beyond our comprehension. The only explanation we can give is that it allows each exhibitor to use his powers of 'placing' with a reasonable hope of success, and that he thinks in that way he can cover the defects in his dogs by his own cleverness. The special clubs have, however, in most cases abandoned this plan, and have each drawn up a code of points, not only describing most minutely the dog they combine to glorify and improve, but appending a numerical value to each point; and in setting this example they have, no doubt, done good service in the cause to support which they have been called into being. It may therefore be concluded that the days of judging by 'rule of thumb' are numbered.

"Having thus reached a stage when it may be laid down as decided that the judges of our shows are to be guided by a written code of laws, it may reasonably be deduced that they shall carry out this code in a practical manner. To show the fallacy of depending on a code theoretically, we may instance the judging of Mr. Bassett at the recent show of fox terriers at Lillie Bridge—under the club specially formed to supervise that fashionable breed of dogs.

Prior to the show the club had drawn up and published a code of points describing each minutely, and alloting to them the following numerical value :—

POINTS OF THE FOX TERRIER.

	Value.		Value.		Value.
Head and ears	15	Back and loin	10	Legs and feet	20
Neck	5	Hind quarters	5	Coat	10
Shoulders and chest	15	Stern	5	Symmetry and character	15
	35		**20**		**45**

Grand Total 100.

"Now, by almost general consent, the above-named gentleman is admitted to have an excellent knowledge of the fox terrier, and, on the whole, his decisions were accepted; but the curious feature attending them is that, with a class of dogs so near together as to take him almost two hours to select the prize winner, no attempt was made to reduce the theory of points into practice with the aid of pencil and paper. At the end of an hour and twenty minutes Mr. Bassett had drawn six from the sixty-seven dogs of which the class was composed, five of them being compact and strong bodied-animals, with slight variations in other points, but all very near together, while the sixth is a dog with a beautiful head, but possessing a body of almost greyhound-like proportions. Now, surely with such opposite types, and with a code of points at his disposal, drawn up by a club who had appointed him, any reasonable man would aid his memory by jotting down in pencil the numerical value of the points in each of the competitors according to the above code. Of what use is such a code, if not thus applied? we ask of all men possessed of common sense. How otherwise can the beautiful head of the winner (Brockenhurst Joe), coupled with his light body, be compared with the inferior head, but wonderfully good body and legs, of the second dog (Moslem)? That it was a near thing between them, as admitted by all, only makes this numerical comparison the more needful; and, though we do not by any means impugn the decision, we think it highly probable that if Mr. Bassett had taken out his pencil he would have come to a different conclusion: at all events, he would have given his estimate of the points exhibited by the six dogs formally selected by him, which would have been of great interest to breeders of the fox terrier, in which every point in detail is now weighed and considered with great care by thousands of both sexes throughout the land. But, much as we think the paper and pencil were wanted in this class, they were still more needed by him in his judging of the rough bitch class. In this small lot of six, Bramble, bred by Mr. Wootton, exhibited as beautiful a head as that of Brockenhurst Joe, coupled with a light body, but not nearly so light as that of Mr. Gibson's dog—though looking more so than usual from the effects of a recent sea voyage—and in addition very good legs and feet. Minx, who was placed first by Mr. Bassett, was also bred by Mr. Wootton, but was by no means equal to Moslem in body; and between her and Bramble, if judged numerically according to the above standard, the decision would, as we think, have been deservedly in favour of the latter, who only took the third prize. In any case, however, these decisions are not consistent, and indicate that even an acknowledged good judge should assist his memory with paper and pencil; and at the same time add to the knowledge of his supporters by giving them the benefit of his opinions, not only as to the prize winners as a whole, but of their respective points when dissected and analysed by him. In practice it has been sometimes found that this use of the pencil has led to a great expenditure of time, and at the show of bulldogs held under the auspices of the club devoted to that breed, the judge retired for some hours, in order to cast up his accounts. Such a proceeding, however, is wholly unnecessary, unless the judge is unable to do a sum of simple addition; for surely it is easier to estimate the proportionate value of any individual head or back, as compared with fifteen or ten, in the dog's presence than in his absence; and, if so, what is the use of retiring? We contend, from practical experience, that, in judging five or six selected dogs near together in merit, it is the simplest and quickest plan to judge numerically by points, and we have not the slightest doubt that before long no other will be used.

"Lastly, we have to consider the best method of election, the choice lying between that by the votes of the subscribers, that by the committee of management made at the last moment, and that by the committee announced at the time of publishing the programme. All these plans have been tried, and experience has shown that there are drawbacks to each, to which it is very difficult to assign an exact value. For this reason, we shall not therefore venture to give a decided opinion on the present occasion."

In addition to the cases mentioned above, numerous instances have occurred in which the advantage of judging by points, had it been acted upon, would have been made manifest; and in the present absence of all written law in many breeds I do not see how it is possible to prevent the recurrence of such cases. A well-known case of the difficulties connected with judging by rule of thumb occurred some few years ago in the large pointer bitch class at Birmingham. One of the bitches, which we will call A., had a bad head and very light ears, combined with a strong useful middle, but spoilt by short shoulders. In addition, she had good legs and feet, an elegant stern, well carried, and an absence of quality, her age being eighteen months, when a small bitch is fully developed. Another, B., showed a better head, but inferior legs and feet, a coarse stern, and a heavy, lumbering middle. A third, C., exhibited a magnificent head, beautiful ears, capital legs and feet, fine stern, good shoulders, with great liberty of action; but these fine points were counterbalanced by a deficient girth of chest, for which, being only twelve months old, some considerable allowance should be made, the judges having a statement of the age of each animal on their books for this special purpose. Here, then, was a case of some difficulty, and though I do not agree with the award, I by no means assert that it was decidedly wrong. But, supposing, for the sake of argument, the pointer were said to have five properties, viz., 1, head and neck; 2, legs and feet; 3, body; 4, stern; 5, quality and coat; and that to each of these were allotted the following proportion of points, viz., head and neck, 30; legs and feet, 24; body, 20; stern, 16; quality and coat, 10—total, 100; the judges (being provided with books for the purpose, with the number and age of the entries duly written in) would only have to insert under each property such a number as would mark the degree of approximation to perfection—this being represented by the maximum figure given at the head of each column.

CLASS 27.

No.	Age.	Head and Neck. Maximum. 30.	Legs and Feet. Maximum. 24.	Body. Maximum. 20.	Stern. Maximum. 16.	Quality and Coat. Maximum. 10.	Total. Maximum. 100.
1	1 yr. 6 mo.	5	20	12	14	4	55
2	2 mo.	10	16	8	6	3	43
3	3 years	rejected					
4	4 years	rejected					
5	1 year	28	20	6	14	8	76

Had such a plan been adopted—and I can conceive nothing more simple or easy to carry out—the dogs A., B., and C. would have been placed in the order 5, 1, and 2, whereas the awards were given in the order the dogs stand on the lists. At present the judges make their notes opposite each entry, but they are so indefinite that afterwards it is necessary that all the animals likely to take a prize shall be compared together at the same time—a far more tedious operation than that which requires them to be carefully examined only once.   I do not for a moment assume that the numbers I have attached to each property are correctly apportioned, or that I should have carried them out in practice exactly in the manner I have indicated for the three pointers; I only contend that, supposing the judges to be each furnished with a book containing definitions of a similar nature for their guidance, they would have far less difficulty in deciding than at present, while the public would be able to ascertain the reasons which guided them, and would know what to expect in sending their animals to a show.   It will no doubt take some time to settle finally the relative value of the head as compared with the locomotive organs, in the several breeds of dogs, for they vary in almost all.   Thus the pointer, however well formed in his back, chest, and shoulders, is perfectly useless unless he has a head which will not only contain a good brain, but also sensitive olfactory organs.   So, also, with the feet and legs; unless these are capable of sustaining work equally with the back, chest, and shoulders, the latter, however good, are thrown away.   The National Dog Club, however, in 1869, made the attempt, which, though it was somewhat hastily and carelessly carried out, has served as a very useful foundation for subsequent labours in the same field. Unfortunately, only a portion of the judges at their Islington show carried out their code of points into practice, great difficulties being thrown in their way by the paucity of attendants, and the distance between the benches and the field in which all the dogs were led out. On the whole, however, this first attempt on the large scale to combine public judging with the aid of a scale of points was eminently successful, but, nevertheless, it has not been followed to the full extent at any other exhibition. The Birmingham council, in spite of the strenuous efforts of Mr. Murchison, have steadily opposed these innovations, and their only concession has been to guarantee that every dog shall be seen by the judges off the bench to which he is chained. In the series of articles now published I have introduced the points adopted by the several special clubs, with short alterations where I think them needed, as in the case of the bulldog, but still they must have the authority of some generally recognised body before they can be made imperative on judges.

In 1869, a great improvement on the then existing mode of judging by points was suggested—by a correspondent in THE FIELD, who was a noted breeder of mastiffs, and as his letter contains the whole of the argument, stated in a clear and convincing manner, I reproduce it at length.

"SIR,—Although I believe it to be most desirable that the judges at our dog shows should be guided in their awards by a settled standard of points and marks, it will, I believe, be found in practice very difficult, if even possible, to give satisfaction by this method, unless some such plan as I venture to suggest be followed.

"In order to have a claim to be classed as a prize dog, it seems to me that an animal ought to be fairly good in every point, and the plan of judgment I would suggest, which is adopted from the method often followed in scholastic examinations, is this: Presupposing that every point in the animal ought to be fairly good, the positive marks scored in the dog's favour would represent degrees of excellence. Should, however, the animal under judgment be notably deficient in any particular point, I consider that not only should no positive marks be allotted for this particular point, but negative marks should be given to it in proportion as the point in question fell below fairly good.

"Possibly the system may be already followed, but if not, I think it would be found to work fairly and well. The book put into the hands of the judges would run thus:

Bull Terrier.		Positive Marks.	Negative Marks.
Head	25		
Chest	10		
Neck	10		
Shoulders	10		
Feet and Legs	10		
Loin	10		
Colour	10		
Temper	10		
Tail	5		
Total	100		

"It might in practice be found advisable that the negative marks should never exceed the possible positive marks in number; or, again, that an animal notably deficient in any one special characteristic of his breed would be considered disqualified.

"These are, however, minor points; but I hope and think that the principle I suggest, unless it has already been thought of, may be found practical and useful.   "MASTIFF."

"April 3, 1869.

This suggestion removed the only objection in my mind to the plan of judging by points, and with its aid every animal shown, whether horse, dog, poultry, bird, or pigeon, should, I think, be judged.   I have endeavoured to persuade the managers of the various shows to adopt this amended system, but hitherto without success.   Still, as it is never too late to mend, and as I am convinced that, sooner or later, it must come into use, I give a specimen table of an open class of large pointers, with the points filled up of half a dozen selected specimens, between which it is obvious to the judges the three prizes given must rest.   Of course it would be an enormous sacrifice of time to set down the points of the whole of the above class, but an experienced judge can readily point out four, five, or six, as the case may be, all of which may be carefully "pointed," as is shown in the following table, which is supposed to be a copy of a page of the judge's book filled up.   In this way I believe that time may be saved rather than wasted, as I have found that the fixing on the numerical value of the several points is much easier than the judging two nearly equal dogs on their general merits.

There is a very general impression in the minds of judges that the method here advocated would be a great waste of time; and on one occasion, at the recent show of bull dogs by the club specially formed for their improvement, the judge thought it necessary to retire for several hours in order to fill up his book.   Now, this proceeding was simply absurd, because the only thing which could possibly be done in the absence of the dog was to cast up the score made when examining them, and that process could not occupy more than a few minutes.   The fact, I have no doubt, was that he was nervous at having to define his opinions on the several points; but a really well informed judge ought surely to have no such feeling.   Having myself tried the experiment several times, I find that I can easily set down the points of six dogs, previously selected, in half an hour, exercising the greatest care, whilst in most cases I can do it in half that time; and I am quite sure that in all important classes fully half an hour is occupied by the usual rule of thumb process.

The following tabular form is suggested as the most convenient.   The figures in italics are those supposed to be filled in by the judge.

16 Open Class—Liver Pointer Dogs.
Special Valuation of Individual Points.

Points	No. 103 Pos.	No. 103 Neg.	No. 119 Pos.	No. 119 Neg.	No. 98 Pos.	No. 98 Neg.	No. 101 Pos.	No. 101 Neg.	No. 116 Pos.	No. 116 Neg.	No. 109 Pos.	No. 109 Neg.
Nose 10 / Head 10 (20)	18		16		14		20		18		12	
Ears 5 / Neck 5 (10)	9		10		10		10		6		5	
Legs 6 / Feet 6 (12)	12		9		6			12	10		10	
Elbows 4 / Hocks 2 / Stifle 2 (8)	7		6		5		8		8		6	
Shoulders and Chest (15)		4		14	15		15		10		15	
Back and Thighs (15)	15		14		11		12		10			10
Coat 5 / Colour 5 (10)	10		9		8		10		10		10	
Quality 5 / Stern 5 (10)	10		8		6		10		10		10	
Positive Total / Negative Total	81	4	72	14	75		85	12	82		68	10
Totals of Positive and Negative Points	81	4	72	14	75		85	12	82		68	10
Nett Totals	77		58		75		73		82		58	

By inserting the points given at the end of each article in the following chapter, instead of those of the pointer, a series of scales may easily be compiled for the use of judges.

CHAPTER II.

ON JUDGING AT FIELD TRIALS.

HE judging at Field Trials has for some years been conducted on the above principles at Stafford and Shrewsbury, without any negative points, which were, however, introduced at Vaynol, in September, 1871, and gave great satisfaction.

The following is the scale adopted at the Stafford and Shrewsbury trials, which prevailed up to that time. Under it a dog, which we will call Pilot, refusing to back, but reasonably good in other points, would score 52, but under the negative scale 10 would be deducted from his totals, and very properly so, that being the amount of the allowance for backing, which is not only not to be calculated in his favour, but is absolutely to be deducted from his total score. Now, as the dog refusing to back does mischief to the sport so far as often to spoil it altogether, it is quite right that he should be severely punished for his offence, and on that account I think the principle is quite sound. It was at first considered that backing is merely the result of breaking, and therefore is no test of the utility or otherwise of a stud dog. Hence, nose, point, pace, and range were made the chief tests, omitting all notice of backing, dropping to shot, &c. This was, I think, a mistake as regards backing, which is as inherent in some breeds as the point, and quite as difficult to impart by education.

MR. BRAILSFORD'S SCALE OF POINTS AS USED AT STAFFORD AND
SHREWSBURY.

Name of Dog.	Pace and Range.	Obedience.	Style in Hunting.	Game-finding Abilities.	Style in Pointing.	Merit in Backing.	Marks, Total.	Good Points on Game.	General Remarks.
	20	20	15	20	15	10	100		
Pilot	15	10	10	5	12	0	52	3	

The scale used at Bedford and Bala was somewhat different; but still it did not introduce the negative points. I insert it as filled up at Bala by "The Prior" in the case of the celebrated Hamlet:

"Idstone's" Scale, as used at Bedford and Bala.

| Name of Dog. | 40 | 30 | 10 | Staunchness. | | | | 100 | Good Points on Game. |
	Nose.	Pace and Range.	Temperament.	10 Before.	10 Behind.	Style.		Marks, Total.	
Hamlet .... First hour	30	20	5	10	10	Indifferent.		75	2
Ditto .... Second hour	40	25	5	10	10	Good.		90	3
Ditto .... Third hour	40	25	10	10	10	Good.		95	3

Now, supposing Hamlet had refused to back, he would only be mulcted 10 points from the above totals; whereas, according to my ideas, he ought to lose 20. Moreover, there is no calculation made for "dropping to wing and shot," two most important items in the utility of a pointer or setter. Taking these considerations into view, I proposed for adoption at the Vaynol trials the following modifications of the Bedford and Bala scale, which was originally intended only to test dogs used for stud purposes. This, when filled up for a dog of average merits, would be as follows :

SCALE OF POINTS.

| Name and Age of Dog. | Value of Points when perfect. | | | | | | | General Remarks. |
| | 30 | 20 | 20 | 15 | 10 | 5 | 100 | |
	Nose.	Pace and Style in Hunting.	Breaking, as shown in working to hand, and dropping to wing and shot.	Style and Steadiness in Pointing.	Backing.	Drawing on Game, or Roading.	Total Value.	A very good dog naturally, but almost wholly unbroken.
Pilot, 4½ years.								
Positive	30	10		5			45	
Deduct Negative...			15		10	5	30	
Net Total of Points...............................							15	

This scale worked admirably at Vaynol for two years in succession, and not only did the judges experience no difficulty in carrying it out, but the spectators were satisfied with the results, to a degree which I have never seen equalled elsewhere.

In the third year, however, one of the subscribers and his confederate, having been previously spoiled by a long series of successes, objected to the decisions, alleging that the dogs were not worked out in pairs, as in coursing; and since then an attempt has been made under the instigation of Mr. Lowe, the Secretary of the Kennel Club, to establish a code of points founded upon the number of times each dog has found game or backed his competitor, without reference to style, pace, &c. Again and again attempts have been made to carry this plan out, but it has uniformly failed, as might be expected, and when put to the vote of the subscribers to a stake, it has always been negatived. During the present season, 1877, and prior to the trials at Horseheath of the Kennel Club Derby dogs, Mr. Brewis, the liberal owner of the estate on which they take place, has attempted to combine the two plans; but as the combination is still in a state of development, no opinion can fairly be given of its merits.

The following article was published by myself recently in the *Field*, being a comparison between the two plans adopted this year at Shrewsbury and Horseheath. It may, I think, be studied with advantage by those who either dislike judging by points, or desire to carry out the system of pairing all the dogs entered, as in coursing, forgetting altogether the difference between that sport and shooting.

"At the risk of incurring the charge of publishing vain repetitions of our opinions on the above subject, we are tempted once more to return to it, in consequence of recent very remarkable events, which tend to show that we have not been without a good foundation for those so often expressed in these columns.

"In regard to the trials, we think that two positions have been established by the late meetings at Shrewsbury and Horseheath. First, that the absolute winner should never be selected until the latest possible time; and secondly, that the same absence of haste should be displayed in finally rejecting each competitor—that is to say, the system of running the dogs in pairs, adopted in coursing, should not be followed in field trials. The great drawback to these trials is the necessarily short time which can be devoted to the several pairs; and, as a consequence, it is desirable to arrange them so that, if possible, a dog should be estimated according to his whole performance, if tried more than once, rather than by that in any separate run. In coursing it is impossible to carry out such a scheme, because the relative amount of work done by the two dogs previously to any particular course after the first round influences their respective powers very considerably, and, therefore, it would be very difficult for a judge to select any two at his discretion for trial; and the result of long experience is, that the only resource is to draw the whole entry out in pairs by lot, and afterwards try the several winners in the successive rounds together, according to their first position on the card. But in pointer and setter trials no such difficulty exists. The amount of work done by each dog is only sufficient to steady him, and the judges can fairly pair any two whenever they like, as has been done at all meetings but those of late years held under the auspices of the Kennel Club. At Shrewsbury the covert has generally been so bad, and game so scarce, that the trials have been only of the nature of a farce; but this year the ground was nearly equally good with that at Horseheath, and it is therefore fair to compare the results of the two meetings conducted as they are on wholly different plans.

"At Shrewsbury a scale of points originally drawn up by Mr. Brailsford is adopted, in which a certain value is attached to the several qualities demanded in the setter and pointer in the abstract, calculating the whole, when perfectly displayed, at 100. This scale is printed, and furnished to the judges, with the addition of the names of the competitors in each stake, and is made up as follows—namely, for pace and range, 20; obedience, 20; style in hunting, 15; game finding abilities, 20; style in pointing, 15; merit in backing, 10—total 100. After trying a brace of dogs, the judges have only to go through the scale with each, and set down under the above heads the comparative degree of merit shown by them. Thus, under "pace and range," if a dog is only of average merit, they put down 10; if three-quarters, 15; or if perfect, 20. Proceeding next to "obedience," they estimate his merits in the same way as compared with perfection, putting down 10 if an average display has been made, and 20 if perfect; and so on through the whole scale, calculating the figures according to the amount of merit.

"After thus estimating A., the next thing is to proceed in the same way with B., and whichever has the higher figure of merit is declared the winner; or, if equal, a further trial is necessary. On concluding the first round or series of pairs, the judges have only to select the dogs with the highest figure of merit, and place them first, second, and third accordingly, unless the figures of two or more are very near together, when it has been customary to give these animals a further trial; and at the last Shrewsbury meeting it was very properly, as we think, decided that in all cases the highest two should have this. Under both the Shrewsbury and Kennel Club plans, it often happens that the two best dogs come together in the first or second round; but in the former plan they may be ultimately placed first and second; whereas in the latter this is impossible, as the inferior of the two in any particular trial is at once *hors de combat*. As an illustration of this statement, we may instance the fact that in the first two pointer stakes at Shrewsbury this actually occurred in the second round; whilst in the third and most important it took place in the first, Bang and Dick meeting in that position, and being ultimately declared the first and second prize holders. No doubt a mistake was here committed, which the Kennel Club plan would have prevented; but this was manifestly a fault in the practice of the judges, and was not incidental to the plan itself, as proved by the general opinion of the spectators declared at the time, and embodied in our report. It occurred in this way. After a long and very tiring day, the first round of the Combermere Stakes had been completed at seven o'clock, and the judges, overlooking the new rule to which we have adverted above, and considering Bang to be undoubtedly the best in the stake, at once declared him the winner, and ordered three dogs, including Dick, beaten by him, to compete next day for second and third prizes. In this decision they overlooked, most probably from inadvertence, Mr. Whitehouse's Rapid, who had just defeated Rector (the winner there for the last two years) in a short trial, confined to one field, in which Rapid made only the pardonable mistake of flushing a brace of birds the moment he was cast off, and with an undeniably bad scent—a mistake also partially condoned by a subsequent good find. Now, if the judges had at once cast up the "points" made by Rapid and Bang, they must, according to the Shrewsbury scale, have made them at least equal, and thus insured a second trial, since "the pace, range, and style" of Rapid are very superior to those of Bang; and these qualities are estimated at the high relative value of thirty-five out of one hundred, whereas "game-finding," the only quality in which the former could be considered to be excelled by the latter, is valued at twenty. As before remarked, the Kennel Club plan would have prevented this; but in rescuing Rapid from Scylla it would have drawn Dick into Charybdis, since his defeat by Bang would have prevented his getting even the third prize, except under the special provision made by the competitors themselves in the case of the Horseheath "Derby," which, though an improvement on the "heats" method, renders it still more complicated and tedious. Curiously enough, Rapid endorsed this opinion formed by the spectators at Shrewsbury, by defeating Bang at Horseheath, though, as we all know the variation of these animals on different days, it does not prove that he would have done the same at Shrewsbury if they had come together. Passing from the pointers to the setters, we find at Shrewsbury Brave Boy, to whom the third prize was allotted, defeated by Nora (the winner) in the first round, which would have stopped his career under the Kennel Club plan. On the other hand, in the "Derby" at Horseheath, according to the opinion of our reporter, the two best performers came together in the first round, when Danger, who was ultimately placed fourth, beat Norna (the winner at Shrewsbury), and the latter was consequently not allowed another trial. These two were first and second at Shrewsbury without dispute, but in a reverse position to that at Horseheath; and with Die behind them both, she being beaten by Norna in the second round, and not tried a third time. At Horseheath, Die, the winner of the first prize, behaved shamefully in her first two trials, and, if estimated on her average performance throughout the Derby, would have come out badly; but, happening to meet in the first two rounds animals worse than herself, she luckily reached the third round, when, being paired with Danger, who did not do so well as in her previous trials, she just managed to score a win, though, according to our reporter, Danger, on the whole, showed herself to be evidently "the better setter of the two;" and this opinion, coming from a supporter of the "heats" plan, is not likely to be prejudiced in favour of Danger.

"Now, if the object of these trials is to reward the owner of the best dog

in each stake with the first prize, we think the evidence afforded by the pro-
ceedings at these two meetings is strongly in favour of the system of judging
by points, without necessarily running in "heats." With the same time at their
disposal, worse ground, and, we will assume, equal knowledge of their task, the
Shrewsbury judges in two days settled the pretensions of eighty-five dogs,
against thirty-one at Horseheath; and in no instance was such an animal as
Norna put out without a second opportunity of showing his or her powers,
except in the single case of Rapid, which, as above shown, was clearly a mistake, caused· by hurriedly coming to a decision without any necessity for it, and
therefore not in any way implicating the system adopted; and, when it is considered that the numbers judged at Shrewsbury in two days were nearly three
times as great as those judged at Horseheath in the same time, the balance in
favour of the plan adopted at the former is at once apparent.

"We are by no means pledging ourselves to the opinion that the scale of
points adopted at Shrewsbury is incapable of improvement, and we prefer that
used at Vaynol and Bala; but we contend that its principle is correct for the
following reasons:

"1st. It is admitted that the great drawback to these trials is the want of
time to test the merits of the competing dogs fully and fairly. 2nd. The
Shrewsbury plan economises time by devoting as much as possible to the best
dogs in each stake, without wasting it on a second, third, or fourth trial of
inferior animals. 3rd. The Kennel Club method of heats often leads to the
entire defeat of one of the best dogs in a stake in the first or second round, by
meeting either the best or the second best in it, which *contretemps* does not
occur in the Shrewsbury plan. 4th. At Shrewsbury the average performance of
each dog is estimated by the judges, whether he is down once, twice, or thrice;
whereas under the Kennel Club plan a dog may, on the average, perform badly,
and yet, from happening to be in luck or in good temper in the third or fourth
trial may be hailed the winner of the stake, as really happened at Horseheath,
even after such a shamefully bad performance as that of Die. We beg most
distinctly to state that in the above observations we cast no reflections on this
fine bitch, which we greatly admired at Shrewsbury; and we have reason to
believe that she will ultimately turn out to be as good as any setter puppy we
have seen this year. What we mean to imply is that every dog should be
judged by the average merit displayed by him or her, and not by the results
of single trials. In short, our object is that, as far as possible, the luck connected with meeting bad or good competitors, or with bad or good ground, should
be eliminated from these trials, which, though not attended by any number of
spectators, are regarded with great interest by a large body of gentlemen possessed
of moors or manors.

"We have not alluded to the exploded plan of judging according to the
number of times each dog finds game during a certain fixed period, because
experience has shown its fallacy, and it has been abandoned after fair trial.
The choice now lies between the two methods which have this year been fairly

tried on nearly equally good ground, with judges of similar powers, and with almost exactly the same dogs competing, but with the great disadvantage at Shrewsbury of having the merits of eighty-five dogs to decide, instead of thirty-one at Horseheath, in the two days devoted to the principal stakes. Under these conditions, that the former should have come out equal with the latter is a strong argument in favour of the plan adopted there, especially when it is recollected that, but for the error in judgment alluded to above, which is not inherent in the plan, its superiority at all points would have been displayed. In this comparison we have not alluded to the subject of byes which have no unfair tendency at Shrewsbury, but are of necessity an evil in the Kennel Club plan."

PART II.
SPORTING DOGS.

—◦)◦⊙◦(◦—

BOOK I.
DOGS USED WITH THE GUN.

—◦)◦⊙◦(◦—

CHAPTER I.
SETTERS.

GENERAL REMARKS—THE ENGLISH SETTER—THE BLACK AND TAN OR
GORDON SETTER—THE IRISH SETTER.

—◦⌒◦/◦⌒◦—

GENERAL REMARKS.

THE four divisions of the United Kingdom may be said to have each a breed of setters peculiar to itself, though of late years many of each variety have been distributed beyond the limits of their respective districts. The English setter may be taken as the true type of the breed, next to which comes the Irish setter, while the old Llanidloes, or Welsh breed, retain more of the spaniel character. Their curly waterproof coats are, however, admirably suited to the wet climate of their native hills. It is said, and I think probably with truth, that the Scotch or Gordon setter is crossed with the bloodhound, which gives the comparatively heavy head and long folding ears often shown by him, and at the same time accounts for the delicacy of his nose and for the coarseness of his coat. At all events, his appearance is not so typical as that of the English and Irish breeds. The Gordons are now usually described as black and tans, to avoid the disputes as to the breeding of the several entries, for while there is no doubt that many black tans are not true Gordons, it is also indisputable that many true Gordons are black, white, and tan. Similar remarks may apply to the Irish setter, but he has not been treated in the same way, though, no doubt, a red setter of English breed, without any Irish blood, if exhibiting the desired points in perfection, would win in an Irish class. I must, however, take things as I find them, and describe the setter according to the definition given

x

in our prize lists, omitting the Welsh setter, which is not of sufficient importance to interest any but the few possessors of him who remain.

The setter is, without doubt, either descended from the spaniel, or both are offshoots from the same parent stock. Originally—that is before the improvements in the gun introduced the practice of "shooting flying,"—it is believed that he was merely a spaniel taught to "stop" or "set" as soon as he came upon the scent of the partridge, when a net was drawn over the covey by two men. Hence he was made to drop close to the ground, an attitude which is now unnecessary; though it is taught by some breakers, and notably to very fast dogs, who could not otherwise stop themselves quickly enough to avoid flushing. Manifestly, a dog prone on the ground allowed the net to be drawn over him better than if he was standing up; and hence the former attitude was preferred, an additional reason for its adoption being probably that it was more easily taught to a dog like the spaniel, which has not the natural cataleptic attitude of the pointer. But when "shooting flying" came into vogue, breakers made the attempt to assimilate the attitude of the setting spaniel, or "setter" as he was now called, to that of the pointer; and in process of time, and possibly also by crossing with that dog they succeeded, though, even after the lapse of more than a century, the cataleptic condition is not so fully displayed by the setter as by the pointer. In the present day, as a rule, the standing position is preferred, though some well known breakers, and notably George Thomas, Mr. Statter's keeper, have preferred the "drop," which certainly enables a fast dog to stop himself more quickly than he could do by standing up. It is, however, attended with the disadvantage that in heather or clover a "dropped" dog cannot be seen nearly so far as if he was standing, and on one occasion, at the Bala Trials of 1873, the celebrated Ranger was lost for many minutes, having "dropped" on game in a slight hollow, surrounded by heather. As a rule, therefore, the standing position is the better one, but in such fast dogs as Ranger and Drake, "dropping" may be excused. At the above meeting, however, after a long and evenly-balanced trial between Mr. Macdona's Ranger and Mr. R. J. Ll. Price's Belle, the latter only won by her superior attitude on the point, and Ranger was again penalised for dropping at Ipswich in 1873.

With regard to the low carriage of the setter's flag when at work, and his spaniel-like lashing of it; I think they indicate his spaniel descent, and are to be considered from that point of view. This "tail action" is now out of fashion with many good sportsmen, who allege that grouse as well as partridge do not lie so well to a dog exhibiting it largely as they do to a quiet trail. In theory this sounds well, but, as far as I know, it was never propounded until it was required to excuse the fox-like trail of Drake and Ranger in particular, and generally of the Laverack setters; and I confess that in practice I never noticed it in a long experience with both kinds of flag carriage. My bias in favour of "tail action" was founded upon the close observation of three successive litters, which I bred from a wonderfully good bitch about thirty years ago. Lucy was extremely handsome, fast, and untiring, which qualities, coupled with a good nose, gave her a considerable local reputation; and I think I may quote the opinion of that excellent sportsman, the present Rector of Wadhurst, who repeatedly shot over her in my company, that no better single-handed setter was ever seen. She had merry " tail action" without being overdone, which indeed her great pace forbade; and I was anxious to breed from her, for which purpose I put her for three successive years to the late Mr. John Clifton's Bacchus, of great renown in Worcestershire, nineteen puppies altogether being reared. Of these about half had the "tail action" of the mother, while the remainder were without it; and in every case, without a single exception, the "trailers" had no nose whatever, or a very bad one, while the "lively" ones possessed excellent scenting powers, and were indeed nearly all first class dogs. This first drew my attention to the two kinds of flag carriage, and since then I have almost always seen the quiet trail accompanied by a nose of equal dulness. In the pointer I have not found the same remark apply, having both seen and myself possessed dogs of that breed with good noses unaccompanied by "tail action" in a proportion fully equal to one-half, if not more, and I have consequently abandoned all idea of connecting the one with the other in the pointer. In the setter, however, I have still thought, from careful observation, that my original fancy held good, and when I saw Sir R. Garth's Grouse and May, produced at Stafford as pure Laveracks, on trial for the first time in public, the absence of all "tail action" and their low carriage of the head prejudiced me against the breed, which their subsequent bad performance confirmed. Even the brilliant pace and style of Countess and Nellie did not entirely dissipate this original bias; for, though I am not induced to believe that this strain is, on the average, possessed of absolutely bad noses, yet I should not say that they come up to the level of the best old English setter strains, or to the Gordons or Irish. Indeed, I consider this their weak point. Countess, Nellie, and Daisy, could find game well enough with a good scent, but they were comparatively useless with a bad one. In addition to Ranger, whose nose is undeniably good, Dash II., a three-quarter Laverack, who has recently won all before him at Horseheath, may be adduced as a notable exception to the above conclusion; but beyond these I cannot recollect any setter who has appeared in public without tail action possessed of an unexceptionably good nose. Hence, rightly or wrongly, I have still regarded these two features as of considerable importance; and, knowing them to be strongly developed in the spaniel, I conclude that they are transmitted to his descendant the setter, and, as such, that they are to be regarded as his natural attributes.

The greater frequency of a good nose without "tail action" in the pointer than in the setter, supposing it to exist, may, I think, be explained in the following way. Both the original pointer and the spaniel undoubtedly always possessed "tail action," which has probably been lost in many examples of each breed by crossing with the hound. Now, the foxhound chiefly tries for the foot scent, and so does the spaniel; while the peculiarity of the true pointer is that he carries his head high in the air, trying for the body scent, in which he is imitated by the best setter strains. As a consequence, according to my theory, the hound cross was borne by the pointer, while it was fatal to the setter, making the latter—who had by a long process of selection lost the spaniel's kind of nose in the hands of the most successful breeders—return to his original low carriage of head and "quest" of the foot scent.

There is a quality of great importance to the enjoyment of a good day's shooting over setters or pointers which has not in our field trials been, I think, sufficiently attended to, namely, the mental development necessary to distinguish between a "false point," and one really on game. Even in partridge shooting it is a great nuisance to be dragged all across a large field without seeing fur or feather before you, your dog standing "as stiff as a crutch;" but on a grouse moor it is still worse. Of course even the best dog will occasionally make a mistake, but to be constantly misleading his master is an unmitigated bore. There are two or even three causes of this "false pointing." 1st. A dog may be so bred as to develop the tendency by association of ideas; that is to say, to point without any scent at all, and only from some indication either of eye or ear. 2ndly. A point often occurs from a dog feeling the scent which has been left behind by birds or "fur" recently gone away; and 3rdly. Some soft or lazy dogs point when they are tired, simply to get a rest from their gallop. Now, as to the first of these causes, I have had little or no personal experience in the setter; but I have certainly seen it strongly developed in the old-fashioned pointer, and notably in a well-known strain kept very pure by the last Lord Foley, which, like the Laverack setters, were very much in-bred. But they were very different from that strain in point of stamina and courage, and required no breaking whatever. I should not, therefore, from their example have suspected its existence in the Laveracks, which are said to require a great deal of breaking; although, since it was alleged against them as a fault by "Setter," I can call to mind the fact that Sir R. Garth's Daisy, when she won at Shrewsbury in 1869, began to point almost as soon as she was cast off by her breaker, and the general impression was that it was a trick, for which E. Armstrong got the blame, as her false point ended in a draw; and this going on till she came on game, Daisy obtained credit which it was thought she did not deserve. Not having seen Blue Belle III. at Horseheath, I must depend on the evidence of the *Field* reporter, who describes her as manifesting the fault five times in succession in a short time, pointing and staring about her when on the point, in a way to show clearly that no game was before her. Assuming this account to be correct—as I have no doubt it is—it certainly corroborates "Setter's" statement in a remarkable manner, and endorses the opinion generally formed that the strain is too much in-bred. Most probably Mr. Laverack selected for stud purposes those animals which showed the greatest tendency to point naturally, and in this way obtained the cataleptic tendency in excess. But this propensity is by no means objectionable when crossed with other strains, and hence we have seen such good dogs as Mr. Field's Daisy, Mr. Macdona's Ranger, Mr. Brewis's Dash II., and Mr. Purcell Llewellin's Norna and Nora.

The second kind of "false point" is the most common, and should be severely

MR. PURCELL LLEWELLIN'S ENGLISH SETTER "COUNTESS."

punished in the fully broken dog by every means short of the whip. Most breakers, and especially when preparing for field trials, are content to get a point, whether false or true, since the practice usually has been, at public trials, to give the dog credit for the point, if in the opinion of the judge game had recently gone away, whether the dog has made out his mistake or not. But the experienced sportsman is not content with such a mental defect, and expects his pointer or setter to tell him clearly whether or no he is certain of a find. The nose should be keen enough to make a dog stop in his gallop however slight the scent, and he should even point; but no sooner is the stop made, than he should set his brains to work to discover the actual presence or absence of game, which is easily made out by a clever dog, who soon finds the scent diminish if not kept up by a fresh supply from the bird or ground game. To be able to say with certainty that "Grouse" or "Duke" has game before him, and to march any distance to him with confidence is a pleasure only equalled by the annoyance suffered, when after a long march a blank is the result. Hence, I think it highly important that a "false point" repeated more than once in a short trial should be regarded as a fatal defect in selecting a dog or bitch for stud purposes.

As to the third kind of false point arising from laziness alone, I need scarcely remark that a dog exhibiting it is only fit for a hempen collar or a charge of shot.

POINTS OF THE SETTER.—The numerical value of the points in each breed is the same, though the description in several of them will vary. I therefore begin by allotting the following figures to each, referring my readers to the three articles for their varying definitions.

VALUE OF POINTS IN SETTER.

	Value.		Value.		Value.		Value.
Skull	10	Shoulders and		Legs, elbows,		Flag	5
Nose	10	chest	15	and hocks	12	Symmetry and	
Ears, lips, and		Back, quarters		Feet	8	quality	5
eyes	4	and stifles	15			Texture of coat	
Neck	6					and feather	5
						Colour	5
	30		30		20		20

*Grand Total—*100.

THE ENGLISH SETTER.

Since the first publication of the articles on the various breeds of dogs in *The Field*, during the years 1865-6, the strain of English setters known by the name of "Laverack," from the gentleman who bred them, has carried all before it, both on the show bench and in the public field trials which have been annually held. For this high character it is greatly indebted to the celebrated Countess, who was certainly an extraordinary animal, both in appearance and at work; for until she came out the only Laverack which had shone to advantage was Sir R. Garth's Daisy, a good average bitch. Though small, Countess was possessed of extraordinary pace, not perhaps quite equal to that of the still more celebrated pointer Drake, but approaching so closely to it that his superiority would be disputed by many of her admirers. On referring to her portrait accompanying this chapter, it will be seen that her frame, though on short legs, is full of elegance, and her beautiful head and neck are absolutely perfect. With her high pace she combined great power of endurance, and her chief fault was that she never could be fully depended on; for, when fresh enough to display her speed and style to the full, she would break away from her master and defy his whistle until she had taken her fling over a thousand acres or so. On a good scenting day it was a high treat to see her at work; but, like most other fast gallopers, she would sometimes flush her game on a bad scenting day, and then she would be wild with shame. An instance of this occurred at the Bala field trials of 1872, when, on her appearance in the stake for braces with her sister Nellie, both of these bitches were utterly beyond the control of Mr. Buckell, who worked them, Nellie even chasing a bird like a raw puppy. To get rid of this wildness, they were worked hard in the day which intervened between their appearance in the braces and Countess's trial in the Rhiwlas Stakes, when she came out as stale as a poster, and was only placed third to Ranger and Belle. Still, though manifestly beaten, she evidently was so from bad judgment alone on the part of those who managed her; and she only injured the character of the stock to which she belongs so far as to show that, like most high-couraged setters, they require a certain amount of work to keep them steady, which it appears she had not done. Nellie (the sister) was of the same size, but not so fast nor so elegant; still she was good enough to beat the crack on one occasion at Vaynol in 1872, but on most days she would have stood no chance against Countess. She served to show that Countess was not wholly exceptional, as was sometimes alleged by the detractors of the " Laverack "; and these two bitches, together with Sir R. Garth's Daisy, may fairly be adduced as indicating that at all events the Laverack bitches are quite first-class. No dog, however, of the pure breed has yet put in an appearance at any field trial with any pretension to high form, but several winners have appeared half or quarter bred of that strain. For example, Mr. Statter's Bruce, by Dash (Laverack) out of owner's Rhœbe, and his Rob Roy, by Fred II. (also Laverack) out of the same bitch, may be adduced; but Dick and Dan, by Duke (of the Corbet and Graham strain) out of Rhœbe, were far superior to these dogs, and serve to show that, at all events as crosses for other breeds, the Laveracks are not to be so highly recommended as Mr. Lort and other disciples of the " Laverack" school would lead us to believe. The cross which has been most successful is that with Mr. Lort's, Sir R. Garth's, and Mr. Paul Hackett's blood, culminating in the third remove from the Laverack kennel in Mr. Macdona's Ranger. This dog was fully as fast as Countess, with a keener nose and far better temperament, being, when in form, as steady and dependable as a steam locomotive. Mr. Macdona's favourite may be classed A 1 among the field trial winners in a quintet including Drake, Countess, Dash II., and Belle; the Irish setter,

Plunket, approaching them very nearly, but not quite reaching their level. Roll and Frank, who won several prizes on the show bench, are of the same cross as the grandsire of Ranger, all being out of Lort's Dip by a Laverack dog, and these last being all the same blood, as I shall presently show, though their sires are respectively named Rock and Fred II. Roll was a grand dog in shape, with the exception of his loin, in which a certain amount of slackness was displayed when a little out of condition, as he generally was when shown, being a shy feeder. I am told by Mr. Lort, who shot over him for some time, that he was as good in the field as on the bench, but when I tried him he had no nose whatever. His pace was very great, with the usual Laverack quiet trail of flag; and the spaniel-like character peculiar to the Laverack dog is also quite lost in him by the cross with the Anglesea bitch Dip. Next to this cross comes that with the Corbet and Graham strains as shewn in Mr. Brewis's Dash II., who this year (1877) has beaten Ranger in two out of three stakes at Shrewsbury and Horseheath, and whose portrait I have selected, with that of Countess, to illustrate this breed as excellent specimens of the high-bred English setter, though the dog is still, in my opinion, a little too spaniel-like in the shape of the body. He and his sister, Daisy, also a field trial winner, are by Laverack's Blue Prince, out of Armstrong's Old Kate. This bitch is by Laverack's old Blue Dash, out of E. Armstrong's Kate, sister to his Duke, the sire of Dan, about whose stock a great deal has been written in the highest terms by "Peveril" and "Setter" in the *Field* and elsewhere, and by Mr. Purcell Llewellin, who has used him as a stud dog almost exclusively to cross with his Laverack bitches, after purchasing him at a very high price, together with his brother Dick, from Mr. Statter at the Shrewsbury meeting of 1871. The opinions expressed by these gentlemen must be taken *cum grano salis*, as they are manifestly interested in the breed, which they style as *par excellence* "the field trial breed" from the successes obtained by its component parts at these trials. I shall therefore confine myself in my remarks on it to their public performances as observed by myself and others, disregarding all private opinions in this as in all other cases, from my experience of the little reliance to be placed upon them.

The most remarkable feature in the Laverack breed of setters is the extraordinary extent to which in-breeding has been carried, as shown in the pedigree of Countess, given by Mr. Laverack in his book on the setter. By examining this carefully, it will be seen that every animal in it is descended from Ponto and Old Moll, which were obtained by Mr. Laverack in 1825 from the Rev. A. Harrison, who lived near Carlisle, and who had kept the breed pure for thirty-five years. Four names only besides these two are found in the right hand column, and these four are all descended from Ponto and Old Moll, as will be seen at a glance by referring to the names in italic in the middle of the table. Thus it appears that they alone formed Mr. Laverack's breed, though he often stated that he had tried the introduction of alien blood, but finding it not to answer he had abandoned the produce, and resorted again to the original stock. This has led to the belief that the pedigree is incorrect, but he was very positive in his statement. If correct, it certainly is the most remarkable case of breeding in and in I ever met with.

PEDIGREE OF MR. PURCELL LLEWELLIN'S COUNTESS, SISTER TO NELLIE AND SAM.

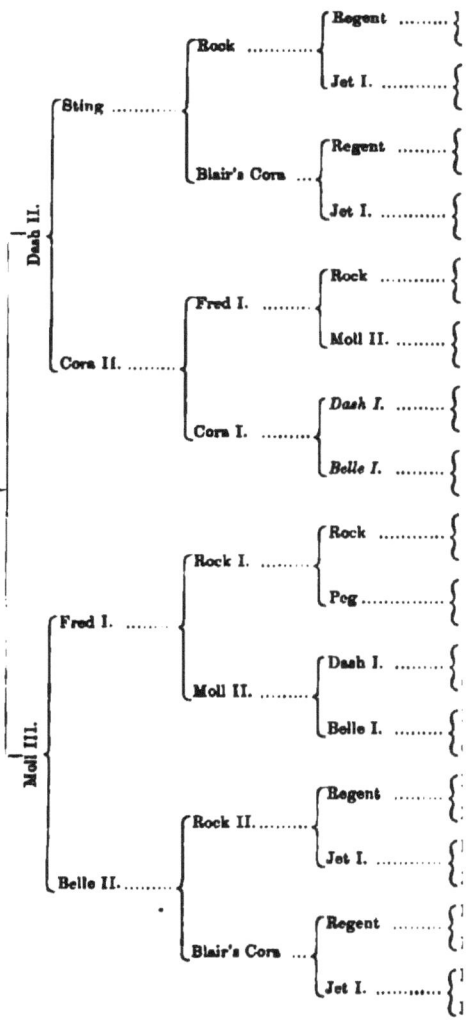

- Dash II.
  - Sting
    - Rock
      - Regent ....
      - Jet I. ....
    - Blair's Cora ...
      - Regent ....
      - Jet I. ....
  - Cora II. ....
    - Fred I. ....
      - Rock ....
      - Moll II. ....
    - Cora I. ....
      - *Dash I.* ....
      - *Belle I.* ....
- Moll III.
  - Fred I. ......
    - Rock I. ....
      - Rock ....
      - Peg ....
    - Moll II. ....
      - Dash I. ....
      - Belle I. ....
  - Belle II. ....
    - Rock II. ....
      - Regent ....
      - Jet I. ....
    - Blair's Cora ...
      - Regent ....
      - Jet I. ....

To this in-breeding is, no doubt, to be attributed the fact that the Laverack setters are very difficult to rear, and that a large proportion of them die of distemper. Whether or no the average working "form" of the breed is a high one, is very difficult to decide; but, undoubtedly, Countess and her sister Nelly were grand specimens of the high-bred setter. Nearly all the pure Laverack dogs which have been shown are too spaniel-like in shape to please my eye, the only exceptions I remember being Prince and Rock, and to some extent the well-known Sam, brother to Countess and Nellie; nevertheless, they have not the spaniel carriage of the flag alluded to above, which is in them generally trailed like that of the fox, and without any lashing or feathering. Probably it is owing to the excessive in-breeding of the Laveracks injuring their health that they have not succeeded as well as might be expected as sires; but at all events, from whatever cause, a good deal of disappointment has been felt by breeders on that score. Nevertheless, for work the breed still maintains the high character gained for it in its purity by Countess, Nellie, and Garth's Daisy, and for its crosses by Ranger, Dick, Dash II., Field's Daisy, Prince, Ginx's Baby, Glen, Rhoda, Druid, Norah and Nora, and, last, but not least, that excellent little bitch, Mr. Lloyd Price's Queen, by Blue Prince out the Rev. S. East's Quaver II.—bred by that gentleman from his own old Shropshire blood.

A great many different strains of English setters might be adduced from all parts of the country, but notably from the north of England, with claims superior to those of Mr. Laverack's strain, up to the time of the institution of field trials. Among these were the Graham and Corbet breeds, those of the Earl of Tankerville, Lord Waterpark, Mr. Bishop, Mr. Bayley, Mr. Lort, Mr. Jones (of Oscott), Major Cowan, Mr. Withington, Mr. Paul Hackett, and Mr. Calver, the last two being a good deal crossed with Gordon blood. None of these strains were, however, so generally known beyond the immediate circle of their owners' friends as to have gained a universal reputation; and it was not till the public appearance of Mr. Garth's Daisy, and afterwards that of Mr. Purcell Llewellyn's Countess and Nelly, that the Laverack strain attained its present high reputation. Before Daisy came out, Mr. Garth had produced a brace of very bad ones at Stafford in 1867; and it was with considerable prejudice against them that the above celebrated bitches first exhibited their powers, in spite of the high character given of them by Mr. Lort, Mr. Withington, and other well-known sportsmen who had shot over them for years. It is Mr. Lort's opinion that Mr. Withington possessed better dogs than even Countess; but it must not be forgotten that private trials are generally more flattering than those before the public.

I come now to consider the value of Mr. Llewellyn's "field trial" strain, as they are somewhat grandiloquently termed by their "promoters," or as I shall term them, the "Dan-Laveracks," being all either by Dan out of Laverack bitches, or by a Laverack dog out of a sister to Dan. As a proof of the superiority of this cross to the pure Laveracks "Setter" states, that "during the last two years ten of this breed" (Laveracks), "and ten of the Duke-Rhœbe and Laverack cross, have been sent to America; the former including Petrel, winner of the champion

prize at Birmingham, Pride of the Border,
Rock, Leicester, Rob Roy, Dart, and Do
sorts. At the Americans Shows both so
has always beaten the Laverack. At fiel
but, first, second, and third prizes were
champion stakes, by dogs of the Rhœbe l
kennel." I confess that, in my opinion
in the one over the other, as far as I
tested together; and in reference to th
the show bench, it is of little interes
hesitatingly state, that, as far as my j
it go, "Setter" is quite correct. Dan h
handsome dog, and his stock might then
the Laverack dogs are nearly all heavy
very elegant, too small and delicate for pei
the Laveracks have not shown very del
always considered them rather deficient
is the worst point of the setter as com
regarded, therefore, as the first essential
though I have always regarded Duke hims
in pace and range, and have estimated
with Mr. Statter's Phœbe, favourably, as
shown in Bruce and Rob Roy, yet I no
the Laverack bitches, because his sire a
that of the Laveracks themselves. Du
correctly, to have received a high charac
as exhibited in private, but he was notoriou
before the public, going with his head l
body scent. In proof of this defect it is
by Hamlet and Young Kent in this qualit
him only thirty-one out of a possible fo
following spring Rex found birds twent;
left his point, and thereby gained the ci
being one of the judges, and loud in ad;
finding fault with that of Duke. Indeed,
for E. Armstrong's constant interference
rightly or wrongly I do not pretent to
breaker's want of confidence in his dog's n
enough to give an opinion as to this qui
produce I do not remember any but Bruce
amount of scenting powers. Rob Roy
Dick, brother to Dan, in his second sea;
and is so described in the report of the
reasons, although I had always considere

two Laverack-Rhœbe litters, I never expected Dan to get such a good bitch as Norna in point of nose and correct carriage of head and flag, according to my ideas. If Nora, as alleged by her owner and "Setter," as well as by *The Field* reporter at Horseheath, is superior to her, I can only make my apology to Dan, and admit that he has turned out a better sire than I expected, and than might have been gathered from the performances of Laura, Leda, and Druid, at the Devon and Cornwall, and Sleaford trials of 1874, which I saw. These two bitches were slow and without any style whatever, while the dog, though moderately fast, was well beaten by Ranger at Sleaford at all points.

In 1875 it is true he turned the tables on Mr. Macdona's dog, who was out of all form at that meeting, but he could only get second to Viscount Downe's Sam, who was consequently at once added to Mr. Llewellin's kennel. Taking into consideration that the dogs which have been exhibited by Mr. Llewellin are picked from a very large kennel, and that as far as I have seen them perform, they have not proved themselves to be above the average, I can only come to the conclusion that Dan has not done any great good in improving the Laveracks, except in size and looks. Neither do I place him or any of his stock in the first rank of field trials winners, which in setters would, I think, include only Countess, Ranger, and Dash II., forming with the pointers Drake and Belle, a quintet in class A1, as remarked above. Dan came out in public only once, it is true, though winning three stakes at that meeting; but he met the same competitors in all, and the victory was virtually a single one. After this he put his shoulder out and never appeared in public, but his brother Dick, who was coupled with him in the braces, and went equally well with him in the short trial accorded them, did nothing worth speaking of next year, except to win the brace prize at Southampton, "by a succession of false points, in which he was splendidly backed" by his companion Ruby; and to divide the Stoneham Stakes with his only competitor Robin, "neither being able to find birds," though Dick "made many points, all of which turned out to be at nothing," according to the report in *The Field*, which is no doubt worthy of all credit from the well known ability of the writer. Moreover, Dan at Shrewsbury had a very narrow escape of defeat by Rake, as recorded by myself at the time, so that on mature reflection I have no hesitation in placing him below the first class; but possibly he is entitled to rank in the second along with Plunket and his son and daughter, Kite and Music (Irish), together with Kate, Rex and Lang (Gordons). To them may probably be added the Dan-Laveracks Nora and Norah, and also Die, the last two winners respectively at Shrewsbury and Horseheath of the puppy stakes, all more or less crossed with the late Mr. Laverack's strain. To sum up, therefore, it may be safely alleged that his setters have been of great service to sportsmen in giving pace and style when crossed with other breeds.

The *points* of the English setter may be described as follows:

1. The *skull* (value 10) has a character peculiar to itself, somewhat between that of the pointer and cocker spaniel, not so heavy as the former's, and larger than the latter's. It is without the prominence of the occipital bone so remarkable in

the pointer, is also narrower between the ears, and there is a decided brow over the eyes.

2. The *nose* (value 5) should be long and wide, without any fullness under the eyes. There should be in the average dog setter at least four inches from the inner corner of the eye to the end of the nose. Between the point and the root of the nose there should be a slight depression—at all events, there should be no fullness—and the eyebrows should rise sharply from it. The nostrils must be wide apart and large in the openings, and the end should be moist and cool, though many a dog with exceptionally good scenting powers has had a remarkably dry nose, amounting in some cases to roughness like that of shagreen. In all setters the end of the nose should be black, or dark liver-coloured, but in the very best bred whites or lemon and whites pink is often met with, and may in them be pardoned. The jaws should be exactly equal in length, a "snipe nose," or " pig jaw," as the receding lower one is called, being greatly against its possessor.

3. *Ears, lips*, and *eyes* (value 4). With regard to ears, they should be shorter than the pointer's and rounded, but not so much so as those of the spaniel. The "leather" should be thin and soft, carried closely to the cheeks, so as not to show the inside, without the slightest tendency to prick the ear, which should be clothed with silky hair little more than two inches in length. The lips also are not so full and pendulous as those of the pointer, but at their angles there should be a slight fullness, not reaching quite to the extent of hanging. The eyes must be full of animation, and of medium size, the best colour being a rich brown, and they should be set with their angles straight across.

4. The *neck* (value 6) has not the full rounded muscularity of the pointer, being considerably thinner, but still slightly arched, and set into the head without that prominence of the occipital bone which is so remarkable in that dog. It must not be "throaty," though the skin is loose.

5. The *shoulders* and *chest* (value 15) should display great liberty in all directions, with sloping deep shoulder blades, and elbows well let down. The chest should be deep rather than wide, though Mr. Laverack insists on the contrary formation, italicising the word *wide* in his remarks at page 22 of his book. Possibly it may be owing to this formation that his dogs have not succeeded at any field trial, as above remarked; for the bitches of his breed, notably Countess and Daisy, which I have seen, were as narrow as any setter breeder could desire. I am quite satisfied that on this point Mr. Laverack is altogether wrong. I fully agree with him, however, that the " ribs should be well sprung behind the shoulder," and great depth of the back ribs should be especially demanded.

6. *Back, quarters*, and *stifles* (value 15). An arched loin is desirable, but not to the extent of being "roached" or "wheel-backed," a defect which generally tends to a slow up-and-down gallop. Stifles well bent, and set wide apart, to allow the hind legs to be brought forward with liberty in the gallop.

7. *Legs, elbows*, and *hocks* (value 12). The elbows and toes, which generally go together, should be set straight; and if not, the "pigeon-toe" or in-turned leg

is less objectionable than the out-turn, in which the elbow is confined by its close attachment to the ribs. The arm should be muscular and the bone fully developed, with strong and broad knees, short pasterns, of which the size in point of bone should be as great as possible (a very important point), and their slope not exceeding a very slight deviation from the straight line. Many good judges insist upon a perfectly upright pastern, like that of the foxhound; but it must not be forgotten that the setter has to stop himself suddenly when at full stretch he catches scent, and to do this with an upright and rigid pastern causes a considerable strain on the ligaments, soon ending in "knuckling over;" hence a very slight bend is to be preferred. The hind legs should be muscular, with plenty of bone, clean strong hocks, and hairy feet.

8. The *feet* (value 8) should be carefully examined, as upon their capability of standing wear and tear depends the utility of the dog. A great difference of opinion exists as to the comparative merits of the cat and hare foot for standing work. Foxhound masters invariably select that of the cat, and, as they have better opportunities than any other class of instituting the necessary comparison, their selection may be accepted as final. But, as setters are specially required to stand wet and heather, it is imperatively necessary that there should be a good growth of hair between the toes, and on this account a hare foot, well clothed with hair, as it generally is, must be preferred to a cat foot naked, as is often the case, except on the upper surface.

9. The *flag* (value 5) is in appearance very characteristic of the breed, although it sometimes happens that one or two puppies in a wellbred litter exhibit a curl or other malformation, usually considered to be indicative of a stain. It is often compared to a scimitar, but it resembles it only in respect of its narrowness, the amount of curl in the blade of this Turkish weapon being far too great to make it the model of the setter's flag. Again, it has been compared to a comb; but as combs are usually straight, here again the simile fails, as the setter's flag should have a gentle sweep; and the nearest resemblance to any familiar form is to the scythe with its curve reversed. The feather must be composed of straight silky hairs, and beyond the root the less short hair on the flag the better, especially towards the point, of which the bone should be fine, and the feather tapering with it.

10. *Symmetry and quality* (value 5). In *character* the setter should display a great amount of "quality," a term which is difficult of explanation, though fully appreciated by all experienced sportsmen. It means a combination of symmetry, as understood by the artist, with the peculiar attributes of the breed under examination, as interpreted by the sportsman. Thus, a setter possessed of such a frame and outline as to charm an artist would be considered by the sportsman defective in "quality" if he possessed a curly or harsh coat, or if he had a heavy head with pendant bloodhoundlike jowl and throaty neck. The *general outline* is very elegant, and more taking to the eye of the artist than that of the pointer.

11. The *texture and feather* of coat (value 5) are much regarded among

setter breeders, a soft silky hair without curl being considered a *sine quâ non*. The feather should be considerable, and should fringe the hind as well as the fore legs.

12. The *colour of coat* (value 5) is not much insisted on among English setters, a great variety being admitted. These are now generally classed as follows, in the order given: (1) Black and white ticked, with large splashes, and more or less marked with black, known as "blue Belton;" (2) orange and white freckled, known as orange Belton; (3) plain orange, or lemon and white; (4) liver and white; (5) black and white, with slight tan markings; (6) black and white; (7) liver and white; (8) pure white; (9) black; (10) liver; (11) red or yellow.

THE BLACK-TAN SETTER.

(SOMETIMES CALLED GORDON.)

The black-tan setter, until the institution of shows, was commonly called "Gordon," from the fact that the Dukes of Gordon had long possessed a strain of setters of that colour, which had obtained a high reputation. At the first dog show held at Newcastle in June, 1859, Mr. Jobling's (of Morpeth) black and tan Dandy was shown with success in an open class; and in November of the same year Mr. Burdett's Brougham followed suit at Birmingham. In 1861 Mr. Burdett's Ned (son of Brougham) won the first prize in an open class at Birmingham, after which a special class was made for dogs of that colour at Birmingham, London, and other large shows, the breeders of English dogs fancying that the beautiful colour of the "Gordons" was too much in their favour. Up to the above-mentioned period the black-tan setter had not been generally introduced into the midland and southern counties of England, Mr. Brown of Melton Mowbray, Mr. Burdett of Birmingham, the Rev. T. Pearce of Morden, and Mr. Calver of East Harling, Norfolk, having been the chief breeders in those districts. Mr. Burdett's Ned was a very handsome, useful-looking dog, and was sold at a good price, together with his brother Rock, to Sir J. Rivett Carnac, of Warborne, Hampshire, by whom they were shot over for two or three seasons. Mr. Pearce won several prizes with Argyll II., Regent, and Ruby at the early shows; but it was not till the appearance of Kent, shown by Sir E. Hoare at the Ashburnham Hall show, London, in 1863, that the strong *furore*, which from that time set in, was displayed. Beating Argyll II., bred by Mr. Pearce (but shown in another name, having being previously sold), he was at once claimed by Mr. Pearce at the selling price (30 guineas), and proved a profitable investment, earning for his owner a large annual income for several years at the stud, and winning several prizes in the champion classes, together with the gold medal at the Paris show of 1865. On the show bench his grand head and rich colour drew general attention to him, and it was only to those who could see him out that his rather weak hind-quarters were visible. Taking prize after prize at Cremorne, Birmingham (four times), Islington (twice), Worcester, and Paris, his extraordinary career naturally

Mr. Coath's Black and Tan Setter "Lang."

caused a great amount of jealousy, and he was called by the opposition party a
"cur," a "mongrel," a "half-bloodhound," and a dozen other bad names. Since
that time, however, the real facts of the case have been revealed; and there is
little doubt that he was descended on his sire's side from Mr. Jobling's kennel,
and on his dam's from that of Mr. Adamson. He was bought when a puppy by
Sir E. Hoare from an old rabbit-catcher on his estate, who had brought him up
under a cat. Probably to his early confinement and bad rearing may be attributed
his weak hind-quarters. So convinced, however, was Mr. Pearce of his purity of
breeding that he determined to put the matter to the test of experiment, and
offered to trust one of his stock out of Regent to the care of the writer of
this article, to be brought up where he could not possibly see game, and at the
proper age, namely, nine or ten months, to be introduced to it without
previously being entered to it in any way. The result was in accordance with
Mr. Pearce's prophecy, for the puppy not only beat his ground in fine style, but
at the end of a few hour's work began to stand his birds as only a well-bred pointer
or setter will do, without any artificial education of any kind. Of course the report
of this trial added greatly to Kent's reputation, and, being followed by the successes
of Rex (the above puppy) at Stafford and Shrewsbury, where he won three cups,
beating in the final trial Mr. Field's Duke, who had gained a high reputation in
previous years, Kent had so strong a run at the stud for several years, that it
would be difficult in the present day to find a black-tan setter without a strain
of his blood. Mr. Pearce's Regent had several large litters by him, including
Rex, Young Kent, Iona, La Reine, Dame, Deal, and Silk—all winners at shows
or field trials. Mr. Stokes's Shot, successful at Birmingham and Islington in
1868-9, was out of La Reine; and Mr. J. H. Salter's Young Rex, winner at
Brighton in 1876, is by Rex.

But, in spite of the above successes, it cannot be denied that the general
opinion of good sportsman in the south has not been in favour of the breed
since the institution of field trials, in which it has been brought into competition
with the English and Irish setter. Both Rex and Young Kent had shown
marvellous powers of scent, but exception was taken to their tiring action, and
it must be admitted that six hours' work was enough at one time for either of
them, and probably too much for Young Kent. Both dogs also were headstrong,
and required severe treatment to keep them under command, and, though neither
showed the slightest disposition to unsteadiness on the point, yet both were
jealous behind, and it was difficult to make them work to hand. Among the
numberless specimens of the breed (black-tan) which I have seen at work, not
one has shown the solicitude to catch the eye of the shooter which is so essential
to the perfect correspondence of man and dog which ensures sport. The pointer
or setter ought always to know where his master is, and if put into high covert,
such as beans, should raise his head at short intervals above them to ascertain
his whereabouts. Now, as far as my experience goes, black-tan setters, and
notably the Kents, never do this, and cannot be taken off a scent without very
great severity, till they have satisfied themselves of its fallacy. Most of those

tried in the field have been dead slow, including Mr. Stokes's Shot, Mr. Purcell Llewellyn's Wick, and Mr. Furner's Dorset; but Lang, by Reuben, was fast enough for anyone, though not showing much nose, and Mr. Adey's Kate in her puppy season was fast and clever, shewing also an excellent nose, while Young Kent displayed fair pace, and Rex was far above the average in this respect. On the whole it may be said that the verdict has gone against the breed in England, and, as far as I know, no breeder of experience in the south adheres to it, with the exception of Mr. J. H. Salter; nor is it much more approved of on the moors by the general public.

The *points* of the black-tan setter are very nearly the same as those of the English dog, the only deviations being as follows:

1. The *skull* is usually a little heavier than that of the English setter, but in other respects it resembles it.

2. The *nose*, also, is like the English setters; but it is usually a trifle wider.

9. The *flag* is usually a trifle shorter than that of the English setter, which it otherwise resembles in shape.

11. The *coat* is generally harder and coarser than that of the English or Irish setter, occasionally with a strong disposition to curl, as in the celebrated champions Reuben and Regent. -

12. The *colour* is much insisted on. The black should be rich, without mixture with the tan, and the latter should be a deep mahogany red without any tendency to fawn. It is admitted that the original Gordons were often black, tan, and white; but, as in all our shows the classes are limited to black-tan, the long arguments which have been adduced on that score are now obsolete. A little white on the chest, and a white toe or two, are not objected to; but a decided frill is considered by most judges to be a blemish. The red tan should be shown on lips, cheeks, throat, spot over the eyes, fore legs nearly to the elbows, hind legs up to stifles, and on the under side of the flag, but not running into its long hair.

I have selected Mr. Coath's Lang to illustrate this breed, and Mr. Baker has furnished a wonderful likeness of this elegant dog. On the show bench he has been very successful since the retirement of his sire Reuben from old age, having won first and champion prizes at Glasgow, Edinburgh, Crystal Palace (twice), Birmingham (thrice), and Alexandra Palace. At the Shrewsbury field trials of 1872 and 1873, he was entered, and showed great pace and a fine style of going; but in the former year his pace was too great for the absence of scent and covert which prevailed there, and he was put out by Mr. Armstrong's Don, in one of those unsatisfactory trials to which owners of dogs have so often been reduced there. In the next year he showed well at first with Mr. Barclay Field's Rake, but was put out from chasing fur. At the same meeting he was bracketed with Mr. Macdona's Ranger in the braces, but not being quite steady behind, they were beaten by Mr. Barclay Field's Bruce and Rose. He is a fine slashing dog, of good size, possessing plenty of bone without lumber, and excellent legs and feet. His pedigree is an excellent one, being as follows:

Mr. Macdona's Irish Setter "Rover."

```
                      ┌ Reuben ......... ┌ Milo (Malcolm's) ...... { Dandy (Jobling's)
                      │                  └ Ruin (Lord Rosslyn's) { Grouse
Lang (Mr. Coath's) ┤                                              { Duchess
                      │                  ┌ Suwarrow (Birch's)... { (Pedigree unknown. From
                      └ Mona ........... │                       {  Duke of Buccleuch's
                                         │                       {  Kennels)
                                         └ Bounce ................ { Kent (Pearce's)
                                                                  { Old Moll, by Jobling's
                                                                  {  Dandy.
```

It will be seen that he goes back to Jobling's Dandy, on the side of both sire and dam.

The black and tan setter crosses well with the Irish, and Mr. Salter possesses an excellent specimen of the cross in his Young Rex, winner of the first prize at Brighton in the black and tan class in 1876. This dog is by Rex (son of Kent and Regent), out of Sal, a well-bred bitch descended from Major Hutchinson's Bob, and is a good looking dog, as well as a fine mover. Mr. Purcell Llewellyn has also crossed the Laveracks with it, the result, in 1872, being a very beautiful orange belton bitch, Flame, out of Carrie, who was by Pilkington's Dash, out of a daughter of Hutchinson's Bob (winner of the champion prize at the Crystal Palace in 1875); and also a 1st prize winner at the Crystal Palace in 1872, and a 2nd at Birmingham in the same year.

THE IRISH SETTER.

This breed has long been known to sportsmen throughout Great Britain as a good one, especially in point of stamina, and a class was set apart for it at Birmingham in 1860, a year before the black and tans were similarly favoured, though, I think, hardly from so flattering a cause, and most probably from the circumstance that Mr. Jones, of Oscott, who was then a prominent member of the committee, possessed two specimens of the breed, which he had recently obtained from Ireland; but, to his disgust, Major Irving, who judged the class, awarded the first prize to Mr. R. F. Onslow, of Herefordshire; Mr. Jones getting a second only with his Carlo, with which dog, however, under the same judge, he beat a better class in 1861, including Mr. Watts' Ranger, a slashing one in appearance, but, unfortunately, with a pedigree which was disputed. In 1863 Major Hutchinson brought out Bob, whose pedigree exhibits a strain of the celebrated La Touche breed, and with him he carried off the chief prizes at Birmingham, Cremorne, and Islington in 1864, leading to his selection for the illustration of the article on the Irish Setter in 1865. He was, however, not a typical specimen, being too heavy both in frame and head, and obviously over-topped, although otherwise useful, and, I have reason to believe, thoroughly good in the field. In 1867 Capt. Allaway exhibited his beautiful brace, Shot and Grouse, which were generally accepted as showing all the peculiarities of the breed, and were of such a fine formation, that Shot, considered by me inferior in shape to his brother, obtained the silver cup for the best setter in the show,

M

after a warm dispute between the two judges, Messrs. Lang and Walker, in which the former, an excellent and experienced judge, stuck to the Irishman throughout, while the latter was as strongly in favour of Fred II., a well-known Laverack, and the referee was called on to decide between them. Capt. Allaway maintained his position till 1871, when Capt. Cooper brought out his Ranger, a son of Hutchinson's Bob, and also straining back on the dam's side to the La Touche kennel. At length, in 1873, Dr. Stone came out with his Dash, who was admitted to be almost perfect in shape, and of the true type. He took every prize until age compelled his retirement in favour of Mr. Hilliard's Palmerston, who may now be considered the best public representative of the breed. Dash is of Dr. Stone's own strain, which he has kept to himself for twenty-five years, in colour blood-red, showing white on his head and toes, and also on his neck, with great quality, and a faultless frame.

There is no reason to suppose that any improvement had taken place in this breed in its native country until very recently, when the institution of local shows seems to have stimulated Irish breeders to fresh exertions; but in the exhibits which have been made on this side the Channel the chain of progress has been unbroken from Carlo to Dash and Palmerston. In the field trials, the Rev. J. C. Macdona has raised its character by producing his Plunket at Shrewsbury in 1870, after which he was sold to Mr. Purcell Llewellyn, and took prizes at Vaynol, Southampton, and Shrewsbury. This dog was very small and bitch-like in appearance, and rather light in colour, but his pace was very great, though not perhaps quite equal to that of the Laverack Countess, while his style of going and his attitude on the point were far superior to hers. He was bred by the Hon. D. Plunket, and combines the blood of that gentleman's kennel with the La Touche and Hutchinson strains. Mr. Purcell Llewellyn purchased him in the height of his successes, and bred several average dogs from him out of Kate (of the Knight of Kerry's strain), including Kimo, Kite, and Kitty; while another litter, out of Buckell's Min, contained Marvel, May, and Knowing, less successful than the former, both on the bench and in the field. With the solitary exception of Plunket and his daughter Music, who was at Vaynol in 1872, however, no Irish setter has shown anything like high form in the field trials, Mr. Purcell Llewellyn's Samson, who is above the average, being crossed with the Laverack Prince through his dam, Carrie, though both are entered in the Stud Book as Irish setters.

After a great deal of discussion, a separate class has been made in Dublin and elsewhere for "reds" and "white and reds," it being shown that there are two distinct strains of the Irish setter, of these colours respectively. The white and reds stand no chance in the open classes, and yet it was considered hard to debar them from all prizes, especially as by some good judges they are thought to possess better noses than the reds. According to my judgment the rich red, or blood-red colour as it is described, is made a little too much of, and I should strongly object to the passing over of excellence in shape because the colour is too pale; a marked instance of which happened at the Brighton show of 1876.

Here one of the grandest bitches I ever saw in shape, size, and quality, who had won several prizes in Ireland, and moreover of excellent blood, succumbed to a very mediocre animal, simply because her coat was too pale in colour, though very little, if any, paler than that of the above-mentioned excellent dog Plunket. If this class had been judged by points, the bitch in question would have distanced her competitors, because she would have been credited with a full allowance for all other qualities, and could only have had ten points altogether knocked off for the negative value of colour.

The old breeds of this dog most celebrated are the O'Connor (generally known as La Touche), Lord Dillon's, Lord Clancarty's, Lord Lismore's, Lord de Fresne's (usually called the French Park), the Mount Hedges, Lord Rossmore's, and the Marquis of Waterford's. In modern days Dr. Stone, Major Hutchinson, Capt. Cooper, Capt. French, Mr. H. B. Knox, Hon. D. Plunket, Capt. W. Allaway, Mr. Hilliard, Mr. Lipscombe, Mr. C. Brien, and Miss Warburton have been most successful on the show bench; but, with the exception of Plunket, none of them have proved the excellence of their strains at any field trials.

In *points* the Irish setter only differs from the English in the following :

1. The *skull* is somewhat longer and narrower, the eyebrows being well raised, and the occipital prominence as marked as in the pointer.

2. The *nose is* a trifle longer, with good width, and square at the end; nostrils wide and open, with the nose itself of a deep mahogany or very dark fleshy-colour, not pink nor black.

3. *Eyes, ears, and lips.*—The *eyes* should be a rich brown or mahogany colour, well set, and full of intelligence; a pale or gooseberry eye is to be avoided. *Ears* long enough to reach within half an inch or an inch of the end of the nose, and, though more tapering than in the English dog, never coming to a point; they should be set low and close, but well back, and not approaching to the hound's in setting and leather. Whiskers red; lips deep, but not pendulous.

5 and 6. In *frame* the Irish dog is higher on the leg than either the English or black and tan, but his elbows are well let down nevertheless; his shoulders are long and sloping; brisket deep, but never wide; and his back ribs are somewhat shorter than those of his English brethren. Loin good, slightly arched, and well coupled to his hips, but not very wide; quarters slightly sloping, and flag set on rather low, but straight, fine in bone, and beautifully carried. Breeders are, however, going for straight backs like that of Palmerston, with flags set on as high as in the English setter.

7. *Legs* very straight, with good hocks, well-bent stifles, and muscular but not heavy haunches.

8. The *feet* are hare-like, and moderately hairy between the toes.

9. The *flag* is clothed with a long, straight comb of hair, never bushy or curly, and this is beautifully displayed on the point.

11. The *coat* should be somewhat coarser than that of the English setter, being midway between that and the black and tan, wavy but not curly, and by no means long. Both hind and fore legs are well feathered, but not profusely,

and the ears are furnished with feather to the same extent, with a slight wave, but no curl.

12. The *colour* should be a rich blood red, without any trace of black on the ears or along the back; in many of the best strains, however, a pale colour or an occasional tinge of black is shown. A little white on the neck, breast, or toes is by no means objectionable, and there is no doubt that the preponderance of white, so as to constitute what is called "white and red," is met with in some good strains.

In his *work* the Irish setter is fast and enduring; his nose is quite up to the average of fast dogs in delicacy, and to those who are limited to a small kennel he is an invaluable aid to the gun. His style of going is very beautiful, with head well up and feeling for the body scent; he has a free action of the shoulders, hind legs brought well under him, and a merry lashing of the flag on the slightest indication of scent—often, indeed, without it. His advocates contend that he is as steady as any other setter when once broken, but, as far as my experience goes, I scarcely think this position can be maintained. Neither Plunket, nor any that I have seen of Mr. Purcell Llewellyn's breeding, nor indeed any of those which I have had out in private, have been always reliable, and I fear that, like almost all other setters of such high courage, it must be admitted that he requires work to keep him in a state of control fit for immediate use with the gun. In this respect, and indeed in delicacy of nose, both the English and Irish setter must yield to the black and tan of the best strains; but to do the same amount of work, at least a double team of the last mentioned must be kept.

Having been charged, by Mr. Adcock, in the case of the bulldog, with selecting inferior specimens for illustration, it is perhaps necessary that I should explain my reasons for choosing a dog without any public reputation to represent the Irish setter in preference to Mr. Hilliard's Palmerston, who has taken all the chief prizes since the last appearance of Dr. Stone's Dash at the Crystal Palace in 1875. As remarked above, no strain but that of the Hon. D. Plunket has been tried in the field; and, as that has done great credit to the breed in the shape of Mr. Macdona's (afterwards Mr. Llewellyn's) Plunket, his daughter Music, and his sons Marvel and Kite, I prefer a portrait of one of this tried strain to that of any dog not similarly tested. Both Plunket and his daughter Music were too small to serve as a type, while Kite and Marvel have faults which render them equally unfit for that purpose. Fortunately, however, I have been able to meet with a grand specimen of the breed in an own brother to Plunket, which Mr. Macdona has recently obtained from Ireland, and which has never yet been shown. The faithful portrait of this dog presented herewith speaks for itself as to his external shape; but for his performances it is necessary to look to his brother Plunket, except that I have ascertained on good evidence that in private he has been tried to be first class. In colour he is of a beautiful rich red with scarcely any white; while he possesses a frame of great size, symmetry, and substance, with good legs and feet. He is thus fit to show in any company; but, as I have not been able to compare him with the celebrated Palmerston, and must depend on memory alone, I do not pretend to settle their respective merits from a show-bench point of view.

The high form of Plunket and his stock in the field is well known to all who have seen the various field trials of 1870-73; and for stud purposes his own brother may be considered as identical with himself. Mr. Baker's drawing of Rover is almost as exact as a photograph, and in particular his rendering of the head is wonderfully good, and shows the character of the breed extremely well. Plunket first appeared at Shrewsbury in 1870 as a puppy, when he was placed second to Mr. Statter's Bruce, by Dash (a Laverack dog) out of Rhœbe. In his first trial he was described in *The Field* as going in fine style, but was afterwards beaten on a bare piece of ground by Bruce, who showed a better nose. He was then so much admired by Mr. Purcell Llewellyn that he gave 150l. for him. In the autumn of the same year he won the all-aged stake at Vaynol without much competition, and he was described in *The Field* as "greatly improved in appearance, having lost none of his grand dash and style," and as having "gained in staunchness." In 1871 he seems to have been out of form at Southampton, being beaten by Capt. Venner's Dandy, a grand dog, in the single stakes, and only dividing the second prize in the braces. In the following week he was still more unsuccessful at Shrewsbury; but, nevertheless, "he completely outpaced March," who defeated him in the single stake, and, though going better in the braces, lost his chance from the bad performance of his companion Shot. At Vaynol in the next autumn, he was selected by Mr. Purcell Llewellyn as the companion of Countess in the Bodfill Stakes for braces; and here, with the exception of two slight mistakes, their performance was described as "faultless," making the large score of ninety nevertheless, and winning easily. He also won the Borough Stakes, going "even better than before, and not making a single mistake." Finally at Vaynol in 1872 he appeared with his son Marvel in the braces, and was second to Countess and Nellie, beating Mr. Statter's Rob Roy and Belton. The description given was that "Plunket and Marvel went beautifully together and each did some pretty work till towards the end of their time, when Plunket making a point, Marvel drew by him, and put the birds up. This, of course, penalised them ten points. Countess and Nellie, going in fine style, made no mistake whatever, and, being credited with their full quota of points, were made the winners without dispute." Plunket therefore lost none of his reputation by this defeat, except through his son Marvel, whose fault was moreover dependent on his breaking only; and as his daughter Music, "going in fine form and very merrily," won the Dinorwig Stakes, at the same meeting, he gained rather than lost from the stud point of view.

Plunket (and his brother Rover of the same litter) are by Beauty out of the Rev. R. Callaghan's Grouse. This gentleman informs me that Plunket was bred by himself, and not by the Hon. D. Plunket, as stated in the "Stud Book"; Beauty by Birtwhistle's Tim out of Hebe; Grouse by Capt. Hutchinson's Bob.

Since the above was written, Rover has been placed above Palmerston at the Kennel Club Show, where he took the first prize

CHAPTER II.

THE MODERN POINTER—THE DROPPER.

THE MODERN POINTER.

IN selecting the setter for the first of the articles on the dog in the present series, I have not intended to settle the comparative claims of these two dogs to superiority in the field. It is alleged that the field trials have not done much towards settling this vexed question, which, however, they could only do irrespective of those enduring qualities not capable of being tested even at Bala, where, on two occasions, several hours have been devoted to a single trial. As far as they go, until this year (1877), the two breeds have been nearly equally successful when first-class specimens have been tried together, excluding that phenomenon, Sir R. Garth's (now Mr. Lloyd Price's) Drake. Countess (setter) and Belle (pointer) have each won once when tried together, while the latter and Ranger (setter) have also exchanged wins; so that, exclusive of Drake, who was never pitted against a setter till long past his prime, the balance has not been struck, except in so far that, while Belle defeated Ranger single-handed, the latter only won from her in the braces. In the present year however, the setters have gone ahead, both at Shrewsbury and Horseheath. At the former trials the two breeds did not come together, but as far as could be judged without this, the setters were far superior to the pointers; and at Horseheath where the same dogs were entered in the Horseheath Stakes the setters had the advantage, two of each breed being left in for the last two rounds, and Dash II. winning the first prize, Mr. Whitehouse's Rapid (pointer) being second. Mr. G. Brewis's dog also won the club cup which was open to both breeds, Blue Bell III. being second to him.

Among pointers there are no national divisions corresponding with those of the setters. There are, however, two distinct varieties, strongly marked by colour, viz., the lemon and white and the liver and white, besides the black and white, the whole liver, and the whole black strains; but these last are not common in the present day, and the appearance of one on the show bench is almost as rare as a black swan. Among the liver and whites the dogs are often too heavy for much speed or endurance—a remarkable exception being the celebrated Drake, bred by Sir R. Garth, and sold by him at a high figure in his seventh season to Mr. R. J. Lloyd Price, of Bala, at which advanced age he went as fast, and showed as good a nose, as most puppies even of high class. This dog was in his day the fastest and most wonderful animal that ever quartered a field, and his race up to a brace of birds at Shrewsbury in the field trials of 1868, when the ground was so dry as to cause

a cloud of dust to rise on his dropping to their scent, was a sight which will probably
never be seen again. He was truly a phenomenon among pointers. His extraordinary pace compelled his dropping in this way, for otherwise he could not have
stopped himself in time, but when he had lost pace in his seventh season he began
frequently to stand up, as represented by Mr. Baker, who never saw him till
then. In appearance he is not taking, having a plain head with a somewhat
throaty neck; but his frame is all through good, and there is no lumber about him.
He could not, therefore, be considered a model for imitation, and consequently
I have added a very beautiful and racing bitch to represent the strain—in which
this sex is generally to be preferred for work, being lighter and more active.
This bitch, Mr. Lloyd Price's Belle, was bred by Lord H. Bentinck, and was bought
by Mr. Price for 10l. after winning a third prize at Manchester. She was at first
fearfully headstrong, and chased hares for many weeks persistently, being far
beyond her puppyhood and unbroken; but the perseverance of a young, and
till then unknown, breaker, Anstey, overcame these defects, and being tried in
private to be good, she was entered at Vaynol field trials in 1872, when she won
the prize for braces, and also that for bitches, being left in to contest the disputed
point of priority in the two breeds with Mr. Whitehouse's Priam against Mr.
Llewellyn's Countess and Nellie, both setters. In this trial she succumbed to
Countess, but turned the tables on her at Bala in 1873. Being possessed of this
beautiful and excellent bitch, Mr. Lloyd Price naturally desired to mate her,
and Drake being put up to auction, together with the whole of Sir R. Garth's
kennel, he was purchased in his seventh season for £150, and retained by his new
owner for his own use alone. Previously, however, Drake had got several dogs
of high class, including Viscount Downe's Bang, Drake II., and Mars; but,
considering the run he had at the stud, his stock could not be said to have come
out as well as might be expected in public, though in private their character was
well maintained. Crossed with Belle, a litter considerably above the average was
obtained, including Mallard and Beau, but none coming up to the form of either
sire or dam, and not equal to Eos, who was subsequently from her by Mr. Wm.
Statter's Major. A third litter by the old dog died when a few days old, so that
Mr. Price has been unfortunate with him; but a litter from a bitch bearing the
euphonious name of Nimble Ninepence promise well, and a younger litter, bred
the same way, are coming on. Mr. Statter has also bred Dick, successful at
Bala and Ipswich, from a daughter of Drake by his Major, who was descended
from the good old-fashioned strains of Lord Derby, Mr. Antrobus, and Mr. Edge.
Major was a fast, resolute dog, and ranged in beautiful style, but he behaved
very badly at Bala in 1867 (his only public appearance), having just returned
from the moors, and not owning the partridge scent, as is often the case with
even the steadiest grouse dogs. It should be remembered that in these days
fast pace is demanded far more than in those when pointers were used in the south
for beating high stubbles in fields of 20 acres or less, and when the heavy breeds
of Mr. Edge, Lord Derby, and Mr. Antrobus were able to do all that was desired,
delicacy of nose and steadiness, both before and behind, being the chief essentials

required. At present the pointer is regarded as a grouse dog rather than a partridge finder, and hence he must be not only fast, but enduring. By careful selection, however, and some luck, Sir R. Garth was able to breed Drake, and Lord H. Bentinck also obtained Belle, while Mr. Statter has been little behind them with his Major, Dick, and Rex. In the south Mr. S. Price has produced his Bang, Mike, and Wagg, the first not quite up to the pace of the above dogs, but closely approaching it. He is descended from Brockton's Bounce, one of the old heavy sort, who, however, showed fair pace at Southill in 1865, but crossed with the lemon and white strain of Mr. Whitehouse, which I must now proceed to describe. Mr. Lloyd Price has recently added Wagg to his kennel for stud purposes, and in the present year (1877) has obtained a very fast and clever puppy from Devonshire, viz., Bow Bells, by Bang out of Leech's Belle—Mr. Whitehouse's Rapid is another Devonshire bred dog of recent celebrity, being by Chang out of Romp.

Up to the time of the institution of dog shows, the lemon and whites were little valued in comparison with the liver and whites; but Mr. H. Gilbert's Bob and Major (the latter sold to Mr. Smith, of Tettenhall, on Mr. Gilbert's death in 1862), brought the lemon and whites into notice on the show bench; while a son of Bob, Mr. Whitehouse's celebrated Hamlet, took 90 points out of a possible 100 at the Bedford field trials in 1865, making a tie with Brockton's Bounce, to whom I have alluded among the liver and whites. Mr. Whitehouse's Hamlet also took several prizes on the show bench, and his stock have quite superseded that of Major, which, handsome as they are admitted to be, have not shown much capacity for the work demanded from them in the field. Mr. Whitehouse has bred from this dog Priam, Rap, Joke, Flirt, and Nina, all winners; besides Macgregor, who is by Sancho out of a grand-daughter of Hamlet. From these successes in the twofold direction of beauty and goodness in the field, Hamlet was in high fashion until the appearance of Sir R. Garth's Drake, since which the contest between the stock of those two dogs has been maintained with varying results, there being little difference in the number of wins between Viscount Downe's Bang II., Mars, Grace II., and Drake II.; together with Mr. Lloyd Price's Mallard and Beau, and Mr. Statter's Dick; and, on the other hand, Mr. Whitehouse's Priam, Rap, Pax, Nora, and Blanche. Besides these may be mentioned Mr. Brackenbury's Romp and her produce by Chang, Mr. Whitehouse's Rapid, and Mr. Fairhead's Romp. Mr. Birkett's black and white dog Rector is the only addition to these strains among the chief prize winners, but he is entirely of blood unknown in the field or on the bench.

Taking, however, these several strains as representing the modern fashionable pointer, it must be admitted that the result of recent efforts in breeding has been manifested in a great increase of pace, so as to bring the pointer up to the level of the setter in that quality, so important to the grouse shooter, for whom both pointers and setters are now, as already remarked, chiefly demanded. For this reason it is absurd to ignore range and pace in judging at field trials, as has been attempted by certain influential members of the Kennel Club. In any case,

MR. SMITH'S POINTER "MAJOR."

to count up the number of times each competitor finds a brace of birds, and decide by that alone, in a trial limited to minutes, is, in my opinion, to give chance too great a "pull"; and, as I before remarked, range and pace, though not necessary in the south, are essential for grouse dogs, and it is for that purpose that pointers as well as setters are now mainly required. One great advantage in pointers is that they do not require water so often as the setter, or to be rebroken every season more or less. They are hardier too, and do not succumb so easily to the ravages of distemper.

In the endeavour to increase the speed and stamina of the pointer, the foxhound has been used as a cross by Col. Thornton and others since his time. It is well known that the foxhound is far superior to all dogs in the latter capacity, and equal to all but the greyhound in the former. I have tried several pointers more or less crossed with the foxhound, and most of them have been very fast and stout; but in every instance there was unsteadiness behind, however carefully the dog was broken, and great difficulty has been experienced in getting any "back" whatever. In both the foxhound and the greyhound jealousy is encouraged to the utmost, while in the pointer it is a fatal defect. Hence, although I believe several of our best strains possess in a remote degree a cross of the foxhound, it is not hastily to be introduced, and it takes several crosses back into steady pointer blood to neutralise the defect alluded to.

The most celebrated breeders of the liver and white strain in modern times have been Sir R. Garth, *facile princeps* with Drake, besides a number of lesser stars—Lord H. Bentinck, Mr. Statter, Lord Lichfield, the Duke of Westminster, Mr. Francis (of Exeter), Mr. S. Price (also of Devon), the late Mr. G. Moore, Viscount Downe, and Mr. R. J. Lloyd Price (of Bala). Sir Dudley Coutts Marjoribanks has a breed of high private reputation, as has also Sir R. Musgrave, of Edenhall; but, as far as I know, none have appeared in public. The old, heavy sort of the Edge, Antrobus, and Sefton strains are now quite out of fashion, except when combined with faster blood.

The best strain of the lemon and whites has been almost entirely in Mr. Whitehouse's hands, he having had a succession of winners from the time of Hamlet to the present day, and his sideboard groaning with silver cups. Beginning with little Hamlet, he has gradually increased their size and substance, and got rid of the delicacy of constitution which was at first a defect in the strain. Priam and Rap are both big enough for any work, and, though not over 60lb., very nearly approaching that standard. Rap is one of the most perfect dogs in symmetry that I ever saw, and is a model of the true type. Mr. Whitehouse's Pearl and Nina are also full of quality, and symmetrical, as well as all over useful in shape. There is, however, so little difference between their appearance and that of Major, whose portrait I gave in the last series, that I have not thought it necessary to supersede it.

The *points* are nearly the same in numerical value as those of the setter, the only difference made being in the texture of coat, which is not so great a sign of breeding in the pointer as the setter.

N

POINTS OF THE POINTER.

	Value.		Value.		Value.		Value.
Skull	10	Shoulders and		Legs, elbows,		Stern	5
Nose	10	chest	15	and hocks	12	Symmetry and	
Ears, eyes, and		Back, quarters,		Feet	8	quality	7
lips	4	and stifles	15			Texture of coat	3
Neck	6					Colour	5
	—		—		—		—
	30		30		20		20

Grand Total, 100.

Describing them in detail, they are as follows:

1. The *skull* (value 10) should be of good size, but not as heavy as in the old Spanish pointer, and in a lesser degree his half-bred descendants. It should be wider across the ears than that of the setter, with a forehead rising well at the brows. A full development of the occipital protuberance is indispensable, and the upper surface should be in two slightly rounded flats, with a furrow between.

2. The *nose* (value 10) should be long (4in. to 4½in.) and broad, with widely-open nostrils. The end must be moist, and in health is cold to the touch. It should be black, or very dark brown, in all but the lemon and whites; but in them it may be a deep flesh colour. It should be cut off square and not pointed—known as the " snipe nose " or " pig jaw." Teeth meeting evenly.

3. The *ears, eyes,* and *lips* (value 4) are as follows: Ears soft in coat, moderately long and thin in leather, not folding like the hound's, but lying flat and close to the cheeks, and set on low, without any tendency to prick. Eyes soft and of medium size; colour brown, varying in shade with that of the coat. Lips well developed, and frothing when in work, but not pendent or flew-like.

4. The *neck* (value 6) should be arched towards the head, long and round, without any approach to dewlap or throatiness. It should come out with a graceful sweep from between the shoulder-blades.

5. The *shoulders* and *chest* (value 15) are dependent on each other for their formation. Thus a wide and hooped chest cannot have the blades lying flat against its sides; and consequently, instead of this and their sloping backwards, as they ought to do in order to give free action, they are upright, short and fixed. Of course, a certain width is required, to give room for the lungs; but the volume required should be obtained by depth rather than width. Behind the blades the ribs should, however, be well arched, but still deep; this depth of back rib is specially important.

6. The *back, quarters,* and *stifles* (value 15) constitute the main propellers of the machine, and on their proper development the speed and power of the dog depend. The loin should be very slightly arched and full of muscle, which should run well over the back ribs; the hips should be wide, with a tendency even to raggedness, and the quarters should droop very slightly from them. These last must be full of firm muscle, and the stifles should be well bent and carried widely apart, so as to allow the hind legs to be brought well forward in the gallop, instituting a form of action which does not tire.

7. *Legs, elbows,* and *hocks* (value 12). These chiefly bony parts, though merely the levers by which the muscles act, must be strong enough to bear the strain given them; and this must act in the straight line of progression. Substance of bone is therefore demanded, not only in the shanks but in the joints, the knees and hocks being specially required to be bony. The elbows should be well let down, giving a long upper arm, and should not be turned in or out; the latter being, however, the lesser fault of the two, as the confined elbow limits the action considerably. The reverse is the case with the hocks, which may be turned in rather than out; the former being generally accompanied by that wideness of stifles which I have already insisted on. Both hind and fore pasterns should be short, nearly upright, and full of bone.

8. The *feet* (value 8) are all-important; for, however fast and strong the action may be, if the feet are not well shaped and their horny covering hard, the dog will soon become foot-sore when at work, and will then refuse to leave his master's heels, however high his courage may be. Breeders have long disputed the comparatively good qualities of the round cat-like foot, and the long one, resembling that of the hare. In the pointer my own opinion is in favour of the cat-foot, with the toes well arched and *close together*. This is the *desideratum* of the M.F.H., and I think stands work better than the hare-foot, in which the toes are not arched but still lie close together. In the setter the greater amount of hair to a certain extent condones the inherent weakness of the hare-foot; but in the pointer no such superiority can be claimed. The main point, however, is the closeness of the pads combined with thickness of the horny covering.

9. The *stern* (value 5) must be strong in bone at the root, but should at once be reduced in size as it leaves the body, and then gradually taper to a point like a bee's sting. It should be very slightly curved, carried a little above the line of the back, and without the slightest approach to curl at the tip.

10. Of *symmetry* and *quality* (value 7) the pointer should display a goodly proportion, no dog showing more difference between the "gentleman" and his opposite. It is impossible to analyse these essentials, but every good judge carries the knowledge with him.

11. The *texture* (value 3) of coat in the pointer should be soft and mellow, but not absolutely silky.

12. In *colour* (value 5) there is now little choice, in point of fashion, between the liver and lemon and whites. After them come the black and whites (with or without tan), then the pure black, and lastly the pure liver. Dark liver-ticked is, perhaps, the most beautiful colour of all to the eye.

THE DROPPER.

This breed, between the setter and pointer, is often very good in the field; but after the first cross it does not succeed. The two varieties do not seem to amalgamate; as in the same litter may be found a portion looking like true pointers, while the rest resemble the setter. The dropper is generally a hardy, useful dog of all work, and is specially good for snipe bogs, single-handed.

CHAPTER III.

SPANIELS.

The Modern Field Spaniel—The Modern Cocker—The Sussex Spaniel —The Clumber Spaniel—The Irish Water Spaniel—The English Water Spaniel.

THE MODERN FIELD SPANIEL.

MONG the earliest records of venerie in England, the spaniel is alluded to as used for hawking and netting, and he claims, with the greyhound, the bulldog, and the mastiff, the honour of having been the first of his species introduced into this country. I do not pretend to settle this moot point; but there can be no doubt that in this century he is remarkable among his compeers for tenderness of nose, high intelligence, devotion to his master, pluck, stamina, and perseverance in the pursuit of his game. Possessed of these high qualities, he is not only useful as a "dog of all work," but he is also a sagacious and faithful companion. Nevertheless, for some years past the spaniel has been supplanted in general estimation by the pointer, setter, or terrier, partly owing to the superior speed of the first two better suiting our modern ideas, and partly also to the fact that the terrier will not only hunt game, but vermin, about which the spaniel is comparatively indifferent. Still there are many excellent sportsmen who adhere to the spaniel, and who use nothing else for beating hedgerows, small coverts, and even turnips or clover, where, of course, this dog is constantly kept within range of the gun by careful breaking. In our modern farming, the large inclosures and the very thin fences which are its distinguishing features also lessen his utility; and even in Wales, Devonshire, and Norfolk—each of which districts used formerly to possess its peculiar breed— spaniels are comparatively rare, and these three strains are no longer to be met with in a typical form. There is, however, one kind of game—the woodcock— which still demands a couple or leash of spaniels; and "cock shooting" being highly valued, a few good sportsmen, for this and other reasons, have recently done their best to improve the breeding of this dog, in externals as well as utility.

In the early days of dog shows Mr. F. Burdett, the secretary of the Birmingham Dog Show, and in fact its prime mover, possessed a breed of black Cockers, collected in the neighbourhood of Lutterworth, where they were bred by an old family of the name of Footman. They were unrivalled in appearance as well as at work, taking every prize for which they competed. Mr. Burdett's early death, however, caused their distribution, and the best specimens passed

MODERN COCKER SPANIEL.—MR. W. GILLETT'S "BRUSH" AND "NELLIE," AND MR. W. LANGDALE'S "LADYBIRD."

into the hands of Mr. Jones, of Oscott, and Mr. Phineas Bullock, of Bilston, the latter of whom has crossed them with the Sussex, and apparently with the water-spaniel. In the last ten years he has almost monopolised the prizes in the spaniel classes, and without doubt he has deserved his success. I regret that I am unable to present to the readers of this book a portrait of any of his dogs, having in vain applied to him for the necessary facilities; but the omission is of the less consequence, because he has gradually introduced so much Sussex blood into the old strain that the produce are almost exactly of that type, with the single exception of the head; and for the illustration of the pure Sussex I prefer the original selection, as represented by Mr. Soames's George. In order to obtain the genuine field spaniel other than Sussex or Clumber, I have consequently been obliged to look outside Mr. P. Bullock's kennel, and have fortunately discovered the very best specimen I have ever seen in the possession of Mr. W. Gillett, of Hull, together with his dam, the former bred by Mr. W. W. Boulton, of Beverley, whose portraits are giving with this chapter, associating with them a little old-fashioned cocker bitch, bred by Mr. Lort, to serve as a contrast. Brush, the young dog above alluded to, has all the bone, symmetry, and quality of Mr. Bullock's dogs, with a flatter, softer, and more silky coat, and without the heavy ears, which are, in my opinion, faults in the Bilston kennel. His ears are of the true spaniel type, lobular in shape without being too heavy, and he has plenty of feather for his age, whilst his middle only requires another six months to be perfect. As to his head, legs, and feet, I have never seen them equalled, and his colour is the finest jet black, with a most beautiful polish. Nell shows signs of age, and has too much ear for my taste; but her success on the show bench qualifies her for her position in the group. As to Ladybird, I have selected her as the type of a working hedgerow spaniel. She is about 18lb. in weight, with excellent legs and feet, and ears not likely to get in her way in pushing through the brambles or gorse. She was bred by Mr. Lort, and combines the Burdett and Lort strains with other old ones unknown to fame.

THE MODERN COCKER.

The above title includes every kind of field spaniel except the Sussex and Clumber, and it is therefore necessary to allude to the Norfolk Spaniel as well as to the Welsh and Devon Cocker. The Norfolk spaniel is still be found scattered throughout the country, and is generally of a liver and white colour, sometimes black and white, and rarely lemon and white; usually a good deal ticked with colour in the white. Higher on the leg than the Clumber or the Sussex, he is generally more active than either, sometimes almost rivalling the setter in lightness of frame; his ears are long, lobular, and heavily feathered, and he is a very useful dog when thoroughly broken, but he is apt to be too wild in his behaviour and too wide in his range until he has had a longer drill than most sportsmen can afford, and in retrieving he is often hard mouthed. When thoroughly broken, however, he is an excellent aid to the gun; but he is so intermixed with other breeds

that it is impossible to select any particular specimen as the true type. With
regard to the Welsh and Devon cocker of former times, they are now scarcely
to be met with in a state of purity and of the regulation size (20lb. to 25lb.);
most of them have been crossed with the springer, or by improved management have been raised in weight to 30lb. at the least, which militates against
their use in some coverts; and in a vast majority of teams the modern field spaniel
must be regarded as more like the springer than the cocker. The Welsh and
Devon cockers are both liver-coloured, not of the Sussex golden hue, but of a
dead true liver colour. Their ears are not too large for work, and on the show
bench would by many judges be considered too small; but they are always lobular,
without the slightest tendency to a vine shape. Throughout the country there
are numberless breeds of cockers of all colours, varying from white, black, or
liver to red and white, lemon and white, liver and white, and black and white.
Ladybird is nearly all red, but she comes of strains usually all liver or all black.

The modern field spaniel should be the best made "all-round" shooting dog
of the day, for he is expected to perform equally well on land and on the water,
in covert, hedgerow, or turnips. He is also called on to retrieve, whilst he must
be thoroughly steady, reliable under all circumstances, however trying to his
nature, and he must never tire. In order to obtain this marvellous combination
of powers and varied qualifications, our modern breeders have crossed the old-
fashioned cocker with the Sussex, and then, by careful selection as to size, points,
and colour, they have established a breed, of which Brush may be taken as the
type in its best form.

The following is the numerical allotment of the

POINTS OF THE FIELD SPANIEL.

	Value.		Value.		Value.
Head	15	Length	5	Colour	5
Ears	5	Legs	10	Coat	10
Neck	5	Feet	10	Tail	10
Chest, back, and loins	20			Symmetry	5
	45		**25**		**30**

Grand Total 100.

1. The *head* (value 15) should be long, with a marked brow but still only
gradually rising from the nose, and the occipital protuberance well defined. Nose
long and broad, without any tendency to the snipe form. Eye expressive, soft,
and gentle, but not too full or watery.

2. The *ear* (value 5) should be set on low down, lobular in shape, not over-
long in the leather, or too heavily clothed with feather, which should always be
wavy and free from ringlets.

3. The *neck* (value 5) should be long enough to allow the nose to reach the
ground easily, strong and arched, coming easily out of well-shaped shoulders.

4. *Chest, back, and loins* (value 20). The chest should be deep, and with a

Mr. Soames's Sussex Spaniel "George."—Bred by Mr. Fuller

good girth; back and loin full of muscle, and running well into one another, with wide couplings, and well-turned hind quarters.

5. The *length* (value 5) of the spaniel should be rather more than twice his height at the shoulder.

6. The *legs* (value 10) must be full of bone and straight; elbows neither in nor out; quarters full of muscle, and stifles strong, but not very much bent.

7. The *feet* (value 10) are round and cat-like, well clothed with hair between the toes, and the pads furnished with very thick horn.

8. The *colour* (value 5) preferred is a brilliant black, but in the best strains of the dog an occasional liver or red puppy will appear.

9. The *coat* (value 10) is flat, slightly wavy, soft and silky; the legs are well fringed or feathered like the setter, as also are the ears; there must be no topknot or curl between the eyes, indicating a cross of the water spaniel.

10. The *tail* (value 10), which is always cropped short, must have a downward carriage, and should not be set on too high.

11. The *symmetry* (value 5) of the spaniel is considerable, and any departure from it should be penalised accordingly.

Mr. Gillett's Brush is by Boulton's Rolf out of Gillett's Nell; Rolf by Boulton's Beaver (4408) out of his Runic; Beaver by Boulton's Bruce (4412) out of Nell; Runic by Rex, brother to Rhea (2228), out of Boulton's Fan. He has only been exhibited twice, viz., at the Islington Kennel Club Show, where Mr. Lort gave him the second prize, and at Stockton, where he was placed first by Major Corven. Mr. Gillett's Nell is of the Burdett strain, but her pedigree is not well made out. While the property of Mr. Boulton, she took the first prize at Manchester and Stockton-on-Tees, and since she changed hands she has been several times exhibited, and always with success. Mr. Boulton's Ladybird is by a black Burdett dog out of a bitch by Withington's Dash out of Lort's Fan. She has only been exhibited once, when she won the first prize at Whitby in 1876. Since the above was written, I understand she has been purchased by Mr. A. W. Langdale, of Scarborough.

THE SUSSEX SPANIEL.

Until the year 1872, Sussex spaniels were never distinguished as a separate class at any of our shows, being admitted only as "other than Clumber," or as "large spaniels." In that year, however, the Committee of the Crystal Palace Show instituted a special prize for the Sussex breed, and their example was followed in October at Nottingham, where the puce-coloured Rufus, bred by Mr. Beesly, defeated Mr. P. Bullock's George, so named from his resemblance to the dog selected by me in 1866 as the type of the breed. Mr. Soames's George has never yet been surpassed, as far as my opinion and observation go, and I shall therefore retain his portrait as efficiently representing the true type of the Sussex spaniel.

Until the above-mentioned constitution of a distinct class under the name

"Sussex," it was of course impossible to criticise the various liver-coloured spaniels exhibited, excepting generally; but almost as soon as the opportunity was thus given it was taken advantage of, and in 1874-5 a host of letters appeared in the *Field* on this subject, under the signatures of C. B. Hodgson, J. Blade, " Castra," " Ruthwell," J. Farrow, J. H. Slater, W. W. Boulton, " Sussex," Phineas Bullock, J. Hughes, and R. Marchant, with a view to show not only that a dog must himself possess a proper liver colour to constitute him a Sussex spaniel, but he must also be descended from parents of that hue. In illustration of this argument, it was proved under protest at Birmingham in 1874, that Mr. Phineas Bullock's George, though himself exhibiting the proper colour and shape of the Sussex breed, was by his celebrated Bob, who was of a rich black colour. The result was that George was from that time withdrawn from the Sussex classes at the chief shows; and it has been since held that the objection was valid. It may be remembered that a portrait of this dog was published in the *Field* in 1872 as a Sussex spaniel, which he closely resembled in appearance; and, though his pedigree was given in the catalogue of the Crystal Palace show, it did not strike me that his sire (the well-known Bob) was black, as was afterwards brought out.

From the year 1872 special classes have been given to the Sussex spaniel at most of our large shows, and in nearly every case a dog with a golden liver coat, or a reasonable approximation to this, has been selected for premier honours; but still I have reason to believe that a good many of the prize winners have been crossed with extraneous strains, and that there are very few really pure specimens of the genuine Sussex spaniel in existence. In 1859, when I published in " The Dog in Health and Disease" the portraits of Mr. Soames's George and Romp, from the Rosehill kennels, it was so rare that many good sportsmen had never heard of its existence, and for several years I looked in vain through the various shows for another good specimen of it. At the early Birmingham shows Mr. F. Burdett's blacks were in fashion; and on his death Mr. Jones, of Oscott, took possession of the show bench with his Bob, a son of Burdett's dog of the same name. Soon after this Mr. Phineas Bullock came to the fore with dogs descended from the same strains, and without any infusion, as far as I know, of the real Sussex spaniel—at all events, not for some years. After a time, Mr. Bowers, of Chester, obtained a dog (Buckingham) and two or three bitches of the Rosehill strain; and Mr. J. H. Salter, of Tolleshunt D'Arcy, in Essex, also purchased Chanco and Chloe, of pure old Sussex blood. Dr. Williams, of Hayward's Heath, Sussex, possesses a bitch from which I believe he has bred some good puppies. Mr. Marchant of Dartford, the Rev. W. Shield of Kirkby Lonsdale, Mr. H. B. Spurgin of Northampton, and Mr. A. W. Langdale of Bishop's Stortford, also have the breed; but beyond this short list I am unable to go, though no doubt there are others with which I am unacquainted.

In work the Sussex spaniel is somewhat faster, and certainly more lasting and persevering, than the Clumber, from whom he also differs in possessing a peculiarly full and bell-like tongue, though still somewhat sharp in note. He is by no means noisy, except when first entered to his game, and it is easy to distinguish by his tongue whether he is on "fur" or "feather." He is readily taught to retrieve with a soft mouth, but there is sometimes a slight tendency to sulk, and he certainly is not so easily kept under command as the Clumber; but for hard work he beats that dog altogether, and is rarely gun-shy. As compared with the indefinite strains of liver-coloured spaniels of such symmetry as to be exhibited at our shows, but descended from Mr. Burdett's Bob and other black dogs, I have no reason to think that the real Sussex is in any way superior to them, either in the field or on the show bench, if judged without regard to purity of blood; and if a class were made for "liver-coloured spaniels" without designating them as "Sussex," I can see no reason to believe that the first prize would of necessity go to either of the gentlemen above named. Classes for "Gordon" setters are now abandoned, on account of the difficulty in defining that dog; and I am by no means sure that it is not desirable to follow this example in reference to the Sussex spaniel, as was to some extent done at the last Brighton show, when a class was formed for "golden-livered Sussex spaniels." But even then, a dog of the true "golden" colour, if proved to be descended from a black strain, would be open to disqualification. Clearly, however, the colour alone is no mark of purity, as was proved in the case of Mr. Phineas Bullock's George above mentioned; and, indeed, I know no breed of dogs in which colour alone can be relied on. The standard points of the Sussex spaniel may be estimated as follows:

POINTS IN THE SUSSEX SPANIEL.

	Value.		Value.		Value.
Skull	15	Neck	5	Tail	10
Eyes	5	Shoulders and chest	10	Colour	10
Nose	10	Back and back ribs	10	Coat	5
Ears	5	Legs and feet	10	Symmetry	5
	35		35		30

Grand Total 100.

1. The *skull* (value 15) should be long, and also wide, with a deep indentation in the middle, and a full stop, projecting well over the eyes; occiput full, but not pointed; the whole giving an appearance of heaviness without dullness.

2. The *eyes* (value 5) are full, soft, and languishing, but not watering so as to stain the coat.

3. The *nose* (value 10) should be long (3in. to 3½in.) and broad, the end liver-coloured, with large open nostrils.

4. The *ears* (value 5) are moderately long and lobe-shaped—that is to say, narrow at the junction with the head, wider in the middle, and rounded below, not pointed. They should be well clothed with soft wavy and silky hair, but not heavily loaded with it.

5. The *neck* (value 5) is rather short, strong, and slightly arched, but not carrying the head much above the level of the back. There is no throatiness in the skin, but a well-marked frill in the coat.

6. *Shoulders and chest* (value 10).—The chest is round, especially behind the shoulders, and moderately deep, giving a good girth. It narrows at the shoulders, which are consequently oblique, though strong, with full points, long arms, and elbows well let down, and these last should not be turned out or in.

7. *Back and back ribs* (value 10).—The back or loin is long, and should be very muscular both in width and depth. For this latter development the back ribs must be very deep. The whole body is characterised as low, long, and strong.

8. *Legs and feet* (value 10).—Owing to the width of chest, the fore legs of the Sussex spaniel are often bowed; but it is a defect notwithstanding, though not a serious one. The arms and thighs must be bony as well as muscular; knees and hocks large, wide, and strong; pasterns very short and bony; feet round, and toes well arched and clothed thickly with hair. The fore legs should be well feathered all down, and the hind ones also above the hocks, but should not have much hair below that point.

9. The *tail* (value 10) is generally cropped, and should be thickly clothed with hair, but not with long feather. The true spaniel's low carriage of the tail at work is well marked in this breed.

10. The *colour* (value 10) of the Sussex is a well-marked but not exactly rich golden liver, on which there is often a washed-out look that detracts from its richness. This colour is often met with in other breeds, however, and is no certain sign of purity in the Sussex spaniel.

11. The *coat* (value 5) is wavy without any curl, abundant, silky, and soft.

12. The *symmetry* (value 5) of the Sussex spaniel is not very marked; but he should not be devoid of this quality.

It being generally admitted that no improvement has taken place on Mr. Soames' George, whose portrait has already been given in the former editions of this book, it is unnecessary to substitute any other for it.

THE CLUMBER SPANIEL.

Since the publication of the article on this spaniel in the year 1865, no change is to be recorded in the opinions on its merits, nor have the specimens exhibited shown any improvement in shape or quality. Mr. R. J. Ll. Price's Bruce may, therefore, still be regarded as a good type of the breed, and I need not replace him by any more modern dog.

The Clumber spaniel takes his name from the seat of the Duke of Newcastle, in Nottinghamshire, where the breed was first established. His distinguishing features are a heavy head, long body, very short legs and consequent slow pace, and absence of tongue, being entirely mute. Coupled with these qualities, on the other hand, there is a necessity for a team of at least three or four, if sufficient ground is to be gone over even for one gun, as the dog never ranges far from his master, and is very slow in his work. He has, however, an excellent nose, is easily kept

MR. PRICE'S CLUMBER SPANIEL "BRUCE."

under command by ordinary means, though he does not readily own a new master; and when a team of Clumbers is composed of dogs well broken, excellent sport may be obtained from them. Like the Laverack setter, the Clumber has been very much in-bred, and is equally difficult to rear, and somewhat inclined to be delicate even at the best. Nevertheless, he is no doubt highly prized by those who can afford to keep an unlimited kennel for only occasional use. The practice of *battue* shooting without dogs by the aid of human beaters has greatly reduced the demand for this dog, which was formerly adopted in beating almost all large woodland preserves.

The points of the Clumber spaniel are as follows:

POINTS OF THE CLUMBER SPANIEL.

	Value.		Value.		Value.
Head	20	Length	15	Colour	5
Ears	10	Shoulders and chest	10	Coat	5
Neck	5	Back	10	Stern	5
		Legs and feet	15		
	35		**50**		**15**

Grand Total 100.

1. The *head* (value 20).—The skull of this dog is large in all dimensions, being flat at the top, with a slight furrow down the middle, and a very large occipital protuberance. Sometimes this part is heavy in excess, but this is far better than the opposite extreme. The nose is very long and broad, with open nostrils. The end should be of a dark flesh colour, but even in the best strains it is sometimes of a cherry or light liver colour. The eye is large and soft, but not watering.

2. The *ears* (value 10) are peculiar in shape as compared with other spaniels, being setter-like or vine-shaped, and indicating that this kind of spaniel is the original "setting spaniel" of olden times, now converted into the setter. They are slightly longer than those of most setters, and feathered, but not heavily, especially on the front edge.

3. The *neck* (value 5) is long and strong, but lean, and free from dewlap in front, where, however, there is a slight ruff of hair.

4. In *length* (value 15) this spaniel should be two and a half times his height.

5. Good *shoulders* (value 10) are very important qualities in so heavy a dog, who tires in any covert rather too soon, and, with heavy shoulders, drops into a walk after a single hour's work. The chest must also have a large girth.

6. A *strong back and loin* (value 10) are equally necessary, and for the same cause. The latter ought to be free from arch, as the back should be from droop, and the back ribs should be very deep.

7. The *legs and feet* (value 15) of the Clumber must be carefully attended to, being of great importance to him in standing his work. He is very apt to be out

at his elbows from his width of chest, and occasionally his legs are bowed from rickets, to which disease he is especially prone. These defects when present should be heavily penalised, as they are faults of great importance.

8. The *colour* (value 5) is always white, with more or less lemon; and when the latter is freckled over the face and legs the colour is perfect. The face should always be white, with lemon head, and at the best a line of white down its middle.

9. The *coat* (value 5) must be soft and silky, slightly wavy, and, though abundant, by no means long, except in feather.

10. The *stern* (value 5) must be set low, and carried considerably downwards, especially when at work.

THE IRISH WATER SPANIEL.

In Ireland two breeds of this dog are known, which are distinguished by the prefixes North and South, the latter being also named after Mr. M'Carthy, a gentleman who, between thirty and forty years ago, alone possessed it in perfection. At the present time the M'Carthy strain may be considered to be *the* type of the Irish water spaniel; and his description published in the *Field* in 1859 is the standard by which the breed is judged, and must therefore be so regarded.

Most of the prize winners of late years have been more " on the leg " than Capt. O'Grady's dog (an engraving of which was published in my first edition in 1865); but several bitches have been successful even lower than he was. They all show, however, in greater perfection one peculiarity of the strain, viz., the total absence of feather both on tail and legs; whereas Capt. O'Grady's dog, though good in tail, was feathered considerably on his legs. I shall therefore substitute portraits from remarkably good photographs of Mr. Lindoe's celebrated brace, Rake and Blarney, which for five or six years shared with Mr. Skidmore's Doctor (half brother to Rake) the chief prizes of the various English shows. Rake was descended from M'Carthy's celebrated dog Boatswain, on the side of his dam; but his grandsire on the other side, also called Boatswain, was from another kennel. He was considered by Capt. Montresor and by Mr. M'Carthy himself to be a good specimen of the breed; and their endorsement must be regarded as final.

The Irish water spaniel has been imported into England in considerable numbers, but not to such an extent as to become common; why, I am at a loss to know, as from Mr. Lindoe's experience, and that of Mr. Englebach (formerly of Teddington), in addition to the account given originally by M'Carthy himself, I am led to believe that he is by far the most useful dog for wildfowl shooting at present in existence. " Notwithstanding their natural impetuosity of disposition," Mr. Lindoe says, " these spaniels, if properly trained, are the most tractable and obedient of all dogs, and possess in a marked degree the invaluable qualities of never giving up or giving in. From real personal experience of almost every kind of dog," he goes on to say, " they are the cleverest, gamest, and most companionable of all." Judging from my knowledge of Mr. Englebach's Pat, bred by Mr. Skidmore, to

MR. LINDOE'S IRISH WATER SPANIELS "RAKE" AND "BLARNEY."

which dog my experience of the breed is confined, I should say he is too quarrel-some to be companionable, except to those who are fond of repeated impromptu dog fights, and he is admitted to be too impetuous for work on land. England appears to have obtained the cream of the strain, as the above-mentioned English-bred dogs, Doctor and Pat, took the first and second prizes at the Dublin show of 1872; while young Doctor was first in the champion class at Belfast in 1876, and Mr. Skidmore's sister to Barney divided the puppy prize at the same show. The chief prizes in England have fallen to dogs belonging to Mr. Skidmore of Nant-wich, Mr. Robson of Hull, Mr. P. J. D. Lindoe, the Rev. W. J. Mellor, Capt. Montresor, and Mr. Englebach, all being of the M'Carthy strain, while Mr. N. Morton of Ballymena is at the head of the Irish breeders. The dog is readily taught to retrieve, but care must be taken to prevent his impetuosity leading to a " hard mouth."

The points of the breed are as follows :

POINTS OF THE IRISH WATER SPANIEL.

	Value.		Value.		Value
Head	10	Chest and shoulders...	7½	Tail	10
Face and eyes	10	Back and quarters	7½	Coat	10
Topknot	10	Legs and feet	10	Colour	10
Ears	10			Symmetry	5
	40		**25**		**35**

Grand Total 100.

1. The *head* (value 10) is by no means long, with very little brow, but moderately wide. It is covered with curls, rather longer and more open than those of the body, nearly to the eyes, but not so as to be wigged like the poodle.

2. The *face and eyes* (value 10) are very peculiar. Face very long, and quite bare of curl, the hair being short and smooth, though not glossy; nose broad, and nostrils well developed; teeth strong and level; eyes small and set almost flush, without eyebrows.

3. The *topknot* (value 10) is a characteristic of the true breed, and is estimated accordingly. It should fall between and over the eyes in a peaked form.

4. The *ears* (value 10) are long, the leather extending, when drawn forward, a little beyond the nose, and the curls with which they are clothed two or three inches beyond. The whole of the ears is thickly covered with curls, which gradually lengthen towards the tips.

5. *Chest and shoulders* (value 7½). There is nothing remarkable about these points, which must, nevertheless, be of sufficient dimensions and muscularity. The chest is small compared with most breeds of similar substance.

6. The *back and quarters* (value 7½) also have no peculiarity, but the stifles are almost always straight, giving an appearance of legginess.

7. *Legs and feet* (value 10). The legs should be straight, and the feet large, but strong; the toes are somewhat open, and covered with short, crisp curls. In all dogs of this breed the legs are thickly clothed with short curls, slightly pendent behind and at the sides, and some have them all round, hanging in ringlets for some time before the annual shedding. No feather like that of the setter should be shown. The front of the hind legs below the hocks is always bare.

The *tail* (value 10) is very thick at the root, where it is clothed with very short hair, as is well shown in the portrait of Blarney. Beyond the root, however, the hair is perfectly short, so as to look as if the tail had been clipped, which it sometimes fraudulently is at our shows; but the natural bareness of tail is a true characteristic of the breed.

9. The *coat* (value 10) is composed of short curls of hair, not *woolly*, which betrays the poodle cross. A soft, flossy coat is objected to as indicative of an admixture with some one of the land spaniels.

10. The *colour* (value 10) must be a deep puce liver without white; but, as in other breeds, a white toe will occasionally appear even on the best-bred litter.

11. The *symmetry* (value 5) of this dog is not very great, and I have consequently only estimated it at 5.

Mr. P. J. D. Lindoe's Rake is by Robson's Jock out of Duck, by Tuffnell's Jack, a son of M'Carthy's Boatswain, Jock by Lord Eglinton's Boatswain out of Flush. He has won nine first prizes, besides several seconds. Blarney is by Tollemache's Boatswain out of Skidmore's Juno, and has won three first prizes, besides seconds and highly commendeds.

THE ENGLISH WATER SPANIEL.

Although a class for this variety of the spaniel is often included in the prize lists of our shows, the exhibits are generally of a most miscellaneous character, and I do not pretend to be able to settle the points of the breed with anything like accuracy or minuteness. The following description will probably serve to include all the variations:

Head, long and narrow; eyes, small; ears, long and clothed with thick curls; body, moderately stout and barrel like, but not so much so as the field spaniel; legs, rather long, straight, and strong; feet, large and spreading; stern, bushy and curly-coated; colour, liver and white, varying in the proportion of these colours.

CHAPTER IV.

RETRIEVERS.

THE RETRIEVER PROPER — THE WAVY-COATED RETRIEVER — THE CURLY-COATED BLACK RETRIEVER—RETRIEVERS OTHER THAN BLACK—WILDFOWL RETRIEVERS—THE DEERHOUND.

AS there are several purposes for which dogs are required to retrieve, so there are special breeds which fulfil those various requirements in the best manner. Thus a dog may be wanted to retrieve partridges in a turnip field; or he may be required to road a running grouse on the moors; or, again, a winged pheasant or a broken-legged hare in covert may test his nose and tender mouth. For these several purposes, what is now called *the* retriever is the fashion of the day, and the same animal may sometimes be called on to take water in order to fetch a wounded duck or widgeon, or even a wild goose or swan. Lastly, the red deer, when wounded by the rifle ball, and not killed, sometimes goes away at a great pace, and tries the speed, and even the stamina, of the deerhound or other dog which is slipped after him. Hence it is necessary, under this article, to describe (1st) the retriever proper, including (a) the wavy-coated black, (b) the curly-coated black, (c) the retriever other than black, (d) the wildfowl retriever; and (2nd) the deerhound.

1.—THE RETRIEVER PROPER.

Until within the last twenty years, many good sportsmen were not satisfied unless their pointers and setters retrieved the game shot to them, and Gen. Hutchinson still maintains that it is a good plan to teach them to do so. Fashion is, however, altogether against this last-mentioned combination, partly because no southern shooter can do without a retriever in walking up birds in turnips; and, as he must have such a dog for part of the year, the more practice that dog has the better, and, consequently, the shooter seldom goes out without one—either on the moors or elsewhere. My own experience is, that with a pointer or setter of very high courage it is almost impossible to keep him steady at "down charge" if he is allowed to retrieve; but, on the other hand, a slack worker will no doubt be encouraged if he is permitted to go to his bird and bring it to his master. Consequently, there are two sides to the argument, as I think; and before attempting to form a reliable opinion, it is well to know the breed of pointers or setters which is to be worked. I am, however, inclined to believe that no retriever proper possesses as good a nose as the pointer or setter, though there are some dogs of these latter breeds who seem incapable of trying for anything but a body scent—and they, of course, are useless as retrievers. Some years ago I endeavoured to devise a plan of trying retrievers in public, and in my experiments I used an old worn-out pointer, which happened to be the only retrieving dog at hand. Constructing a trap on a tripod, which, on pulling a string, would drop a bird with its wing feathers cut in a field of turnips or other covert, I found the old dog invariably bring it to hand, although on one occasion the bird had reached the next field, fully three hundred yards from the trap; and, as the result of these private experiments, I produced the machine at Vaynol in 1871, in full confidence that it would serve the purpose of the retriever trials. But there the retrievers proper could do nothing with a winged partridge dropped on turnips exactly as I had done in private, and if the bird happened to get away more than fifty yards, the scent was very seldom taken up; and if found at all, the success was owing to perseverance in seeking at random, and to accident, rather than nose. Mr. R. J. Lloyd Price's Devil, a curly liver-coloured dog, apparently a cross between the Irish water-spaniel and the poodle, bred by Sir P. Nugent, is the only dog I have ever seen perform in public to my satisfaction, showing great perseverance in hunting, with a good nose, but not coming up to the level of the old pointer above alluded to. With this exception, the best private retrieving I have ever seen has been with crosses of the terrier and beagle; for with one of these little dogs I never yet lost either fur or feather, though of course he could not carry a hare across a brook or over a gate. Still, we must take the world as we find it, and the world of 1877 demands a retriever proper, black by preference, and either wavy-coated or curly.

In the early shows, up to 1864, the classes for retrievers were open to all, and it was not till after the second and third held at Birmingham that any decided opinions began to be expressed. In 1860 the celebrated Wyndham was brought out by Mr. R. Brailsford with success, and he was at once accepted as the type of the wavy-coated strain, being apparently nearly or quite pure Labrador. Next year, at Leeds, Wyndham was second to Mr. Riley's Sam, a curly-coated dog of good shape, but inferior to that gentleman's Royal, afterwards winner of several prizes in England, and of the gold medal at Paris. In 1861 Mr. Riley again succeeded in taking the first prize with his Cato, of about the same pretensions as Sam; the second prize being awarded to a curly-coated dog exhibited by myself, bred by Mr. Whitbread's keeper at Cardington, with an admitted colley cross, and, though handsome in shape, without any of the points which would now be demanded by the judges of the strain, and notably deficient in that bareness of face at present considered a *sine quâ non*. At Islington in 1862 Mr. Riley's Royal was in high form; but at Birmingham in the same year Wyndham again came out first. In the following year Mr. Hill bought Wyndham, and showed him with his Jet at Islington, with which latter he took the first prize, Wyndham only getting the third. In 1863 Wyndham came out as champion at Birmingham : and, after these ups and downs of the wavy and curly coats, the committee of the Chelsea Show decided on dividing the retrievers into distinct classes, their example being followed at Birmingham and elsewhere. In this year Wyndham and Jet again changed hands, Mr. Gorse, who had long before been engaged in breeding retrievers, becoming their new master, and succeeding in getting first at Birmingham with Jet in the curly-coated class, but, curiously enough, being only second in the wavy-coated class to another Wyndham, belonging to Mr. Meyrick, of Pembroke, but bred by Capt. Sparling. The two Wyndhams were much of the same type, nearly or quite pure Labrador, and were about equally successful on the show bench. For some years Mr. Gorse carried all before him in the curly-coated classes of the various shows with Jet and his son Jet II.; but in 1872 Mr. Morris, of Rochdale, brought out True, a magnificent specimen of the breed, with which he has since that time swept the board in the champion classes, his grand bitch X L being almost equally successful in her own class. From the year 1870, when Meyrick's Wyndham only took a third prize at Birmingham, Mr. Gorse, Mr. Shirley, and the various owners of Morley have shared the prizes in the smooth-coated classes, Major Allison's Victor being their chief competitor. This dog shows more of the setter than is approved of by Dr. Bond Moore, who takes the lead as a retriever judge, and who has apparently influenced his coadjutor, whether Mr. Lort or Mr. Shirley, in the case of Victor; but has nevertheless, in conjunction with those gentlemen respectively, at the Alexandra Palace and Birmingham Shows of 1874, and more recently at the Islington Show of 1877, awarded a first prize to Melody, a bitch showing even more of the setter than Victor, according to my judgment. In each case the class was a large one, and that at Birmingham was noted by the judges as "extraordinarily good." With such conflicting fiats, it is difficult to arrive at any definite opinion of the strain considered by the *cognoscenti* to be the proper type of the smooth-coated retriever, and I have therefore selected one of each kind, my own impression being decidedly in favour of the setter cross, as likely to possess the best nose. Melody is a beautiful bitch, no doubt, but she has no pretensions to superiority in any respect over Victor, and hence the above-mentioned decisions are the more incompatible. Both Paris and Morley are said to be pure Labradors, the former being by Sir Henry Paulett's imported Labrador Lion, out of Bess, an imported Labrador bitch. Paris has won repeatedly the champion prizes at the Crystal Palace and Dublin shows. Melody's pedigree is unusually long in comparison with other retrievers, and is as follows:

Mr. G. Brewis's Melody .... { Sailor (Gorse) .... { Moses by Nap (West). / Di (Adm. Curry). } / Midnight (Shirley) ... { Wyndham (Meyrick). / Young Bounce (Hull). }

How she gets her setter blood I am at a loss to know, but her ears, flag, and feather show it in a most unmistakable manner.

(a) THE WAVY-COATED RETRIEVER.

It is generally supposed that this breed is a cross between the Labrador dog, or the small St. John's Newfoundland, and the setter; but in the present day the most successful on the show bench, as above remarked, have been apparently, and often

P

admittedly, pure. In the belief that the nose of the pure Labrador is inferior to that of the setter, I certainly should advise the cross-bred dog for use; but to be successful on the show bench, under such judges as Dr. Bond Moore, Mr. Handley, and Mr. Lort, the competitor should display as little as possible of the setter. In all other respects Major Allison's Victor was perfect, his symmetry being of the most beautiful order; but Dr. Bond Moore could not forgive his setter-like ears, and his fiat was against him. According to my general rule, I shall therefore describe this breed in its show form, the following being the numerical value of the points:

POINTS OF THE BLACK WAVY-COATED RETRIEVER.

	Value.		Value.		Value.
Skull	10	Quarters and stifles ...	10	Tail	5
Nose and jaws	10	Shoulders	6	Coat	5
Ears and eyes	5	Chest	4	Colour	5
Neck	5	Legs, knees, and hocks	10	Symmetry and temperament	10
Loins and back	10	Feet	5		
	40		**35**		**25**

Grand Total 100.

1. The *skull* (value 10) should be long, wide, and flat at the top, with a very slight furrow down the middle. Brow by no means pronounced; but the skull is not absolutely in a straight line with the nose.

2. The *nose and jaws* (value 10) are to be considered from two points of view—first, as to the powers of scent; and secondly, as to the capacity for carrying a hare or pheasant without risk of damage. For both purposes the jaws should be long, and for the development of scenting powers the nose should be wide, the nostrils open, and its end moist and cool.

3. The *ears and eyes* (value 5).—The ears must be small to suit the ideas of the Labrador fancier. With the setter cross they are considerably larger. In any case they should lie close to the head, and be set on low. With regard to the hair on them, it must be short in the Labrador; but in the setter cross it is nearly as long as in the setter itself. The eyes should be of medium size, intelligent-looking, and mild in expression, indicating a good temperament.

4. *Neck* (value 5).—Whatever be the breed of this dog, his neck should be long enough to allow him to stoop in seeking for the trail. A chumpy neck is especially bad; for, while a little dog may get along on a foot scent with a short neck, a comparatively large and unwieldy dog tries himself terribly by the necessity for crouching in his fast pace.

5. The *loins and back* (value 10) must be wide and deep, to enable the retriever to carry a hare over a stone wall, a brook, or gate.

6. The *quarters and stifles* (value 10) must be muscular, for the same reason; and, to enable the retriever to do his work fast enough to please the modern sportsman, with ease to himself, the stifles should be set wide apart.

7. The *shoulders* (value 10) should be long and sloping; otherwise, even with a proper length of neck, the dog cannot stoop to a foot scent without fatigue.

8. The *chest* (value 4) should be broad as well as deep, with well-developed back ribs.

9. *Legs, knees,* and *hocks* (value 10).—When tolerably fast work is to be done by a heavy dog, it is important that these parts should be strong and free from disease in their joints. Hence the legs must not only be long and muscular, but they must be clean and free from gumminess. The knees should be broad, and the hocks well developed, and clean.

10. The *feet* (value 5) are rather larger proportionately than in the setter, but they should be compact, and the toes well arched. Soles thick and strong.

11. The *tail* (value 5) in the "Bond Moore" type should be bushy, and not feathered, which is a sign of the setter cross. It should be carried gaily, but not curled over the back.

12. The *coat* (value 5) is short, but not so short as in the pointer or hound; set close, slightly wavy, and glossy.

13. The *colour* (value 5) should be a rich black, free from rustiness. In many good imported dogs there is a white star on the breast, and a white toe or two; but the fashionable breeders now go in for a total absence of white, and this point is therefore to be estimated accordingly, as long as Dr. Bond Moore and his coadjutors maintain their position. That the public do not agree with him is plain from the fact that, in answer to an advertisement offering to give away several puppies bred by him with white on their toes, &c., he received more than 150 applications. It also shows that even his own breed cannot be depended on for absence of white, and that it is purely an arbitrary sign, altogether independent of race. Hence, in my opinion, it is absurd to disqualify a dog absolutely because he shows a small white star or a white toe; but it is quite within the powers of the judge to penalise him to the extent of the allowance for colour in the scale of points.

14. *Symmetry and temperament* (value 10).—The symmetry of this dog is often considerable; and, though there is no grandeur, as in the large Newfoundland and St. Bernard, still there is a due proportion of size and strength, with elegance all through, which takes the eye, and should be valued highly. The walk of the Labrador is not so loose and shambling as that of the large Newfoundland. The evidences of good temperament should be regarded with great care, since the utility of this dog mainly depends on it. A sour-headed brute, with a vicious look about the eyes, should at once be penalised to the full extent of this point, and a retriever shown with a muzzle on, as has often happened, should be regarded with great suspicion. Of course a dog *may* be so savage in a show as to require a muzzle, yet perfectly mild and inoffensive in the field; but such cases are exceptional, and a judge ought always to satisfy himself of the general good temper of a retriever requiring a muzzle.

Mr. G. Brewis's Paris has been very successful on the show bench, and has a fine body and good coat, but I confess I neither like his head nor his short jaw. Nevertheless, it is impossible at present to find a better type of the pure Labrador. Melody is a beautiful specimen of the setter cross.

(b) THE BLACK CURLY-COATED RETRIEVER.

Little or nothing seems to be known of the history of this dog, now so extensively bred throughout the United Kingdom. At all events, there is no getting at the exact source of the breed, and on that account I am led to think that some non-sporting dog, such as the poodle, has been used. Possibly successful breeders do not like to give information which may lead to a repetition of their success in other hands; but my experience does not lead me to place much reliance on this interpretation of their secresy. It is admitted that the curly-coated dog is remarkably sagacious, and more "tricky" than the smooth, and this confirms the above suspicion; but I confess that I have no proof whatever to allege in its support, and my theory must be taken for what it is worth as such. The general belief is that the water spaniel and small Newfoundland have been used in establishing the breed, and there is little doubt of the truth of this theory.

This variety of the dog has certainly not increased in numbers of late years, or improved in symmetry, and has notably gone off in the shape of head, which is now too narrow by far. The falling off numerically is probably due to the fact that the public have pronounced in favour of the Labrador, which has been largely imported by "Idstone" and others, as well as extensively bred by Dr. Bond Moore and Mr. Shirley, who have, with Mr. Lort and Mr. Handley, composed the goodly company of judges in this department. From whatever cause, however, the curly-coated dogs of the present day are not exhibited in such large and good classes as they were about ten years ago, and they are notably deficient in those indications of good temper which should always be looked for in the retriever. There is some little difference in the points of the two breeds, the main ones being those connected with bareness of face and texture of coat. I insert the altered scale :

POINTS OF THE CURLY-COATED RETRIEVER.

	Value.		Value.		Value.
Skull	10	Shoulders	6	Texture of coat and bareness of face	15
Nose and jaws	10	Chest	4	Colour	5
Ears and eyes	5	Legs, knees, and hocks	5	Symmetry and temperament	10
Neck	5	Feet	5		
Loins and back	10	Tail	5		
Quarters and stifles	5				
	45		25		30

Grand Total—100.

11. The *tail* (value 5) is the first point in the list above given wherein the curly-coated dog differs from the wavy-coated retriever. In the latter, as described in the points of that variety, it may be either bushy or setter-like; but in the curly-coated retriever the hair must be short and curly, and though not quite bare as in the Irish water spaniel, it should be nearly so towards the tip. The tail also should be stiff, and only slightly bent, without any approach to a curl beyond a very gentle bend, as shown in the illustration which accompanies this chapter.

12. The *texture of coat and bareness of face* (value 15) constitute the chief difference between the two breeds. The texture of coat should be intermediate between wool and hair, like that of the Astrakan sheep, with even a crisper curl, each of which should be quite distinct. The breed has naturally a very oily coat, which serves to protect the skin when in the water; but for show purposes artificial oil is often added to such an extent as to soil the hand considerably when stroking the dog. This fraud, though not so great as dyeing or clipping, is still one which should be deprecated, and, if clearly established, ought to disqualify a dog from competition. On the whole face, up to nearly the middle of the ears, the coat should be quite short, without the slightest wave even; and here clipping is some-times resorted to, and should be punished in the same way—it can easily be detected by the absence of bloom at the parts clipped. Plucking is useless, as it leaves the skin bare. With the above exceptions, the whole body should be clothed with short curls, and the occurrence of a patch of uncurled hair on the back, called a "saddle," is greatly objected to.

The illustrations accompanying this chapter are portraits of Mr. Bartrum's Nell and Mr. Morris's True. Nell obtained the remarkable distinction of being placed above True as "the best retriever in the show" at Birmingham in 1875, by Dr. Bond Moore and Mr. Shirley, and I have therefore coupled her with that dog in the most prominent position. The following is her pedigree:

Mr. Bartram's Nell .... { Oscar (Schofield) ... { Sweep (Hodgson) { Hector (Riley)
(late Mr. E. W. Richards) { Jet (Mr. J. Holmes) { Bess (Gill) .... { Old Bess (Ferraud).

Mr. Morris's True is by Challoner's Sam, of the Duke of Portland's breed, out of Watson's bitch. He is a winner of a host of first and champion prizes, including that of the Kennel Club Show, at Islington, in 1877.

(c) THE RETRIEVERS OTHER THAN BLACK.

Classes defined as above have been made specially with a view to include those liver-coloured specimens which are met with constantly in litters bred from black curly-coated parents, indicating the spaniel cross. Thus, in 1866, Mr. Jones and Mr. Harrison took the first and second prizes at Birmingham with Neptune and Sailor respectively, both being by the celebrated Jet, and the former out of a black daughter of that dog, while the latter was out of Gorse's Gyp, also black. Both were liver-coated dogs; and in 1865 Sailor was placed second to Mr. Gorse's Jet, Mr. Harrison asserting his superiority to that dog in all other respects, and on that account a separate class was made next year; but the result was not more favourable to the then treasurer and prime mover of the show, as he only got a second to Neptune, as above stated. This class is not defined at all, so that the judges may have to decide between curly-coated of both colours, wavy-coated of a black, brindled, black and tabby, black and tan, or red colour; and of course, can have no rule but the rule of thumb to guide them. In such a class, colour must be left out of consideration ; but a well-coated and finely-shaped curly-coated liver dog would generally achieve success.

The *weight* of the modern retriever proper is about 80lb ; height, 25 to 26 inches.

(d) WILDFOWL RETRIEVERS.

A great difference of opinion exists as to the comparative merits of the Labrador and the curly-coated retriever for water. In any case, the latter is not improved by the setter cross for this purpose, as the coat of that dog is not nearly so oily as the Labrador's. As far as I can learn from wildfowlers, there is no reliable evidence to found an opinion on.

In *tenderness of mouth* the wavy-coated dog is said to be superior to his rival, but without doubt there are many curly-coated retrievers whose mouths are tender enough. Notably Mr. Gorse's Jet was so ; and, indeed, from reliable "information received," I am led to believe that he was far above the average in this respect as well as in nose. The Irish water spaniel makes an excellent water retriever.

2.—THE DEERHOUND.

This dog is now more ornamental than useful, his former trade of retrieving wounded deer in Scotland being often entrusted to colleys, whole or half-bred, and cross-bred dogs of various kinds, but in the south his grand size and outline make him a great favourite with country gentlemen, and more especially with the ladies of their families. For this fashion Sir Walter Scott with his Ban and Buskar, immortalised in "Waverley," is mainly responsible, as with the Dandie Dinmonts in "Guy Mannering."

There is no doubt that the Scotch deerhound and the thorough Scotch greyhound were identical in shape, and could scarcely be distinguished by good judges, and even by them only when at work, the deerhound galloping with his head considerably higher than the greyhound. *Pari passu* with the disappearance of the rough greyhound has been the rarity of the deerhound in modern days, the former being displaced by the smooth breed, and the latter by various crosses, *e.g.*, that between the foxhound and greyhound advocated by Mr. Scrope ; the mastiff and greyhound cross of the Earl of Stamford, and all sorts of crosses between the colley and greyhound, rough as well as smooth, as mentioned above. In the present day pure deerhounds *kept for the retrieving of deer* are comparatively rare, and I believe even those in Her Majesty's kennel are not used for that purpose. Hence it is idle to attempt to describe this dog solely from the deer-stalker's point of view, and he must be estimated rather from an artistic stand-point, in which capacity he rivals, and perhaps surpasses, all his brethren, having the elegant frame of the greyhound united with a rough shaggy coat, which takes off the hardness of outline complained of by the lovers of the picturesque as attaching to the English "longtail." Still, though the deerhound of modern days is to be considered as a companionable dog rather than as a deer retriever, as he has always hitherto been regarded as coming under the latter category, and is

MR. FIELD'S DEERHOUND "BRAN."

so classed in all our shows, I shall not attempt to displace him from his old time-honoured position. As a companion he must depend for a good character on his ornamental appearance, rather than on his utility as a protector of dames, in which capacity he is quite useless as compared with the mastiff, St. Bernard, or Newfoundland. He is not so quarrelsome as the colley, but when attacked defends himself with great power, quickness, and courage. His chief defect as a companion is his proneness to chase any moving object, and he will even pick up little dogs, especially if they attempt to run away from him; and if not broken early from this habit, he often occasions trouble to his owner. On the other hand, he is seldom offensive to strangers, but he does not take to children, and is seldom to be trusted with them. Unless well broken, he will chase hares and rabbits, and of course deer, and on that account he should not be taken into deer parks or game preserves by those who are not sure of being able to control him.

The disproportion between the sexes is greater than in any other breed of dogs, the average difference in height in the same litter being often from five to six inches.

When this dog is slipped at a wounded deer, he pursues it by either scent or sight, the latter being, of course, used in preference, but the nose being lowered for the trail the moment the deer is lost to the eye. In hunting the trail, however hot and fresh, the deerhound does not throw his tongue as a rule, though, as is the case even with some of the highest bred greyhounds, occasionally a low whimper is heard. When a stag stands at bay, the dog opens with a loud sharp bark, and continues till his master appears to give the *coup de grace*, unless his quarry is sufficiently exhausted by loss of blood to permit his pinioning him; but a stag in possession of his full powers is beyond the reach of any dog from the front, and a well-bred deerhound does not make the attempt unless he sees an opening from behind. A cross with the bulldog was tried some years ago in order to give courage, which it did; but it also gave the peculiar bulldog tendency to go at the head of the deer, and led to the loss of so many valuable animals that it was abandoned.

The numerical value of the points of this dog is as follows:

POINTS OF THE DEERHOUND.

	Value.		Value.		Value.
Skull	10	Chest and shoulders...	10	Legs and quarters	7½
Nose and jaws	5	Back and back ribs...	10	Feet	7½
Ears and eyes	5	Elbows and stifles	10	Colour and coat	10
Neck	10	Symmetry and quality	10	Tail	5
	30		40		30

Grand Total 100.

1. In *skull* (value 10) the deerhound resembles the large coarse greyhound, it being long and moderately wide, especially between the ears. There is a very slight rise at the eyebrows so as to take off what would otherwise be a straight line from tip of nose to occiput. The upper surface is level in both directions.

2. *Nose and jaws* (value 5).—The jaws should be long and the teeth level and strong. Nostrils open but not very wide, and the end pointed and black; cheeks well clothed with muscle, but the bone under the eye neither prominent nor hollow.

3. *Ears and eyes* (value 5).—The *ears* should be small and thin and carried a trifle higher than those of the smooth greyhound, but should turn over at the tips. Pricked ears are sometimes met with, as in the rough greyhound, but they are not correct. They should be thinly fringed with hair at the edges only ; that on their surfaces should be soft and smooth. Eyes full and dark hazel, sometimes by preference blue.

4. The *neck* (value 10) should be long enough to allow the dog to stoop to the scent at a fast pace, but not so long and tapering as the greyhound. It is usually also a little thinner than the corresponding part in that dog.

5. *Chest and shoulders* (value 10).—The chest is deep rather than wide, and in its general formation it resembles that of the greyhound, being shaped with great elegance, and at the same time so that the shoulders can play freely on its sides. The girth of a full sized dog deerhound should be at least two inches greater than his height, often an inch or two more, but a round unwieldly chest is not to be desired, even if girthing well. Shoulders long, oblique, and muscular.

6. *Back and back ribs* (value 10).—Without a powerful loin a large dog like this cannot sustain the sweeping stride which he possesses, and therefore a deep and wide development of muscle filling up the space between wide back ribs and somewhat ragged hips is the *desideratum*. A good loin should measure 25 or 26 inches in show condition. The back ribs are often rather shallow, but they must be wide, or what is called "well sprung," and the loin should be arched, drooping to the root of the tail.

7. *Elbows and stifles* (value 10), if well placed, give great liberty of action, and the contrary if they are confined by being too close together. These points should therefore be carefully examined. The elbows must be well let down to give length to the true arm, and should be quite straight, that is, neither turned in or out. The stifles should be wide apart and set well forward to give length to the upper thigh. Many otherwise well-made deerhounds are very straight in their stifles.

8. The *high symmetry* (value 10) of this dog is essential to his position as a companionable dog, and it is therefore estimated accordingly. *Quality* is also to be regarded as of great importance.

9. *Legs and quarters* (value 7½).—Great bone and muscle must go to the formation of these parts, and the bones must be well put together at the knees and hocks, which should be long and well developed. The quarters are deep but seldom wide, and there is often a considerable slope to the tail. Some of the most successful dogs lately exhibited, and notably Mr. Musters's Torunn and Mr. Beasley's Countess, have been nearly straight backed, but this shape is not approved of by deerstalkers.

10. The *feet* (value 7½) should be well arched in the toes and catlike—a wide spreading foot is often met with, but should be specially condemned.

11. *Colour and coat* (value 10).—The *colours* most in request are dark blue,

fawn, grizzle, and brindled, the latter with a more or less tint of blue. The fawn should have the tips of the ears dark, but some otherwise good fawns are pale throughout. The grizzle generally has a decided tint of blue in it. White is to be avoided either on breast or toes, but it should not disqualify a dog. The *coat* (value 5) is coarser on the back than elsewhere, and by many good judges it is thought that even on the back it should be intermediate between silk and wool, and not the coarse hair often met with; and there is no doubt that both kinds of coat are found in some of the best strains. The whole body is clothed with a rough coat sometimes amounting to shagginess, that of the muzzle is longer in proportion than elsewhere, but the moustache should not be wiry, and should stand out in irregular tufts. There should be no approach to feather on the legs as in the setter, but their inside should be hairy.

12. The *tail* (value 5) should be long and gently curved, without any twist. It should be thinly clothed with hair only.

The most successful exhibitor at our shows for the last ten years is Mr. Chaworth Musters, of Kirk Langton, with his two Torunns, father and son. The old dog was of the Monzie strain, and was the sire of several prize winners, including Brenda, Hylda, Meg, Mr. Parkes's Bevis, Hilda and Teeldar, the younger Torunn, and Mr. Fitt's Bruce, all which (except the first two) were from sister to Morni, his chief competitor on the show bench. Next to him comes Mr. J. N. Beasley, of Brampton House, Northampton, with Alder and Countess, both with unknown pedigrees; and third, very nearly approaching them indeed, is Mr. Hickman, of Birmingham, whose Morni alone has taken eight first or champion prizes, whereas Old Torunn stopped short at five. Countess was undoubtedly, in my opinion, the most beautiful deerhound I ever saw, and quite unapproached by either dog or bitch; Mr. Allen's fawn bitch Hylda (the dam of Morni), who took the second prize to her at Birmingham in 1867, being also a splendid specimen of the breed. The latter was by a dog in Her Majesty's kennels. Bran, whose portrait is retained as showing well all the points of the deerhound, was by Mr. Stewart Hodgson's Oscar, son of a dog belonging to Colonel Lennard, of Wickham-cross, and of the breed of Mr. M'Kenzie, of Applecross, Ross-shire. His dam was Mr. Cole's (Her Majesty's keeper) Hylda, by his Old Kieldar out of Tank; Old Kieldar by Hector, a dog presented to Her Majesty by Mr. Campbell, of Monzie.

The measurement of Bran was as follows: From nose to setting on of tail, 47 inches; tail, 22 inches; height, 32 inches; length of head, 12 inches; circumference of head, 17½ inches; round arm at elbow, 9½ inches; girth at chest, 33½ inches; girth at loin, 24 inches; round thigh, 17½ inches; round lower thigh hock, 7 inches; knee, 7 inches.

BOOK II.
HOUNDS AND THEIR ALLIES.

———

CHAPTER I.
THE GREYHOUND.

———

AS ITS NAME IMPLIES, this variety of the dog must be classed with the hounds, but it differs from all the others of this division in being used for the pursuit of hares by the eye alone. Its congener, the deerhound, fills up the gap between the two, being encouraged to take up the scent of its game when it loses view. But it must not be supposed that our modern greyhound is entirely without the power of scent, as there are numberless proofs to the contrary in the shape of pure-bred dogs of this kind which are used as lurchers. A good dog of this sort will run from view to scent and back again as often as is required by the nature of the ground, and will account for every hare he is allowed to hunt undisturbed. Indeed, the chief difficulty with the trainer of greyhounds is to keep his charge from using their noses, which many strains are very apt to do, to the great disgust of the public courser; though the tendency of this development of the olfactory organ is so much in favour of "currant jelly" that the private courser does not always object to it. On the whole, however, the greyhound may be defined as the only British dog hunting its game by the eye alone.

As the points of this dog have been fully described in "The Greyhound," and as it is desirable to keep them before the public without any alteration, I shall insert them in the *ipsissima verba* which are introduced in that book.

"Experience has convinced all coursers that a dog with plenty of length from his hip to his hock is likely to be speedy, because there is a greater than usual length of muscle to act upon the hock, and also a longer stride. The same unerring criterion has also led us to believe that a good back will give increase of power; in fact, that, *cæteris paribus*, size is power. But this law must not be taken without exceptions, since there must of necessity be a due proportion of parts, or else the successive actions necessary for speed will not take place in due order and with the proper regularity of stroke, and also because, by a well-known mechanical law, what is gained in power is lost in speed or time. This framework, then, of bones and muscles, when obtained of good form and proportions, is so

much gained towards our object; but still, without a good brain and nervous system to stimulate it to action, it is utterly useless; and without a good heart and lungs to carry on the circulation during its active employment, it will still fail us in our need. Again, even if all these organs are sound and formed of good proportions by nature, if mismanagement or other causes interrupt their proper nutrition by digestion and assimilation, the framework speedily falls away, and our hopes are irrecoverably wrecked."

The following are the points in the greyhound:

	Value.		Value.		Value.
Head	10	Loin and back ribs	15	Tail	5
Neck	10	Hind quarters	20	Colour and coat	5
Chest and fore quarters	20	Feet	15		
	40		50		10

Grand Total 100

1. The head (value 10).—"I have already said that, in my opinion, the head should be large between the ears, and in a dog from 25in. to 26in high, should measure at least 14½in. in circumference midway between the eyes and ears. This point is one which is not usually insisted on, many coursers preferring the narrow and elegant head, which will easily allow the neck-strap to slip over it. My own conviction is so strong that I do not hesitate to advise the selection of the head with a wider neck to it, and as narrow and low as it can be obtained between the eyes. Very little intelligence is required in the greyhound; and if it were possible to obtain the full development of the appetite for his game (the seat of which is no doubt in the back of the brain) without any corresponding increase of intellectual faculties, it would be desirable to do so. But, unfortunately, this is not attainable without some slight drawback; for, though it may be possible to select heads in which there is very great increase in volume in the back of the head, in proportion to the enlargement of the forehead, still the latter part is more or less developed, and in these animals greater care is necessary in the rearing to prevent them from self-hunting, or from assisting the sheepdog of the farm in finding and killing what rabbits and hares are in the neighbourhood. But when that care has been taken, this greyhound is really valuable; his courage is immense; no amount of injury or work seems to cow him (though he is not necessarily stout, for this quality, I believe, resides in the whole nervous system, and not in any part of it), and even the whip only subdues for a time his appetite for blood. The jaw can hardly be too lean, but the muscle should be full, and there should be little or no development of the nasal sinuses. I am not fond of long-nosed greyhounds; but I have seen good ones possessing that appendage in almost every variety of shape. The eye should be full and bright, giving the idea of high spirits and animation. As to the ears, there is a very great variety in the different breeds, from the large upstanding ones of the Heatherjock variety to the small and elegantly-falling ear of most of our modern greyhounds. The bitch has always a neater and more compact head than her brothers, and there is generally a livelier look about the eye; but though the

head is smaller, it is still in the same relative proportion to the whole body, which
is more neat and elegant also. No courser should omit to examine the teeth,
which require to be strong and long enough to hold the hare when taken."

2. The *neck* (value 10) of the greyhound, in the old rhyme, was compared
to that of a drake, and of all the comparisons therein contained this is the nearest to
the truth. It certainly is not so long or so round as a drake's, but sometimes
approaches very nearly to it. This form will enable the greyhound to seize his game
while in full stride without losing his balance; but I have known many good killers
with short necks, almost like that of a bull; still, as a rule, a long neck is of great
importance, and should be well considered in selecting a cross. Too often the thick
compact form has also the bull neck; but in some breeds, as in the Curler and
Vraye Foy family, which are very muscular, the neck is proportionally long.

" The points I have been considering are not immediately connected with speed;
but now I have to describe the framework by which locomotion is effected. It
must be apparent to anyone who watches the gallop, that its perfection depends
upon the power of extending the shoulders and fore legs as far as possible, as well
as of bringing the hind legs rapidly forward to give the propulsive stroke. Upon
the due relation between these two parts of the action everything depends; and if
the one part is more perfect than the other—that is to say, if the hind quarters are
well brought into action, while the shoulders do not thrust the forelegs well forward
—the action is laboured and slow; whilst, on the contrary, if the shoulders do their
duty, but the hind legs are not brought well forward, or do not thrust the body
onwards with sufficient force, the action may be elegant, but it is not powerful and
rapid. For these various purposes, therefore, we require good shoulders, good
thighs, a good back, and good legs, and, lastly, for lodging the lungs and heart,
whose actions are essential to the maintenance of speed, a well-formed and capacious
chest."

3. *Chest and fore quarters* (value 20).—" With regard to the *chest*, there are
two things to be considered—namely, capacity for the lodgment of the lungs and
heart, and the attainment of that form most conducive to speed and working.
It must not be too deep, or the animal is constantly striking it against obstacles;
it must not be too wide, or the shoulders are unable to play smoothly upon it, as
they must do in the action of this quarter; but it must be of sufficient capacity
to lodge the heart and lungs. A just relation between these three counterbalancing
essentials is therefore the best form—neither too small for good wind, nor too wide
for speed, nor too deep to keep free from the irregularities of the ground, but that
happy medium which we see in our best specimens, and which the portraits of most
of our best dogs will exhibit to the eye of the courser. The shoulders must be so
formed as to thrust the forelegs well forward, and to do this the shoulder-blade
must be as oblique as possible. The reason for this is, that its muscles may be able
to exert their full power upon the true arm, in bringing it into a straight line with
the axis of the shoulder-blade. This alone is a great advantage; but, by the greater
angle which it forms with the arm, it also enables the greyhound to bear the shock
of a fall upon his legs in coming down from a leap without injury, which is another

most important feature. An oblique shoulder is likewise usually accompanied by a longer true arm, because the point of the shoulder must be raised higher from the elbow to allow of the obliquity, and in proportion to the increased length will the fore foot be extended forward; thus this form gives longer levers with greater power of leverage, and *more space for the lodgment of muscles.* If, then, we have this form, combined with good length from the elbow down to the knee, compared with that from the knee to the ground, and with a good development of bone and muscle in addition, perfection in this essential part of the frame is insured. In this last point (from the elbow to the knee) there is a very great difference in greyhounds; but, by a careful measurement of various well-formed legs, I am inclined to think that from the elbow to the knee ought to be at least twice the length from the same point to the ground. In this measurement the dog would be standing on a level surface with his weight bearing upon both legs, and I think the measure should be taken in this way, and not from the base of the two middle nails, because in the stride the action is from the ball of the foot, and not from the end of the toes. In variously-formed feet there is a difference of nearly an inch in length of toes; and many a dog with short toes would measure from the ground nearly an inch less than another with long toes; which latter would nevertheless measure, from his toe-nails to his knee, nearly an inch more than the former.

"Such are the general points of importance in the fore quarter; the minor ones are, good bony and well-developed shoulder points, elbows neither turned in nor out, muscular arms, good bony knees, not too much bent back, and large strong pasterns, the bones composing which are of full size."

4. *Loin and back ribs* (value 15).—"In order to unite the hind and fore quarters, and to assist in fixing the pelvis, from which the muscles composing the haunch take their fulcrum, a good back is required, and when of a good form it has been compared to a beam. Now the back is composed of a series of vertebræ, having the ribs attached to the sides of the first thirteen, but in those of the loins depending alone upon the hip bones and lateral processes for the lodgment and attachment of muscles. It must be self-evident that every additional inch in length of back increases the stride by that amount exactly, and therefore if prolonged indefinitely it would be advantageous, till counter-balanced by the disadvantages inseparably connected with this form, in consequence of the diminished strength. The length of back should therefore be looked for between the neck and the last rib, rather than between the last rib and the hip bone; and this is a very important consideration too often neglected. The back ribs should be well spread and deep; for, unless they are in this form, a sufficient attachment cannot be afforded to the muscles of the loins, which constitute the chief moving power in drawing the hind legs forward, and in fixing the pelvis. The loins must therefore be broad, strong, and deep, and the measure of their strength must be a circular one. Breadth alone will not do, since the lower muscles require to be well developed as well as the upper, but a good measurement *round* the loin is a good test of power in that quarter. It was the fashion from 1840 to 1850 to select flat and straight backs, and these certainly are handsomer than the high-arched backs previously so much in

vogue. Either form may be qualified to do its duty, if there is only the power of straightening the line in the arched back; but if permanently arched it becomes what is called the 'wheel back,' and the power of extension in the gallop is very much limited. Since the time of Bedlamite, who was very drooping in his quarters, and possibly partly in consequence of the attention which he drew to this point, the very level back is not so much in fashion, and the arched loin, coupled with the Bedlamite quarter, is much sought after."

5. *Hind quarters* (value 20).—These are " of more importance than the fore quarter, and are composed of three separate divisions, varying greatly in total and comparative length in different individuals. These three divisions are—the true thigh, between the hip and stifle joints; the false or lower thigh, answering to the leg of a man, and situated between the stifle and hock; and, lastly, the leg, between the hock and foot. The first two of these divisions should be nearly equal in length, and in most well-proportioned greyhounds are each about one-fifth longer than the lower arm; whilst the leg, from the hock to the ground, should bear about the same relation to each of the thigh bones as the fore pastern does to the arm—that is to say, it should be about one-half, generally rather more than less. Many good greyhounds vary much in these proportions; and the stifle joint is often placed far from midway between the hip joint and the hock—generally it is a little nearer the hip—but I have seen it much lower than the mid-point, but never in a greyhound of good pace and performance. With a greyhound thus formed, having both the upper and lower thigh bone one-fifth longer than the lower arm, with the hock also placed a little above the level of the knee, and the top of the shoulder-blade only the length of the thigh bone above the elbow, it follows either that the top of the hind quarter will be considerably higher than the fore, or that the hind legs will be bent at the hock and stifle joint considerably out of the straight line. Either of these forms is conducive to speed; but the latter is the more elegant, and also appears to be the best calculated for preserving the equilibrium in the turn. If the hind legs are straight, and yet the back is level, the fore legs must be long, or else there can scarcely be sufficient speed. This form is, however, inferior to the bent hind legs, and correspondingly short anterior extremities. The type of the best formation is seen in the hare, in which there is a still greater disproportion; and as the greyhound has to cope with her in speed and working, he must, to a certain extent, be formed upon the same model, and so he really is when the proportions are carefully examined in a skinned hare. In the portraits of Mr. Randell's Ruby and Mr. Brown's Bedlamite (given in " The Greyhound "), the best form of stifles may be seen. The latter dog himself possessed remarkably developed stifles, which have been transmitted to many of his descendants, and on which I believe much of their success has depended. This peculiarity consists in the stifles being set on wide apart, so that they can be brought well forward in the stride without any difficulty. Good bony stifles and powerful hocks are essentially requisite for the attachment and leverage of the various muscles; and unless these are large and powerful in the haunches and thighs no greyhound can be of first class powers. This point is, however, so well known, that it is scarcely necessary to insist upon it."

6. The *feet* (value 15) of the greyhound are met with in two varying but useful forms, namely, the catlike and the hare foot. In the former case they are round and close with upstanding knuckles, and by many people they are much preferred. Such toes are, however, very likely to "break down;" and for use the hare foot, longer and flatter, is by many coursers preferred. In any case a flat open foot is to be discarded.

7. The *tail* (value 5) should be fine and nicely curved; but this point is only to be looked at as a mark of good breed.

8. The *colours* (value 5) preferred are black and red, or fawn with black muzzles. Black-tan is very rarely seen, but almost every other colour is occasionally met with. White greyhounds are by many disliked, being considered delicate; but I do not know that this objection is founded upon reliable premises. The brindled colour is also supposed, without reason, to be a mark of the bulldog cross, as I am satisfied it existed before there is any evidence of that cross having been used.

The relative value of these several points varies a good deal from those of dogs whose breeding can chiefly be arrived at by external signs—*e.g.*, the stern, colour, and coat in the pointer and setter. Here the pedigree is well known for many generations; and therefore, although the breeding may be guessed at from the appearance of the individual, it is far better to depend upon the evidence afforded by the *Coursing Calendar*, or, if that is not forthcoming, to avoid having anything to do with breeding from the strain.

"In measuring a dog I should take only the following points, which should be nearly of the proportions here given in one of average size:

"*Principal points:* Height at the shoulder, 25in.; length from shoulder point to apex of last rib, 15in.; length of apex of last rib to back of buttock, 13in. to 15in.; length from front of thigh round buttock to front of other thigh, 21in.

"But to be more minute, it is as well to measure also the *subordinate points* as under: Circumference of head between eyes and ears, 14½in. to 15in.; length of neck, 9in. to 10in.; circumference of chest, 28in. to 30in. in condition; length of arm, 9in.; length of knee to the ground, 4½in.; circumference of the loin, 18in. to 19in., in running condition; length of upper thigh, 10½in.; lower thigh, 11in.; and leg from hock to ground, 5½in. to 6in.

"In taking these measurements the fore legs should, as nearly as possible, be perpendicular, and the hind ones only moderately extended backwards."

The specimens selected to illustrate this chapter are Riot and David, which were perhaps the best greyhounds for all kinds of ground which ever ran, not even excepting the two treble winners of the Waterloo Cup, as they were not tried over the downs. Riot was the property of Mr. C. Randell, of Chadbury, and was not only the winner of seventy-four courses in public, with the loss of only ten, but she was also the dam of several good greyhounds. David had also the same double distinction, but was not quite so celebrated in the coursing field as the bitch. He had, however, the advantage at the stud, as might be expected from his sex, and a goodly list of winners are credited to him. Curiously enough, both were bred in the same kennel, from which they were transferred as whelps, in the case of the bitch, to Chadbury, and in that of the dog, to Mr. W. Long, of Amesbury, both distinguished in the south as public coursers, and pitted against one another in many a stake.

I might point to the numerous descendants of Beacon and Scotland Yet, and to Cerito and Master McGrath, as having been more successful over the plains of Altcar; but I believe that no strain of blood has done more over all sorts of ground than the combination of Bedlamite and Blackfly in Riot, and that of Motley and Wanton in David, and again in his son Patent.

CHAPTER II.
MODERN HOUNDS HUNTING BY NOSE.

GENERAL REMARKS—THE BLOODHOUND—THE FOXHOUND—THE HARRIER—THE BEAGLE—THE OTTERHOUND.

NDER this general heading are included by sportsmen those varieties of the dog which pursue and kill their game by the nose only, and above ground. As a consequence, greyhounds, deerhounds, pointers, setters, spaniels, and terriers, are excluded from the list—greyhounds, because they do not ordinarily hunt by scent; deerhounds, because they are only used to retrieve their quarry when wounded by the rifle; pointers, setters, and spaniels, for the reason that though they find their game by the nose they leave the gun to kill it; and terriers, because they work underground as well as above it. From the latter half of the word greyhound and deerhound, it might naturally be inferred that they could be considered hounds; but in sportsman's language they are not so, and if a man was heard to say that he saw a lot of hounds out on a certain farm, when it turned out that they were greyhounds, he would at once be set down as ignorant of sport and its belongings. The term is therefore confined in the present day to the bloodhound, staghound, foxhound, harrier, beagle, and otterhound. Except in Devonshire and Somerset, the staghound is not allowed to kill his quarry, being whipped off as soon as the deer stands at bay; and in all other packs either a pure foxhound of full size is used, as in Her Majesty's, or a bloodhound, as in Mr. Nevill's and Lord Wolverton's, and hence these last are included under the bloodhound or foxhound classes. The Devon, and Somerset are, however, said to be of the pure old Southern hound strain

MR. RAY'S BLOODHOUNDS "ST. HUBERT" AND "BARONESS."

drafted for speed until they are now able to go such pace as fits them for the modern ideas of hunting, which demands a good gallop as the essential to sport. Never having seen them, I can only form an opinion of them on second hand testimony, but it appears to me from this evidence, that they only differ in colour from Mr. Nevill's black tans, being in fact light and corky bloodhounds, and in all probability derived from the same source. It is quite clear, from the series of portraits published in the *Field*, three years ago, that in France a much greater variety has been developed in the hound than in England, where the foxhound has absorbed nearly all the others into its own capacious net. Even the harrier is now very seldom met with pure, and the old fashioned beagle is equally rare. Patience is no longer a virtue cultivated by English sportsmen, by whom the dash and forward cast of the foxhound are greatly preferred, to the careful puzzling out of a cold scent on which our forefathers set so much value. Many good sportsmen contend that a modern foxhound, even of the fastest strains, can make out a cold scent as well as a bloodhound or a beagle, and that it is the change in our farm management from that of former times, which makes the existing foxhound appear to have a worse nose than his predecessors. That there has been such a change is indisputable in the corn districts, but in the grass lands—at all events during a wet season—no such excuse can be made, and yet it is notorious that after the lapse of a very few minutes there is now little chance of doing any good with a fox, whereas a hundred years ago no huntsman would think of giving up, if he was sure of the line a full hour after a fox had been viewed. All the hounds—pure and simple—have heads of average size, long and broad noses, and full pendulous ears. They all give tongue when on a scent, and their note is musical, not like that of the terrier, shrill and squeaky. With the exception of the otterhound and the Welsh harrier, which closely resemble one another, all our modern hounds have stout coats, but their sterns show a fringe of hair underneath. All carry their sterns "gaily," that is, with a considerable upward tendency, but not curled over their backs beyond a right angle. With these characters in common, I now proceed to distinguish each breed from the others.

As the series of articles in the present edition of the "Dogs of the British Islands" is confined to the description of existing varieties, I do not include among them any of those which, though formerly common enough, are now extinct. Consequently, no notice is taken of the Talbot, or of the old Southern hound.

THE BLOODHOUND.

The majestic head of this dog has frequently attracted the notice of the poetical and pictorial artist, and, without doubt, he is deserving of it; indeed, from this point of view, he probably excels the whole animal creation as far as the greyhound surpasses them in elegance of outline and grace of movement. It is somewhat remarkable that these two attributes, so different in themselves, should be possessed to this full extent by two members of the canine race. The prefix "blood" has been given to this hound in consequence of his being used to track deer and sheep stealers by the scent of the blood dropped on the line; but his fine nose was also employed to follow the body scent, whether of man or animals; and in this way he was employed in former days to pursue runaway slaves, but being rather unmanageable when he reached them, the Cuban mastiff, or a cross between this mastiff and the bloodhound, was generally preferred on account of his greater amenity to the discipline and control of his master. At present the bloodhound is little used in this country, two packs of staghounds comprising the whole extent to which his employment in hunting reaches; Lord Wolverton's is said to be pure, but Mr. Nevill's differs greatly in appearance from the recognised type of the breed. The bloodhound in the hands of our chief exhibitors is now kept for ornament only, or for the purpose of exhibition and prize taking; and it must be estimated accordingly from the artistic point of view alone.

Until within the last twenty years, or thereabouts, the bloodhound has been almost entirely confined to the kennels of the English nobility; but at about that distance of time Mr. Jennings, of Pickering, in Yorkshire, obtained a draft or two from Lord Faversham and Baron Rothschild, and in a few years, by his skill and care, produced his Druid and Welcome, a magnificent couple of hounds, which he afterwards sold, at what was then considered a high price, to Prince Napoleon for breeding purposes. In the course of time, and probably from the fame acquired by these dogs at the various shows, his example was followed by his north-country neighbours, Major Cowen and Mr. J. W. Pease, who monopolised the prizes of the show bench with successive Druids, descended from Mr. Jennings's dog of that name, and aided by Draco, Dingle, Dauntless, &c., all of the same strain. Up to 1869 the only other largely successful dogs in this class were the two Rufuses (Mr. Boom's and Mr. Brough's), whose pedigrees are chiefly composed of Faversham and Rothschild blood, either through Jennings's Druid, or other channels. In 1869, however, another candidate for fame appeared in Mr. Holford's Regent, a magnificent dog, both in shape and colour, but still of the same strains, and until the appearance of Mr. Reynold Ray's Roswell in 1870, no fresh blood was introduced among the first-prize winners at our chief shows. His pedigree is not well ascertained, but no doubt from his stock it is a good one. This dog, who died last year, maintained his position for the same period almost without dispute, and even in his old age it took a good dog to beat him. The head of the bitch is so very inferior in majesty to that of the dog, that as this is the peculiar feature in the breed, it is by the male alone that it is adequately represented.

As above remarked, the bloodhound must now be regarded chiefly as a companionable dog, though he is always included at our shows in the division comprising the "Dogs Used in Field Sports." He is in considerable demand amongst country gentlemen; but, having been much in-bred for many years, there is a great difficulty in rearing puppies in this country, though in France and Germany, probably from the change of climate and soil, bloodhounds have been successfully bred and reared from the stock imported from England. From the keen nose possessed by this hound, he has no doubt been employed as a cross for the black and tan setter, and some mastiff breeders have resorted to him to give majesty to the heads of their favourites; but in both cases I think there has been a loss in point of temperament; for there can be no doubt that the bloodhound is not very amenable to the discipline required in these two breeds. Occasionally an exception is met with, in which a pure bloodhound is controllable under all circumstances; but, as a rule, I have no doubt that he is a very unmanageable dog, and can only be employed usefully by letting him have his own way, to work out his own instinctive promptings and appetite. The Hon. Grantley Berkeley's celebrated dog Druid was beyond even his control when excited, and, with the long experience of dogs and well-known pluck of that gentleman, it must be something out of the common that would make him give way to any animal. Like the bulldog, the bloodhound is amiable enough when not excited; but once get his "hackles up," and he is not easily turned from his object. It is sometimes asserted that this character only belongs to badly-bred animals; but whenever I have had the opportunity of visiting a kennel of highly bred bloodhounds, I have put the matter to the test by asking the master to show a whip to his dog, and, with the exception of Mr. Ray's dogs, which seem remarkably amiable, the result has always satisfied me that he dared not use it—that is to say, if the dog was at liberty. Personally, I have had no experience of the breed except in the case of the bitch, two of which (both very highly bred) I have possessed at different times, and certainly their tempers were not to be depended on, though they would not turn on me, as I have more than once seen a dog hound do on his master. My experience and the evidence afforded by that of others lead me, therefore, to conclude that the temper of the bloodhound is not of such a nature as to make him a pleasant and safe companion; but I am bound to state that several breeders who have considerable practical acquaintance with this dog have recently given an entirely opposite opinion in the columns of the *Field*, and the question must therefore be considered undecided. In his style of hunting he usually carries his head very low, and is slow in his quest, dwelling on the scent when at all doubtful until he has assured himself of its truth. In pace and stamina he cannot compare with the foxhound, who could beat him by one-half at the very least in both respects. His voice is full, deep in tone, and melodious; and this in itself is regarded by many as a claim entitling him to very high consideration.

The points are numerically as follows:

POINTS OF THE BLOODHOUND.

	Value.		Value.		Value.
Head	15	Chest and shoulders...	10	Colour and coat	10
Ears and eyes	10	Back and back ribs ...	10	Stern	5
Flews	5	Legs and feet	20	Symmetry	10
Neck	5				
	35		**40**		**25**

Grand Total 100.

1. The *head* (value 15) is the peculiar feature of this breed; and I have accordingly estimated it at a very high rate. In the male it is large in all its

dimensions but width, in which there is a remarkable deficiency. The upper surface is domed, ending in a blunt point at the occiput; but the brain case is not developed to the same extent, as the jaws, which are very long and wide at the nostrils, hollow and very lean in the cheeks and notably under the eyes. The brows are moderately prominent, and the general expression of the whole head is very grand and majestic. The skin covering the forehead and cheeks is wrinkled in a remarkable manner, wholly unlike any other dog. These points are not nearly so fully developed in the bitch; but still they are to be demanded in the same proportionate degree.

2. *Ears* and *eyes* (value 10).—The ears are long enough to overlap one another considerably when drawn together in front of the nose; the "leather" should be very thin, and should hang very forward and close to the cheeks, never showing the slightest tendency to " prick ;" they should be covered with very short, soft, and silky hair. The *eyes* are generally hazel, rather small, and deeply sunk, showing the third eyelid or "haw," which is frequently but not always of a deep red colour; this redness of the haw is, as a rule, an indication of bloodhound cross wherever it is met with, whether in the mastiff, Gordon setter, or St. Bernard, though occasionally I have met with it in breeds in which no trace of the bloodhound could be detected.

3. The *flews* (value 5) are remarkably long and pendent, sometimes falling fully two inches below the angle of the mouth.

4. The *neck* (value 5) is long, so as to enable this hound to drop his nose to the ground without altering his pace. In front of the throat there is a considerable dewlap.

5. *Chest* and *shoulders* (value 10).—The chest is rather wide than deep, but in any case there should be a good girth; shoulders sloping and muscular.

6. The *back* and *back ribs* (value 10) should be wide and deep, the size of the dog necessitating great power in this department. The hips, or " couples," should be specially attended to, and they should be wide, or almost ragged.

7. *Legs* and *feet* (value 20).—Many bloodhounds are very deficient in these important parts, owing to confinement. The legs must be straight and muscular, and the angles of full size; but it is not to be expected that the upright and powerful pasterns so dear to the M.F.H. should be found in the bloodhound. The feet also are often flat, but they should be, if possible, round and catlike.

8. *Colour* and *coat* (value 10).—In colour the bloodhound is either black and tan, or tan only, as is the case with all black and tan breeds. The absence of black is a great defect, but many well bred litters contain one or two tan puppies without it. The black should extend to the back, the sides, top of the neck, and top of the head. It is seldom a pure black, but more or less mixed with the tan, which should be a deep rich red. There should be little or no white. The *coat* should be short and hard on the body, but silky on the ear and top of the head.

9. The *stern* (value 5) is, like that of all hounds, carried gaily in a gentle curve, but should not be raised beyond it a right angle with the back. The lower side is fringed with hair about two inches long, ending in a point.

10. The *symmetry* (value 10) of the bloodhound as regarded from an artistic point of view should be examined carefully, and valued in proportion to the degree in which it is developed.

The engraving of the celebrated Druid, which illustrated this breed in the "Dogs of the British Islands," gives a good view of his frame and legs; but it is on too small a scale to convey an adequate idea of the remarkable head which the bloodhound possesses. I have therefore confined Mr. Baker's attention to this feature alone, and have selected that of Mr. Ray's St. Hubert as the type of the male, while his Baroness is an excellent example of the female, the contrast between the two being, as usual in this breed, very great. St. Hubert is a son of Roswell, and presents the most wonderful head I have ever seen, but, having deformed legs, from a bad attack of distemper, he has never been exhibited. Mr. Baker's sketch is a wonderfully careful copy of this dog's head; and I thing bloodhound breeders generally will admit that the choice I have made is fully deserved. Baroness is good throughout, and has taken two prizes.

The following are the pedigrees of this fine couple of bloodhounds—that of Roswell is given in the Kennel Club Stud Book as by the Duke of Beaufort's Warrior out of sister to Field's Rufus; but I believe this pedigree is not very reliable, and, therefore, I have not included it in that of either:

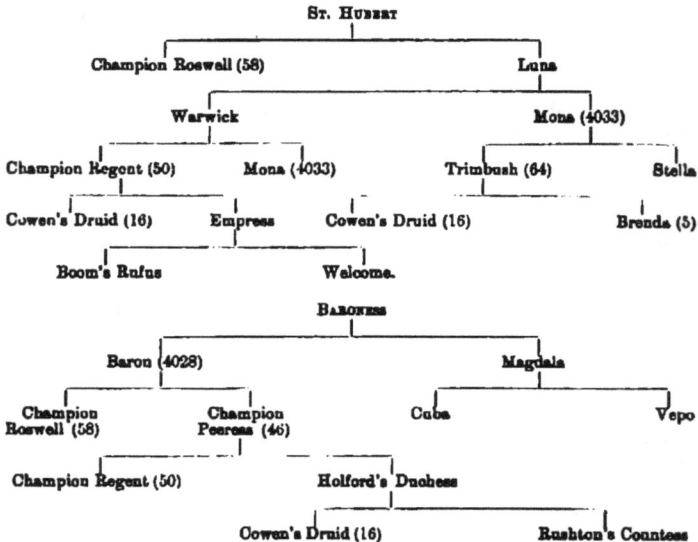

St. Hubert
— Champion Roswell (58) — Luna
— — Warwick — Mona (4033)
— — — Champion Regent (50) — Mona (4033) — Trimbush (64) — Stella
— — — — Cowen's Druid (16) — Empress — Cowen's Druid (16) — Brenda (5)
— — — — — Boom's Rufus — Welcome.

Baroness
— Baron (4028) — Magdala
— — Champion Roswell (58) — Champion Peeress (46) — Cuba — Vepo
— — — Champion Regent (50) — Holford's Duchess
— — — — Cowen's Druid (16) — Rushton's Countess

THE FOXHOUND.

No dog has for so long a time been carefully bred, reared, and trained in large numbers as the English foxhound. Up to the time of the passing of the present Game Laws, the public greyhound was confined to a very few kennels, and in them only were pedigrees preserved with anything like care; but in many foxhound kennels careful records have been kept of the breeding of every litter for, at least, 150 years; and, I believe, there is no instance in which a cross of any kind has been tried—masters being content with improving the breed by selection of the best within its limits, taking care to go out of their several kennels for sires to prevent the close in-breeding which would otherwise inevitably lead to a delicacy of constitution inconsistent with the severe work demanded from the foxhound. When it is remembered that this hound is often kept moving for eleven or twelve hours without food, and after a fast from the previous noon, and that during the greater part of that time he is either forcing his way through thick covert in "drawing," or running at his best pace in pursuit of his game, the amount of stamina required is at once apparent. To be sure of obtaining this constitutional quality, it is necessary to attend carefully to pedigree; for, without it, a handsome and useful hound, as far as appearance goes, might often be preferred on account of his exterior to another of lesser pretensions to beauty, who might yet from his breeding prove to be far the better animal when both had been entered to their game. As in the case of the racehorse, with regard to the Darley Arabian, most of our best hounds now trace back to the Osbaldeston Furrier, Sir R. Sutton's Hercules, or the Belvoir Comus; but since their days masters of foxhounds in every hunting country have vied with each other in breeding, not only a single hound of their form and quality, but a whole pack so "suity," as to vie with them in all important points. Nose combined with speed and stoutness have always been considered as *the* essentials for the foxhound; but of late years, owing to the enormous "fields" which have attended our leading packs, and the forward riding displayed by them, another feature has been demanded, and the supply in the "grass countries" has been obtained in a remarkable manner. I allude to the gift peculiar to our best modern hounds, of getting through a crowd of horses when accidentally "slipped" by the pack. This faculty is developed to a very wonderful extent in all the packs hunting "the shires," varying, of course, slightly in each; and it is no less remarkably absent in certain packs otherwise equal to the Quorn and its neighbours, or even superior to them. The peculiarity is well known to hunting men; but no little annoyance is felt by the members of the several hunts to which I allude when reference is made to individuals; and having great respect for the tender feelings of every master of foxhounds and his followers, I shall not venture to make any attempt to allude more particularly to this matter.

The appearance of the modern foxhound is greatly altered by the universal practice of "rounding" the ears, which has existed during the whole of the present

LORD POLTIMORE'S FOXHOUND " LEXICON."

THE NORTH WARWICKSHIRE FOXHOUND "ROSY."

century, if not longer. That the custom is useful in preventing "canker," either from foul blood or mechanical injury, is clear enough, and I can see no possible objection to it except from Mr. Colam's point of view. "Idstone" dislikes it on the score that the full ear "is a natural protection to the eye in drawing a covert or thorny brake, and that it is given by Nature for that purpose;" but I confess I cannot understand how this can be the case unless the drawing is performed in a retrograde manner, as, even when at rest, the ear does not approach the eye; and in drawing a thorny brake, it must be pushed back some inches behind the organ which, he says, it covers. The sole use of an abnormally large ear, as far as I can see, is to aid the internal organ of hearing, and it is only found in hounds which depend on co-operation for success—that is to say, who hunt in packs. In this kind of hunting, the ear is required to ascertain what is given out by the tongues of the leading hounds, so as to enable "the tail" to come up; but whether or no "rounding" diminishes the sensitiveness of the organ of hearing, I am by no means prepared to say. It is, however, admitted by physiologists that the external ear aids the sense of hearing, and as this large folding ear is confined to hounds hunting in packs, which, as above remarked, depend on hearing for co-operation, it is reasonable to suppose that the hound's large ear is given him to aid in this kind of hunting; and, if so, it is by no means clear that rounding is an unmixed good, but that it has not the disadvantages attributed to it by "Idstone," is as clear to me as noonday.

Another mental peculiarity of the foxhound is his superior "dash" and tendency to cast forward rather than backward, for the bloodhound, otter hound, and old-fashioned heavy harrier still have a tendency to dwell on a scent, and sitting on their haunches mark their enjoyment of it by throwing their tongues heavily and with a prolonged series of notes, during which their game is getting away from them. Such a deed would sentence any foxhound to the halter if seen by his master, and undoubtedly it is by selection, or possibly by crossing with the greyhound, that the change has been effected. However produced, there is no doubt that it exists, and that the foxhound is distinguished by it from all other varieties of his class.

The points of the foxhound are as follows:

POINTS OF THE FOXHOUND.

	Value.		Value.		Value.
Head	15	Back and loin	10	Colour and coat	5
Neck	5	Hind quarters	10	Stern	5
Shoulders	10	Elbows	5	Symmetry	5
Chest and back ribs	10	Legs and feet	20		
	40		**45**		**15**

Grand Total—100.

1. The *head* (value 15) should be of full size, but by no means heavy. Brow pronounced but not high or sharp. There must be good length and breadth,

sufficient to give in the dog hound a girth in front of the ears of fully 16in. The nose should be long (4½in.) and wide with open nostrils. Ears set on low and lying close to the cheeks.

2. The *neck* (value 5) must be long and clean, without the slightest throatiness. It should taper nicely from the shoulders to the head, and the upper outline should be slightly convex.

3. The *shoulders* (value 10) should be long and well clothed with muscle without being heavy, especially at the points. They must be well sloped, and the true arm between the front and the elbow must be long and muscular, but free from fat or lumber.

4. *Chest and back ribs* (value 10).—The chest should girth over 30in. in a 24in. hound, and the back ribs must be very deep.

5. The *back and loin* (value 10) must both be very muscular, running into each other without any contraction or "nipping" between them. The couples must be wide even to raggedness, and there should be the very slightest arch in the loin, so as to be scarcely perceptible.

6. The *hind quarters* (value 10) or propellers are required to be very strong, and as endurance is of even more consequence than speed, straight stifles are preferred to those much bent as in the greyhound.

7. *Elbows* (value 5) set quite straight, and neither turned in nor out are a *sine quâ non*. They must be well let down by means of the long true arm above mentioned.

8. *Legs and feet* (value 20).—Every master of foxhounds insists on legs as straight as a post, and as strong; size of bone at the ankle being specially regarded as all important. The desire for straightness is, I think, carried to excess, as the very straight leg soon knuckles over, and this defect may almost always be seen more or less in old stallion hounds. The bone cannot, in my opinion, be too large, but I prefer a slight angle at the knee to a perfectly straight line. With the exception, however, of Mr. Anstruther Thompson I never yet met with a master of foxhounds who would hear of such an heretical opinion without scorn. The feet in all cases should be round and cat like, with well developed knuckles, and strong horn, which last is of the utmost importance.

9. The *colour and coat* (value 5) are not regarded as very important, so long as the former is a "hound colour," and the latter is short, dense, hard, and glossy. Hound colours are black tan and white—black and white, and the various "pies" compounded of white and the colour of the hare and badger, or yellow, or tan. In some old strains the blue mottle of the southern hound is still preserved, but it is generally voted "slow."

10. The *stern* (value 5) is gently arched, carried gaily over the back, and slightly fringed with hair below. The end should taper to a point.

11. The *symmetry* (value 5) of the foxhound is considerable, and what is called "quality" is highly regarded by all good judges.

Lord Poltimore's Lexicon, and the north Warwickshire Rosy may still serve to illustrate the foxhound as well as any more modern specimen.

MR. EVANS'S HARRIER "CLAMOROUS."

THE HARRIER.

In the present day it is very difficult to meet with a harrier possessed of blood entirely unmixed with that of the foxhound, though many a master will no doubt put in a claim to that distinction. The most beautiful pack I have ever seen is that of Sir Vincent Corbett, which is said to be pure, and no doubt has as good a claim to be so distinguished as any other, and if their breeding had been confined within the limits of their own kennels during the lifetime of their master, I should accept his statement to that effect as proving their purity, but he has had recourse —as all masters must—to other strains for occasional crosses, and in that way the evidence is rendered somewhat doubtful. In any case the modern harrier is very unlike his predecessor of forty or fifty years, and is assimilated in appearance and style of hunting to the foxhound, from which he differs very slightly, even in the most pure specimens, in either particular. Breeders still take special care to have a combination of intelligence and high scenting power sufficient to meet the wiles of the hare, which are much more varied than those of the fox, and hence in most good harriers the head will be found wider and altogether heavier than that of the foxhound, and the nose longer and broader. The ears also are set on rather more backward, and are not usually rounded, but with these exceptions there are no distinguished marks between these two hounds, and even they are often exceedingly small. In the field there is often a marked and peculiar style differing from that of the foxhound, but I have seen it displayed almost equally in packs admitted to be of pure foxhound blood, and believe it to depend more on the huntsman than on the hound. If hounds are not interfered with *as long as they are industrious*, they work very differently from the style they show when constantly capped and lifted. The modern harrier which should sit down on his haunches and "lift up his voice" on a scent would not suit even the most bigoted "thistlewhipper," and yet our ancestors rather liked it than otherwise so long as the sitting was not too prolonged —and that it was only exhibited when first owning the scent—especially that left in a form from which "puss" had just gone. The tongues of these old-fashioned harriers were full and melodious, and I confess until I once more hear the "merry peal" which I can so well remember in my youthful days, I shall not believe in pure harrier blood.

The *points* of the modern harrier with the above slight difference are the same as those of the foxhound, and I need not, therefore, repeat them. In height he varies from 16in. to 20in..

Mr. Evans' Clansman, which illustrated the article on the harrier in the last edition of this book, will serve the purpose now as well as any that I know.

The Rough Welsh harrier still exists in a state of comparative purity, and resembles in appearance the otter hound, which will presently be described, when unmixed with other strains. When so crossed, every intermediate condition occurs, some being only slightly rough, and others approaching the otter hound in that respect as well as all others.

B

THE BEAGLE.

This little hound is probably as old a breed as the northern hound, being, in fact, a miniature specimen of it. It was formerly very much in demand for hunting the hare on foot; but went out of fashion for some years, to be again revived as a form of modern athletics. The intention has always been to obtain a hound of delicate nose, united with so slow a pace as to allow of "the field" keeping up without the aid of horses. With the exception of the head and ears, the modern beagle has all the points of the foxhound. The former is much larger proportionally, both in width and height, while the latter are almost like those of the bloodhound in size and hanging. Foot beagles should not much exceed nine inches in height; but for "Young England" they are now often used up to eleven and even twelve inches, going a pace which requires a good runner, in prime condition, to keep up with them A great many packs of "foot beagles" are now kept throughout the country, some for hunting rabbits, others for hare, and others again for "drag." Usually these little packs are of a "scratch" character, and would not show to advantage by the side of Mr. Crane's beauties, two of which served to illustrate the article in the last edition, and cannot well be improved on, and which I have therefore retained. The following description of the pack is reproduced from the last edition :—

"A diminutive pack of rabbit-beagles, the property of Mr. Crane, of Southover House, near Bere Regis, Dorset, contains the best 'patterns' we have ever known. We have seen them on a cold bad scenting day work up a rabbit and run him in the most extraordinary manner, and although the nature of the ground compelled the pack to run almost in Indian file, and thus to carry a very narrow line of scent, if they threw it up it was but for a moment. Mr. Crane's standard is 9in., and every little hound is absolutely perfect. We saw but one hound at all differing from his companions, a little black-tanned one. This one on the flags we should have drafted, but when we saw him in his work we quite forgave him for being of a conspicuous colour. Giant was perhaps the very best of the pack, a black-white-and-tanned dog hound, always at work and never wrong. He has a capital tongue, and plenty of it. A bitch, Lily, has the most beautiful points we have ever seen, and is nearly all white, as her name implies. Damper, Dutchman, Tyrant, are also all of them beautiful models. We give the measurement of Damper: Height, 9in.; round the chest, 16in.; across the ears, 12in.; extreme length, 2ft. 4in.; eye to nose, 2½in.

"The beagle was in great force in the reign of Queen Elizabeth, and 'singing beagles' were bred as small as possible. A pack of the Virgin Queen's (it is said) could be carried in a man's glove.

"Mr. Crane's standard is kept up with great difficulty. He has reduced the beagle to the minimum. Many of his mothers do not rear their offspring, and distemper carries them off in troops. Single specimens may occasionally be found excessively dwarfed and proportionately deformed. These hounds would

MR. CRANE'S BEAGLES "GIANT" AND "RINGLET."

MR. CARRICK'S OTTER HOUND "STANLEY."

perhaps be wanting in nose or intelligence if they could be produced in sufficient force to form a pack; but Mr. Crane's are all models of symmetry and power, and are as accomplished and as steady as Lord Portsmouth's hounds.

"The Southover beagles are as small as it is possible to breed them (in sufficient numbers to form a pack) without losing symmetry, nose, intelligence, and strength; and we hold those to be the best which possess all the requisites for rabbit hunting in the smallest compass. Our experience warrants us in asserting that it would not be prudent to attempt forming a pack of less height than 9in.

"We sincerely wish every pack of beagles was multiplied by twenty; and we express this wish, not only because we believe hunting on foot a most healthy and inspiring exercise, but because we are bitter foes to the rabbit, which has been the bane for years of the English yeoman. A pack like Mr. Crane's, steady from hare and hunted on heath and common with ability and discretion, could in no way injure fox or hare hounds, and would provide recreation for many an embryo foxhunter. We believe we are correct in stating that ten or more of the most celebrated masters of the day learnt their first lessons with the merry beagles.

"The dwarf beagle should be formed on the model of the foxhound. He should be a 'Pocket Lexicon.' As in the case of the harrier, it is not customary to round his ears. He should be of a hound colour, and smooth-coated. The rough beagle is similar to the smooth in all but coat, which, like the Welsh harrier's, resembles that of the otterhound."

Since the above was written, Mr. J. Grimwood, of Stanton House, near Swindon, and Sir Thomas Davin Lloyd, of Bromwyd, Carmarthenshire, have been the chief prize winners in the beagle classes of our various shows, Mr. Crane having, however, been 1st and 2nd in 1865, with Pilgrim, Crafty, Gossip, and Famous; Mr. D. Everett, and Mr. E. Loftus Bevan, have also shown some very neat little hounds of this breed.

The points of the beagle are similar to those given for the foxhound, except as to head and ears mentioned above, and I must refer to the article on that animal for their numerical value.

THE OTTER HOUND.

This hound, by an oversight, was entirely overlooked in the last edition of the "Dogs of the British Islands," although there are few breeds of a more distinct character and type. Packs of these hounds possess a great advantage in being able to show sport during the summer, and by some it is alleged that otter hunting and angling may be made to dovetail with each other on alternate days of the week; but this is scarcely practicable, inasmuch as the artificial preservation of the otter, in any considerable numbers, is antagonistic to the preservation of the fish on which he wastefully feeds. The angler consequently shows him no mercy, and

on "good rivers" the appearance of an otter is the signal for a foray against
him with gun, trap, and spear.   In Cumberland, Devonshire, and some parts of
Wales there are, however, many large brooks and embryo rivers, where the fish
run too small for good sport with the rod, and yet afford the otter sufficient food.
Here hunting him is prosecuted with great zest, and no one can possibly object to
such an amount of preservation as will not supply the adjacent districts with more
than a casual visitor, whose appearance is soon signalled to the master of the
nearest pack, and a short shrift is given him when once his "spraint" is discovered
there.   It is alleged by many good sportsmen that the otter does little or no damage
to a fishery, but the above is the general impression among the angling fraternity.

The otter hound is no doubt a lineal descendant of the southern hound,
with his coat roughened by a long process of selection and careful breeding.   He
evidently has not been crossed with any breed other than hound, or he would have
lost some one or more of the characteristics peculiar to the hunting dog, either in
shape of body, length of ear, style of hunting, or tongue.   In all these qualities
he is a southern hound to the letter, with the addition of a rough coat, the history
of which is not known.   In many cases a pure foxhound has been used with
success against the otter, and, as far as the mere hunting goes, he fulfils the task
set him admirably ; but it has usually been found that in a very short time the wet
tells on him, and he either becomes rheumatic or is attacked by disease of the chest
in some shape.   It is not the long hair of the true otter hound which saves him
from these penalties, but the thick woolly under-coat, with which he is furnished for
the same purpose as in the colley and Dandy Dinmont terrier.   He also strongly
resembles the southern hound in his style of hunting, which is low and slow, but
very sure, his nose being of the tenderest kind, and often owning an air bubble
or "vent" at the distance of some yards.   Like him, he is apt to sit down on
his haunches and throw his tongue with delight at first touching on a scent, as
is shown in the engraving, in a most characteristic manner.   Subscription packs of
otter hounds are kept at Garlisle under the mastership of Mr. Carrick ; in North-
umberland, near Morpeth, under Mr. A. Fenwick ; and at Cockermouth hunted
by a committee.   In South Wales, Col. Pryse and Mr. Moore have each a pack ;
while in England the Hon. Geoffrey Hill hunts the otter from his kennels at
Hawkeston, Salop, and Mr. Collier's from Culmstock, near Wellington.   In the
west, Mr. Cheriton and Mr. Mildmay also pursue the sport.

The points of the otter hound are like those of the bloodhound, except
as to the coat, which should be composed of hard and long hair, somewhat
rough in its lying, and mixed with a short, woolly under-coat, which serves
to keep the body warm even when wetted by long immersion.   The colour
differs also, in not being confined to black-and-tan or tan—the former, however,
being often met with, as in the case of Mr. Carrick's Stanley, whose portrait
accompanies this article.   This dog is of a grizzled black-and-tan colour, and of a
very fine shape both in head and body.   He is by Mr. Carrick's Ringwood out
of Harrison's Glory, and took several first prizes at Glasgow, Birmingham, and
Nottingham in 1872-3.

MR. MURCHISON'S FOX TERRIER "OLIVE" AND MR. BURDON'S FOX TERRIER "BITTERN."

CHAPTER III.

THE FOX TERRIER (SMOOTH AND ROUGH) AND THE DACHSHUND.

THE SMOOTH FOX TERRIER.

ROM the very commencement of foxhunting in this country, small terriers were kept at each of the various kennels, for the purpose of bolting the fox from his earth when run to ground by the hounds. Originally these dogs were for the most part black and tan in colour; but from this cause they were so frequently mistaken for a fox when drawing a covert, that they were bred white or pied.

The dogs used for bolting foxes by some of the most famous masters of hounds and their families for generations were similar to the old English terrier, and were many of them white, slightly wire-haired, and with no more of the bulldog in them than in the Italian greyhound, that cross making them so savage as to kill rather than bolt the fox; they had plenty of pluck; their noses were sharp, and they were small enough to go to ground wherever a fox or badger could go—indeed, they would "lay on" either, if they could not bolt them, till they were dug out. A terrier was a thoroughbred animal *per se*, but it could only be called a *fox* terrier when fit to be used for the bolting of a fox.

About forty years ago, Sir Watkin Wynn and Mr. Foljambe were famous for their breeds of fox terriers. These strains closely resembled each other, and were short-headed, full in the eye, with fair stop, and what would be called well chiselled out under the eye. They were remarkably strong—indeed, rather inclined to be cobby and bull-necked, with very short straight legs. They were particularly wide sprung in their ribs and broad in the brisket, short-backed, light in the hind quarters, and generally with the stern carried too high. Their colour was invariably white, with red ears or patch, and often a spot in the centre between the ears. The coat was very thick, and somewhat coarse. Mr. Ffrance, of Cheshire, had another breed, which were very different, being rather leggy, with fine light oval bone; and they had a sharp foxy face, showing more of the Italian greyhound style, with small eye and fine coat.

After a time the Badsworth blood was crossed with the Wynnstay, the result being a coarser dog altogether, with black ears or spot on the head. In those days a black and tan headed fox terrier was never seen. The late Duke of Rutland is said to have used some of his black and tan terriers to cross with the Belvoir terriers, and so produced the coloured head so much coveted in the present day; but the deep red is the original Foljambe and Wynnstay colour. Jack Morgan's dogs had all red ears, till Grove Nettle appeared. The celebrated Old Jock was by a black and tan dog, and he and Old Trap brought out the coloured heads, being very much used to every kind of fox terrier bitch.

During the last ten years the fox terrier has risen into great celebrity; but among the multitude of his admirers and patrons there is a strange difference about his necessary qualifications, as evidenced by the various distinct types which meet with favour at dog shows. It is important, therefore, to recall attention to the purposes for which the dog is intended, and consider how far they can be carried out by the possession or otherwise of certain points in his make; and in discussing the subject I shall confine myself to this feature, and exclude his *fighting* and *killing* merits, which among many people seem to be the chief objects of their desire in breeding this dog, though they are a positive disqualification for his intended use in bolting the fox. When brought up and employed solely for fighting and cat slaughter he ceases to be a fox terrier.

With regard to size, I cannot describe what it should be better than in the language of a letter which has recently appeared from that old and thoroughly experienced master of foxhounds, the Hon. Grantley Berkeley, who says: "What is wanted with foxhounds is a terrier so small as to be well able to go to ground, with pluck enough to keep to or bark at a fox, to bolt the fox, or prevent his earthing further." For real work—that is, going to ground to fox or badger—no terrier should be higher than 13in. to 14in. at the shoulder, or heavier than 16lb. With the Trelawny hunt small terriers of 10lb. and 12lb. are used, and in the S.D.H. country the late master had them of 12lb. and 14lb. Mr. A. F. Ross, the present master of the latter hunt, is using a brace by Mr. Murchison's old dog Lancer which are about 14lb. each, with plenty of bone and quality, and he is very fond of them, as they work wonderfully well. The chest, also, should not be too wide, as it is impossible for such dogs to go to ground in most rabbit earths, or up drains frequented by foxes, so as to reach the end. The Wynnstay and Grove terriers of forty years ago did not exceed 15lb. to 16lb. at the outside, though the Yorkshire dogs were larger; but the former were very plucky, and in those days cherry noses and red eyes were not uncommon.

The question of length of leg depends much upon the configuration of the dog, and it is difficult to lay down any defined "hard and fast" line as to their form *per se*. For instance, a dog with a deep brisket, sloping shoulders, and elbows well let down, can race away with short forelegs; for the pace comes from the loins and hind legs as the propelling power. Again, a long-backed dog, always remembering he is well-loined, so as to give breadth enough, does not require such length of leg as a short-backed dog. The famous bitch Grove Nettle was very long in her back. A dog to race must have freedom of action, and this he gets from length; but the fox terrier must also have good back ribs, as well as muscular development in shoulders and loins, to do his work well underground. The legs should be good round-boned ones, and strong at the pasterns (the part immediately above the toes), to enable them to travel easily over wet or rough ground.

It is not absolutely necessary that the fox terrier should be a fast galloper, and, indeed, it can scarcely be expected that he can keep up with foxhounds, particularly in a long run; and if he could, it would scarcely be fair to send him half exhausted to hard work underground. In some countries they do run with the pack, but in most cases they are either carried on horseback, or are taken in panniers, a boy riding on a pony with them; while sometimes a man is sent out with them, to follow on foot, otherwise, in many instances, their presence when required could not be depended on. A long-legged terrier cannot travel over all descriptions of ground like a short-legged one, nor can he last out a long day so well. The smooth-coated dog is generally preferred to the wire-coated fox terrier; but he should be stout in constitution, so as to withstand wet, cold, or fatigue; and he must have courage enough to face punishment, without showing unnecessary irritation.

The greatest care should be taken in first entering terriers, as with hounds. If a deerhound is not properly entered, he will seize the haunch of a stag, and there hold him. A well-known keen sportsman tells me that he used to wound most severely a deer, get up to him, and sit on the body if he could, and then enter the hound at the neck only. The dog would always afterwards seize that part. So with fox terriers, if entered on large rats, or on a very savage dog fox, or on a vixen with cubs, they never do well. The teaching should be gradual till the dog has confidence in his own abilities.

With the exception of some foxhounds and greyhounds, there is not a dog in England with an authentic pedigree that will go back to the year 1800; but with regard to fox terriers their pedigrees are specially obscure, and it is singular that most of those which became noted at the commencement of the popularity of the breed had no known reliable pedigrees, though they had specific parentage given to them. The establishment of the "Kennel Club Stud Book" will to some extent remedy this in the future, but it will require much caution in compilation.

The following are the points of the fox terrier, chiefly as settled by the club specially formed for his improvement. I have not altered the numerical value, but in the description of one or two points I have changed the wording without greatly interfering with the sense.

POINTS OF THE FOX TERRIER.

	Value.		Value.		Value.
Head and ears	15	Hind quarters	5	Coat	5
Neck	5	Stern	5	Colour	5
Shoulders and chest	15	Legs	10	Size and symmetry	15
Back and loin	15	Feet	10		
	50		**30**		**25**

Grand Total, **100.**

1. *Head* and *ears* (value 15):

a. The *skull* should be flat and moderately narrow; broader between the ears and gradually decreasing in width to the eyes. Not much "stop" should be apparent; but there should be more dip in the profile, between the forehead and top jaw, than is seen in the case of a greyhound.

b. The *ears* should be V-shaped, and rather small; of moderate thickness, and dropping forward closely to the cheek, not hanging by the side of the head, like a foxhound's.

c. The *jaw* should be strong and muscular, but not too full in the cheek; should be of fair punishing length, but not so as in any way to resemble the grey-hound or modern English terrier. There should not be much falling away below the eyes; this part of the head should, however, be moderately chiselled out, so as not to go down in a straight slope like a wedge.

d. The *nose*, towards which the muzzle must slightly taper, should be black.

e. The *eyes* should be dark rimmed, small, and rather deep set; full of fire and life.

f. The *teeth* should be level and strong.

2. The *neck* (value 5) should be clean and muscular, without throatiness, of fair length, and gradually widening to the shoulders.

3. *Shoulders* and *chest* (value 15).—The shoulders should be fine at the points, long, and sloping. The chest deep and not too broad.

4. *Back* and *loin* (value 10).—The back should be straight and strong, with no appearance of slackness behind the shoulders; the loin broad and powerful (and particularly so if the back is long), and very slightly arched. The dog should be well ribbed up with deep back ribs, and should not be flat-sided.

5. The *hind quarters* (value 5) should be strong and muscular, quite free from droop or crouch; the *thighs* long and powerful; *hocks* near the ground, the dog standing well up on them, like a foxhound, without much bend in the stifles.

6. The *stern* (value 5) should be set on rather high, and carried gaily; but not over the back, or curled. It should be of good strength, anything approaching a pipe-stopper tail being especially objectionable.

7. The *legs* (value 10), viewed in any direction, must be straight, showing little or no diminution in the size of the ankles when viewed in front. They should be of strong bone throughout, the elbows working freely just clear of the sides. Both fore and hind legs should be carried straight forward in travelling, the stifles not turning outwards.

8. The *feet* (value 10) should be round, compact, and not too large, the toes moderately arched, and turned neither in nor out. There should be no dew claws behind.

9. The *coat* (value 5) should be smooth, but hard, dense and abundant.

10. In *colour* (value 5) white should predominate. Brindle or liver markings are objectionable. Otherwise this point is of little or no importance.

11. *Symmetry, size,* and *character* (value 15).—The dog must present a generally gay, lively, and active appearance. Bone and strength in a small compass are essentials; but this must not be taken to mean that a fox terrier should be cloggy or in any way coarse. Speed to some extent, and endurance, must be looked to as well as power, and the symmetry of the foxhound taken as a model. The terrier, like the hound, must on no account be leggy; neither must he be too short on the leg. He should stand like a cleverly-made hunter—covering a lot of ground,

yet with a broad and powerful loin, as before stated. He will thus attain the highest degree of propelling power, together with the greatest length of stride that is compatible with the length of the body. *Weight*, within certain limits, is not a certain criterion of a terrier's fitness for his work. General shape, size, and contour are the main points; and if a dog can gallop and stay, and follow his fox up a drain, it matters little what his weight is to a pound or so, though, roughly speaking, it may be said he should not scale over 20lb. in show condition. *In my opinion the weight should be little, if any, over 16lb.*

Disqualifying Points.

1. *Nose*, white, cherry, or spotted to a considerable extent with either of these colours.

2. *Ears*, prick, tulip, or rose.

3. *Mouth*, much undershot.

There is no breed of dog that has risen so high and so quickly in popular favour and estimation as the fox terrier has done since 1866, but a large proportion of those bred at the present day are useless for the practical purpose of bolting a fox or badger, from their size alone.

There was not even a class for this breed at the first two or three Birmingham shows; but in 1862 Mr. Wootton entered there the first *fox* terriers—as such—in a class for "white and other smooth-haired English terriers (except black and tan)," when Jock won. In 1863 a distinct class for fox terriers was given at Birmingham, when Mr. Wootton entered a considerable number, and again won with Jock. In 1864 there were more than forty exhibited at Nottingham; and, if I mistake not, it was here that the celebrated Tartar made his *debut.* At the Dublin Show, in the same year, there was a fair fox terrier class, and Mr. Stevenson's Patch took the first prize back to Chester—a feat she repeated at Birmingham soon after.

In 1867 and 1868 there were respectively 62 fox terriers exhibited at Birmingham, being on each occasion about one-twelfth and one-thirteenth of the total number of dogs at the show. In 1869 there were 69 at Islington, or one-fifteenth of all the dogs exhibited; while at Birmingham that year the number increased to 115, or nearly one-seventh the whole exhibition.

At the Crystal Palace in 1870 the number was 104, or nearly one-ninth of the total number of dogs; and in the same year at Birmingham it was 116, or one-eight the whole show.

In 1876 the number at the Crystal Palace was 141, or one-eighth of all the show; at Brighton 166, or one-fifth; and at Birmingham 120, or one-ninth.

Two shows have lately been held specially for fox terriers (smooth and wire-haired), at Nottingham and Lillie Bridge. At the former (of the smooth alone) the number exhibited was 157, and at the latter 190. I believe the largest number at any one show was at Nottingham, about five years ago, when it was above 270, or about one-third of all the show.

T

As regards Scotland, at the Glasgow Show in 1871 there were only 11 fox terriers; at Edinburgh the other day there were 41.

In the past, the most famous fox terriers as prize winners have been Jock (known better perhaps as Old Jock), Trap (or Old Trap), Trimmer, Vandal, and Grove Nettle—names which have become household words among the fanciers of this breed.

Jock won 33 first prizes (8 of which were champion) and 4 second prizes (one of which was champion), beginning at Birmingham in 1862, and ending at the Crystal Palace in 1870. He was long considered the beau idéal of a terrier, and by many people is still referred to as a model. From Mr. Wootton he passed into the hands of Captain Kindersley, and thence into those of Mr. Cropper, who sold him to Mr. Murchison, in whose possession he died of old age in November, 1872.

Old Trap was not exhibited often, but he won a few prizes, and I believe he was about the best fox-terrier dog as to size and make that has yet been seen. According to my view, he was a better dog than Jock, and any of his blood is much sought after. He also became the property of Mr. Murchison, in whose hands he died a few years ago, having lived his full time.

Trimmer had a splendid career of prize winning from 1868 to 1871, having in that time won no less than forty first prizes, nearly the whole of them consecutively. On two occasions he won the champion prize at the Crystal Palace, and also the special prize for the best fox terrier in the show. Had he possessed a little more bone and substance, this dog would have been as near perfection as could be. In 1874 Mr. Murchison sold Trimmer to Sir E. Kerrison, some time after which the dog was killed through an accident.

Vandal was another of Mr. Murchison's dogs, and a grand one in appearance, shape, size, and pluck. He won twenty-four first prizes, and he also was killed by an unfortunate accident on his way home from his last victory, in December, 1874, being then only in his prime, and a great loss to his owner.

Grove Nettle, though not much shown, was a prize winner; but irrespective of this, she was considered by far the best bitch of her day. When about 7½ years old, the late Mr. Bishop, of Nottingham, sold her at a high price to Mr. Murchison, and she subsequently died of milk fever.

At the present time the most noted show fox terriers are Mr. Burbidge's Bitters, Nimrod, Royal, Nettle, and Dorcas, Mr. Abbott's Moslem, Mr. Hyde's Buffett, Mr. Murchison's Forceps, Olive, Natty, and Whisky, Mr. Gibson's Boxer and Joe, Mr. Fletcher's Rattler, and Mr. Whittle's Yorick. The most successful breeders of these have been Mr. Luke Turner and Mr. Gibson, the former having bred Nettle, Olive, and Joe, besides the first bitch puppy at the Lillie Bridge show, while the latter has bred Dorcas, Buffett, Natty, and Boxer.

I have selected for the engraving, as the best specimens, Bitters and Olive, the former being, I believe, the nearest of any of the dogs to the requirements of a fox terrier, and the latter more close to perfection as a bitch than any I have ever

لز

Mr. O. Brewis's Wavy-coated Retrievers "Paris" and "Melody."

ROUGH FOX TERRIER—MR. G. F. RICHARDSON'S "BRAMBLE" AND MR. LINDSAY-HOGG'S "TOPPER."

seen. Bitters won his first prize (under the name of Jock) at Epworth in 1872, and has altogether won nine first and nine second prizes. He was first shown by Mr. Denton, of Doncaster, who sold him to Mr. Murchison (who changed his name to Bitters); then he came into the hands of Mr. Gibson, and now belongs to Mr. Burbidge. In 1876 Bitters was first in the champion class at Maidstone, and second champion at Brighton; in 1877 he has already been second champion at Nottingham. He is said to be by Tyrant, but the name of his dam is very doubtful. Olive has been shown only twice, namely, at Brighton and Bristol, winning first each time, and also the special prize at Brighton for the best fox terrier never shown before, beating at the same time Burbidge's Nettle, who was first at the Crystal Palace in 1876, and at Lillie Bridge in 1877. Olive is by Belgrave Joe—Tricksey by Chance; Belgrave Joe by Belvoir Joe—Branstone's Vic, great granddam of Burbidge's Nettle.

THE ROUGH FOX TERRIER.

Until within the last thirty years a rough or broken-haired terrier, differing altogether from the modern Skye, Dandie, and Yorkshire blue-tan, was commonly met with throughout England, where, curiously enough, he was often called "Scotch"—*lucus a non lucendo*—such a dog being almost unknown across the Tweed. He closely resembled the dog now called the rough fox terrier; but had usually rather a longer coat on the body, and of a coarser texture, the beard being considerably more prominent than that approved of in the present day. Somewhat of this kind was the Rev. Thomas Pearce's Venture, whose portrait was given in the *Field* among the "Terriers of no Definite Breed" in 1866; but she more nearly approached the modern rough fox terrier than the old-fashioned wire-haired breed, and indeed was from strains used with foxhounds by Mr. Radclyffe and the Rev. J. Russell in the West of England, some of which were rough and others smooth. In general character she closely resembled Mr. Lindsay Hogg's Topper, selected by me to illustrate the rough fox terrier dog, partly on account of his beautiful shape throughout and remarkable quality, and partly from his close resemblance to my first pet, a wonderfully game "ratter" and badger terrier. Undoubtedly he is not quite deep enough in his back ribs for perfection; nor, indeed, is Bramble, my other selection; but it would be difficult to find any other fault with either of them, and, until I see a specimen of the breed with deep back ribs, united with all their other good points, I am content to take them to represent the type of the rough fox terrier of the day. A white colour, more or less marked with tan or black, was always preferred for vermin terriers; but a great many black and tans, or rather grey and fawn were met with, and also grey throughout, or a very dark grizzled tan, brown, or badger-grey, as in Mr. Radclyffe's breed, of Cherwell Grange, Shropshire, which last, however, were possessed of tulip ears, a fault no doubt in the opinion of the "fancy," and therefore condemning them to private life at the shows, where they were exhibited by that gentleman some ten years ago. In my young days the broken-haired terrier was always cropped; and, never having seen one *au naturel*, I am not aware whether the ears were originally tulip, rose, or falling; but I imagine that they would resemble that of the modern dog, many of which are more or less pricked, even in the best bred litters. Partly, or wholly, in consequence of the correspondence which appeared in the *Field* some years ago, a special class for rough fox terriers was introduced into the Glasgow Show of 1872; and this example has been followed since then at most of our large shows, the classes being sometimes called "wire" or "broken-haired," and at others "rough fox." At Birmingham, in 1872, in a broken-haired class, Mr. Sanderson, formerly of Cottingham, now residing at Beverley, took a second prize with his afterwards celebrated dog, Venture, *the first being withheld for want [of merit* in the opinion of the judge, Mr. S. Nisbet, who was here a little out of his element, being specially retained for Skyes and Dandies. Next year, at Manchester and the Crystal Palace, Mr. Sanderson exhibited a grand team, including Venture, Tip, and Turpin, with which he took several prizes, and also the fancy of Mr. Wootton, who purchased the lot, and, after gaining prizes with them at the Crystal Palace and Wolverhampton, sold Venture to Mr. Carrick, jun., for use with the otterhounds at Carlisle, where he is much valued. In the interval, I suppose, Mr. Nisbet has seen his error; for at the Birmingham Show of 1874 he gave Venture the first prize in the wire-haired class, that dog having previously been awarded a similar honour at Nottingham. But time and hard work in the water have told their tale too much for him to show the type in perfection; besides which, he is more leggy than Topper, with even less claim to perfection in his back ribs. At the late Show at Lillie Bridge several good dogs of this breed were shown, Venture being placed first, Mr. Easten's Tip second, and Mr. Lindsay Hogg's Topper third, the three being so close together that the choice must always be, in my opinion, a matter of fancy.

The *points* of the rough fox terrier are the same as those of the smooth (described on p. 135), with the exception of the coat, the proper nature of which is correctly given in the points of the Fox Terrier Club, quoted in the *Field*. The club description does not, however, I think, sufficiently insist on the thick and soft under-coat, which, as in the Dandie Dinmont, should always be regarded as of great importance in resisting wet and cold. An open, long coat is even worse than a thick, short one for this purpose, as it admits the wet to the skin, and keeps it there; whereas the short coat speedily dries.

Topper, bred by Sir F. Johnson, is about three years old, white in colour, with very slight lemon markings on the ear and hip; and his blood has been in the Legard family for more than ninety years, he being by Sir F. Johnson's Topper out of Mr. R. Crowle's Vic; she by the Rev. — Legard's Sam—Nettle; Nettle by Tartar—Missy. He has won the following prizes and commendations, never having been elsewhere exhibited, viz.: 1866, h.c. Filey; 2nd Maidstone; v.h.c., Crystal Palace; 2nd, Cork; and 2nd, Brighton. 1877, 3rd, Nottingham; and 3rd, Lillie Bridge.

Bramble, bred by Mr. Wootton, is by Turpin—Vic. Besides a third prize at Lillie Bridge, she took first prize at Cork in 1876, and the same at Dublin in 1877. Since the article appeared in the *Field* she has taken several first prizes.

MR. BARCLAY HANBURY'S DACHSHUNDS "FRITZ" AND "DINA."

THE DACHSHUND, OR GERMAN BADGER-DOG.

This dog is generally considered in Germany to be of a pure and independent breed, for a long time confined to the mountain chain and high forests of Southern and Central Europe, extending through Germany and into France, where he is probably the original of the *basset à jambes torses*. The old English turnspit somewhat resembled him, but differed in his ears, which were more terrier-like, and also in his nose, which had even less of the hound character than that of the dachshund.

During the last ten or fifteen years this breed has been largely inported into England, where it has also been bred by the Earl of Onslow, Mr. Schweizer, and Mr. Fisher (the most successful exhibitor), and to a small extent in the Royal as well as several private kennels. Several hundred specimens have been imported and sold by Mr. Schuller, and the breed has been well tried in England as badger dogs, as well as for hare hunting. Opinions differ as to their merits in these capacities, some declaring, with Mr. Barclay Hanbury, that they are inferior to our own beagles and terriers; while others, including Mr. Schweizer—whose German proclivities may, however, render him partial—maintain that a good one will face any badger with as much pluck as our gamest terrier. The balance of evidence in my possession is, however, strongly against this last opinion, and I think it may be alleged that any of our terriers will beat him in going to ground to fox or badger. As to nose, I am induced to believe that it is, on the average, better than that of our modern beagles, who certainly do not equal in that respect the old miniature southern hounds, which in my young days used to be commonly met with throughout England.

Dr. L. J. Fitzinger, in his book on dogs, mentions twelve varieties of the dachshund, but it is generally believed that all but one of these are cross-bred. The one pure strain is that described by him as *der krummbeinige*, or crooked-legged, which is known in this country as *the* dachshund *par excellence*, and will be alluded to here only. This dog, in proportion to his height and weight, possesses great strength; but his muscular power can be better displayed in digging than in running, wherein his remarkable short and crooked fore legs render his gait ungainly and rolling to a degree amounting to the ridiculous; hence his use in Germany is mainly to mark the badger or fox to his earth, for which also his keen nose is well suited; and, as the entrance to the sleeping chamber of the former is kept as small as is consistent with his size, the dachshund is able to dig away the earth, so as to reach the exact spot, which his tongue at the same time serves to show his master, and thus enable him to dig down to it. In the extensive vineyards of Germany and France, which are often on hillsides, the badger makes numerous earths, and here he is diligently pursued by the peasants, either from love of sport or to get rid of a troublesome intruder. The dachshund is also used for driving deer to the gun; but for this purpose the straight-legged cross, *geradbeinige dachshund*, is most in demand, which variety is generally also larger in size and more hound-like in character. In constitution the dog is hardy, but in temper somewhat wild and headstrong, so that he is often difficult to get under command when once on the scent. He is also snappish in kennel, and inclined to fight on the slightest provocation, or often without it. His tongue is loud and shrill, without the deep bell-note of the old-fashioned hound. The best breeds are met with in the vicinity of the Schwarzwald, Stuttgard, Lonberg, and Eberstein, near Baden Baden. Mr. Fisher's celebrated dogs are from the kennels of Prince Edward of Saxe-Weimar.

The *points* of the dachshund are as follows in numerical value and description. For much valuable information on this breed I am indebted to Dr. Fitzinger's work (kindly translated for me by Mr. Perceval de Castro, of Kensington, who is an enthusiastic lover of the dachshund), Prince Albert Solms, Mr. Barclay Hanbury, Mr. Fisher, Mr. Schuller, and Mr. Schweizer.

POINTS OF THE DACHSHUND.

	Value.		Value.		Value.
Skull	10	Legs	15	Colour	7½
Jaw	10	Feet	7½	Size, symmetry, and	
Ears, eyes, and lips	10	Stern	10	quality	10
Length of body, including neck	15	Coat	5		
	45		**37½**		**17½**

Grand Total 100.

1. The *skull* (value 10) is long and slightly arched, the occiput being wide, and its protuberance well developed; eyebrows raised, but without any marked " stop."

2. The *jaw* (value 10) is long, and tapering gradually from the eyes; but, nevertheless, it should not be " pig-jawed "—the end, though narrow, being cut off nearly square, with the teeth level and very strong.

3. The *ears*, *eyes*, and *lips* (value 10). — The *ears* are long enough to reach nearly to the tip of the nose when brought over the jaw without force. They are broad, rounded at the ends, and soft in " leather " and coat, hanging back in graceful folds; but, when excited, brought forward so as to lie close to the cheeks. *Eyes* rather small, piercing, and deeply set. In the black and tan variety they should be dark-brown, or almost black; but in the red or chocolate deep hazel. Dr. Fitzinger has often observed the two eyes vary in colour, and even in size. The *lips* are short, but with some little flew towards the angles; not at all approaching, however, to that of the bloodhound. The skin is quite tight over the cheeks, and indeed over the whole head, showing no bloodhound wrinkle.

4. *Length of body* (value 15).—In taking this into consideration the neck is included : this part, however, is somewhat short, thick, and rather throaty. The *chest* is long, round, and roomy, but not so as to be unwieldy. It gradually narrows towards the back ribs, which are rather short. The brisket should be only 2½in. to

3in. from the ground, and the breast bone should project considerably. The loin is elegantly arched, and the flanks drawn up so as to make the waist look slim, the dog measuring higher behind than before. The quarters are strong in muscle as well as the shoulders, the latter being especially powerful.

5. *Legs* (value 15).—The *fore legs* should be very short, strong in bone, and well clothed with muscle. The elbows should not turn out or in, the latter being a great defect. The knees should be close together, never being more than 2½in. apart, causing a considerable bend from the elbows inwards, so as to make the leg crooked, and then again turning outwards to the foot, but this bend at the knees should not be carried to the extent of deformity. In order that the brisket should approach the ground as above described, the fore legs must be very short. On the hind leg there is often a dew claw, but this is not essential either way.

6. The *feet* (value 7½) should be of full size, but very strong and cat-like, with hard, horny soles to the pads. The fore feet are generally turned out, thus increasing the appearance of crookedness in the legs. This formation gives assistance to the out-throw of the earth in digging.

7. The *stern* (value 10) is somewhat short and thick at the root, tapering gradually to the point, with a slight curve upwards, and clothed with hair of moderate length on its under-surface. When excited, as in hunting, it is carried in a hound-like attitude over the back. Its shape and carriage indicate high breeding, and are valued accordingly.

8. The *coat* (value 5) is short and smooth, but coarse in texture, and by no means silky, except on the ears, where it should be very soft and shiny.

9. The *colour* (value 7½).—The best colours are red, and black-and-tan, which last should be deep and rich, and this variety should always have a black nose. The red strain may have a flesh-coloured nose, and some good judges in England maintain that this is indispensable, but in Germany it is not considered of any importance. In the black-and-tans, the tan should extend to the lips, cheeks, a spot over each eye, the belly and flank, under-side of tail, and a spot on each side of breast bone; also to the lower part of both fore and hind legs and feet. Thumb marks and pencilling of the toes are not approved of in this country; but they are often met with in Germany. Whole chocolate dogs are often well bred, but they are not liked in England, even with tan markings, which are, however, an improvement. Whole blacks and whites are unknown out of Germany, where they are rare. In England white on toes or breast is objected to, but not in Germany.

10. *Size, symmetry, and quality* (value 10).—In *size* the dachshund should be in an average specimen from 39in. to 42in. long, from tip to tip, and in height 10in. to 11in. at the shoulder; the weight should be from 11lb. to 18lb., the bitches being considerably smaller than the dogs. In *symmetry* the dachshund is above the average, as may be judged from a reference to the excellent examples belonging to Mr. Barclay Hanbury, which I have had drawn by Mr. Baker, who has caught the peculiar characteristics of the breed with marvellous truth. Though not able to show as many first prizes as Mr. Fisher's Feldmann or the Earl of

Onslow's Waldmann, they are quite up to the level of those dogs, and being within easy reach of Mr. Baker, I have selected them accordingly. Their dimensions are as follows :

FRITZ (red tan).—Imported by Mr. Schuller from the royal kennels, Stuttgard (pedigree unknown) : Height, 10½in. ; length from tip to tip, 42½in. ; head, 8in. ; ears, 7in. ; age 1½ years.

DINA (black and tan).—Imported by Mr. Schuller (pedigree unknown) : Height, 10in. ; length, 40½in. ; head, 7½in. ; ears, 6in. ; age, 2½ years.

I append the following interesting and very valuable letter received from Germany, which, in the main, confirms the information previously obtained from the various sources above-mentioned ; although in unimportant details there is, of course, some difference of opinion. I may observe, in reference to Herr Beck-mann's insisting on the propriety of regarding the dachshund as used only underground in Germany, that I have nothing to do with the *intentions* of those who originally bred the dog ; all that is now within my province is to describe him as he exists.

NOTES ON THE GERMAN TYPE OF THE DACHSHUND.

(By HERR LUDWIG BECKMANN, of Dusseldorf.)

SIR,—There has been a great deal of correspondence in the *Field* and other sporting papers regarding the points of the dachshund, and yet the question seems to be still unsettled. This uncertainty is rather striking, if we notice that hundreds of dachshunds have already been imported into England, and among them certainly many well-bred, if not even high-bred, dogs, which might serve as a model for the real dachshund type every moment. The writer of these lines has bred and worked dachshunds all his life, and, as he has given the subject peculiar attention, he begs to state his opinion as to what may be the cause of this uncertainty, and in what respect some English fanciers might perhaps be in error regarding points, size, colours, or employment of this ancient German breed.

1. *The Houndlike Type.*—The dachshund has had the misfortune, on his intro-duction into England, to be confounded by some authors with the French basset. This mistake was favoured by the fact that even our modern German and French kynologists* make no difference between the two races. M. A. Pierre Pichot, editor of the *Revue Britannique*, was the first who cautioned the English dachshund fanciers

* *Vide* Prof. Fitzinger, " Der Hund und seine Racen," p. 179 ; and De la Blanchère in his excellent book, " Les Chiens de Chasse." De la B. says verbally (p. 110 : " Les bassets sont extrèmement nombreux en Allemagne, et quelques races ont les oreilles tellement énormes, qu'elles traînent jusqu'à terre." I beg to state here that dachshunds of that kind have never existed. The French basset was identical with the German dachshund in days of yore, and was most probably imported from Germany into Flanders, and from there to France (compare Jacques du Fouilloux, " Vénerie," Paris, 1573, p. 89, et Verrier de la Conterie, " Ecole de Chasse," Rouen, tom. ii., p. 172). But, as the dachshund has been employed in France chiefly to hunt above ground, and is crossed with most races of the French hound (chien courant), he has lost his original frame and character, and has become completely a *hound* in course of time.—HERR L. BECKMANN.

against confounding the dachshund with the basset, "the dachshund being quite a different breed."* Nevertheless, the desire for "long ears, houndlike head, and much throatiness" was going on, though one of our first and most successful breeders protested in the *Field* † against these erroneous points in several accounts. Some fanciers of the dachshund breed went even a step further, and regarded the bloodhound, with its peaked skull and "drapery-like" ears, as the *beau idéal* of our little dachshunds! (I beg to state here that the Germans have never had a native breed of dogs with head and ears like the present English bloodhound, and least of all a breed of dachshunds.)

In recent times those points are somewhat modified, but the desire for "hound-like type" seems to prevail still. In the *Field* of January 13, 1877, I find published a short scheme of points on dachshunds, from which I beg to quote the following points: "Head thoroughly houndlike, occiput very decided, ears of good length and full of fold, lips 'lippy,' nose large with open nostrils, much throatiness, and chest round without much breadth (like the bloodhound)." I suggest that the author of this scheme has not at all the intention to create a new breed, but that he really is desirous to find out the true type of the German dachshund. If so, I am very sorry to say that those points will certainly turn out to be untenable, and to be quite opposite to the opinions of most of our sportsmen and breeders. Dogs of that kind are no longer "dachshunds," but "dachsbracken" ‡ (in English perhaps dachs-talbots).

It is much to be regretted that the advocates of the hound-like type in dachshunds, who have evidently so much sympathy for these little courageous dogs, are endeavouring still to support an imaginary *beau idéal* of the breed, which neither is derived from the antecedents of the breed, nor accords in any respect with the points of our present high-bred dachshunds and their chief employment— "underground work."

The German dachshund is perhaps one of the most ancient forms of the domesticated dog. The fact is that he has for centuries represented an isolated class between the hound and the terrier, without being more nearly connected with the one than the other. His obstinate, independent character, and his incapacity to be trained or broken to anything beyond his inborn, game-like disposition, are quite unrivalled among all other races of the dog. Regarding his frame, he differs from the hound, not only by his crooked fore legs and small size, but by the most refined modification of all parts of his body according to his chief task—to work underground. It is not possible to imagine a more favourable frame for an "earth dog" than the real dachshund type, which I shall describe afterwards. I beg to say that some of our high-bred dachshunds are near perfection, according to German points; they do not want much improvement, but propagation, for they are seldom met with even in northern Germany. If I had to choose a likeness or model

---

* In the *Live Stock Journal*, 1875, vol. ii., No. 87.
† May 27, 1876, and following numbers, signed "S."
‡ Bracke or Braken is the old German hound (from Bracco); the German word *Hund* is equivalent to dog in English.

U

for these active little dogs, it would certainly not be the bloodhound, but the weasel!

The desire for " hound-like type " in dachshunds would never have originated if the natural vocation of this breed (underground work) had not been overlooked. The consequence of this erroneous idea will be that well-bred dachshunds will be regarded as a " terrier cross," and that it will be next to impossible for many dog fanciers to get a clear idea of the real type of the dachshund.

Having concentrated all varieties of the badger dog to one single class—the crook-legged, short-haired dog, with head neither hound nor terrier like, weight from 8lb. to 20lb., colour black-tan and its variations—we shall still meet here many varying forms. With some attention we shall soon distinguish the *common* breed (*Landschlag*) and the *well* or *high-bred* dachshund. The first is a stout, strong-boned, muscularly built dog, with large head and strong teeth; the back not much arched, sometimes even straight; tail long and heavy; forelegs strong and regularly formed; the head and tail often appear to be too large in the dog; the hair is rather coarse, thick set, short, and wiry, lengthened at the underside of the tail, without forming a brush or feather, and covering a good deal of the belly. These dogs are good workmen, and are less affected by weather than high-bred ones; but they are very apt to exceed 18lb. and even 20lb. weight, and soon get fat if not worked frequently. From this common breed originates the well and high-bred dog, which may at any time be produced again from it by careful selection and inbreeding without any cross. The *well* and *high-bred* dog is smaller in size, finer in bone, more elegantly built, and seldom exceeds 16lb. to 17lb. weight; the thin, slight tapering tail is only of medium length; the hair is very short, glossy like silk, but not soft; the under part of the body is very thin-haired, rendering these nervous and high-spirited dogs rather sensitive to wet ground and rain. These two breeds are seldom met with in their purity, the vast majority of dachshunds in Germany ranging between the two, and differing in shape very much, as they are more or less well bred or neglected. In this third large group we still meet with many good and useful dogs, but also all those aberrant forms, with pig snouts and short under jaws, apple-headed skulls, deep set or staring eyes, short necks, wheel backs, ring tails, fore legs joining at the knees, and long hind legs bent too much in the stifles and hocks.

The following points of the dachshund are fixed by the author, in strict conjunction with one of our best connoisseurs, Mr. Gustav Lang, of Stuttgart, and in agreement with some of our first breeders, with the judges on dachshunds at the dog shows in Hamburg and Cologne in 1876, and with the editor of the periodical *Der Hund*. As these points are taken from the best existing specimens of the breed, and with regard to the employment, anatomy, and history of this dog, they may give a true picture of the real dachshund type as far as this is possible at present.

Points.

Head, elongated, large, and combined with the neck in a rather obtuse angle. When viewed from the side, the protuberance of the occiput is not much developed;

skull not high vaulted; forehead descending to the eyes without any marked stop, but eyebrows raised; space between eye and ear comparatively much wider than in the hound and pointer, owing to the ears being placed high and far back; nose straight or very slightly arched between top and root, nostrils not too large; jaw neither pig-snouted nor square, but moderately pointed by a sloping line from tip of nose to the chin, and widening gradually from there towards the throat; lips short, not overlapping the lower jaw, but with a little flew at the angles. The superior maxillary bone and the jaw muscle protrude so much as to give the face a hollow-cheeked appearance. When viewed from above and in front, the skull is broad between the ears, and only slightly vaulted (neither narrow and conical nor perfectly flat; the jaw or muzzle tapering gradually from the eyes; skin rather tight over the whole head, showing no wrinkles when the dog is not excited. The shape of bone and muscles must be marked sharply and distinctly in the head, and this lean and plastical appearance (*trockner Kopf*) must remain in the head, even when the body of the dog is laden with fat.

Eyes, ears, and *teeth.*—In good heads, with long jaw, the centre of the space between tip of nose and occiput will be found to be in the hind angle of the eyes. The *eye* should be of medium size, open, bright, intelligent, and fiery (small deep-set eyes, showing the "haw," are even as objectionable in dachshunds as protruding eyes); iris rich brown in black-tan dogs, never brighter than the tan except in the bluish varieties (wall eyes). The *ear* is a very important point in dachshunds, and its situation, shape, and carriage are quite peculiar to the breed; but it should by no means be noticeable in the head from its largeness, ornamental folding, and low situation. The ear of the dachshund is set on so high that its base is nearly even with the outline of the skull and neck; and it is situated so far backwards and distant from the eyes (*vide* head), that it covers a good deal more of the neck than of the cheeks; it should be broad at the base, of equal width, and the lower edge bluntly rounded, not filbert-shaped or pointed; it should hang down quite close and smooth to the cheek, without the slightest inclination to any twisting, folding, or curl. The ears are of sufficient length if they are half as long as the head; they should not over-reach the outline of throat, and should cover about half-an-inch of the angle of the mouth when stretched gently towards the nose. There is no blemish in their being somewhat longer, but, as long as ears are neither useful nor characteristic of the breed, they should never be brought to an excess. The leather of the ears should be very thin, but the hair of the upper surface very short, smooth, and silky. In fighting and attacking, an ear of this description is drawn back and upwards suddenly, and knitted together so much that it is scarcely to be seen in front of the dog. When the dachshund pricks his ears they are not lifted above their usual level, but only bent forwards, until they stand out rectangularly from both sides of the face in their whole usual breadth, without any folding, the fore edge of the ear lying close to the cheek. The *teeth* of the dachshund should be level, strong, and well shot, with sharp fangs. A peculiar arrangement of the teeth is to be found in more than one-third of our dachshunds. The two first or corner teeth of the incisors in the upper jaw are developed to a remarkable size and strength, so as to form, with the corresponding tusk or fang, a deep and narrow notch, in which the fang of the under-jaw glides. These "double fangs" (*saa-gengebiss*) are not to be found in any other breed of German dogs besides dachshunds. But as this criterion of the breed seems every year to disappear more, and as there are at present so many good dachshunds without this peculiarity, it cannot be regarded as a "point," except perhaps in such a case where the judge had to decide between two dogs of equal merits.

The *neck* should be long, strong, clean, and flexible. When viewed from the side, it should be finer where it joins the head, and gradually widening to the full proportions of the chest. The upper outline of neck should not be much arched, the lower outline sloping from the throat down to the protuberance of the breastbone. Throatiness is very objectionable in dachshunds, only the common dog having sometimes a tendency to "looseness" of skin in the throat. When viewed from above, the neck is wide, strong, and not too much tapering towards the broad skull.

The *trunk* (including shoulders and haunches) of the dachshund is not at all hound-like; in many respects it is more like that of the pointer, in others like that of the greyhound. When viewed from the side, it is long; the chest very deep and roomy, with breast-bone projecting; back ribs rather short, and the flanks well drawn up; shoulders rather low, with slight drop in back behind, and corresponding elegant arch of the long and deep loins; quarters not very sloping, and stern set on rather high, these dogs being somewhat higher in the hind quarters than in shoulders. When viewed from the front, the chest is very wide between the joints of the shoulder, but, being neither barrel-like nor square, it slopes gradually between the forelegs, and is rather narrow beneath at the fore-end of the brisket, but widening again towards the belly. When viewed from above, the largest diameter of the dog is to be found in the middle of the shoulders behind the joint, owing to the powerfully developed muscles of the upper arm and blade; from there the trunk narrows gradually towards the stern. The ribs spring up well behind the shoulders, and the muscular haunches project suddenly at the quarters, but not to such an extent of width as in the shoulders, even not fully in bitches. Dachshunds with narrow chest and wide hind-quarters are unfit for hunting underground: they are soon tired, and are very apt to get squeezed in narrow passages.

Forelegs very short, strong in bone; forearm well clothed with muscles; knee broad and clean; pasterns strong, broad, and not too short; feet broad, rounded, with thick large toes, hard soles, and strong, long nails. Owing to the original employment of the dachshund, his forefeet are much larger and stronger than the hind ones. When viewed from the side, the foreleg should appear pretty straight, the knees not protruding much, the slope of the pasterns not exceeding a slight deviation from the straight line, the toes not twisted or turned out too much. When viewed from above, the elbows should not be turned out (out of shoulders) nor in when the dog is standing quietly; in walking they will always be turned out more than in other dogs. When viewed from the front, the forelegs should have

by no means a crippled appearance, as if the dog had rickets, or as if the legs were
not able to resist the pressure of the weight of the body, and had broken down so
much as to join at the knees. Forelegs of that kind will do pretty well for
bassets and dachsbraken, to prevent their running too fast in hunting above ground,
but not for our badger dog. His forelegs must appear as firm supports of the body,
and as powerful shovels in digging away the ground, but without too much
arresting the movableness of the dog in other respects; therefore the forearm
should be bent inwards in a slight regular curve, the inside of the knees not
projecting too much, and the inner outline of the pasterns (from knee to sole of foot)
nearly straight. The pasterns should by no means slope too much sideways
("splayed feet"); if so, they will not be able to support the forearm sufficiently,
and will give way every year more. All that is wanted is that the foot should be
turned somewhat outwards; and this turning should begin already in the joint of
the knee. Therefore, the inner edge of the knee will project very slightly in front,
while its outer edge is turned more backwards. In some dogs the pastern and feet
are standing perfectly straight, only the *toes* being twisted outside, which is very
bad. The shape of the forelegs in dachshunds has often been mistaken, even by
German breeders. They should have a simple, pleasing sweep, like that of the
leg of an elegant but solid piece of rococo furniture. The bending of the forearm
should harmonise with the shape of the chest, and the pasterns and feet be not
more splayed and turned out than is required to restore the *equilibre*. When the
dog is lying on his back the whole foreleg from elbow to tip of toes should lie
quite close to his body, like the flippers of a seal. Owing to the movableness
of the forequarters in dachshunds, it is next to impossible to take exact measures
from the positions and width of the legs. In regularly built dogs with wide chest,
I always found the distance between the knees to be equal to one-third of the
diameter (measured across and outside) of the shoulders. The distance between
the feet (from heel to heel) should never exceed the width between the knees more
than about half or three-quarters of an inch. The toes should not fully reach
sideways to a line which is drawn perpendicularly from the most prominent point
of the shoulder to the ground.

Hind legs comparatively higher and less powerfully developed than the fore ones;
the haunches muscular; the under thigh remarkably short; the leg (or that part
from hock to heel) high; the feet small, but, like the fore ones, round, with thick,
well-closed toes and strong nails. When viewed from the side, the hind leg
appears rather straight, as it is not much bent in the stifles and hocks, that part
from hock to heel standing nearly straight. When viewed from behind, quarters
wide, the haunches showing great development of muscle; the legs should be wide
through them, the hocks being turned in very slightly, and the feet standing out
a little; but this deviation from the straight line should not be very noticeable. In
common dogs the feet sometimes stand out so much that the hocks touch. This is
a blemish, though not so objectionable as the contrary, when the hocks are turned
out and the feet in. Dew-claws are seldom met with in dachshunds, and should be
removed directly where they appear in a whelp.

Stern, set on rather high, strong at the root, tapering slightly to a fine point, short-haired, length not much exceeding that of the head, and not touching the ground when hanging straight down. Carriage of stern: the root or first third should be nearly straight, the two remaining thirds bent into a rather wide curve, the slender point standing straight again, or even sweeping upwards a little. The tail should be carried gaily, like that of the foxhound, either upright over the back, or straight down when the dog is tired. Horizontal carriage is not objectionable, but it usually indicates a drowsy temper; if the stern is at the same time very thin and long, it gives an objectionable appearance, when it becomes stiff and bare, by old age of the dog. The common dog has the stern longer and heavier, the hair on its under side longer; the lower two-thirds of the stern are in some specimens nearly straight, and the last third crooked suddenly in a short semicircle, forming a hook at the end of the stern. This is a blemish, as well as the " ring tail " and much leaning to the right or left. I have mentioned already the "otter-tailed" dachshund, a peculiar old strain—but now seldom to be found—with short, broad, or flat stern, very hairy beneath, and carried straight down.

Coat (skin and hair): The *skin* of the dachshund is (with the exception of the head and extremities) rather full, but of sufficient elasticity to prevent looseness, which is only to be found in the common dog to a certain degree. The *hair* should be short, glossy, smooth, but wiry—not soft and silky, except on the ears, where it is extremely short and thin, the "leather" becoming often quite bare and shiny when the dog gets old. The longest and coarsest hair is to be found under the stern, lying close to the tail in well bred dogs; and even in the common breed it should never form a perfect brush. The hair is often very scarce under the chest and belly, which is not at all favourable for a dog standing so close to the ground.

Colour: black and tan is the most ancient and legitimate colour of the class; but this colour is not so constant as to prevent the accidental appearance of a puppy whose colour varies into any tinge or shading, produced by combination, separation, or blending of the black ground colour and the tan of the marks—such as *black, chocolate, light brown,* and *hare-pied* with blackish ears and dark stripes along the back, either whole coloured or with tan marks. Sometimes the colour of the marks (tan) appears alone, and produces the "*whole-coloured tan,*" with all its varieties of shading through red, ochre, fawn, and sandy. In all the darker varieties of the black-tan dog the nose and nails should be perfectly black, and even in the brightest whole or self-coloured tan, fawn, and sandy dogs, they should be at least as dark as possible. Rosy or fleshy noses and nails indicate that there is white in the breed; they cannot be excused by the colour of the coat —not even in whole-coloured tan and sandy dogs—or else the *nails in the low-coloured paws of our black-tan dogs* must also be changed into fleshy or horn coloured ones. Besides, the original ground colour of the dog is black, and will appear again sooner or later in the whole-coloured tan offspring. The extension and design of the marks in black-tan dachshunds is nearly the same as in the English terrier. The tan of the cheek should not be divided in dachshunds, but ascend abruptly towards the jaw-muscle, so as to give the eye the appearance as if it was surrounded beneath by a black semicircle. On the hind legs the tan is not limited to the inside of the legs, but extends over the whole front of them, and the half outside of the feet; from hock to heel runs a black stripe. *Pencilled toes* in the forefeet are nothing else but the imperfect repetition of this black stripe, both according pretty well to the position and bending of the extremities during the embryonal state of the dog. (The tan marks seem to be limited chiefly to those parts which are covered and pressed by the bending of the extremities in the embryo.) Pencilled toes appear and disappear in black-tan puppies of any breed in Germany; therefore they cannot be regarded as indicating a "terrier cross" in dachshunds, the English terrier being quite an unknown animal in many of those remote places in Germany where good dachshunds are bred. On the forearm and the under-thigh the black melts gradually into the tan; but on all other parts of the body the two colours should be divided distinctly, and without any blending. *White* toes, and indeed white anywhere, are great blemishes; but there are few black-tan dachshunds to be found without having at least a small greyish tuft of hair on the breast-bone, or a narrow line along the brisket, which is only to be seen when the dog is sitting on his haunches.

More rarely met with are the *bluish* alterations of the black-and-tan (for instance, slate-grey, mouse, silvery-grey, and the "tigerdachs"), which are all to be regarded as a more or less "*imperfect albinism*," originating in want of pigment in the hair. The "tigerdachs" is nothing else but a black-tan dog whose ground colour is altered only on *some parts* of the coat into a bluish tinge, while other parts have preserved the original ground colour ("*partial* imperfect albinism"), and form now irregular black or brown stripes and blotches. None of these bluish varieties can be regarded as a distinct breed, nor are they only limited to the dachshund class.[*] Nose and nails of the bluish varieties are dark, fleshy, even rosy or black-spotted, as the ground colour of the coat has been altered more or less. The eyes are bluish, or quite colourless (wall-eyed). All these bluish dogs should have no white marks, except the tiger-dachs, which should be as variegated as possible, and therefore white on the breast and belly of these dogs is no blemish; but they should not have white toes or white marks on the head, body, nor end of stern.

White, as a ground colour, with hound-like blotches, spotted, or mottled, is much disliked by most of our breeders; and these colours should disappear entirely from the dachshund class, and be limited to the basset and the various "dachsdracken." White dachshunds are kept and bred as a curiosity, and the origin of most of them is very dubious. The only reason for breeding them is that white dogs are easier kept in sight when hunting a covert. But the qualification for hunting above ground is not at all the criterion of the dachshund class.

[*] The bluish colours are to be found among all possible breeds of German dogs which are not crossed too much, and even in black cats. A beautiful specimen of a tiger-dachs-coloured *colley* I saw at Kyle-Rhea, near Skye, in September, 1874.

The legitimate colours of the dachshund may be divided into four groups:

1. *With tan marks:* Black, chocolate, light brown, hare-pied; the brighter varieties often showing a blackish stripe along the back, and black ears; eyes, rich brown, never brighter than the tan marks; nose and nails black; *no white.*

2. *Whole coloured:* Black, chocolate, light brown, hare-pied; and also the tan varieties—red, tan, ochre, fawn, sandy; the brighter varieties often with a darker stripe along the back; ears and muzzle also often darker than the body; no tan marks; eyes, rich brown or light brown, never brighter than the colour of the coat; nose and nails, black, no white. In bright tan and sandy dogs the nose and nails should be at least much darker than the coat, and never fleshy.

3. *Bluish varieties:* Slate, mouse, silver-grey, either whole coloured or with tan marks; eyes, bluish or colourless (wall-eyed); nose and nails blackish, fleshy, rosy; no white.

4. *Variegated varieties* (tiger-dachs): Slate, mouse, silvery-grey, with irregular black chocolate or tan stripes and blotches, with or without tan marks; eyes, at least one of them, bluish or colourless; nose and nails, fleshy or spotted; white marks on throat and breast are not objectionable in the tiger-dachs.

In judging dachshunds no difference should be made between the four groups of colours, except when there were two dogs of equal merit; there the black-tan dog should be preferred, or that dog would have developed the marks most exactly, in the richest tone, and with no white at all.

Size, symmetry, and quality.—The height of an average specimen is from 9in. to 10in. at the shoulder; the weight should be from 15lb. to 17lb., bitches being always smaller than dogs of the same litter. I have mentioned already that the class will most probably embrace dogs from 9lb. to 20lb. weight, owing to the different sized dogs used to hunt underground by our sportsmen. In a regularly built dog of 17lb. weight I found these proportions: head, from nose to occiput over the skull, 8in.; neck to shoulders, 4½in.; back, 15in.; stern, 8in.; distance from ground to brisket, 2½in.; from ground to elbow, 6in.; to shoulders, 10in.; to hip, 10½in.

In judging dachshunds it must be borne in mind that the frame of these dogs has preserved pretty well all the proportion of a large or middle-sized dog, only the legs are shortened; while in the terriers all parts of the body have been reduced equally. A cross with the terrier will be directly indicated in the offspring by alteration of the peculiar proportions of the dachshund, and therefore the badger dog cannot be called "dachs-terrier," it not being a cross. We must also notice that the reduction of the legs is not quite equal in all parts of the legs, but is chiefly limited to the bones of the forearm (radius and ulna) and those of the *lower thigh* (tibia and fibula). The consequence is that the paws of the fore-feet appear large and broad, and the hind-leg (from hock to heel) rather high and straight. These peculiar proportions become unfavourable when carried to excess; but even then they are not so bad as the contrary (too long forearms being out at the shoulders and joining at the knees, and too long under-thighs being bent too much in the stifle and hocks). The disadvantage of the short lever in the hind-legs must be compensated by powerful arched loins. The dachshund runs pretty fast on level ground; he must even be able to jump and to climb, which will often save his life in steep passages underground, where an unwieldy dog is quite helpless.

A good dachshund should be built long and low, but never to such an extent as to become unwieldy. The whole outline must be most elegant, something like a weasel; head and neck carried neither quite horizontally nor straight upright.

The two dachshunds, Fritz and Dina, are pretty good representations of the breed respecting their bodies; and I was very glad to find them not corresponding much to the hound-type scheme of points proposed in the *Field* of Jan. 13. But there is something very strange in their heads, particularly in the foremost dog: there the skull is far too much vaulted, the ears are set on too low, and not at all of a dachshund-like shape and carriage. The jaw should be larger and stronger, and the tail somewhat shorter. Heads of this kind are the mistaken qualities (*missverstandne Schonheit*) in *dachshunds*, and more fit for house pets and for dogs used in hunting above ground than for an earth dog.

If I had to fix the value of the points, I should rank them thus:

	Value.		Value.		Value.
Head	15	Body	10	Stern	10
Ears, eyes, teeth	10	Fore legs	15	Coat	10
Neck	10	Hind legs	10	Size,symmetry,quality	10
	35		35		30

Grand Total, 100.

Many particulars will have to remain open to conclusion till we have had a show for dachshunds only (*e.g.*, extension or division of the class, white ground colour, carriage of stern, and so on).

Where opinions differ among our fanciers, I have always added the arguments for my assertions. Perhaps my description of the dog has become too minute by these additions; but I hope it has not thereby been rendered unintelligible. I know very well that there are few dogs to be found that will agree in all respects with the particulars I have mentioned in describing the points. But nobody who is acquainted with the endless variety of animal forms will expect to find all well-bred dachshunds having exactly the same proportions. No dog is perfect, and those particulars are taken from the best head, best neck, best leg, &c., which were to be found among a number of regularly-built dogs, in order to find out the arche-type of the breed, which is rarely, if ever, reached in a single specimen.

Before I conclude my writing I may mention shortly some particulars about breeding, disposition, and employment of the badger dog.

I have seldom found bitches whelping more than four or five pups; they are born with straight forelegs, only the paws turn outside somewhat more than in other dogs. This would lead to the old theory of "hereditary rachitis" in dachshunds; and I have offered already a number of hopeful puppies for osteological researches in this direction, but without any noticeable success. Dachshunds are not much subject to distemper if kept in a dry, warm, and clean place. When they are full grown—say when twelve or eighteen months old—they will mostly be ready for business, when once seeing an old dog doing his work underground. By frequent exercise with rats, foxes, &c., their education will be completed sooner; but they should not be used to badgers before having reached their second year and their full development. When going to the burrows the dogs should not be allowed to tire themselves out during the walk, but should be carried in a basket in a wheelbarrow, or taken in the box of the dogcart when driving. Young dogs should always be taken up as soon as they show an indisposition to go to ground, or return too often from the earths. Many old dogs have the habit of coming out when they have received a first blow from the badger or fox. Some people say, "He comes to show his wound"; but the dog only wants to have a glance round above to see if all is right there, and, if so, he will go in again without being asked. There are many badger dogs that will kill their fox under ground, and drag the dead body out to the surface if possible; but I remember only two dachshunds who had the strength and the will to "draw" an old badger from its den, and this was only managed when they had the good fortune to seize the unlucky badger from behind in the haunches, the channel at the same time being neither too narrow nor too steep. I have already said that this is not at all the task of our dachshund, who has only to hunt and to attack his game till it quits the den or stands at bay. For bolting a fox (*sprengen*) one small game dachshund will be sufficient when the shooters (for the fox is shot in Germany) have been posted cautiously and noiselessly; but, in digging out a badger or fox, one small dog will seldom be able to resist his enemy at the moment when the drain is opened, and the badger or fox is frightened by the daylight. Therefore, at least one large dog, or two small ones, should be used for this purpose. Dogs which are used often to hunt coverts are seldom persevering earth dogs; besides, they are accustomed to give tongue as soon as they come upon the track, which is the worst an earth dog can do (*weidelaut*). On the contrary, we find often good earth dogs hunting quite silent above ground till they get sight of the game.

In hunting above ground the dachshund follows more the track than the general scent (*witterung*) of the game; therefore he follows rather slowly, but surely, and with the nose pretty close to the ground. His noise in barking is very loud, far sounding, and of surprising depth for a dog of so small a frame; but, in giving tongue while hunting, he pours forth from time to time short, shrill notes, which are quickened as the scent gets hotter, and, at sight of the game the notes are often resolved into an indescribable scream, as if the dog were being punished in a most cruel manner.

Though not a pack hound, the dachshund will soon learn to run in couples; and two or three of these couples, when acquainted with one another, or forming a little family, will hunt pretty well together. They do not frighten their game so much as the larger hounds, and, when frequently used, they will learn to stay when arrived at the line of the shooters. not by obedience to their master, but because they are intelligent enough as to see that it is quite useless to run longer after the game.

For tracking wounded deer or a roebuck a dachshund may be used when no bloodhound (*schweisshund*) is to be had; but they must be accustomed to collar and line for this purpose, and then they are rather troublesome to lead in rough ground or coverts. They retrieve better by running free or slipped, but must carry a bell, for they are apt to keep silence when they find their game dead; and, beginning to lick at the wound where the ball has gone into the body, they will slowly advance to tearing and to eating their prey.

No dog is so sensitive to rain and wet ground as the dachshund. They will often steal away from the coverts on a wet day, and sneak homewards.

Dachshunds are very headstrong and difficult to keep under command; and, as they are at the same time very sensitive to chastisement, it is next to impossible to force them to do anything against their will. Many good badger dogs have been made cowards for their whole life by one severe whipping. They must be taken as they are—with all their faults, as well as their virtues. When treated always kindly, the dachshund is very faithful to his master, and not only a useful, but a most amusing dog—a very humorist among the canine family. In spite of his small frame, he has always an air of consequence and independence about him; but, at the same time, he is very inquisitive, and always ready to interfere with things with which he has no concern. He seems to have an antipathy to large dogs, and, if they object to be domineered over, the dachshund will certainly quarrel with them. When his blood is up he will care neither for blows nor for wounds, and is often bitten dreadfully in such encounters. Therefore dachshunds should not be kept in kennels with larger dogs. When kept in houses and accustomed to children, they will make good pets, for they are clean, intelligent, and watchful, without being noisy, though often snappish with strangers.

The names which are given to dachshunds in Northern Germany are usually the same old-fashioned ones, indicating chiefly their employment or their quarrelsome disposition. For instance : Names for dogs—Bergmann (miner), Erdmann (earth-man), Judas, Krup-in (creep-in !), Kuhlmann (pit-man, miner), Waldmann (forester), Zänker (quarreller); for bitches, Bergine, Erdine, Hertha, Valda, Waldine, Zang (tongs, nippers).

In England the earth dog is already represented by the various terriers, and, with respect to the great difference between English field sports and German "Jägerei," I doubt if the dachshund will ever become so useful and favourite a sporting dog in England as he has for centuries been in Germany. Foxes and their cubs are sacred personages in most English districts, badgers are comparatively rare, and the destruction of vermin is generally left to the gamekeepers. Therefore, I believe that dachshunds will be kept and bred in England chiefly for hunting coverts, or to serve as housepets and for show purposes, as an object of fashion or fancy. Both employments will inevitably alter the type and disposition of the dog as soon as his qualification for underground work is regarded to be only secondary. But I believe there are also many sportsmen and fanciers of the dachshund in England who would like to preserve these dogs as they are bred originally, and who wish to know how we in Germany are going to fix the points of this breed—as we Germans are desirous of becoming acquainted with the English points of English breeds of dogs.

To describe the real old type of dachshund, and to prevent, if possible, the creation of a new cross breed, was my intention in sending these notes.

MR. VERO SHAW'S BULL DOGS "SMASHER" AND "SUGAR."

PART III.
NON-SPORTING DOGS.

BOOK 1.
WATCH DOGS.

CHAPTER I.
THE BULLDOG AND MASTIFF.

THE BULLDOG.

NTIL the early part of the nineteenth century the bulldog was bred with great care in this country for the purpose of baiting the bull, which up to that time formed one of the most popular out-of-door amusements of the lower orders, to whom also his cross with the terrier, then known as "half-and-half," afforded indoor entertainment by means of dog-fights and rat-killing. Bear baiting was occasionally added to this list, but never to any great extent, on account of the cost of procuring the bear; but the three other kinds of sport, as they were then considered, were extensively patronised, and notably in London, Birmingham, and the manufacturing districts of Staffordshire and Yorkshire. Bull-baiting was chiefly confined to the potteries, but London had still its Westminster dog-pit till the passing of the Act for the prevention to cruelty of animals in 1835, which put a stop to all public exhibitions of this kind, with the exception of an occasional sly run at a bull by the Staffordshire miners during their weekly holiday above ground, and to the private cockfights, which until very recently were carried on even in circles considerably higher. The bulldog was used for the bull-bait, because he was exactly suited to the purpose; his nature being to run at the head of the animal he attacks, and after laying hold ("pinning") to maintain it in spite of any amount of punishment, short of insensibility from injury to his brain. Whether this peculiar attribute is natural or bred artificially, I believe there is no sufficient evidence to prove; except that if, as I shall presently show, the superior antiquity of the greyhound is satisfactorily established, it may be assumed that the bulldog is a subsequent production. To permit his keeping his wind while thus holding on to the bull, the nostrils must be set back as far as possible behind the level of

his teeth, or the soft and yielding substance of the lip of the bull would suffocate
the dog, and hence the breeders have always insisted on the necessity of a shortness
of the face to an extent such as is never seen in any other variety of the species,
and also on wide and open nostrils.   The large head is indispensable to give courage;
and though no great amount of intelligence was necessary for bull-baiting, some
cleverness was required to avoid the horns of the bull.   There is no doubt that
this dog is capable of great attachment to his master, and even of learning tricks,
as might be expected from the size of his brain; but he has always been troublesome
as a companion on account of his losing all control over his actions when excited,
so as to be beyond the management even of the most determined master, whom,
when calm, he would fondle like a spaniel.   Mr. Adcock, who is an enthusiastic
lover of the breed, in a letter to me lately announcing the death of his celebrated
dog Ajax, writes that until the dog came into his possession " he exhibited the
greatest ferocity, going straight at man, beast, or vehicle, if in motion, and, in the
case of animals, invariably selecting the head for attack, and becoming the more
determined if beaten with whip or stick."   It was not, he writes, until he engaged
in a *naked-handed* contest, in which, by continually throwing him, he showed the
dog that he was his master, that he could do anything with him in safety.   " From
that time," he goes on to say, " the dog's temper gradually improved, the chain
was no longer used, and he readily learnt to fetch and carry, and other tricks, such
as jumping a hurdle, &c."   This anecdote certainly would lead one to believe that
in breeding for size one of the peculiar attributes of the bulldog has been lost or
greatly reduced; for, according to the statements of all experienced owners of the
bulldog in his purity, with whom I have conversed on his temperament both in
past and present times, such a feat would be impossible with a well-bred animal
even of 50lb. weight or less, whereas Ajax weighed 65lb.   The notorious account
published in the *Daily Telegraph* some years ago of the fight between the man with
his fist alone, and the dog chained in a room, was asserted to be apocryphal as
being incredible, although according to my experience perfectly feasible, for in it
the dog was described as chained, whereas in the above-mentioned contest Mr.
Adcock with his naked hands must have been fully within reach of Ajax, or he could
not have thrown him as he states he repeatedly did.   Either, therefore, Mr. Adcock
performed a feat of a superhuman character, or Ajax did not display the average
courage and tenacity of the pure bulldog; and if so, his case goes to show that the
speciality of the breed has been sacrificed to some extent in order to procure the
increase of size, which made him the champion of his day in the various dog shows.
This accords with my own opinion of him, as I considered him deficient in length
of skull, though no doubt *for his size* I thought him a grand specimen of the breed,
knowing as I do how difficult it is to procure increased bulk in all parts of the
body of any animal.   Giants are almost invariably out of proportion in some part
or parts, and to this rule I fear I must contend that Ajax was no exception, *malgré*
his owner's opinion that he was the " finest example of the breed ever exhibited."
In comparison with the head of Lamphier's King Dick or Romanie, or with that
of Henshall's Duke, the skull of Ajax would, I think, be found greatly reduced in

size, taking into consideration the difference in the respective weights of their whole bodies. However, *de mortuis nil nisi bonum*, and I should not have alluded to this asserted deficiency except for the purpose of considering size *per se* in this breed, of which, as I think, too great importance has been made.

Up to the stoppage of the above-mentioned amusements, which are now generally stigmatised as brutal, the bulldog might justly be estimated by the points he exhibited which were best adapted to the office he was required to fulfil. At present he is "out of place," and is only wanted to impart some portion of his extraordinary courage to other breeds; and here, indeed, the demand is more theoretical than practical, as the crosses in which he has been used are now established; and it is very seldom indeed that a new infusion of his blood is required. These crosses are chiefly that with the mastiff, resulting in the keeper's night dog; with the greyhound, in which after several generations the cross retains a certain degree of additional courage and power of bearing punishment; and with the terrier, the result of which, after many generations, is the modern bull terrier —one of the most companionable of all the dogs of the present day, and gradually creeping into favour with the public. In the cross with the greyhound the peculiar shapes of the bulldog are soon lost in the elegant lines of the longtail; and this bears strongly on another point in his natural history, to which I shall now allude. Before proceeding to that subject I may, however, wind up the present one by stating that, for the reasons given above, the bulldog is only to be regarded as a remarkable curiosity in natural history; but as such it would be a great pity to lose him.

A warm controversy has long been maintained among dog fanciers as to the antiquity of the bulldog; but the above-mentioned fact would serve to show that the greyhound, at all events, is the older and purer variety of dog, since it is admitted by all experienced breeders that whenever a cross is attempted between two animals of different strains, the older and purer strain very soon shows and maintains a marked predominance. In my first attempt at defining our various breeds of dogs, published in the year 1859, I describe a series of crosses made by the late Mr. Hanley, who was an enthusiastic courser of that period, with a view to further improve the greyhound by a second infusion of bull blood, which had previously been found advantageous by Lord Orford and others. Putting a high-bred bulldog "Chicken" (by Burn's Turk out of sister to Viper) to a greyhound bitch, the produce showed very little of the bull, having not the slightest vestige of "stop," no lip, and a pointed muzzle, with a body nearly as light as that of the dam. The produce of the next cross with the greyhound were wholly greyhound-like in appearance, but, though they were moderately fast, they could not stay a course; and this defect continued to the last, when the experiment was terminated in the sixth generation by Mr. Hanley's death. His want of success has most probably prevented a repetition of the cross; but, as far as one example goes, it tends to show that the bulldog is not, what many of his admirers contend he is— the oldest and purest breed of modern dogs.

Soon after the enforced cessation of bull-baiting, the breeding of bulldogs was in great measure put a stop to, and indeed was confined to a very limited number, including, in London, the celebrated dealer in dogs, familiarly known as "Bill George," and a few of the prize-fighting fraternity, who, however, never attempted a "bait;" while around Birmingham, as already stated, and in the Potteries, a sly run at the bull was still occasionally held. Gradually, however, for want of encouragement, the pure breed became more and more rare, even with the aid of the original Bulldog Club, and its acknowledged head, Mr. H. Brown, of Hampstead, who was enthusiastically supported by the late Mr. Mundell, Q.C., Mr. Stockdale, and one or two others of similar position; but, with these exceptions, the breed in London fell into the hands of the publicans, who from time to time held shows in their tap rooms, to draw custom; and mainly for the same purpose it was kept up at Birmingham, which has always rivalled London in its breed of these dogs—as well as Sheffield, where the late Mr. Lamphier long held undisputed sway. Still, however, it has been artificially stimulated as a variety of "the fancy," and, consequently its value cannot now be tested by any rules founded on a special purpose for it, as is the case with the various kinds of sporting dogs and with its congener the mastiff, as well as with the St. Bernard and Newfoundland; in which size forms an element of great importance when regarded as protectors of man. Nevertheless, it has lately been assumed by Mr. Adcock and his followers that this point is to be taken as *per se* a mark of superiority; and that gentleman has at great trouble imported a dog from Spain to improve his strain, for the sole reason, as it appears to me, that he is of great size, which he undoubtedly is; but, being already in possession of Ajax, a dog confessedly of full size, being 65lb. in weight, I cannot understand why he should wish to increase the bulk of his breed by crossing with a dog exhibiting no single bulldog point in anything like perfection. Nevertheless, his example has been followed by Mr. Dawes, of Leamington, and one or two other noted breeders of the bulldog, but hitherto without producing anything fit for the show bench, as far as I know; and, as before remarked, the description of his encounter with Ajax would lead me to consider that dog as showing anything but a good example of the courage and tenacity of purpose which are the attributes specially insisted on, even by Mr. Adcock himself, as all-important.

With a desire to stop this attempt at improvement (after a short interval from the death by inanition of the old Bulldog Club above mentioned), several influential breeders lately established the present Bulldog Club, which commenced their labours by drawing up a scale of points very similar to that of the old club given in the first edition of "The Dogs of the British Islands," the chief difference being in the allowance for skull, which is reduced from 25 to 15, the balance being given to symmetrical formation.

THE NEW BULLDOG CLUB'S SCALE OF MARKS FOR JUDGING BULLDOGS BY POINTS.

"In adopting the principle of distributing 100 marks amongst the several points of the bulldog, the Bulldog Club has followed the example of the old National Dog Club, with whose valuation of the separate points of the bulldog (as given in Stonehenge's 'Dogs of the British Isles') the present scale is almost identical.

"The opinions of all (whether members or not) were solicited and received, and the steps to define and obtain the establishment of a recognised standard for the breed have been carefully and impartially taken."

Point mentioned in standard.	Details for consideration of Judge.	Distribution of 100 marks for perfection in each point.
1st General appearance	Symmetrical formation; shape, make, style, action, and finish	10
2nd Skull	Size, height, breadth, and squareness of skull; shape, flatness, and wrinkles of forehead ...	15
3rd Stop	Depth, breadth, and extent	5
4th Eyes	Position, shape, size, and colour	5
5th Ears	Position, size, shape, carriage, thinness	5
6th Face	Shortness, breadth, and wrinkles of face; breadth, bluntness, squareness, and upward turn of muzzle; position, breadth, size, and backward inclination of top of nose; size, width, blackness of, and cleft between nostrils	5
7th Chop..................	Size and complete covering of front teeth	5
8th Mouth	Width and squareness of jaws, projection and upward turn of lower jaw; size and condition of teeth, and if the six lower front teeth are in an even row	5
9th Neck and chest ...	Length, thickness, arching, and dewlap of neck; width, depth, and roundness of chest	5
10th Shoulders	Size, breadth, and muscle	5
11th Body..................	Capacity, depth, and thickness of brisket; roundness of ribs..............................	5
12th Roach back	Shortness, width at shoulder, and height, strength, and arch at loins	5
13th Tail	Fineness, shortness, shape, position, and carriage	5
14th Fore legs and feet	Stoutness, shortness, and straightness of legs, development of calves and outward turn of elbows; straightness and strength of ankles, roundness, size, and position of feet, compactness of toes, height and prominence of knuckles	5
15th Hind legs and feet	Stoutness, length, and size of legs, development of muscles, strength, shape, and position of hocks and stifles, formation of feet and toes as in fore	5
16th Size	Approaching 50lb.	5
17th Coat	Fineness, shortness, evenness, and closeness of coat; uniformity, purity, and brilliancy of colour....................................	5
	Total for perfection in all points	100

This scale is given here *in extenso*, out of consideration for the high authority from which it emanates; but I cannot help thinking that the skull, which is the essential point of the breed, has been sacrificed in favour of another, which can far more readily be obtained, and is of comparatively little importance.

If the dog is to be regarded as useful in himself for any purpose whatever demanding symmetry, by all means value that point accordingly ; but as I do not so regard him for the reasons above given, and as I consider his courage, which depends for its development on that of his brain, as the peculiar attribute of the breed, I must confess that I do not accept this alteration without protest, and I therefore put forth the following scale, in which I have added five points for skull, leaving it still lower than the old estimate :

PROPOSED SCALE OF POINTS.

	Value.		Value.		Value.
Skull	20	Chop	5	Fore legs and feet ...	5
Stop	5	Mouth and lower jaw	5	Hind legs and feet ...	5
Eyes	5	Neck	5	Size	5
Ears	5	Shoulders and chest	10	Coat and colour	5
Face, upper jaw, and		Back	5	Symmetry and action	5
nostrils	5	Tail	5		
	40		**35**		**25**

Grand Total **100.**

1. *Skull* (value 20) should be as large as possible, square in all directions, and the skin covering it well wrinkled. The distance between the eye and ear passage should be considerable.

2. The *stop* (value 5), or indentation between the eyes, should be well developed in depth as well as width, and should extend up the skull, or be "well broken up the face," as this is called in canine phraseology. This term is an appropriate one, the conformation giving the animal possessing it an appearance as if his skull was split in two beneath the skin at this part.

3. The *eyes* (value 5) should be dark and large, but not too full ("goggle"). Their setting should be straight across, not oblique or fox-like, and should be wide apart.

4. The *ears* (value 5) should be small and fine. Three shapes are known, under the names "rose," "button," and "tulip." In the "rose" ear, which is considered by far the best, the tip laps over outwards, showing part of the inside. The "button" shows scarcely anything of the inside, from the tip falling forwards, while the "tulip" stands erect like that of the fox. Many dogs are in the habit of cocking up their rose or button ears into the shape of the tulip when excited; but this, though objectionable, and sufficient to make a good judge take off a proportionate amount from the allotted value of this point, should not make him estimate them as if they were absolute tulips. In all cases the ears should be set on at the edges of the upper surface of the skull, and not on its top, which gives an unnaturally narrow appearance to the head.

5. *Face, upper jaw,* and *nostrils* (value 5).—In the upper jaw there should be no

falling away under the eyes, the cheek-bones being prominent, showing a good girth from depth as well as breadth. The nasal bones and cartilages must be very short, so that the end of the nose lies sloping back considerably behind the level of the teeth, reducing the distance between it and the eyes to a *minimum*. The "shortness of face," as it is called, is considered of great importance, for the reason given in the introductory remarks. The nose itself should be broad, damp, and black, with the nostrils wide open, having a cleft between them. A light-coloured ("Dudley") or a parti-coloured ("butterfly") nose is especially objected to.

6. The *chop* (value 5) or lips should completely cover the teeth, the more the better.

7. The *mouth* and *lower jaw* (value 5) must be wide and square. The lower jaw should be well turned up, and project beyond the upper. The canine teeth (tusks) should be strong and set wide apart, and the incisors in an even row and of regular size.

8. The *neck* (value 5) should be moderately long, but arched and very muscular, and should be clothed with a quantity of loose skin hanging down in the form of a double dewlap.

9. *Shoulders* and *chest* (value 10).—The shoulder-blades should be long, and strongly covered with muscle. The *chest* must be very wide and deep, giving a great girth, the thickness of brisket being specially to be noted as different from that of all other dogs in reference to the width between the elbows.

10. The *back* (value 5) must be short, and arched at the loin ("roached"), showing a great width of the dorsal muscles running up in a hollow between the shoulder blades, which, combined with the arched loin, should make the dog look lower before than behind. There is rather a "tucked-up" appearance at the loins, from the shortness of the back ribs as compared with those in front, a "cobby" shape being undesirable.

11. The *tail* (value 5) or stern should be set on low. It should be very fine, and by no means long. A twist is considered desirable rather than otherwise, and many go so far as to admire what is called "a screw." It must not be carried over the back, and a hooked end is a bad fault.

12. *Fore legs* and *feet* (value 5).—The legs should be short, straight, and well clothed at the arms—or "calves'" as they are called—with muscle. This, being chiefly on the outside, often gives the bulldog's forelegs an appearance as if crooked, which they ought not really to be, and really are not in a well-made dog. The elbows should be set on to the true arm wide apart, the arm itself sloping out from the shoulder joint. The ankles, or pasterns, must be as nearly upright and straight as possible, showing plenty of bone; but very few even of the best dogs quite come up in this point, and it must not, therefore, be much insisted on. The feet should have the toes well split up and arched, but most of the best dogs exhibit rather a wide or "splayed" formation of the feet.

13. *Hind legs* and *feet* (value 5).—The hind legs should be well turned out at the stifles, and in at the hocks, giving an appearance of what is called "cow hocks."

The hocks should be straight and near the ground; the feet should turn out, but in other respects resemble the fore feet.

14. The *size* (value 5) should, on the average, in the male, not exceed 50lb.

15. *Coat* and *colour* (value 5).—The coat should be fine, short, even, and close; the colours are white, brindled, fallow, or red, or pied with one of these colours; and white or red smut, fallow or fawn smut—that is, with black faces. Black is objected to.

16. *Symmetry* (value 5) depends on shape, style, and finish, united with action; this last is peculiar, and consists in a lurch or roll, depending on the width of this dog's shoulders, and the formation of his hind legs rendering it difficult for him to raise them high from the ground.

Since the last edition of the "Dogs of the British Islands" was published, several well-known breeders of the bulldog have either died, or have retired from the fancy, as is the case with Mr. H. Brown, Mr. Mundell, and the two Lamphiers. Among the latter, Mr. Shirley and Mr. R. J. Ll. Price have given up the breed, and the names of Messrs. Henshall, Stockdale, Tyser, Fulton, and many others, have disappeared from the prize-list. In the present day, Mr. G. A. Dawes, of Leamington; Mr. G. Raper, of Stockton on-Tees; Mr. James Taylor, of Rochdale; Mr. Harding Cox; Mr. Adcock, of Wigan; Mr. James Berrie (one of the oldest and most enthusiastic fanciers now), Mr. Layton, Mr. T. H. Joyce, and Mr. Vero Shaw, of London, have many good specimens of the type I have endeavoured to describe in the foregoing notes.

Mr. Vero Shaw has kindly placed his kennel at my disposal for illustration, and I have selected two specimens from it which show the peculiarities of the breed in a marked degree. The foreshortened sketch of the dog exhibits the formation of the chest, shoulders, width of skull, and "rose" carriage of ears, peculiar to the breed, while the bitch's side view shows her wonderfully short face and "roached" loin, rarely met with to the same extent. Their pedigrees are as follow: The dog, Smasher, by Master Gully out of Nettle, by Sir Anthony. The bitch, Sugar (formerly Lily), is by the Abbot out of Mr. J. L. Ashburne's Lola, and was bred by the latter gentleman.

THE ENGLISH MASTIFF.

Like the bulldog, the old English mastiff was bred in this country in the earliest times of which we have any reliable record; but, whether in these former ages the two breeds were distinctly separate, and whether the modern bulldog and mastiff can be traced to one or the other of them, are points which must ever remain unsettled. Mr. F. Adcock and Mr. Kingdon would no doubt write half a dozen volumes in support of the superior antiquity and purity of their respective *protegé's*; but after all, a jury empanelled to deliver a verdict between them would probably be discharged without agreement upon it, and I shall not certainly attempt to do that which I think a 12-man engine would fail in doing. My object is simply to describe the mastiff as I find him: but, nevertheless, I

MR. LUKEY'S MASTIFF "GOVERNOR."

shall not refuse to lay before my readers Mr. Kingdon's views of the origin of the pure breed, which he believes to be now confined to Lyme Hall, in Cheshire, and his own kennels, but most of his dogs are now more or less crossed with the modern mastiff. He says : " There appear to be recorded only four ancient seats of the mastiff in its purity, and these four most celebrated strains have been preserved, each in its integrity ; the oldest of these, pre-eminent for its antiquity and purity, has been thus preserved by the ancient family of Legh, at Lyme Hall in Cheshire, where it seems to have been even previous to 1415, and has been handed down by them in its integrity and purity ; another at Chatsworth, by the Duke of Devonshire ; a third at Elvaston Castle, by Lord Harrington ; and a fourth at Hadzor Hall, by the Galtons." Two of these four are said to be extinct, and, as he says, " there remains only the Lyme Hall and Elvaston breeds in their legitimacy, and of these the Lyme Hall stands pre-eminent." But, unfortunately, although it is readily admitted that a breed of mastiffs has been maintained at Lyme Hall for many generations, there is no written evidence that it has been kept pure, and we may just as well depend on the purity of Mr. Lukey's brindled bitch with which he started his kennel, and which was bred by the Duke of Devonshire, as on that of the Lyme Hall strain. The fact really is, that there is no breed among existing British dogs which can be traced through all its generations for 200 years, and very few individuals for half that time. Foxhound and greyhound pedigrees are the oldest and most carefully kept, but with very few exceptions even they do not extend much beyond the latter period ; and excluding them no breed goes back even for half a century without a doubtful link in the chain of pedigrees.

In determining the points which are desired in any individual of a particular breed, it is idle to go back for centuries and select some strain of which we have no reliable record, and which, if obtained, would probably prove to be very different from what we want. For example, the foxhound is admitted to be descended from a hound which was very different from him in many important respects ; yet, according to Mr. Kingdon, we ought to take the old type and reject the modern one. Instead of proceeding in this illogical way, the master of hounds nowadays improves upon the old type by every possible means, and the result is a hound which does what is asked from him, in a manner which would be far beyond the powers of his ancestors. So with the mastiff—we want a large and handsome dog, possessed of a temperament which will bear restraint under provocation, and, at the same time, of courage to defend his master till the death. These mental properties were carefully attended to by Mr. Lukey, who may be considered to be the founder of the modern English mastiff, and his example has been carefully followed in this respect by Mr. E. Hanbury, Capt. Garnier, Miss Aglionby, Miss Hales, Mr. M. B. Lynn, Mr. Lindoe, Mr. Nichols, and Mr. W. George. All these eminent breeders have taken Mr. Lukey's breed as typical of what they desire to produce, and the results of their efforts may be compared with Mr. Kingdon's dogs on perfectly equal terms, inasmuch as it is admitted that full attention has been paid to the demand for a mild temperament and other mental attributes which

z

are peculiarly essential to this breed. Now Barry is without doubt Mr. Kingdon's *pièce de résistance*, and yet he is as a satyr to Hyperion when compared with Lukey's Governor or Baron, Hanbury's Prince, Green's Monarch, Wallace's Turk, Field's King, Miss Hales's Lion, or Miss Aglionby's Wolf, besides some dozen or more other dogs of nearly equal merit and celebrity. For these reasons I shall discard all further mention of the Lyme Hall strain, and proceed to describe the modern mastiff as founded by Mr. Lukey, and improved on by Capt. Garnier, Mr. Hanbury, and the other eminent breeders mentioned above.

Mr. Lukey began to breed mastiffs rather more than forty years ago, taking a brindled bitch bred by the then Duke of Devonshire as his foundation. Putting her to Lord Waldegrave's celebrated dog Turk, and her puppies to the Marquis of Hertford's Pluto, he obtained a strain with which he stood for some years almost alone as the celebrated mastiff breeder of the day, without any outcross. At length, fearing deterioration by further in-breeding, he resorted to Capt. Garnier's kennel for a sire, the produce being that magnificent dog Governor, by Capt. Garnier's Lion out of his own Countess, a daughter of his Duchess by his Bruce II., who was by his Bruce I. out of his Nell. Of the breeding of his own Lion, and Lord Waldegrave's Turk, Capt. Garnier writes as follows, in a letter which was published at length in the last edition of "Dogs of the British Islands" :—

"About this time I bought of Bill George a pair of mastiffs, whose produce, by good luck, afterwards turned out some of the finest specimens of the breed I ever saw. The dog Adam was one of a pair of Lyme Hall mastiffs, bought by Bill George at Tattersall's. He was a different stamp of dog to the present Lyme breed. He stood 30½in. at the shoulder, with length of body and good muscular shoulders and loins, but was just slightly deficient in depth of body and breadth of forehead; and from the peculiar forward lay of his small ears, and from his produce, I have since suspected a remote dash of boarhound in him. The bitch was obtained by Bill George from a dealer in Leadenhall Market. Nothing was known of her pedigree, but I am as convinced of its purity as I am doubtful of that of the dog. There was nothing striking about her. She was old, her shoulders a trifle flat, and she had a grey muzzle, but withal stood 29in. at the shoulder, had a broad round head, good loin, and deep lengthy frame. From crossing these dogs with various strains I was easily able to analyse their produce, and I found in them two distinct types—one due to the dog, very tall, but a little short in the body and high on the leg, while their heads were slightly deficient in breadth; the other due to the bitch, equally tall, but deep, lengthy, and muscular, with broad massive heads and muzzles. Some of these latter stood 33in. at the shoulder, and by the time they were two years old weighed upwards of 190lb. They had invariably a fifth toe on each hind leg, which toe was quite distinct from a dew-claw, and formed an integral portion of their feet. By bad management, I was only able to bring a somewhat indifferent specimen with me on my return to England from America—a badly reared animal, who nevertheless stood 32in. at the shoulder, and weighed 170lb. This dog Lion was the sire of

Governor and Harold, by Mr. Lukey's bitch Countess, and so certain was I of the vast size of the breed in him that I stated beforehand, much to Mr. Lukey's incredulity, that the produce would be dogs standing 33in. at the shoulder—the result being that both Governor and his brother Harold were fully that height. In choosing the whelps Mr. Lukey retained for himself the best marked one, an animal that took after the lighter of the two strains that existed in the sire; for Governor, grand dog and perfect mastiff as he was, compared to most others of the breed, was nevertheless shorter in the body, higher on the leg, and with less muscular development than Harold, while his head, large as it was, barely measured as much round as did his brother's. I, who went by the development of the fifth toe (in this case only a dew-claw), chose Harold, a dog which combined all the best points except colour of both strains, and was a very perfect reproduction on a larger scale of his dam Countess. This dog was the finest male specimen of the breed I have met with. His breast at ten months old, standing up, measured 13in. across, with a girth of 41in., and he weighed in moderate condition 140lb., and at twelve months old 160lb., while at 13½ months old Governor only weighed in excellent condition 150lb. with a girth of 40in.; and inasmuch as Governor eventually weighed 180lb. or even more, the size to which Harold probably attained must have been very great. His head also in size and shape promised to be perfect.

"I will mention three other dogs. The first, Lord Waldegrave's Turk, better known as 'Couchez,' was the foundation of Mr. Lukey's breed. This dog has frequently been described to me by Bill George and Mr. Lukey, and I have a painting of his head at the present moment. He stood about 29½in. or 30in. at the shoulder, with great length and muscular development, and, although he was never anything but thin, weighed about 130lb. Muzzle broad and heavy, with deep flews; skin over the eyes and about the neck very loose; colour red, with very black muzzle. He was a most savage animal; was fought several times with other animals, and was invariably victorious. The second was a tailless brindled bitch, bought by Mr. Lukey from George White of Knightsbridge. She was a very large massively built animal, standing 30in. at the shoulder. Her produce with Couchez were remarkably fine. 'Long-bodied, big-limbed, heavy-headed bitches. They were mastiffs Mr. Lukey had in those days!' is Bill George's eulogium of them. This bitch was bred by the Duke of Devonshire, and must therefore have been one of the Chatsworth breed. The third animal, L'Ami, was a brindled dog of such vast size and weight that he was taken about and shown in England, in the year 1829, the price of admission being one shilling. Of the head of this dog also I have a drawing, and it shows him to be very full and round above the eyes, with a broad heavy muzzle and remarkably deep flews, the ears being cropped close. This dog, with the exception of rather heavier flews, answered exactly to the type of Vandyke's mastiff.

"Now the point to which I wish to draw attention is, that both Couchez and L'Ami came direct from the Convent of Mount St. Bernard. The mighty dogs which used to be kept at Chatsworth (and one of which stood 34in. at the shoulder) were pure Alpine mastiffs, as also were the two magnificent animals I have mentioned as having seen at Bill George's kennels some sixteen years ago; while others that I frequently used to meet with at that time were of the same character. These, one and all, presented the same type—a strong proof of their purity—and that type was in all respects the same as the old English mastiff portrayed by Vandyke. The same may be said of the dogs in Landseer's picture of Alpine mastiffs, which have all the points of the true mastiffs, although their tails, as might be expected from the cold climate, are hairier than they should be. At that time one used to meet with good English mastiffs also, but they were few compared to the number of half-bred animals that went by that name; and, with the exception of Mr. Lukey's breed, the good ones have nearly all come from Lancashire, Cheshire, and the north of England generally, where some years ago they were still in considerable request for guarding the large bleaching grounds. Between these and the Alpine dogs I never could discover the slightest difference except in size—the best English dogs varying from 29in. to 33in. at the shoulder, while the Alpine male specimens were seldom under 32in.

"Now, it is ridiculous to suppose that the dogs that used to be found at the convent, and in a few of the Swiss valleys, were a breed indigenous to that small part of the continent of Europe; and yet it was there only that the breed existed. When, therefore, we find the same animal common in England two hundred years ago, and still to be met with in considerable numbers, though more rarely than formerly, it is only reasonable to conclude that the English and Mount St. Bernard mastiffs are identical breeds, and that the monks, requiring large, powerful, generous, and high-couraged animals for their benevolent purposes, selected the old English dog in preference to all other breeds. It is very easy to understand that with the disuse of the breed for combating wild animals they should have been allowed to die out and degenerate in England; and it is equally easy to understand that the mastiffs kept at the Convent of St. Bernard for a particular purpose, requiring strength and courage, should have been kept up, and thus that the best specimens of the breed in modern times have come from there."

According to Captain Garnier, therefore, Mr. Lukey's original breed was composed of Chatsworth and Alpine mastiffs, to which was added, by means of Lion, a strain of the Lyme Hall breed. But, whatever may have been the origin, there can be no doubt that no finer specimen of the mastiff than Governor has ever been exhibited, and I have therefore retained his portrait, which is undoubtedly a faithful one, as representing the true type of the modern English mastiff. Mr. Green's Monarch was larger, but his head and ears were not so good as those of Governor, who showed moreover no trace of the bulldog, supposed to have existed in King and in Miss Aglionby's celebrated litter by that dog, including Wolf and Turk, as well as in Lukey's Baron, also by him. This cross is traced to Lord Darnley's Nell, supposed to be nearly or quite half bull.

As I stated in the last edition of this book, there is probably no variety of the species which combines so much strength and power of doing mischief with such docility and amiability, and hence he is, *par excellence*, the keeper's dog. A well-broken mastiff may be taken out at all hours, and in any company, by the most delicate lady, without the slightest fear of leading her into a scrape, and with the most perfect confidence in his protection. There are few Newfoundlands even, docile as they are generally considered to be, from whom it would be safe to take away a bone, but this may be fearlessly done by the master or mistress of the mastiff; and with children he is gentleness itself; yet when roused, and set at man or animal, his courage is second only to that of the bulldog. His sense of smell is acute; Mr. Hanbury tells me that his Duchess will track him with the truth of a bloodhound, and he has seen her draw up to a covey of partridges like a pointer. These dogs are not good at water, and do not voluntarily take it, except in the heat of summer. According to my experience the English mastiff is more reliable in temper than the modern St. Bernard, and bears the chain much better, confinement having a greater tendency to produce disease both of body and mind in the latter. Indeed, I know no dog that stands confinement so well as the mastiff, and it is probably owing to the unfair advantage taken of this peculiarity that we see so many mastiffs deficient in legs and feet, as the result of want of exercise.

A great deal has been written lately, on the bad effect of the bull cross, as exhibited in King and his stock; but I quite agree with Capt. Garnier in thinking that the injurious results complained of have been greatly exaggerated, though I do not go the full length with him of asserting that a century or two ago the two breeds were identical; for, much as I am inclined to think he is right, there seems to be no absolute proof of the truth of his opinion. The sole objection to the cross, as it appears to me, rests in the danger of spoiling the temper of the produce; but every one of experience knows that many keeper's dogs, which are fully half-bull, are perfectly under control even with severe provocation. Still, unless a bulldog is selected of specially amiable temperament, there would be great risk of the effect alluded to, and in any case the proportion of bull ought to be small, not exceeding one-eighth. Capt. Garnier's opinion of the bull cross for the mastiff may be gathered from the following remarks, which form part of the letter above alluded to:—

"By crossing, then, the bulldog with the mastiff, we merely combine two breeds which a century or two ago were identical. This fact is also proved by the colour of the two breeds, which are the same, viz., brindled, fallow, and red with black muzzles; while the known effects of domestication and warmth in producing white in all animals would have full play in the bulldog—the fireside companion of the working man—and would quite account for the change of a light fallow into that colour, and its presence in the bulldog of the present day. In using the cross, however, it would, of course, be advisable to select a brindled or fallow dog.

"We have an illustration of the bull cross in King and his produce; but here I think it has proved of but slight use. King combines in him some of the best strains of the pure mastiff, and his good qualities are quite as much derived from them as from the bull strain in him. His great-granddam, Mr. Lukey's Countess, had a longer and more muscular body than he has, and his head and muzzle are not one whit fuller than any of Mr. Lukey's old strain; while Baron, his son, who is the result of another cross with the old strain, has, I think, a slightly fuller head than he himself. His ears also are more probably inherited from his great-granddam Countess than from the bull cross. The only effects produced by the latter are the under jaw slightly underhung, a full prominent eye, short muzzle, and square forehead. The two first are objectionable, and the two latter produce certain illusive effects on the eye. The shortness of the muzzle makes it look broader than it really is, and the squareness of the forehead makes that part look fuller. These latter so far are advantages, but mastiff critics should remember that the effects produced by them are more apparent than real. Thus Turk's square forehead measures no more round in proportion to his size than does Druid's; and yet, while the eye can detect no great fault in Turk's head, the want of breadth in Druid's is evident at once. So also the contrast of a strongly-marked muzzle with the rest of the head makes it look fuller than it really is. While on this subject, I may as well notice another effect. Some of the correspondents in the *Field* have written of Druid as having a narrow and pointed muzzle. If, however, they measure the girth of his muzzle and that of King's, they will find that they are in the same proportion as the relative sizes of the two dogs, while Druid's muzzle is actually more truncated than King's, and as much so as Baron's; but let the owner of Druid slightly lift the skin on each side of his dog's head, so as to give the forehead an appearance of greater breadth, and the supposed faults in the muzzle will at once disappear. So deceptive are these little tricks of effect, that I never depend on my eye alone, but always assist my judgment with the tape. The fact that in the particular case of King the bull cross has had no very decided effect need not prove an objection to that cross, unless it can be shown that the bulldog used was the best of his class. For there are "bulldogs and bulldogs;" and it is only in the best specimens that the head will measure more round in proportion to their size than the heads of well-bred mastiffs, the squareness of forehead and shortness of muzzle in the bulldog contributing to make their heads look larger and fuller in proportion to their size than they really are. From what I know of the strain from which the bull cross in King came, I expect that his bulldog ancestor was not of the largest-headed type. But take such a dog as Bill George's Young Dan, whose head measures 20½in. round, and who stands 22in. at the shoulder. If he stood 32in., the height of Peveril, his head would measure nearly 31in., while Peveril's only measures 27in.; and the volume of the two heads would then be as 3 to 2."

A much worse stain in the pedigree of the mastiff is the cross with the bloodhound, which has been tried in order to give majesty to the expression. The result is perhaps in accordance with that object, but the temperament is sadly interfered with, and the general size, as well as the relatively large dimensions of head to body, are lost. Instead of the peculiar breadth of the head, it becomes long and narrow, the lips are too pendulous, and the eye sunken, with an exhibition of the haw in the bloodhound form, often to the extent of being absolutely red. I should certainly object to this cross to the full extent of disqualification if exhibited. The following is—

THE NUMERICAL VALUE OF THE MASTIFF'S POINTS.

	Value.		Value.		Value.
Head	20	Neck	5	Size and symmetry	15
Eyes	5	Shoulders and chest	10	Colour	5
Ears	5	Legs and feet	10	Coat	5
Muzzle	5	Loin	10	Tail	5
	35		**35**		**30**

Grand Total 100.

1. The *head* (value 20) is broad, full, and flat in its general character; but this flatness is made up of two gentle swells with a furrow between, as well shown in the portrait of Governor. Eyebrows well marked, but not high. Jaws square in outline and broad, moderately long, and without flews; for though the upper lip is full, it should by no means be pendulous, which formation only exists when there is a cross of the bloodhound.

2. The *eyes* (value 5) are small and somewhat sunken, but mild in expression, and without the sad and solemn look exhibited by the bloodhound. They are generally hazel or brown.

3. The *ears* (value 5) should be small and pendant, lying close to the cheek, without the slightest approach to a fold, which indicates the bloodhound cross. They should be set well back, and should be vine shaped, neither lobular nor houndlike.

4. The *muzzle* (value 5) must be short, with level teeth and square at the nose. The flews should be distinctly marked so as to make the square distinctly pronounced; but they must not be pendulous to anything like the same degree as is exhibited by the bloodhound. A slight projection of the lower teeth may be overlooked.

5. The *neck* (value 5) is muscular, and of sufficient length to avoid loss of symmetry. There is a well-marked prominence at its junction with the head. No throatiness should be allowed, as it indicates the bloodhound cross.

6. The *shoulders and chest* (value 10) must be taken together, as with a full development of the latter there is generally a slight want of obliquity in the former. The girth is, however, the important point, and it should always be at least one third greater than the height. Thus a dog 32in. high should girth 41½in. In such a case the shoulders are apt to be rather short, but they must in any event be well clothed with muscle.

7. *Legs and feet* (value 10). Both these important organs are too apt to be defective in the mastiff, owing greatly to the confinement in which he is usually reared from generation to generation. The consequence is that, however well a puppy is treated, even if left at full liberty, his feet are often weak and flat, his legs small in bone and bent at the knees, he has frequently cat-hams, and a gallop is quite beyond his powers. Hence, these points should be specially attended to in

estimating the merits of any individual. The *desideratum* for the feet is that of the cat—round, with the knuckles well up. A dew-claw is often met with behind, but it is not considered important either way.

8. The *loin* (value 10) must be wide and deep, and should girth nearly as much as the height at the shoulder. The back ribs being apt to be short, a nipped loin is often met with, but it takes away greatly from the strength of the back.

9. *Size and symmetry* (value 15). From the peculiar formation of this breed as a guard for his master, size is all-important, and a dog ought to be at least 29in. or 30in. high to be considered perfect, while any increase on this, if combined with symmetry, is to be counted in his favour. Bitches are usually about 2in. less than the dogs of the same litter. Few breeds are more symmetrical in their proportions when the best specimens are examined.

10. The *colour* (value 5) is regarded as of some considerable importance by mastiff breeders, most of whom now confine themselves to a stone fawn, with black muzzle and ear tips. It is, however, indisputable that the brindle is a true mastiff colour, and if we take Mr. Lukey's breed as the foundation of most of our strains, and as his dog Wallace was of that colour, the question is at once settled. Capt. Garnier thinks that a cross of brindle is necessary to keep up the black points; but I scarcely think this can be correct, for the black is well marked in the Lyme Hall strain, as well as in Mr. Kingdon's crosses, none of which are derived from brindled sires or dams. Nor is it the case in greyhounds, in which black muzzles occur in certain red and fawn strains without a brindled or black cross, whereas they are absent in others, although even a black sire or dam has been used, as in the case of Effort and The Brewer, descended from a long line of fawns, although crossed with the Bedlamite black in their dam Hopmarket. Sometimes white is shown on the face, but this is certainly a defect, though not a great one. A white star on the breast, or a few white toes, may be passed over. Red, with black muzzle is admitted, but not admired.

11. The *coat* (value 5) must be fine and short, even on the tail, which, however, may be allowed to be a little more rough than the body.

12. The *tail* (value 5) is long and strong at the root, without any curl or twist, but carried high when the dog is excited, not otherwise.

The following are the dimensions, in inches, of Mr. Lukey's Governor, whose portrait illustrates this article: Height at shoulder, 33in.; length, nose to tip of tail, 86; girth, 40; girth round loin, 31; round fore leg, 10½; round thigh, 22; round head before ears, 28; skull, 9½; muzzle, 5½—conjoined, 15; ears, 7½. Weight, 180lb. His pedigree is as follows:—

```
                      ┌ Lion ............  ┌ Adam.        ┌ Bruce I. ............  ┌ Couches.
                      │ (Garnier).        { Eve.         │ (Lukey).              { Yarrow.
                      │                    ┌ Bruce II. ......                      ┌ White's Dog.
Governor ........    {                    │ (Lukey).          Nell.................  { Yarrow.
(Lukey).              │                    │                   (Lukey).            ( (Lukey).
                      │ Countess  ......  {                    Tiger.
                      └ (Lukey).           └ Duchess ........  (Armitage).
                                            (Lukey).           Countess.
                                                               (Thompson).
```

CHAPTER II.

THE NEWFOUNDLAND, LABRADOR, ST. BERNARD, AND DALMATIAN DOGS.

THE NEWFOUNDLAND DOG.

TWO distinct types of this breed are now generally admitted—one considerably larger than the other, and known as *the* Newfoundland, from its being generally found on the island of that name; while the other, distributed over the state of Labrador chiefly, though also met with in the island of Newfoundland, is now known as the Labrador, otherwise called the St. John or Lesser Newfoundland. In addition to these distinct types there are numberless nondescript dogs to be found in both of the above districts, and notably a breed of black and white dogs with curly coats and fine heads and frames, which, from one of them having been selected by Landseer to serve as a model for his celebrated picture denominated "A Distinguished Member of the Humane Society," are now known as the "Landseer Newfoundland." In spite, however, of the immortality thus conferred on them, our judges refuse to recognise their merits as compared with the whole blacks, and they are relegated to a separate class in those shows which recognise them at all. Independently of the difference in colour, they also vary from the black type in being more open in their frames, weaker in their middles, and generally displaying a more shambling and ungraceful gait in walking. All the varieties of the breed are excellent swimmers.

The large black Newfoundland is remarkable for his majestic appearance, combined with a benevolent expression of countenance. The latter quality, being really in accordance with his disposition, and frequently displayed by his life-saving capacities in cases of threatened drowning, has made him for many years a great favourite as a companion, especially, with those who live near the sea or any great river. With these points in view, judges have naturally made a full size of great importance, since it not only adds to the majestic aspect of the dog, but renders him really more capable of distinguishing himself in the career so beautifully commemorated by Landseer in the picture above alluded to.

The general opinion now is, as first pointed out by "Index" in the *Field*, that a dog of this breed above 26in. is almost unknown in Newfoundland; but it is also allowed that puppies bred and reared in England of the pure strains, which in the island never attain a greater height than 26in., will grow to 30in. or even 32in. Such an animal is Mr. Mapplebeck's Leo, who has recently taken the first prize at Islington in the Kennel Club Show, after distinguishing himself previously at Bath,

Swindon, and other exhibitions. He is, I believe, descended from an imported Newfoundland on both sides, and shows his pure descent in all respects, being the grandest specimen I ever saw. For this reason I have displaced the portrait of that fine dog, Mr. Robinson's Carlo, who represented the breed in the last edition of "Dogs of the British Islands," although I had intended to retain him; but Leo is so magnificent an animal that I could not leave him in the cold. By many people the rusty tinge in his coat is objected to, and no doubt it is slightly against him; but it is admitted by "Index," Mr. Lort, the late Mr. Wheelwright ("Old Bushman"), and others who are acquainted with the breed in its native districts, that the rusty black is very common among the best strains, though considered by the native breeders to be a slight defect. The last-named gentleman left behind him on his death in 1865 a very fine Newfoundland dog of this rusty colour, imported by himself, which his sister offered to me, and I gladly accepted the present, partly from respect for the memory of so good a sportsman and writer, and partly from my fondness for the breed. This dog was fully 28in. high, which militates against the truth of "Index's" theory on that point, and had double dew claws on both hind legs, in which Mr. Mapplebeck's Leo is altogether wanting, but showing marks of their having been removed in his puppyhood. In all other respects he closely resembles Mr. Wheelwright's dog, but exceeds him in size by about 2½in. to 3in., being nearly 31in. in height. But although not absolutely perfect in colour, the texture of his coat is so beautiful, that the rusty tinge on it may be almost overlooked; and, even if penalised, the dog must score fully 97½ points out of a possible 100, so perfect is he in all other respects; and we all know the difficulty of getting any dog so nearly correct in all his points as this estimate would make Leo to be. "Index," in his final letter, published in the *Field* of July 31, 1869, writes with regard to this tinge as follows: "The black dogs, especially when young, often appear to have a brown tinge on their coats. It is to be seen more or less in almost all these dogs, though not in all. Combing will often remove it if the dog has not been well kept; but I don't think much combing is advisable, for it sometimes would remove the brown-tinged black hair at the sacrifice of the length and thickness and beauty of the coat. Nor is the slight brown tinge (not visible in all lights) ugly; nor is it inconsistent with purity of breed, though it would be always better absent." This extract is exactly in accordance with the evidence I have obtained on this point from Mr. Lort and other good judges who have visited Newfoundland. With regard to size, the same gentleman further writes in the same letter: "While from 24in. to 26in. is the average height of dogs on the island, I have seen that the standard often reached in England is considerably higher; and I cannot, either in theory or as a matter of taste, object to size if it be united with perfection of shape. All I have said, and all I maintain, is that size apart from colour is worthless, and that very large dogs would often (in my experience almost invariably, though I have not had the presumption to advocate any rule on this experience) be found much inferior to dogs which stood in height in proportion as 24 or 26 is to 31 or 34. Whether young imported Newfoundlands do generally or frequently reach 30in. or 31in., or whether such cases as those adduced as being within the knowledge of the *Field* are exceptional cases, has not been discussed by me."

Numberless anecdotes are told of the sagacity and fidelity of this dog, and notably of his desire to save life in cases of threatened drowning. The Rev. S. Atkinson, of Gateshead, had a narrow escape in trying to rescue one of two ladies who were immersed in the sea at Newbiggin, being himself unable to swim; but his fine dog Cato came to their aid from some considerable distance without being called, and, with his help, Mr. Atkinson was safely brought to shore, together with his utterly exhausted charge. Hundreds of similar cases, and of ropes being carried on shore from wrecked vessels, have been published, so that it is needless to gild the refined gold with which these deeds are emblazoned. This dog's fame as a member of the Humane Society is as firmly established as that of the St. Bernard in the snow; and as the numbers of the former until recently have been greatly in excess of those of the latter, and the area for their operations is almost unlimited, while the St. Bernard is confined to a couple of monasteries, it is scarcely fair to compare the escapes carried through by the two breeds in point of numbers. Suffice it to say that the gratitude of mankind has been earned by both.

The numerical value of the points in this breed is as follows:

POINTS OF THE NEWFOUNDLAND.

	Value.		Value.		Value.
The head	25	Back	10	Symmetry	10
Ears and eyes	5	Legs	10	Colour	5
Neck	10	Feet	5	Coat	5
Chest	5	Size	10	Tail	5
	45		**35**		**25**

Grand Total 100.

1. The *head* (value 25) is very broad, and nearly flat on the top in each direction, exhibiting a well-marked occipital protuberance, and also a considerable brow over the eye, often rising three-quarters of an inch from the line of the nose, as is well shown in the case of my present illustration, Mr. Mapplebeck's Leo, in which it exists to a greater extent than usual. The Labrador shows the brow also, but not nearly in so marked a manner. There is a slight furrow down the middle of the top of the head, but nothing approaching to a stop. The skin on the forehead is slightly wrinkled, and the coat on the face and top of the head is short, but not so much so as in the curly retriever. Nose wide in all directions, but of average length, and moderately square at the end, with open nostrils; the whole of the jaws covered with short hair.

2. *Eyes and ears* (value 5).—The eyes of this dog are small, and rather deeply set; but there should be no display of the haw or third eyelid. They are generally brown, of various shades, but light rather than dark. The *ears* are small, clothed with short hair on all but the edges, which are fringed with longer hair.

3. The *neck* (value 10) is often short, making the dog look chumpy and inelegant. This defect should always be attended to, and a dog with a sufficiently lengthy neck should have the full allowance; but, on the other hand, a short chumpy one is so often met with that, even if present, the possessor of it should not be penalised with negative points. The throat is clean, without any development of frill, though thickly clothed with hair.

4. The *chest* (value 5) is capacious, and rather round than flat; back ribs generally short.

5. The *back* (value 10) is often slack and weak, but in some specimens, and notably in Leo, there is a fine development of muscle; accompanying this weak back there is often a rolling and weak walk.

6. The *legs* (value 10) should be very bony and straight, well clothed with muscle on the arms and lower thighs. Elbows well let down, and neither in nor out. Both the fore and hind legs are thickly feathered, but not to any great length. There is also often a double dew claw.

7. The *feet* (value 5) are large and wide, with thin soles. The toes are generally flat, and consequently this dog soon becomes foot-sore in road work, and cannot accompany a horse or carriage at a fast pace.

8. In *size* (value 10) the Newfoundland should be at least 25 inches in height, and if he is beyond this it is a merit rather than a defect, as explained in the above remarks. Many very fine and purely-bred specimens reared in this country have been from 30 to 32 inches high.

9. The *symmetry* (value 10) of this dog is often defective, owing to the tendency to a short neck and weak loin. As a consequence, a symmetrical dog like Leo is highly to be approved of.

10. The *colour* (value 5) should be black, the richer the better; but a rusty stain in it is so common in the native breed that it should by no means be penalised. Still, the jet black is so handsome in comparison with it, that I think, other points being equal, it should count above the rusty stain in judging two dogs. A white star on the breast is often met with. The white and black colour exhibited in the Landseer type never occurs in the true Newfoundland.

11. The *coat* (value 5) of the Newfoundland is shaggy, without much undercoat, and at first sight it would appear unfit for much exposure to wet. It is, however, so thick and oily that it takes some time for the water to reach the skin through it. There is often a natural parting down the back, and the surface is very glossy.

12. The *tail* (value 5) is long and gently curled on one side, but not carried high. It is clothed thickly with long hair, which is quite bushy, but often naturally parted down the middle.

Mr. Mapplebeck's Leo, whose portrait accompanies this article, is the finest Newfoundland I have ever seen, exhibiting all his best points in proportion, without the short neck and weak back which are so often met with. He is by Windle's Don out of Meg of Maldon, and is a great grandson of Mr. Robinson's Carlo, a first-prize winner at Birmingham and Islington in 1864 and 1865.

THE REV. J. C. MACDONA'S ST. BERNARD "TELL."

The Landseer type of Newfoundland differs from the true type chiefly in the colour and texture of his coat. The former is always white with black patches, and the latter is more woolly, without the gloss of the true Newfoundland. He is also generally higher on the leg and more slack on the loin, giving a remarkably shambling and awkward gait.

THE LABRADOR OR LESSER NEWFOUNDLAND DOG.

This dog, also called the St. John Newfoundland, is described in the article on the wavy-coated retriever in the 2nd part of this book; and as his use in this country is almost entirely confined to retrieving game, he cannot be included among the non-sporting dogs.

THE ST. BERNARD DOG.

Until about twelve years ago, this variety of the dog was comparatively unknown in the British Isles, except on canvas. Landseer and Ansdell had repeatedly portrayed the majestic form and benevolent expression which have long been traditionally attached to this breed, and some few specimens have been imported; but their numbers were so small that it was rare to meet with an Englishman who had seen one in this country. About the time above mentioned, however, the Rev. J. Cumming Macdona determined to make the attempt to naturalise the dog here, and, with that view, twice visited the monasteries of St. Bernard and the Simplon, where his enthusiastic efforts were on the first occasion rewarded by the attainment of a dog and bitch, which formed the nucleus of his subsequent large and valuable collection, aided by subsequent additions from other sources. By his unwearied efforts and skill in breeding, the St. Bernard dog has now become so generally diffused throughout Great Britain that thirty or forty specimens are generally exhibited at each of our large shows; and these being the cream of the whole breed, it may easily be imagined that the milk from which it has been skimmed is in abundance.

In the year 1815 the old and true Alpine breed was reduced to so small a number that the monks began to fear it would be exterminated. This result was no doubt due to an accident by which several dogs were destroyed in an avalanche; but it was also to be traced to continued in-breeding, causing sterility or such delicacy of constitution as to end in early death. Consequently they determined to introduce a cross with the Newfoundland; but, as this did not answer, they procured a couple of bitches descended from the old strain, yet kept distinct from it, in other kennels, belonging to gentlemen residing in the adjacent valleys. When Mr. Macdona was at the Hospice they had recently obtained a noble dog, named after the celebrated Barry, and resembling him in colour and shape, from M. Schumacher, belonging to a strain of the old breed, but kept in the family of the Baron Youde for half a century. With the aid of this dog, the monks have been able to replenish their kennels, and there appears to be at present no necessity

for them to reimport dogs from Mr. Macdona's stock, which he promised to allow
them to do, if necessary, when he obtained his first drafts from them. In 1868
the monks gave Mr. Macdona a bitch puppy by this dog, which he named Hospice.
She was rougher in the coat and had more white about her than is approved of on the
Alps, and was probably on that account undervalued by them. He also obtained his
Monarque (a smooth-coated dog, brother to Barry), from the Rev. Mr. Dillon, chaplain
at Berne, who had him from M. Schumacher in the same year, having previously
imported his celebrated rough dogs Tell and Hedwig, brother and sister, bred by
M. Schindler, and with a pedigree derived from the original Barry, who died in 1815.
Mr. Murchison has imported Thor from M. Schumacher's kennel, and from the
same source Miss Hales' Jura also came. Mr. Stone's Barry and Mr. Tyler's Thunn,
said to be bred from a dog at the Hospice, and Mr Macdona's fine dog Gessler,
imported by Capt. Eastwood from Switzerland, but without a pedigree, complete
the list of the chief sources of the present extensive collection of dogs spread
throughout the length and breadth of the land—a very large proportion of which
are descended from those imported by the Rev. J. Cumming Macdona; but of late
years the stock of Thor have been in the ascendant, including Mr. Gresham's very
strong kennel chiefly composed of Hector, Oscar, The Shah, and Dagmar by this
dog, with the addition of Monk by Sir Charles Isham's Leo, but who, like his sire,
has too much of the Newfoundland type for my taste.

In this country the St. Bernard dog is only useful as a guard and companion,
being in fact chiefly valued for his ornamental qualities, in which his grand head
and intelligent expression, coupled with his massive proportions, render him even
superior to the bloodhound; though in the case of Hilda, given by Mr. Macdona
to Lady Frances Cecil, the St. Bernard has proved a very valuable deerstalker,
well known in the forest of Glentannar. In the Alpine snows the rough coat
is considered to unfit the dog for the work he has to do; but there is not the
same objection to it here; and, as it is far more pictorial in its effect, the rough
variety is preferred in England, as represented by Tell, Hedwig, Thor, Gessler,
Alp, Hospice, Jura, Hector, Oscar, Chang, and Menthon—the last a very fine black
and tan dog imported by Mr. Macdona, without a pedigree, and not showing all the
characteristics of the true breed, but still very successful on the show bench, owing
to his size and beauty of form and coat.

In order to understand the reason of this preference of the short coat on the
Alps, it is necessary to consider the work demanded from the dog. Every morning
during the prevalence of the snow-drifts four monks in pairs, each being attended
by their servants and a couple of dogs, leave the Hospice at eight o'clock, and
descend the mountain, one pair on each side. The dogs run on in front, often
having to clear the path of the snow, and enabled by their instinct and nose to
keep to it without danger of falling into the drifts, which are not cognisable by the
eye. For six hours the party daily remain out, continuing their search for
travellers bewildered and lost, the dogs in stormy weather keeping up a loud
barking, which is of course easily followed, and serves to instil hope even into
the breast of the dying. Stone refuges are built at various spots, and these

MR. MACDONA'S SMOOTH ST. BERNARD "MONARQUE."

are regularly visited, and their inmates, if any, delivered from death, which inevitably follows on long exposure to the cold of these regions. In their arduous struggles to reach these stations, the rough-coated dogs become matted with icicles, the weight of which seriously interferes with their efforts; and, as in the case of the over-coated colley, experience teaches that where active work is to be done, a short coat is the best. Sometimes the dog is required to follow a lost traveller by the scent which he crosses, and for this purpose a keen nose is necessary, and there is plenty of evidence that it is well developed. Mr. Macdona's Tell, whose portrait illustrated the article published in *The Field* in 1865, once tracked his master for sixteen miles in the snow, in which his intelligence was taxed severely to ascertain the mode in which the Mersey had been crossed, the scent failing him at the pier. Watching the various steamers as they came alongside, he visited each in succession, until by his nose he discovered the right one; and crossing over in that, and again taking up the scent on the opposite shore, he followed it for ten miles till he reached the object of his persevering search. Most of the St. Bernards will, like the Newfoundland, "fetch and carry;" and, in relation to this habit, an excellent story is told by Mr. Macdona of his dog Sultan, which shows their sagacity in a remarkable manner. This dog was employed regularly to fetch the daily newspaper from the village, and on one occasion he was engaged in this duty, when a Sunday-school boy, who had been previously allowed to play with him at a school feast, met him, and, presuming on the good temper shown by the dog before, tried to take the paper out of his mouth. Sultan at once quietly dropped the paper, to avoid a struggle, and jumped at the boy's cap, which he took off and held as the ransom for the paper. The boy, objecting to the loss of his cap, quickly made the exchange, and off marched Sultan in triumph with it to his master.

The two strains, rough and smooth, are considered to be distinct enough to require separate classes, but sometimes a litter is composed of specimens of each. Except in coat, there is little or no difference between them.

Having enumerated the principal specimens of the rough strain, I may now mention that Monarque, now dead (whose portrait accompanies this article, drawn by Mr. Baker from an excellent photograph), stands at the head of the smooth division—*facile princeps*. He was bred by M. Schumacher, of Berne, and was by Souldan from Diane, being own brother to Schumacher's Barry, above mentioned. In colour he was white and yellowish red, of immense size and substance, and with wonderfully good legs and feet. Until his death he maintained his supremacy on the show bench, being the winner of about a dozen first prizes at the best shows, besides those given at smaller ones. In addition to him, Mr. Macdona also possessed Victor, Sultan, Bernard (imported from the Monastery), Swiss, Jura, and Jungfrau, daughters of Monarque, and several others of lesser note; while Miss Aglionby's Jura (bred at the Monastery of St. Bernard) Mr. Layland's Le Moine, and Mr. Gresham's The Shah have met with a certain amount of success. But, in spite of the above list of grand dogs, as a lot the smooth-coated St. Bernards will not bear comparison with the rough in this country.

Amongst other noted breeders of St. Bernards of both kinds are Lady Emily Peel, Lord Lindsay (who purchased the cream of Mr. Macdona's kennels), the Rev. G. A. Sneyd, Mr. Gresham, Miss Hales, Dr. Seton, Miss Aglionby, Prince Albert Solmes, and the Princess of Wales, who takes a great interest in the breed, having at Sandringham several of Mr. Macdona's strain.

The following are the

POINTS OF THE ST. BERNARD DOG.

	Value.		Value.		Value.
Head	30	Size and symmetry	20	Temperament	5
Line up poll	10	Legs and feet	10	Colour	5
Shape of body and neck	10	Dewclaws	5	Coat	5
	50		**35**		**15**

Grand Total 100.

The *Head* (value 30) is large and massive, but is without the width of the mastiff. The dimensions are extended chiefly in height and length, the occipital protuberance being specially marked, and coupled with the height of brow, serving also to distinguish it from the Newfoundland. The face is long, and cut off square at the nose, which is intermediate in width between those of the Newfoundland and mastiff. Lips pendulous, approaching in character to the bloodhound type, but much smaller. Ears of medium size, carried close to the cheeks, and covered with silky hair. Eyes full in size, but deeply sunk, and showing the haw, which is often as red as that of the bloodhound.

Line up Poll (value 10).—Great stress is laid by the monks on this marking, which is supposed to resemble the white lace bands round the neck and waist of the gown worn by the Benedictine monks, the two being connected by a strip carried up the back. A dog marked with white in the same manner is supposed to be peculiarly consecrated to his work, and is kept most carefully to it. Hence it is in this country also regarded as a characteristic of the breed, but it is seldom met with in anything like a perfect state of development; Monarque being more perfect in this respect than any dog ever exhibited. Being, as I before observed, chiefly used for ornamental purposes in this country, there is no rational objection to the value apportioned to this point.

Shape of Body and Neck (value 10).—There is nothing remarkable about the neck, except that there is generally a certain amount of throatiness, to which there is no objection. The body ought to be well proportioned, with a full chest, the girth of which should be double that of the head, and half the length of the body from nose to tip of tail; the loins should be full, and the hips wide.

In *Size and Symmetry* (value 20) this breed should be up to a full standard, that is to say, equal to the English mastiff. Indeed, excepting in colour, in the dewclaws, and in the shape of head, the smooth St. Bernard very closely resembles that dog. He is generally more active in his movements, from having been more worked than his English compeer, who for generations has been kept on the chain.

Legs and Feet (value 10).—Of course, in so large a dog the legs must be straight and strong ; while the feet also must be large, in order to avoid sinking through the snow. The last point is greatly insisted on by the monks, who prefer even what would be considered here a splay foot to a small and compact one.

Dewclaws (value 5).—There is no doubt that the double dewclaw on the hind legs has in some way been introduced into the strain of dogs used at the two Alpine monasteries, but how it is now impossible to say. Both Tell and Monarque exhibited this peculiarity, as well as most of the dogs admitted to be imported from the Hospice. Gessler, however, who showed every other point of the breed in a very marked degree, had no dewclaw at all on his hind legs, and his son Alp, though out of Hedwig, sister to Tell, was equally deficient. It is very doubtful whether this peculiarity is sufficiently permanent in any strain to be an evidence of purity or impurity, and consequently its value is only placed at 5, making the negative deduction 10 when wholly absent.

The *Temperament* (value 5) of the St. Bernard is very similar to that of the mastiff—that is to say, if suitably managed, the dog is capable of great control over his actions, whether in the absence or presence of his owner. When kept on the chain he is, like other dogs, apt to become savage, and there is almost always an instinctive dislike to tramps and vagabonds. He is a capital watch and guard, and attaches himself strongly to his master or mistress.

The *Colour* (value 5) of this dog varies greatly. The most common is red and white, the white being preferred when distributed after the pattern described above. Fawn and white and brindled and white come next, marked in the same way, the brindle being a very rich one, with an orange-tawny shade in it, as shown in Tell, and in a lesser degree by his nephew, Alp. Sometimes the dog is wholly white, or very nearly so, as in the case of Hospice and Sir C. H. Isham's Leo.

The *Coat* (value 5) in the rough variety is wavy over the body, bushy in the tail, and feathering the legs, being generally silky, but sparsely so, on the ears. In the smooth variety the depth and thickness of the coat are the points to be regarded.

Mr. Macdona's rough dog Tell (dead) was by Hero (descended from the celebrated Hospice dog Barry) out of Diane. He was a winner of twenty-five first prizes at various shows between the years 1865 and 1870 inclusive. He was own brother to Hedwig, dam of Alp.

Mr. Macdona's smooth dog Monarque, afterwards Mr. Murchison's (also dead), was bred by Mr. Schumacher, of Berne, by his Souldan out of Diane. First shown in 1869, he went on winning numberless prizes up to 1873, being about equally successful with Tell in this respect.

THE DALMATIAN DOG.

Without doubt, the Dalmatian is a pointer when at home; but in this country he has never been used, so far as I know, except to accompany a carriage, in which capacity he is unrivalled. Our English pointers will follow a dogcart quite as closely, and I have had more than one which would occupy the place generally selected by the Dalmatian, close behind the horse's heels; but then they were accustomed to be taken out in the same dogcart to a distance from home, for the purpose of hunting their game; and, associating the idea of hunting with the presence of the dogcart, they clung closely to it, if not allowed to ride. Now, when I have treated greyhounds exactly in the same way, they have not shown the same tendency, but have lagged behind at a distance of at least 100 yards, although in better condition as to wind and feet than the pointers. This peculiarity serves to show that there is a mental capacity common to both the English pointer and the Dalmatian, and confirms the opinion that the latter is a true pointer, differing only in colour from the English breeds of that dog. So long as it was the fashion to crop the ears of the Dalmatian, the above resemblance was not so close in the eyes of the casual observer, as it was usually thought that the bull-terrier was the nearest approach to him in shape; but now that cropping is never practised the pointer type stands out clearly and prominently, and, saving the peculiar distribution of the black and white on the skin, the external differences are *nil*. But, whether or not this dog is by nature a game dog, in this country he has so long been confined to the stable that he is now pre-eminently a carriage dog, and he seems to care for no other occupation. Whether quietly resting in a stall or a loose box, or accompanying a carriage, he is equally content, and in the latter capacity he is jubilant, though, unlike the colley, he does not display his joy in barking at the horses' heads, but quietly and closely follows their heels between the fore-wheels. Most other varieties of the species soon tire of going long journeys on the road at a fast pace; but the Dalmatian perseveres year after year, and never seems to lose the zest which he originally displayed.

In spite, however, of the authority of Youatt, who states that " this dog is said to be used in his native country for the chase," the Dalmatian has always been included in our shows among the "dogs not used in field sports," and for this reason I have classed him among the watch dogs. In the time of Youatt, as would appear from the illustration given by him, the peculiar marking now insisted on was not so imperative; and it would be easy to find an English pointer almost exactly resembling his engraving in this respect. The colour of the Devonshire pointer bitch Romp, well known at recent field trials, very nearly approaches this standard, and, no doubt by a judicious selection from her puppies, a moderately good Dalmatian might soon be produced.

From the prevalence of the breed at the institution of shows, it is not surprising that a class was soon formed for it, the first being at the Birmingham exhibition of 1860; but on that occasion the dogs were so bad that, acting as judge, I withheld

Mr. Fawdry's Dalmatian Dog "Captain."

the prizes altogether. In the following year, at Leeds, a fairly good class appeared, and for some time after this the breed seemed to be rising in public estimation and in appearance; but latterly the colley has superseded it as a carriage dog, and, though some very fine specimens are occasionally exhibited, the classes, on the average, are badly filled. Mr. Harrison's Carlo was the chief prize winner until his son, Mr. R. J. Ll. Price's Crib, appeared at Birmingham in 1866, since which time the latter maintained his supremacy until 1874, when age had begun to tell upon him. In that year his younger brother of the same name, belonging to Mr. Hall, of Burton-on-Trent, beat him at Birmingham, and he retired from competition. Since then Mr. Fawdry's Captain has been the chief prize winner, his colour and markings being specially good. He was bred by Mr. Burgess, by Captain out of Countess; and, commencing at Nottingham in 1875, has since then monopolised all the first prizes at the London, Birmingham, and other important shows.

THE FOLLOWING IS THE NUMERICAL VALUE OF THE POINTS OF THE DALMATIAN.

	Value.		Value.		Value.
Head	10	Legs and feet	10	Coat	5
Neck	5	Tail	5	Colour	10
Body	5	Symmetry	10	Markings	40
	20		25		55

Grand Total 100.

1. The *head* (value 10) exactly resembles that of the pointer, but so long as the nose is cleanly cut under the eyes, and square at the point, great breadth is not insisted on, and there should be no flews. The ears should not be long and hound-like, but flat, thin, and vine-shaped, lying close to the cheeks, and rather smaller than those of the pointer. Eyes small, dark, and brilliant.

2. The *neck* (value 5) should be arched like that of the pointer, without any throatiness or approach to dewlap.

3. The *body* (value 5) must be moderately strong, but not heavy and lumbering; sloping shoulders and a muscular loin are imperative.

4. In *legs* and *feet* (value 10) the Dalmatian ought to be perfect, as his sole employment is on the road; very strong bone is, however, not demanded, as he has no shocks to withstand, and useless lumber of any kind is to be deprecated. However, straight limbs, united with elbows well let down, and clean hocks, form the *desideratum* in this breed. The *feet* must be strong and close, whether hare or cat-like; and the horny sole should specially be regarded as of necessity thick and tough.

5. The *tail* (value 5) should be small in bone after it leaves the root, and should be gently curved in one direction only, not with any approach to a corkscrew twist.

6. The *symmetry* (value 10) should be examined closely, and, if deficient, penalised accordingly.

7. In *coat* (value 5) this dog resembles the pointer in all respects, being short, without any approach to silkiness.

8. The *colour* (value 10) is either black, liver, or dark blue. Sometimes there is a stain of tan about the head and legs, which is not objected to. A clear jet black is more highly valued than black and tan, the liver and blue being of equal value.

9. The *marking* (value 40) is the point on which the judging of this dog mainly depends, some breeders valuing it at 50 out of the 100. I cannot, however, think that a well-marked cripple should prevail over a moderately well-marked dog perfect in all other respects, and I have consequently lowered the valuation of this point to 40. In no case should there be a black patch on any part of the body or head exceeding the size of half a crown, and the nearer the spots approach to the size intermediate between a shilling and half a crown, and to the circular shape, the higher the estimate made. None should be smaller (if possible) than the shilling; but no dog has ever yet appeared without a few such "flecks" or "freckles." A well-spotted tail is greatly admired, but it is very rarely met with. The white ground should be quite distinct from the spots, without any approach to freckles on it, and the more regularly the spots are distributed the better. It is usual to divide the valuation of the several qualities in the markings as follows: Size, 15; shape and well-defined edges, 15; regular distribution so as to avoid patches of white, 10.

COLLEY DOOM.—MR. M. SKINNER'S "VERO" AND MR. H. MAPPLEBECK'S "FAM."

BOOK II.
SHEEP AND CATTLE DOGS.

CHAPTER I.
THE COLLEY AND OTHER SHEEPDOGS.

THE COLLEY DOG.

WHENEVER a serious controversy occurs in relation to the general character of any breed of our domestic animals, or to any peculiarity said to exist in it, there is often strong reason to conclude that the arguments *pro* and *con.* are founded upon unsubstantial premises. It happens in canine matters, as in most others, that facts are sometimes invented to support a theory which has been previously evolved out of the author's inner consciousness, the theory itself owing its birth to a desire on the part of its inventor to explain the existence of some peculiarity connected with a bantling belonging to himself, either in the shape of an individual or a breed. For example, some years ago that good sportsman, the late Mr. Lang, introduced a strain of lemon and white pointers, which was taken up so successfully by Mr. Whitehouse that he gained nearly every prize in the medium-sized classes of our shows. Straightway several of those who have possessed themselves of one or two of the colour contended that it was in itself a proof of high breeding; but, I am happy to say, neither Mr. Lang nor Mr. Whitehouse was of that opinion, both of them resorting to a liver and white dog when they wanted a cross, and one of that colour happened to be the best at their command. Time has shown the propriety of that decision, and good judges of the breed now accept either colour without scruple. In all breeds of dogs which are useful to man there are certain attributes which are essential to the full development of their powers in the right direction, and by these attributes it is easy to estimate any animal of the breed under consideration. Thus a greyhound must have a form calculated to develop high speed, and for distances averaging somewhat less than a mile. A foxhound should have speed also, but united with high powers of scent, and stamina sufficient to carry him at a speed somewhat less than that of the greyhound for ten times the above

distance. Pointers and setters require a combination of these qualities in about
the same proportion as the foxhound; while the fox terrier demands certain other
qualities enabling him to dig his way to his prey underground, and "mark" him
there without injuring him to any serious extent. All these dogs are exposed to
the weather, but they do not stand about for hours in the cold and wet on a hill
side, and the sheepdog is the only one of his kind, except the water spaniel and
water retriever, whose trade renders it all important that the coat should be of a
texture to resist the depressing influence of rain or melting snow when exposed to a
strong wind. Hence it follows that, in addition to speed, stamina, and intelligence
which he requires in common with all the breeds I have named, the proper texture
of his coat for facing bad weather is the first point which requires to be settled
before we can estimate a specimen of the colley, and this attribute must be valued
accordingly in the scale of points allotted to him. In the Irish water spaniel, whose
coat is oily, and of a texture calculated absolutely to resist the entrance of water
into it, even when immersed in that fluid, the legs are clothed with short curls down
to the toes, and this point is of great importance to his resistance for a length of
time of the effects of wet. But he is always actively employed, except when used
for wildfowl shooting in a boat or in ambush, and even then he can protect himself
from the wind. The colley, on the other hand, is often for hours doing little or
nothing on a Scotch, Welsh, or north-country hill side after tramping through
melting snow or wet heather, and in him legs covered with short hair are a *sine
quâ non* on the principle which is admitted to apply to the horse. If that animal
is at grass he must have a long winter coat in order to resist bad weather; but
whenever he is to be worked and then exposed to the wind with his coat wet either
from sweat or rain, he is far less likely to take cold if clipped than if his full coat
is left on. Hence it follows that by the general consent of practical men a peculiar
coat is required on the body of the colley which I shall presently describe,
calculated to keep the whole animal warm, and especially on the neck and breast;
and in addition they have decided that the legs must be clothed with short hair
only, showing little or no feather as in the setter and land spaniel, nor even the
short curls of the water spaniel. This is the main reason for the objections which
are taken to the cross of the Gordon setter, which have been used with the hope of
adding to the beauty of the colley; and from the "toy-dog" point of view no doubt
it has that effect, imparting brilliancy and rich colour to the coat, but at the expense
of its texture, and also feathering the legs, though this last alteration is of comparatively little importance.

The whole variety included under the term "sheepdogs" approaches more
nearly than any other to the Dingo of Australia and the Pariah of India, which
are the only wild dogs now in existence; but whether the former are derived from
the wild breed and have become tame, or the latter are merely wild sheep dogs, I
do not pretend to say. My own opinion is that we know nothing of the history of
the dog sufficiently minute and reliable to identify the ancient breeds as compared
with the modern, and that our knowledge only extends to the proof afforded by
Roman remains that the greyhound and either the mastiff or bulldog, or a dog

intermediate between the two, existed in old Rome; while Arrian describes only three varieties as known in Greece, viz.; the *celeres*, probably greyhounds; *pugnaces*, mastiffs; and *sagaces*, answering either to our trick dogs or to dogs hunting by nose. But, leaving the history of the colley, we must now consider his present condition; and here experience has decided that he should either have a moderately long coat with a woolly undergrowth over the body, increased in length round the neck in the shape of what is called a "ruff" or "frill," and with very short hair on the legs below the elbows and hocks, or that he shall have a short hard coat over the whole body. A very long coat is found to mat and hold the wet, so as to tire the dog, while the short coat is well suited to the lowland sheep, and is even found to answer in some hill countries. At all events, there is no doubt that many good shepherds use, and have long done so, the short-coated colley; and he must therefore be accepted as typical of the true breed as well as the rough variety, and, except in coat, there is not much difference between them.

A great deal of discussion has also lately taken place in regard to the colley's proper colour and general appearance, and various descriptions have been given of what each writer considers the genuine breed, differing in every respect but the one to which I have drawn attention, which in almost all cases has been admitted to be essential. Some gentlemen, however, who have obtained specimens with beautiful but open coats of a glossy black, pointed with tan, have contended that this is the *desideratum*; and so it is for the dog, considered simply as a companion. Hitherto, however, no one has ventured to propound the theory that he is to be so regarded; and, until I find that a separate class is made at some one or more of our important shows for "toy colleys," I must continue to describe the breed from the shepherd's point of view, only—regarding any suspicion of a setter cross, and especially if shown in coat, as injuring his value for the reasons given above. Only those who have seen one or more of the public sheepdog trials (instituted about four years ago by Mr. Lloyd Price, and many of which have of late years been held in Wales as well as in England), or have privately seen these animals at their usual work, can realise the amount of intelligence displayed by them. In these trials the slightest sign from the shepherd is understood and obeyed, and even the exact amount of driving calculated to make the sheep go quietly forward to the pen without breaking away is regulated to a nicety. A curious case which a short time ago happened to myself would almost lead to the belief that the colley understands the meaning of a conversation between members of the human family. Entering the drawing-room of a lady who has a celebrated dog of this variety as a pet, I was met with the question, "What do you think of my dog—is he not a perfect beauty?" After looking him over as he lay on the rug, and with a desire to tease my hostess, to whom I owed a Roland or two, for her previous many Olivers administered in badinage, I replied very quietly, "Yes certainly, if he had but a colley coat and a little more ruff." The words were hardly out of my mouth when the dog rose from his recumbent position, seized one of my feet in his mouth, gave it a gentle but vicious little shake, not sufficient to scratch the leather of my boot, and then lay down again. There was no emphasis on my part, and not a word uttered by the lady until after the act was completed, when I need scarcely say that eyes and tongue told me that I was rightly served. Anyhow, it was a remarkable coincidence; but from a long knowledge of the dog I really am inclined to believe that G—— knew I was "picking holes in his coat," and resented the injustice accordingly. Possibly, as in many human beings, he prides himself most on his only weak point, being absolutely perfect in every other, and not much amiss there. But, irrespective of his obedience to his master's orders, the independent intelligence of the colley is very high, and it is interesting to watch him or some other sheepdog manage a wild sheep which is to be driven against his will in a certain direction. Very frequently the sheep turns round and stands facing the dog, and the natural expectation on the part of a spectator is that the latter would try by barking to make the sheep turn round and progress somewhere. Not so, however; such a proceeding would inevitably cause a "break away," and the course pursued is to lie quietly down and face the sheep. By this method in a short time the facing is changed to a quiet retreat, or sometimes to a slight backing, when the dog quietly moves a step or two forward and again lies down, till at last, by this kind of coaxing, the weaker animal of the two is quietly managed. In such cases a high degree of intelligence and tact is required which is partly innate and partly acquired from the shepherd by education. As a consequence there must be a due development of brain in the sheepdog, and there must be a disposition to learn and obey the orders given. So clever is the colley that he will not be imposed on for any purpose not evidently useful, and it is seldom that he can be taught to execute tricks for the gratification of idle spectators, although there is no difficulty in getting him to perform them once or twice to please his master. If exhibited beyond this extent he is apt to sulk and refuse to show off; but when he is wanted to do really useful work, such as is required for the shepherd's purposes, he is untiring, and will go on till utterly exhausted.

No other dog in this country is so constantly with his master engaged in his proper calling—taking the breed as a whole. Occasionally, it is true, pet dogs are as much so, but by no means universally, nor are they even then so frequently employed in carrying out their masters' orders. This naturally increases the intelligence of each individual and reacts on the whole breed; so that, independently of the constant weeding-out of puppies rendered useless from a want of intelligence, the superiority of the whole variety in mental attributes is easily accounted for. For the same reason, when the pet colley gets old and is submitted to the rebuffs of children or strangers, he is apt to become crusty in temper, and sometimes even savage; but he is always most affectionate to his master, and no dog seems to be more sincerely repentant when he has done wrong.

Within the last ten years the colley has become very fashionable as a pet, and his market price has risen from 3l. to 30l., or even more for animals good-looking enough to take a prize at our shows. For this kind of colley beauty of form and a brilliant black coat are the chief requisites, and these are greatly aided by the cross with the Gordon setter; that is to say, without any consideration for the purposes to which this dog was originally bred, and is still extensively used. The pet colley, not being exposed to weather, is quite as useful to his master with an open setter coat and feathered legs; while regarded from an artistic point of view he is more handsome from the superior brilliancy of his colour, and from the addition of feather. His ears, when thus bred, are, however, seldom good, being neither pricked like the colley's, nor falling close like the setter's; and this is the chief objection to the cross from the pet dog point of view, though no doubt it is and has been easily bred out by careful selection. Moreover, if a pet is wanted solely as such, the Gordon setter in his purity is a handsomer dog than the colley with a more pettable disposition, and it would be better to select him accordingly.

In Scotland and the north of England, as well as in Wales, a great variety of breeds is used for tending sheep, depending greatly on the locality in which they are employed, and on the kind of sheep adopted in it. The Welsh sheep is so wild that he requires a faster dog than even the Highlander of Scotland, while in the lowlands of the latter country a heavier, tamer, and slower sheep is generally introduced. Hence it follows that a different dog is required to adapt itself to these varying circumstances, and it is no wonder that the strains are as numerous as they are. In Wales there is certainly, as far as I know, no special breed of sheepdog, and the same may be said of the north of England, where, however, the colley (often improperly called Scotch), more or less pure, is employed by nearly half the shepherds of that district, the remainder resembling the type known by that name in many respects, but not all. For instance, some show a total absence of "ruff" or "frill;" others have an open coat of a pied black and white colour, with a setter shaped body; while others, again, resemble the ordinary drover's dog in all respects. But, without doubt, the modern "true and accepted" colley has been in existence for at least thirty years, as proved by the engraving published in Youatt's book on "The Dog," nearly thirty years ago, which, by permission of his publisher, was accepted by me as the proper type in 1859, in my first treatise on the varieties of the canine race. This portrait was, I believe, copied from a specimen in the gardens of the Zoological Society, who for some years after its formation possessed a most interesting collection of dogs, now unfortunately abandoned. Up to the time of the last Brighton show I had never seen a single living example of this type in perfection, but on the appearance there of the celebrated Vero in the show ring, I at once picked him out as not only the best in the class, but the best I had ever seen, embodying nearly all the points exhibited in Youatt's engraving, which severally I had previously met with scattered throughout various prize-winners, such as the Nottingham Cockie, the Birmingham Laddie, Mr. Lacey's Mec, and Mr. Shirley's Shamrock, Trefoil, and Tricolour, and since that time Mr. Shirley has again given him a first prize at the Islington Show of the Kennel Club. No doubt in point of beauty some of the above dogs would compare favourably with him, and notably Shamrock, but, taking every point into consideration, I consider Vero to exhibit the true type of the breed in all respects to an extent bordering on perfection, and as such I offer his portrait to the readers of the *Field*. Hogg, the Ettrick Shepherd, describes his colley, Sirrah, as possessing a somewhat surly and

c c

unsocial temper, disdaining all flattery, and refusing to be caressed; "but," he says, "his attention to my commands and interests will never again be equalled by any of the canine race." Such is the colley of the present day of the type I describe, and the colour attributed to Sirrah by Hogg was "almost black, with a grim face striped with dark brown;" and here, allowing for the language of a shepherd belonging to a class whose notions are likely to be indefinite in their idea of colour, the true colley colour is described with as much accuracy as can be expected. The black was a bad black, and the tan rather brown, not the rich tan of the Gordon type.

With this general description of the colley, I now proceed to analyse his points, the numerical estimate of which I allot as follows:

POINTS OF THE COLLEY, ROUGH AS WELL AS SMOOTH.

	Value.		Value.		Value.
Head	10	Chest	7½	Coat	15
Muzzle	5	Loin	10	Colour	10
Ears and eyes	5	Legs	10	Tail	5
Shoulders	7½	Feet	10	Symmetry	5
	27½		37½		35

Grand Total—100.

1. The *head* (value 10), which resembles that of the fox, should be wide between the ears, tapering towards the eyes, which are in consequence set rather close together. The top of the head is flat, and there is little or no occipital protuberance, and a very slightly raised brow; but the facial line is not absolutely straight. The volume of brain is considerable, and the skull looks smaller than it really is, in consequence of the amount of frill in which the occiput is embedded.

2. The *muzzle* (value 5) is very tapering and lean, teeth strong and even, and the muscles of the jaw well developed. The whole face is covered with very short hair.

3. The *ears and eyes* (value 5). The ears are small and pricked, but turn over at the top outwards and slightly forwards, with very short hair clothing them. The eyes are set rather close together, and somewhat obliquely, giving a foxy look to the dog characteristic of the colley in common with the Spitz or Pomeranian dog, which resembles him in many other particulars. They are of medium size, and generally of a brown colour.

4. The *shoulders* (value 7½) must be oblique and muscular, as the dog has to carry himself without falling over all sorts of ground, and often to stop himself when going down hill at full speed.

5. The *chest* (value 7½) is moderately wide, but should have the necessary volume in depth rather than width, on account of the activity required, which a very wide chest interferes with, giving a rolling heavy action unfitted for sheep tending.

6. The *loin* (value 10) is strong and very slightly arched, but not more than elegance requires. The back ribs are often shallow, and, if too much so, the defect should be properly estimated.

7. The *legs* (value 10) are all-important, both behind and before; they must be straight in front and well bent behind, all being of necessity muscular. The arms should be of full size both in bone and flesh, elbows quite straight and well let down, and the hocks powerful, clean, and low. On the hind legs there is often a double dew claw hanging only by the skin; but many excellent strains are without one, owing probably to their having been removed for many generations.

8. The *feet* (value 10) are long rather than round, but the toes are well arched, and the pads very tough and horny. A large flat foot is an abomination.

9. The *coat* (value 15) is, as before remarked, the peculiar feature in this breed; though I am sorry to say that, in my opinion, sufficient stress is not laid on this point by most of our judges. In the *rough* colley it should be shaggy and very thick, so as to create some difficulty in seeing the skin when the hair is separated by the hands with that view, the undergrowth being of a woolly nature, which adds to this difficulty. This undercoat is almost always lighter in colour than the upper, and even in those parts which appear black outside it has a yellowish or brownish tinge. Round the neck, and especially on its under side, the outer coat is greatly lengthened, constituting what is called a "ruff" or "frill," which is found in no other English dog, but is well marked in the Pomeranian. In the smooth colley the coat is short, hard, and very close.

10. The *colour* (value 10) most commonly met with is black and tan. In best breeds the black is seldom brilliant, showing the lighter colour of the undercoat through more or less, and often itself tinged with tan. The face, spots over the eyes, breast, belly, and legs below the elbow and hocks are tan, which should be of a reddish fawn rather than deep red tinge. The under side of the tail is also tinged with this colour. In the smooth colley the black is generally deeper and richer, but the tan should be of the same tinge and extent. A mottled strain, one of which I have selected as the type of the smooth colley, is highly valued in the North of England and also in Wales. A good deal of white is met with in some strains, and sometimes the tan is altogether absent, but, *cæteris paribus*, a black and tan colour without much white is highly preferred. In both varieties the whole body is sometimes tan, or tan mixed with white.

11. The *tail* (value 5) is bushy, and always has a decided curl in it. As described by Burns:

> His gaucie tail wi' upward curl,
> Hung ower his hurdies wi' a swurl,

being carried gaily, though not over the back, as in the Spitz.

12. In *symmetry* (value 5) the colley is fully up to the average dog, or perhaps above it, and artistically he is much admired.

Both Vero and Fan are without any reliable pedigree.

THE BOB-TAILED SHEEPDOG.

Until within the last half-century sheepdogs without tails were exempt from taxation, it being supposed that no one would keep a tailless dog who could afford to pay the tax. As a consequence, almost every sheepdog had his tail cut off, and owing to this cause the tailless sheepdog, still met with in some localities, is supposed to have arisen. Bob-tailed pointers, however, were at one time not uncommon, though their tails never were cut short, fashion only leading to their being cropped to the same extent as our fox terriers and spaniels, among whom I never heard of a bob-tailed strain. It is far more probable that the bob is derived from a cross with the bulldog, which is subject to the natural loss of tail in a greater or less degree, and was probably used to give courage to the pointer, as was known to be done with the greyhound, and also to the drover's dog, to which class the "bob-tails" belong, rather than to the sheepdogs. Usually these "bobs" are strongly made and symmetrical dogs, but without any definite type; they have frequently a tendency to the brindle colour, which favours the theory of the derivation of short tails from the bulldog, though it cuts equally against a similar derivation in the pointer, in whom the brindle is absolutely unknown. Not being able to arrive at any definite type of the "bob-tail," I shall not attempt to describe him. He has the peculiar habit of running over the backs of sheep when in flock in order to head them, and on that account is highly valued for fairs and markets.

CHAPTER II.

THE POMERANIAN OR SPITZ DOG; ALSO CALLED LOUP-LOUP.

WITHIN the last twenty years this dog has been largely imported from Germany and France, in addition to those bred in this country; but, nevertheless, he has not become so general a favourite as was expected, owing in some measure to the fashion of the day tending towards the fox terrier and colley, and also to the temper of the Spitz, which is too short and snappish to make him fit to be trusted with children. It is true that the colley has the same disposition, but not quite to the same extent; and, being a better traveller with horses and carriages, he is more suited to act as a companion in country rides and drives than his more delicate rival.

MRS. M. E. PROSSER'S POMERANIAN DOG "JOE."

Whatever may be the cause, it cannot be denied that the colley is the more general favourite; and at our large dog shows, while his classes are filled by scores, those of the Pomeranian dog are only made up of units.

In his native country the Pomeranian dog is employed as a sheep dog, for which he is fitted by his peculiarly woolly coat and ample frill, rendering him to a great degree proof against wet and cold. Like the colley, he is impatient of control in playing tricks, and indeed can seldom be taught to display them even for a time, his intelligence not being of a very high order—at all events, if the attempt is made in any direction but that of his peculiar calling, for which, as far as I know, he has never been employed in this country. But he is always cheerful in the house, generally free from smell either of coat or breath, and readily taught to be cleanly in all his habits. He has not the fondness for game generally exhibited by the colley, and on that account is more suited to be a ladies' pet, nor is he so pugnacious as that dog, being as a rule inclined to run away rather than fight, when the choice lies between those alternatives. From these peculiarities it may be gathered that he is quite up to the average in his fitness to fill the position of companion.

The following are the generally recognised points of this dog, though hitherto no attempt has been made to define them:

POINTS OF THE POMERANIAN DOG.

	Value.		Value.		Value.
Head	10	Chest	5	Coat	15
Muzzle	5	Loin	10	Colour	15
Ears and eyes	5	Legs	10	Tail	5
Shoulders	5	Feet	10	Symmetry	5
	25		**35**		**40**

Grand Total, 100.

1. The *head* (value 10) is very wide between the ears, and tapers towards the eyes still more than in the colley, resembling the head of the fox almost exactly. Upper surface flat, with a slight furrow down the middle. There is a marked occipital protuberance, but not so much pronounced as in some breeds. Brow sufficiently raised to prevent a straight line.

2. The *muzzle* (value 5) tapers from the cheeks, which are wide, to the point of the nose, which is very fine and fox-like. The tip should be black. Lower jaw generally shorter than the upper.

3. *Ears* and *eyes* (value 5).—The *ears* must be small and pricked, resembling those of the fox in shape, and only very slightly exceeding them in size. A large ear is a great defect, even if properly pricked. The *eyes* rather large, and generally of a dark brown or hazel colour. Eyelids generally set obliquely.

4. The *shoulders* (value 5) are greatly hidden by the frill, but they must be oblique and muscular.

5. *Chest* (value 5) round, and rather deep; but the back ribs are generally very short, leading to a nipped loin.

6. The *loin* (value 10), owing to the above cause, is often weak if examined carefully beneath the thick coat, which conceals this defect.

7. The *legs* (value 10) are generally straight and strong, with elbows well let down, and clean hocks. Any defect therefore in these points will be severely penalised.

8. The *feet* (value 10) are cat-like, and rather small; toes well arched; but the soles are apt to be thin and unfit for road work.

9. The *coat* (value 15) is of a peculiar texture, differing from that of all other dogs in its resemblance to coarse fur rather than hair. It is so marked in this respect that the under-coat, which exists as in the colley, can scarcely be distinguished from it. The frill is of the same character, but rather more hairy in the texture of its long fibres. It is quite as full as in the colley, in the best specimens, and when deficient should be estimated accordingly. In the black varieties the coat is more hairy, and has even a tendency to be silky. In the best strains the coat stands out uniformly from the body like that of the fox or cat, without any disposition to collect in flecks or wavy curls. The fore legs are slightly feathered, but the hind are quite clean. The face is quite bare of all but very short hair.

10. The *colour* (value 15) should be a dead flake white, without any mixture of yellow. A patch of fawn is often to be seen on the head or body, but it is very objectionable. There is a black variety highly prized in Germany, though apparently the produce of a cross, as the texture of coat and size of ears are very different from the best specimens of the white breed. A red strain, closely resembling the fox in texture of coat, and in all respects but the tail, is also met with occasionally on the continent of Europe. This strain is in all respects like the Chinese sheepdog, of which many specimens exist in England, and one or two of them usually go to make up the foreign class in our large shows.

11. The *tail* (value 5) is tightly curled over the back, shaggy, and rather short than otherwise.

12. In *symmetry* (value 5) this dog equals most of his compeers, all his several component parts being in good proportion.

The specimen I have selected for illustration is only of average perfection in the shape of body and head, but his coat is highly characteristic of the true breed. He took the first prize at the late Islington Show of the Kennel Club.

BOOK III.

TERRIERS

(OTHER THAN FOX AND TOY).

CHAPTER I.

NONDESCRIPT TERRIERS.

SINCE the first edition of this book was published, a considerable change has taken place in the type of several of the terrier family. At that time the Yorkshire terrier was represented by an animal only slightly differing from the old Scotch dog, his shape being nearly exactly the same, and his coat differing simply in being more silky. Such an animal was Mr. Spink's Bounce as introduced in the accompanying engraving, and by comparing his portrait with that of Mrs. Foster's Huddersfield Ben, illustrating the article on the Yorkshire terrier, it will readily be seen that a great development of coat has been accomplished in the latter; and, indeed, that except in colour there is a vast difference between the two. A *fac-simile* of Bounce would have a faint chance of taking a prize even in a small show, under the present state of canine law, whether exhibited as a Yorkshire "blue tan," or simply as a broken-haired terrier; and though the strain to which he belongs is common enough, it can scarcely be considered as anything but nondescript. So also with the type represented by Mr. Radclyffe's Rough; many such dogs are scattered about through England and Wales, but they have no *locus standi* on the show bench; and, as Mr. Radclyffe himself found by experience, it is useless to exhibit them if successful prize-taking is the aim of their owners. "Rough" took my fancy greatly when shown unsuccessfully at Islington in 1865, and I have understood that the breed is remarkably game and excellent as a vermin killer. Mr. Pearce's Venture represents what is now called the rough fox terrier, but formerly known as the white Scotch terrier; and, lastly, Mr. Fitter's Dandy is of the old-fashioned black and tan English breed which still keeps its place on the show bench, being commonly, though without good reason, denominated the Manchester terrier. The small English white terrier formerly bred in large numbers by Mr. White of Clapham, has developed into a larger dog, and has now exactly the same points as the black and tan. Having a separate class allotted to him at Birmingham and the Kennel

Club Shows, I have added his portrait to the series, but it is scarcely necessary, inasmuch as the points are identical with those of the black and tan as above mentioned.

Having thus cursorily alluded to the various nondescripts, I must now address myself first to the special breeds of rough terriers, known as (1) The Skye (drop and prick eared); (2) The Dandie; (3) The Bedlington; (4) The Yorkshire; (5) The Irish; and afterwards to the smooth strains, including (1) The black and tan; (2) The white; and (3) The bull terrier; omitting the toy terrier, which will be considered in a separate chapter, and the fox terrier which has been included in the sporting division.

CHAPTER II.

SPECIAL BREEDS OF ROUGH TERRIERS.

THE SKYE (DROP AND PRICK EARED)—THE DANDIE DINMONT—THE BEDLINGTON—THE YORKSHIRE—THE IRISH TERRIERS.

THE SKYE TERRIER.

FOLLOWING the plan which I have adopted throughout the present series of articles, I shall not pretend to ascertain what was the original type of the Skye Terrier, as bred in the island to which he owes his name, but shall describe him as he is now usually exhibited at our various shows. The peculiar length of body, and long coat incidental to the breed, are said to have been introduced into it by means of some Spanish white dogs, which were on board a ship belonging to the Spanish Armada, wrecked on the coast of the Island of Skye, but, like many other "doggy sayings" there does not appear to be much foundation for the statement. All that can be ascertained on reliable evidence about this breed, is that it has existed in some shape or other for many years on the west coast of Scotland, and the adjacent islands, but as to the definite strains recently described by Mr. J. Gordon Murray under the various names of "Mogstads," "Drynocks," and "Camusennaries," I confess I am not a little sceptical. In any case it is premature to attempt a description of them until some further evidence is afforded, which has not yet appeared, although his article and portrait of a specimen brought by him to London appeared several months ago,—and if the likeness is a good one a very ugly brute he is.

MR. MARTIN'S PRICK-EARED SKYE TERRIER.

MR. RUSSELL ENGLAND'S DROP-EARED SKYE TERRIER "LADDIE."

The Skye as known to the frequenters of our shows, is a low weasel-like dog, whether possessed of drop or prick ears, but the former variety is considerably longer than the latter, and more elegant in shape; for this reason he is more popular in the south, where until recently he was very fashionable as a ladies' pet, in which capacity however he is now superseded by the dachshund, fox terrier, or colley. Without any further reference to Mr. Gordon Murray's type, I shall describe this breed under its two recognised varieties, the drop-eared and prick-eared, merely remarking that though both are used, or said to be used in Scotland for the pursuit of vermin, in England they are solely bred as companionable dogs.

THE DROP-EARED SKYE TERRIER.

This dog is the longest of our native breeds, with the single exception of the turnspit, now almost or quite extinct. He is however rivalled in this respect by the dachshund, each being as nearly as may be three and a half times as long as he is high—when stretched out and measured from tip of tail to end of nose. He is a very good house dog, being clean and possessed of an even temperament, not nearly so quarrelsome as the Dandie, or the fox terrier, and although long in coat not at all inclined to be proportionately offensive to the owner; indeed, with the exception of the pug, the Maltese, and smooth terrier, I know no dog less objectionable on that score. To keep his long coat clean is, however, a troublesome task, as it is greatly inclined to mat when the dog is exercised on dirty roads, and if it is allowed to get dry when in this state, nothing but a long soaking in warm water and the careful use of the comb will get it straight again. This difficulty no doubt has operated against the more general adoption of the Skye terrier as a ladies' pet.

The following are the points of the Skye terrier :—

	Value.		Value.		Value.
Head	15	Symmetry	15	Colour	5
Ears and eyes	10	Length of coat	10	Carriage of tail	10
Length of body and neck	15	Texture of coat	10	Legs and feet	10
	40		**35**		**25**

Grand Total 100.

1. The *head* (value 15) looks large when the coat is dry, but when wetted it is found to be long and rather narrow between the ears, increasing in width between the eyes, with a flat skull, little or no brow, and a pointed nose. The teeth should meet level, and be very strong. Nose and roof of mouth black, or very dark brown.

2. *Ears and eyes* (value 10).—The *ears* are set on rather high, and are by no means large in leather, being barely three inches long, but the hair on them makes them look much longer, mixing with that arising from the head, neck, and cheeks. In this variety they should fall perpendicularly and close to the cheeks. The eyes are brown, varying in shade from a hazel to a dark brown. They are of medium size, and sharp in expression rather than soft.

D D

3. *Length of body and neck* (value 15).—The back is very long but strongly coated with muscle, and quite straight, the roach back of the Dandie being specially objected to. The neck also is long, and unless the whole length amounts to three-and-a-half times the height of the dog at the shoulders it is not considered sufficient, a greater proportional length being preferred. In spite of the great length of the back the ribs are round, and the chest barrel-like, the back ribs extending far towards the hips. Shoulders strong and often rather upright.

4. The *symmetry* (value 15) of this variety of the Skye terrier is very considerable, as will be seen by referring to the illustration retained from the last edition on account of the perfection of shape and points generally displayed therein.

5. The *length of coat* (value 10) on the body should be considerable, but should not be so great as entirely to eclipse all his shapes—and to touch the ground—the proper length is well displayed in the illustration accompanying this article. On the head it should be long, and over-hanging the eyes, and often so as to completely conceal them. The tail should be also well feathered, but not so as to make it look bushy or woolly. On the legs also is a certain amount of feather, without matting.

6. In *texture of coat* (value 10).—It is generally admitted that there should be a mixture of hard long and straight hair, with a soft and woolly undercoat. On the back the coat should be so straight and free from curl as to part naturally down the middle; and though this parting is usually assisted by the comb, it cannot be shown by this means if the coat is by nature full of curl, and of a woolly texture. But although the outer coat is hard and straight, the inner wool is so thick on the body that when wetted it prevents the outer from collapsing and adhering to the sides. On the head this is not, however, the case, and when wet it shows its shape to be very different from that displayed in the dry state. In many dogs brought from Skye, the coat is woolly throughout, and on that account it has been contended that this is the true type, but I have described it as approved of by all the best judges without reference to any other source.

7. The *colours* (value 5) most in demand are slate and black, or black with white hairs (grizzle) silver grey and fawn are not now so much fancied as formerly, but the former is certainly very handsome, and is in great demand for ladies' pets. It should always be tipped with black, and the fawn with that colour or dark brown.

8. The *carriage of tail* (value 10) should be low, not being raised above the back except under great excitement, when this defect may be excused.

9. *Legs and feet* (value 10).—The legs should be straight, and the elbows as well as stifles by no means out. The thighs are fully clothed with muscle down to the hocks. Feet round and well clothed with hair, but not overdone. There should be no dew claws. The height of the Skye should be about nine to ten inches, and the length thirty-five to forty inches, weight sixteen to twenty pounds.

The Prick-Eared Skye Terrier

Differs from the variety above described, in having a larger head, a shorter body, and usually a rougher coat. The ears should stand well up without any outward inclination, and they are only covered with short hair, which, like that on the rest of the head, should be silky.

The above description of the drop-eared breed is that of the type to which all ought to be compared, but it is not often that I have seen a specimen fully coming up to it. At the Birmingham show of 1865, however, the prize winner Laddie, whose portrait I now present to my readers, fully realised my ideas of the points of the Skye. He was exhibited by Mr. Russell England, Junior United Service Club, London, and was by a dog belonging to Mr. Daniel Cameron, of Lochiel, out of Mr. James's Lassie, his granddam belonging to his owner. He was a silver grey, with black tips to his ears and tail, and I have never since that time seen his equal. The portrait of the prick-eared variety is that of a dog belonging to Mr. H. Martin, of Glasgow.

The following letter in relation to this breed, will probably be of interest to many lovers of the dog.

"To the Editor of 'Dogs of the British Islands.'"

"Sir,—In answer to your request I may remind you of some letters which appeared in *The Field* three or four years ago, from Mr. Robert Jewell, Lydiates, Herefordshire, and myself, regarding the Scotch terriers. Our object, at the time, being to direct attention to the merits of this fine old breed, which, though plentiful enough forty years ago, has now become scarce, with the view of having it re-established.

" If I am not mistaken, there was a discussion in one or other of the London sporting papers on the same subject, twelve or eighteen months ago, which you may have seen. This, I think occurred shortly after the Inverness Dog Show of 1875, when the question was mooted as to what the Skye terrier *really was*, one party maintaining the silky, and the other the wiry haired Skyes was the original type. Both varieties were shown at Inverness, and it would be difficult to say which was the handsomest. I suspect the former had the most admirers. But be this as it may, no doubt should exist as to which was the original and true terrier. In fact the wiry-haired dog had been bred up for a *special* purpose, namely to hunt and go to ground after the larger kinds of wild animals, with which the Highlands of Scotland formerly abounded, while the soft haired, *blue* and *tan* as they are called, are the result of a cross between the old breed and the French poodle. At all events nothing could be more natural than to suppose, as some Skye gentlemen allege, that the sailors of a French vessel, stranded on the Skye coast, should leave some of these dogs with the inhabitants of the island. But, it is curious and remarkable, if this theory be correct, that the poodle should have *nicked in* so nicely with the native terrier. When I use the word *native*, I should perhaps mention that the wiry

Skye is smaller, and in other respects somewhat different from his congener on the mainland but not in any essential particular. In fact their pluck, colour, hair, hardihood and general contour are, and have always been, much the same, the difference of *build* merely arising from the desire to have them of a suitable size for hunting the *otter*, the only *varmint* of any consequence peculiar to Skye. Of course the cairns and caverns of that rugged seaboard afford the animals the best of shelter, while the inland fresh water lakes and streams, as well as the sea, yield a never-failing supply of food. I am informed hunting and bolting the otter from these fastnesses with a small pack of the *right sort*, such as those still to be seen at Waternish, in all their pristine purity, affords excellent sport.

"But while this is the sort of work for which terriers are chiefly used on the Island of Skye and throughout the Hebrides, it can be readily imagined, their duties were very different on the mainland, where fox, foumart, marten and wild cat, at one time abounded, and hence the necessity for breeding the mainland terrier of greater strength. It is but fair, however, to say these wiry dogs with their punishing heads—no matter whether small or large, prick or drop eared—could hardly be excelled for pluck, nose, and endurance. They had courage to face anything, and often paid dearly for their temerity, as the mutilated heads of the *heroes* I have frequently seen and heard of could testify.

"As I have already stated, the Skye type is still to be found pure on the island as well as occasionally on the mainland, but the latter, or larger-sized terrier, is now very rare. And what it may be asked is the cause of their disappearance and deterioration? The question is easily answered, namely, to nothing but *injudicious crossing*. After the cross with the poodle was *bred-up*, the "blue and tan beauties" became greater favourites; everybody praised them, and the hardy old-fashioned terrier was in due time completely superseded. The new variety appears even to have been credited with all the merits of the old, and, as a natural consequence, connoisseurs, fanciers, ladies, and even gamekeepers went in for the fashionable and pretty silky Skyes. So in this way the old breed, especially on the mainland, has been reduced to a parcel of mongrels.

"I have no doubt the circumstances of four-footed vermin having been decimated by trapping was another reason for keepers being less careful to breed courageous dogs. At any rate, such a thing as a good specimen, as I have said is hardly to be seen nowadays. After much inquiry I have only been able to discover the whereabouts of a few which have any pretensions to the original mainland breed.—P.R.L."

THE DANDIE DINMONT TERRIER.

No variety of the dog has caused such constantly recurring controversies as the Dandie. In the early days of dog shows the classes allotted to it were very badly filled, the breed not having largely penetrated into the south, to which, with the exception of the Newcastle show, and those held at Leeds and Manchester in 1861, canine exhibitions were for some years confined. In 1861 a class for Dandies was

Mr. J. Locke's Dandie Dinmonts "Doctor" and "Tib Mump"

first instituted at Manchester, the example being followed at the London and Birmingham shows of 1862, and since then none of the large shows have been without a prize for the breed. At that held at Cremorne in 1863, the first true Dandie shown (as far as I know), was from the kennel of the well-known breeder Mr. Aitken, of Edinburgh; but he was but a moderate specimen, and received a third prize only, the first and second being withheld for want of merit. A similar result occurred at the Agricultural Hall exhibition held in the same year; but at Birmingham the judges were more lenient, and rewarded Mr. Van Wart of that town, with a first and second prize for two specimens, both very moderate. In 1864 Mr. Hinks, of Birmingham, produced his "Dandie" at Cremorne, and took the first prize, Mr. Van Wart getting a second. Being the best I had then seen, and being again successful at Birmingham in that year, I took this dog to serve as an illustration of the breed, remarking, however, that his coat was too silky for perfection. In 1867 began the paper war on the Dandie, which has, with few intervals, been carried on up to the present day. Its origin must be attributed to the refusal of the judges (Messrs. Collins and Smith) at Birmingham to award any prize for want of merit; one of them describing what he considered the typical dog as having prick ears, among other points altogether foreign to the real breed as now admitted. In the class thus stigmatised was the Rev. J. W. Mellor's Bandy, who, though he would now stand no chance in an average class, had been placed first in 1866 by Messrs. Perceval and Hedley, and except in coat was fairly typical of the breed, though nothing whatever was known of his pedigree. This dog afterwards maintained a successful career on the show bench for some years, being opposed at Birmingham in 1868, and at the Islington Dairy Farm exhibition in 1869, by the Rev. Tennison Mosse's Shamrock, who only gained a second prize at the former, and a third at the latter. Shamrock has been kept well before the public ever since; but·his small head and weak jaws have told against him with most judges, those defective points in his formation being considered, with justice, as inimical to a very high position; and at the recent Dandie show at Carlisle, though he gained premier honours, he was only credited with 78 points out of a possible 100, and with the advantage accruing to him of the disuse of negative points, which, if employed, would have reduced him still more. He is no doubt a very neat little dog and of the true type, but, lacking the above essentials, he can never be regarded as quite first class. Of late years, Melrose, bred by Mr. Broadwith, of St. Boswell's, N.B., has been the most successful up to 1873, but Mr. Locke's Sporran with his son Doctor have since that year been established as the favourites of the various experts employed to judge this breed, and as I think, deservedly, until the last Brighton show, where naturally enough the immediate descendants of Shamrock had the best of it under the fiat of his owner.

Since my first acquaintance with the Dandie, pictorially and in the flesh, going back nearly half a century, a considerable elongation has taken place in the body as well as the ears of that dog. In the well-known portrait of Sir W. Scott, by Landseer, a mustard-coloured Dandie is introduced, which is said to have been painted from a dog then at Abbotsford, and which, as far as my memory serves me, exactly resembles one belonging to a friend of mine, brought by him about forty-five years ago from the Teviot district at considerable trouble and expense, the breed being then in high repute owing to the notice of it in "Guy Mannering" by the "Wizard of the North." With this dog I was very familiar in my ratting and rabbiting days, and consequently the impression made by him is, as it were, photographed in my mind's eye. Now this dog, like that in Landseer's picture, had a body considerably shorter than that of the typical Dandie of the present day, and ears little longer than those of a fox terrier. The only high-bred dog with such ears which I have seen of late years was given me as a puppy by Mr. Murchison about five years ago, being by Mr. Bradshaw Smith's celebrated Dirk Hatteraick; but, though possessed of every other essential point in perfection, it would have been useless to show him against Melrose or the Doctor on account of his ears, and I gave him away to a gentleman, who has him now in India, where he is highly prized. My impression is very strong that the modern Dandie is the result of a cross with the dachshund, by which the ears and body have been lengthened, and the tendency to crooked legs and wide chests also introduced. Mr. Murchison's Rhoderick Dhu when he belonged to me also exhibited a mental peculiarity of the dachshund, quite foreign to any breed of English terrier, in that he was incapable of being broken to leave a rabbit or fox trail at command. No punishment, however severe, could get him off it at such a time, and after breaking away into a fox covert, and killing a whole litter of cubs, I was obliged to get rid of him: and some years afterwards, in other hands, he repeated this offence, and was finally lost on a rabbit scent, which he would not leave. Nevertheless, he was at other times possessed of an excellent temper; but once put his blood up, either by the scent of ground game or a fight by one of his own species, and he was as completely beyond control as an excited bulldog. How or when the cross was introduced I am at a loss to say, but that it is there I am strongly of opinion. All the most celebrated breeders strongly maintain that they have kept to the lineal descendants of the original "Pepper" and "Mustard" immortalised by Scott; but I confess I have no great faith in such statements, knowing how completely every master is in the hands of his servants. This is the most probable explanation I can offer of the cross; but in any case I cannot believe that any terrier could be produced with points so unlike those of our indigenous breeds without the aid of foreign blood; and when I find all those points combined in the dachshund, the probabilities in favour of that dog being used are so great as to amount almost to a demonstration. In summing up these arguments, I may state in short that (1) I remember a terrier, forty-five years ago, reputed to be a pure Dandie, with comparatively short ears and body, narrow chest, and under good command. (2) Such a dog is represented by Landseer in his portrait of Sir Walter Scott. (3) No Scottish terrier has either long ears, or a broad chest combined with crooked legs, and an ungovernable thirst for scent. Yet the Dandie is asserted to be originally bred by Davidson of pure Scotch blood. (4) Such a combination is found in the dachshund. Now, taking all these facts into consideration, I think I am justified in coming to the conclusion which I have arrived at, not without long and careful weighing of the evidence *pro* and *con*, and in spite of the old theory that the Dandie was originally produced from a cross of the Scotch terrier with the otterhound, which would support the opinion that he always has possessed ears as long as those now met with in all the best specimens of the breed. At all events I have, as I think fairly, delivered myself of the arguments on both sides of the question, and shall leave the dachshund cross to be accepted or rejected, with the statement that in my opinion it is purely a matter of curiosity, and not of the slightest real importance. For, even granting the truth of the above conclusions, we must now take the dog as we find him, and a very game and companionable dog he is; generally under fair control, but almost always showing a tendency to have his own way. He is an excellent ratter, but apt to be severe on ferrets, from which he is not very easily broken, and in the case of such a temperament as Rhoderick Dhu's it would be useless to attempt it. This dog has left no stock behind him, so that I am not injuring the reputation of any living animal by the above remarks, which are only made in elucidation of what I consider a mystery connected with this breed.

In the following letter recently published in *The Field*, Mr. Bradshaw Smith denies this asserted elongation of the body and ears of the Dandie, and also of the dachshund cross; and, as his authority stands deservedly at the highest point, I insert it at length, though I confess I am not convinced on either of these points, as my memory is quite distinct upon the elongation, and is supported by the portraits of Sir Walter Scott's dog, which are easily referred to for confirmation:

"Sir,—If not trespassing too much on your valuable space I may here be allowed to show how I first became possessed of this historic breed.

"During my residence in Roxburghshire my fancy was greatly taken by several specimens I saw of this game little animal. In 1841 I bought the first Dandie I ever possessed, and since that date I have no hesitation in stating that more Dandie Dinmonts have passed through my hands than through those of any half dozen of fanciers. I feel myself competent, therefore, to give a decided opinion on the article penned by 'Stonehenge,' although it be at variance with his remarks.

"In the first place, it seems to me an entire mistake on his part that the Dandie Dinmont of the present day is longer in the body than formerly. My observation tends rather in the opposite direction.

"Secondly, a strong characteristic of the breed has ever been tenacity of purpose, and I have only known two of my dogs which could be taught at command to leave the trail of either fox or rabbit; certainly it would be a hopeless task to prevent a Dandie Dinmont from engaging with a fox were an opportunity to offer. I consider the animal as naturally good-tempered, but when once roused he is ready to seize hold of anything within reach. When I first kept these dogs I was ignorant of their extremely excitable nature, and had many killed from time to time in fights, either in the kennels or at the entrance of rabbit holes; in short, when once their blood is fairly up they become utterly unmanageable. On this account for years past (though I keep a number) I do not allow more than one dog and one bitch in a kennel, but sometimes a dog and two bitches if very harmonious.   The first I had worried, many years ago, was a beautiful little fellow 14lb. weight, bred by Mr. Kerss (Bowhill), from a sister of Stoddart's old Dandie and his own old Pepper.   He was killed in the night time by another of my dogs, to my great annoyance.   When I mentioned the circumstance to Mr. Kerss, he informed me that during the time the little animal belonged to him he had worried some of his, amongst the number a Newfoundland pup six months old.   Yet it is by no means always the most excitable and pugnacious animal that stands the severe test, viz., to face alone two badgers at once, and fasten upon one of them whilst the other in turn attacks him, as I have known very many do.   For my part, I prefer the dog who encounters his antagonist coolly and without any fuss.

   " In conclusion, I annex a list of the kennels I purchased, viz., that of Mr. Somner (including his crack dog Shem), those of Messrs Purves, Frain, M'Dougald (including his famous Old Mayday), J. Stoddart (who sold to me his celebrated Old Dandie), and many other Dandies from Mr. Milne, of Faldonside, bred from his famous Old Jenny, from Mr. Jas. Kerss (Bowhill), and likewise from the Haining, near Selkirk.   From these ancestors my dogs are purely and lineally descended.

   " Apologising for having occupied so much of your columns,

                                          " E. Bradshaw Smith."
" Zürich, Switzerland, November, 1877.

   The accepted history of the Dandie is on this wise.   Early in the present century a Scottish tenant farmer named Davidson, possessed a breed of terriers for which he was so famous, that Sir Walter Scott introduced him into "Guy Mannering," under the name of Dandie Dinmont, and as a consequence his own dogs became celebrated wherever the English language was spoken, and the terriers were henceforward known by the name assumed in the novel.   Davidson and his neighbour, Mr. Somner, of West Morriston, near Kelso, bred great numbers of Dandies to meet the demand created by Scott and the breed gradually spread, the Duke of Buccleuch and Sir G. Douglas adding to their *prestige* by each obtained a supply, which they kept up for some years in great purity.   Mr. Stoddart, of Selkirk ; Mr. Milne, of Faldonside ; Mr. Frain, of the Trews ; Mr. M'Dougall, of Cessford ; Mr. Nisbit, of Rumbleton ; Dr. Brown, of Melrose ; Mr. Hugh Purvis, of Leaderfoot ; Mr. Aitken, of Edinburgh ; Mr. N. Milne, of Faldonside ; and last, but not least, Mr. Bradshaw Smith, of Ecclefechan, also obtained the breed ; and to one or other of these several kennels, all the dogs of the present day possessed of a pedigree trace their descent.   Mr. Bradshaw Smith bought most of his dogs from Mr. Somner about thirty-five years ago, in consequence of the latter exchanging country for a town life, the list of kennels purchased being given above by himself.   These several strains, crossed with great care by Mr. Bradshaw Smith, have kept him "at the head of the poll" for many years and "from Mr. Bradshaw Smith's kennel" is always a certificate of high merit.

   In order to set at rest the contested points of this breed, a club was established about two years ago, and they speedily appointed a committee to draw up a scale of points, with which I fully agree, and which were afterwards circulated, and revised at a general meeting of the club. They are as follows:

POINTS OF THE DANDIE DINMONT AS SETTLED BY THE D.D. CLUB.

	Value.		Value.		Value.
Head	10	Body	20	Colour	5
Eyes	5	Tail	5	Size and weight	10
Ears	5	Legs and feet	10	General appearance	10
Neck	5	Coat	15		
	25		**50**		**25**

Grand Total, 100.

1. *Head* (value 10).—Strongly made and large, not out of proportion to the dog's size, the muscles showing extraordinary development, more especially the maxillary. Skull broad between the ears, getting gradually less towards the eyes, and measuring about the same from the inner corner of the eye to back of skull as it does from ear to ear. The forehead is well domed. The head is *covered* with very soft silky hair, which should not be confined to a mere topknot, and the lighter in colour and silkier it is the better. The cheeks, starting from the ears proportionately with the skull, have a gradual taper towards the muzzle, which is deep and strongly made, and measures about three inches in length, or in proportion to skull as three is to five. The muzzle is covered with hair of a little darker shade than the topknot, and of the same texture as the feather of the fore legs. The top of the muzzle is generally bare for about an inch from the black part of the nose, the bareness coming to a point towards the eye, and being about one inch broad at the nose. The nose and inside of mouth black or dark coloured. The teeth very strong, especially the canine, which are of extraordinary size for such a small dog. The canines fit well into each other, so as to give the greatest available holding and punishing power, and the teeth are level in front, the upper ones very slightly overlapping the under ones. [Many of the finest specimens have a "swine mouth," which is very objectionable; but it is not so great an objection as the protrusion of the under jaw.]

2. *Eyes* (value 5).—Set wide apart, large, full round, bright, expressive of great determination, intelligence, and dignity; set low and prominent in front of the head; colour a rich dark hazel.

3. *Ears* (value 5).—Large and pendulous, set well back, wide apart and low on the skull, hanging close to the cheek, with a very slight projection at the base, broad at the junction of the head, and tapering almost to a point, the fore part of the ear tapering very little—the taper being mostly on the back part, the fore part of the ear coming almost straight down from its junction with the head to the tip. They are covered with a soft, straight brown hair (in some cases almost black), and have a thin feather of light hair starting about two inches from the tip, and of nearly the same colour and texture as the topknot, which gives the ear the appearance of a *distinct point*. The animal is often one or two

E E

years old before the feather is shown. The cartilage and skin of the ear should not be thick, but rather thin. Length of ear, from three to four inches.

4. *Neck* (value 5).—Very muscular, well developed, and strong, showing great power of resistance, being well set into the shoulders.

5. *Body* (value 20).—Long, strong, and flexible; ribs well sprung and round, chest well developed and let well down between the fore legs; the back rather low at the shoulder, having a slight downward curve and a corresponding arch over the loins, with a very slight gradual droop from top of loins to root of tail; both sides of backbone well supplied with muscle.

6. *Tail* (value 5).—Rather short, say from 8in. to 10in., and covered on the upper side with wiry hair of darker colour than that of the body, the hair on the under side being lighter in colour, and not so wiry, with a nice feather about two inches long, getting shorter as it nears the tip; rather thick at the root, getting thicker for about four inches, then tapering off to a point. It should not be twisted or curled in any way, but should come up with a regular curve like a scimitar, the tip when excited being in a perpendicular line with the root of the tail. It should neither be set on too high nor too low. When not excited it is carried gaily, and a little above the level of the body.

7. *Legs and feet* (value 10).—The forelegs short, with immense muscular development and bone, set wide apart, the chest coming well down between them. The feet well formed, *and not flat*, with very strong brown or dark-coloured claws. Bandy legs and flat feet are objectionable, but may be avoided—the bandy legs by the use of splints when first noticed, and the flat feet by exercise, and a dry bed and floor to kennel. The hair on the forelegs and feet of a blue dog should be tan, varying according to the body colour from a rich tan to a pale fawn; of a mustard dog they are of a darker shade than its head, which is a creamy white. In both colours there is a nice feather, about two inches long, rather lighter in colour than the hair on the fore part of the leg. The hind legs are a little longer than the fore ones, and are set rather wide apart, but not spread out in an unnatural manner, while the feet are much smaller; the thighs are well developed, and the hair of the same colour and texture as the fore ones, but having no feather or dew claws; the whole claws should be dark; but the claws of all vary in shade according to the colour of the dog's body.

8. *Coat* (value 5).—This is a very important point; the hair should be about two inches long, that from skull to root of tail a mixture of hardish and soft hair, which gives a sort of crisp feel to the hand. The hard should not be wiry; the coat is what is termed pily or pencilled. The hair on the under part of the body is lighter in colour and softer than that on the top. The skin on the belly accords with the colour of dog.

9. *Colour* (value 5).—The colour is pepper or mustard. The pepper colour ranges from a dark bluish black to a light silvery grey, the intermediate shades being preferred, the body colour coming well down the shoulder and hips, gradually merging into the leg colour. The mustards vary from a reddish-brown to a pale fawn, the head being a creamy white, the legs and feet of a shade darker than the

head. The claws are dark, as in other colours. [Nearly all Dandie Dinmont terriers have some white on the chest, and some have also white claws].

10. *Size and Weight* (value 10).—The height should be from 8in to 11in. at the top of shoulder. Length from top of shoulder to root of tail should not be more than twice the dog's height, but, preferably, one or two inches less. Weight from 14lb. to 24lb.; the best weight as near 18lb. as possible. These weights are for dogs in good working order.

Doctor and Tib Mumps, the originals of the accompanying excellent portraits. are the property of that well-known judge of the breed, Mr. Jas. Locke, of Selkirk. Doctor, who has won ten first prizes besides sundry seconds and h.c.'s., is certainly the most perfect Dandie I have ever seen, and richly deserves the high position he has obtained. Fully equal to Mr. Mosso's Shamrock in body and legs, he beats him completely in head and jaw; being, in my opinion, absolutely perfect according to the above standard of points wherein the full-sized car, to which I have alluded in them, is recognised as correct. He is by Mr. Locke's Sporran (son of Mr. Nicol Milne's Tug), out of Ailie by Shamrock.

Tib Mumps is almost equally neat with Doctor, and exactly like him in colour and appearance. She took the first prize at the Crystal Palace in 1876, Nell Gwynne being second; but at the following show at Birmingham their positions were reversed. She is by Mr. Jas. Locke's Dandie III. out of Mr. Patterson's Old Miss.

In corroboration of my opinions as to the change of shape in the Dandie Dinmont, I insert with the writer's kind permission, the following letter, published in *The Field* subsequently to the appearance of the article as reproduced above:

"To the Editor of *The Field.*"

"SIR,—I have read with pleasure the notices of late in your paper about Dandie Dinmont terriers. The description by 'Stonehenge' of the original dogs agrees with what I recollect of them more than fifty years ago, and I have kept them ever since.

"My school vacations were spent at the house of a friend near Kelso, and there I made my first acquaintance with a Dandie, Matcham by name. He belonged to Lady Diana Scott, Rosebank, Kelso, and, to the best of my recollection, in all respects resembled 'Stonehenge's' description of the old kind: an active, well-proportioned dog, with small thin ears close to his cheeks, straight legs and good feet, well suited for a long day's work. Matcham was fond of fun. The first shot we fired at rabbits brought him up to us, and he rarely left the door until we returned to Edinburgh. 'Lady D——'s' coachman was very wrathful at the absence of the dog; but the sport he got with the lads was so much more to Matcham's taste than following the carriage, that he was little at Rosemount, and enjoyed the rabbit shooting as long as he could, returning home, where he lived a quiet and respectable life till the next year's holidays brought back his friends. Afterwards I had several of Mr. Davidson's breed given me by my friend; they were all much alike in shape, and very unlike the prize dog of the present day. I was able to keep the old type, with fine eyes, small ears, and straight legs, until about fifteen years since; but the cross breed then came to me, and I have not been able to get back to what I consider the true one. I have seen partridges as well as ground game shot to a little pepper of the old sort; he pointed after a fashion, holding up his hind leg instead of a fore one. He was obedient to signs, and a wounded hare had little chance of escaping from him. He had a curious way of taking a wounded hare by the neck, and then lying on his breast close to the ground, and so avoiding the kicks of its hind feet. I suppose that was a natural habit in the breed, as I have seen a young Dandie treat the first cat he encountered in the same way—holding it by the neck and never rising off the ground so long as the cat lived. I think some of the prize dogs at a year old, would find 'a cat on rabbits fed' as much as they were able for. The old kind had fine tempers, not much given to fight; but I have had two dogs killed stone dead, in a private battle, although they had never been allowed to fight when there was anyone at hand to separate them. Having been so long in possession of Dandies, I was glad to see an accurate description of the old race, which to my mind were nicer dogs than what we see in the present long-eared, bent-legged prize ones. Indeed, the first time I saw them at a dog show the thought immediately occurred to me that these are not Dandies."

"ALEX. J. ADIE."

" Rockville, Linlithgow."

THE BEDLINGTON TERRIER.
BY HUGH DALZIEL.

Of all the varieties of terriers, not one owes more to dog shows than the Bedlington. Until these institutions came in vogue they were almost unknown out of their own district, having the strictly local habitation which their name imports; indeed, so much was this the case that, when first brought before the general public, and their merits and claims to long descent descanted on by some of their admirers in *The Field* eight or nine years ago, there were not a few to question their good qualities, and to deny them the right to be considered a distinct variety. Now no one doubts that they possess characteristics clearly distinguishing them from every other variety of terrier; nor would anyone, I imagine, now be rash enough to assert that a Bedlington could be produced in a few years by crossing certain other varieties, as was boldly stated in the discussion on the breed in *The Field* in 1869. The Bedlingtons, however originally produced, exhibit pronounced distinctive features separating them from all other terriers; and this is so thoroughly recognised that separate classes are made for them at all our principal shows.

The history of the breed, and the long pedigree claimed for them, are not quite so clear, resting, as they do, to a great extent on traditional evidence, which is never severely accurate in such matters. I have before me, by the kindness of Major J. A. Cowen, the pedigree of his blue and tan dog Askim II., pupped in 1874, which goes back to about 1792; |the oldest named progenitors being A. Evan's Vixen, by the Miller of Felton's dog, out of a bitch of Carr's, of Felton Hall. The

BEDLINGTON TERRIERS.—MR. F. ARMSTRONG'S "ROSEBUD" AND MR. A. ARMSTRONG'S "NAILOR."

pedigrees of Nailor and Rosebud, the subjects of our engraving, as furnished me by the secretary of the Bedlington Terrier Club, Mr. W. J. Donkin, go back through the same channel, claiming as the fountain head Old Flint, the property of Squire Trevellyan, of Netherwitton, the same date being given as the limit to which the breed can be traced. Granting, however, that these facts are correct—and I think there is very good evidence that they are at least approximately so, which is all that can be reasonably expected in such a case—there is no proof that Old Flint or the Miller's dog had the characteristics of the modern Bedlington; and I think, had there existed a breed in that district at the date referred to differing so widely from the ordinary run of terriers, we might expect to find some notice of it in Bewick, whose book was first published at Newcastle in 1790. But the terrier shown in his woodcut is a totally different animal, being a heavy, coarse, unshapely dog, with rather short and thick legs, the fore ones heavily feathered, a rough bearded muzzle, prick ears, and coarse tail turned over the back; and of terriers he writes: "There are two kinds, the one rough, short-legged, long-backed, very strong, and most commonly of a black or yellowish colour, mixed with white; the other is smooth, sleek, and beautifully formed, having a shorter body, and more sprightly appearance; it is generally of a reddish brown colour, or black with tanned legs, and is similar to the rough terrier in disposition and faculties, but inferior in size, strength, and fierceness."

Neither of these varieties, it will be seen, bears any resemblance to the modern Bedlington; and how this dog, as he is, was produced must be to a great extent matter of conjecture. If we go beyond the present century—or I might fix a much more recent date—there does not exist, so far as I have been able to discover, an engraving of a terrier with other than prick ears; and I imagine the Bedlington owes his hanging filbert-shaped ones to otter-hound blood, whilst his general conformation suggests a combination of greyhound and terrier. When once the properties desired—if the breeder had a design—were developed, they would be improved and fixed by selection; but, as often happens, the first real Bedlington, as we now understand it, may have been the result of haphazard breeding. It was not, however, until the year 1825 that the name Bedlington was given to this breed of terriers by Mr. Ainsley, the breeder of a celebrated dog, Young Piper; and this date gives some confirmation to the claim that the pedigree dates back to 1792, for Young Piper was by Anderson's Piper out of a bitch known as Coate's Phœbe. This bitch was brought from Bedlington in the year 1820, and given to Mr. Andrew Riddle, of Framlington, and subsequently passed into the hands of Mr. Ainsley; and as her pedigree is traced for four generations, and that of Piper, with which dog she was mated, for five generations, it is just barely possible that it might take us back to 1792. The names of the principal breeders before the Young Piper era were Messrs. R. Cowen, Rocklaw, Dixon, Longhursley, Anderson, Rothbury, and Edward Donkin, known during the first quarter of this century to sportsmen of Coquetdale as "hunting Ned." He was the owner of two celebrated dogs, Peachem and Pincher, whose blood runs in the veins of all our best dogs.

Before proceeding to give a description of the Bedlington as he is, I will put on record descriptions of these two famous progenitors of the modern dog.   Anderson's Piper was a slender-built dog, 15in. high, and weighing only 15lb.; he was liver colour, the hair being of a hard, linty texture; ears large, hanging close to the cheek, and slightly feathered at the tips.   Phœbe was black, with brindled legs, and with a tuft of light-coloured hair on the top of her head; she was 13in. high, and weighed 14lb.   This shows that more than fifty years ago some of the features peculiar to the Bedlington of to-day characterised their ancestors.

In general appearance the Bedlington terrier has little to recommend him; to strangers he must be known to be appreciated.   He looks lean and leggy, his flat sides, cut-up flank, and light thighs give him a starved appearance; in fact, as a rule, he is an indifferent feeder, and never carries much flesh; he has, too, in quiescence, a soft look, although when roused he is all fire; he is a remarkably courageous dog—deadly to vermin of every kind, from the rat to the otter and badger; rather too fond of a free fight, but not the vicious brute he has been described.   I may mention that the two dogs, Nailor and Rosebud, were in my keeping for two days whilst Mr. Baker sketched them; and, although I had never seen them, except a few times on the show bench, I let them run loose in the street and fields, and found them most tractable, under perfect command, and instantly obedient to voice or whistle.

The points are:—

1. *Head.*—This is long and narrow, and wedge-shaped; the skull, however, is not long, it is the jaw that gives the length, and in thickness it is a medium between the tapering muzzle of the English terrier and the broader muzzle of the Dandie Dinmont; the skull is high, narrow, and peaked at the occiput.

2. *Ears.*—These are filbert-shaped, lying close to the cheek, and set on low, leaving the outline of the head clear.   They should be slightly feathered at the tips.

3. *Eyes.*—In blue and blue and tans the eyes have a dark amber shade; in livers and sandy specimens they are lighter, commonly called "hazel eyes."   They should be small, well sunk in the head, and placed close together.

4. *Jaws and teeth.*—As already said, the jaw is long, lean, and powerful.   In most specimens the upper jaw is slightly longer, making the dog overshot.   The level-mouthed dogs are termed "pincer-jawed."   The teeth should be large, regular, and white.

5. *Nose.*—The nose should be large, standing out rather prominently.   The blue and blue and tans have black noses; the livers and linties have them red or flesh coloured.

6. *Neck and shoulders.*—The neck long and muscular, rising gradually from the shoulders to the head; the shoulder is flat and light, set much like the grey-hound's.

7. *Body.*—Moderately long, with rather flat ribs, low at the shoulder, especially in the bitches; arched light and muscular loins, slightly tucked up flank, deep chest.

8. *Legs and feet.*—Fore legs perfectly straight and rather long; feet large, furnished with long, strong claws.

YORKSHIRE TERRIERS.—MRS. FOSTER'S "HUDDERSFIELD BEN" AND LADY GIFFARD'S "KATIE."

9. *Coat.*—The coat is rather soft, about the texture of fine flax, hence called "linty," with a few hard hairs scattered through it; but a decidedly wiry coat is not orthodox.

10. *Colour.*—The recognised colours are blue, blue and tan, liver, liver and tan, and various hues of sandy, the lightest called "linty"; but this term is objectionable, as it originally referred to the texture—therefore, it would be better, to prevent confusion, to call them "light sandy" or "flaxen," as there are often special classes for this colour. The coat should be open and straight, but some are slightly curly.

11. *The tail.*—This should be of moderate length, 8in. to 10in., set on low, carried straight, or with a slight curve, not curled, over the back.

12. *Weight.*—This varies considerably, running from 16lb. up to 25lb.; but 18lb. to 20lb. is the most desirable weight.

I place the numerical value of the points as follows:—

	Value.		Value.		Value.
Head, including jaws	15	Teeth	5	Coat	10
Ears	5	Neck and shoulders	10	Colour	5
Eyes	5	Body, chest, ribs, loin	20	Tail	5
Nose	5	Legs and feet	10	Weight	5
	30		**45**		**25**

Grand Total 100.

The most successful breeders and exhibitors of late years have been Mr. S. Taprel Holland and the late Mr. Pickett, who was so well known in the fancy as to gain for himself the sobriquet of "The Duke of Bedlington." Mr. J. Parker, Mr. Wheatley, Mr. J. Stoddard, and last, though not least, the various members of the Bedlington Club.

THE YORKSHIRE TERRIER.

By HUGH DALZIEL.

This terrier is a genuine product of the county from which he takes his name. Undoubtedly a manufactured article, and the most recent addition to our varieties, he may be described as the newest goods of this class from the Yorkshire looms; with the greater propriety that his distinctive character is in his coat—well carded, soft, and long as it is, and beautifully tinted with "cunning Huddersfield dyes," and free from even a suspicion of "shoddy."

Visitors to our dog shows who look out for the beautiful as well as the useful cannot fail to be attracted by this little exquisite, as he reclines on his cushion of silk or velvet, in the centre of his little palace of crystal and mahogany, or struts round his mansion, with the consequential airs of the dandy that he is; yet, with all his self-assertion of dignity, his beard of approved cut and colour, faultless whiskers of Dundreary type, and coat of absolute perfection, without one hair awry, one cannot help feeling that he is but a dandy after all, and would

look but a poor scarecrow in dishabille, and, possibly too, on account of his dwelling
or reception room, in the construction of which art is mostly set at defiance, one
is apt to leave him with the scarcely concealed contempt for a scion of the
" Veneering family," who in aping the aristocrat fails, as all parvenues do ; such
as he is, however, there can be little doubt that should ever a canine Teufelsdröckh
promulgate a philosophy of clothes for the benefit of his species, the Yorkshire
terrier will represent the " dandiacal body ;" whilst, in striking contrast, those
every-day drudges, the Irish terriers and the Scotch terriers, with their coarse,
ragged, unkempt coats, will be exhibited as the " bog trotters" and "stock o' duds"
sects of the doggy family.

Although so very modern, it is difficult to trace satisfactorily the pedigree of
this breed ; indeed, pedigree he may be said at present to have none, and it is
hard to say out of what materials he was manufactured ; but the warp and woof
of him appear to have been the common long-coated black and tan, and the
lighter-coloured specimens of what is known as the Glasgow or Paisley Skye
terrier, the former of no certain purity, and the latter an admitted mongrel ; and
from which I think the Yorkshire gets the softness and length of coat due to
Maltese blood.   In shape this dog is in the proportion of height to length between
the Skye and English terrier—rather nearer to the latter ; a long back is objected
to, and was a fault found by many breeders with that excellent dog, Miss Alderson's
Mozart. As they are always shown in full dress, little more than outline of shape
is looked for ; the eye, except when the hair is tied up, is invisible ; the tail is
shortened, and the ear is generally cut ; when uncut it must be small, and is
preferred when it drops slightly at the tip, but this is a trivial point, and sinks
into insignificance before coat and colour ; the coat must be abundant over the
whole body, head, legs, and tail, and artificial means are used to encourage its
growth ; length and straightness, freedom from curl and waviness, being sought
for ; the body colour should be clear, soft, silvery blue, of course varying in shade ;
with this is preferred a golden tan head, with darker tan about the ears, and rich
tan legs. The style in which the coat is arranged for exhibition is beautifully
shown by Mr. Baker in the sketch of Huddersfield Ben ; but that stage of perfection is not attained without much time, trouble, and patience. When the pups
are born they are black in colour, as are pepper Dandie Dinmonts and others ;
at an early age the tip of the tail is nipped off to the desired length, the ears
if cut at all not until the age of six to eight months ; and before this the coat
will be changing colour, getting gradually lighter. To prevent the hair being
scratched and broken, little or no meat is given—all food likely to heat the blood
and create irritation of the skin being avoided ; and, as a further precaution, the
hind feet are carefully kept in stockings ; but, as "muffed cats are never good
mousers," so a terrier in stockings stands a poor chance against his active enemy
of the genus Pulex. Therefore, he should be kept free from these insects, and
once a week must be washed and carefully brushed until quite dry ; and to assist
the growth of hair, and keep it soft and from getting matted, it must be well
greased, cocoanut and other oils being used for this purpose.

MR. G. JAMISON'S IRISH TERRIER "SPUDS."

Of the oldest dogs of note of this breed were Walshaw's Sandy, Ramsden's Bounce, Inman's Don, Burgess's Kitty, and the celebrated Huddersfield Ben, represented in our engraving; and he, sharing the blood of three of the above, proved the best of his day, and there is now scarcely a dog exhibited that is not a descendant of Ben—his companion in the engraving, Lady Giffard's Katie, being also of his blood. Huddersfield Ben was the property of Mrs. M. A. Foster, of Bradford, a very large and successful exhibitor of this breed; the dog was bred by Mr. W. Eastwood, of Huddersfield, and was sire to Benson, Bright, Bruce, Bounce, Cobden, Emperor, Mozart, and numerous other winners at first-class shows.

The classification of these dogs at shows and in the Kennel Club Stud Book is confusing and absurd, as shown by the fact that some of the above, all being of the same breed and blood, are classed as Yorkshire terriers; others as rough or broken-haired toy terriers. It would be much better to divide them by weight, and classify them as large and small Yorkshire terriers. In assessing the value of points, shape, coat, and colour absorb nearly all. I would, however, give ten points for ears, and five for tail, and deduct points for cropped ears and docked tail; also for carriage of the tail over the back. There is no reason for mutilating pet dogs, and perfect tails and ears should be bred, not clipped into shape with scissors. Lady Giffard's Katie, in the engraving, has natural ears, and very good ones.

VALUE OF POINTS.

	Value.		Value.		Value.
Symmetry	15	Length of coat	10	Tail	5
Clearness in blue	15	Texture of coat	10	Condition in which	
Distinctness and rich-		Straightness of coat	10	shown	10
ness of tan	15	Ears	10		
	45		40		15

Grand Total 100.

THE IRISH TERRIER.

BY R. G. RIDGWAY, WATERFORD.

That the Irish terrier is and has been a pure breed of dog indigenous to Ireland is a fact undoubted and undisputed by the oldest fanciers and breeders still living, who can well remember this dog fifty and sixty years ago, and at a time before the introduction to this country of the Skye, Yorkshire, or English bull terriers now so fashionable in many parts; as a breed they are peculiarly adapted to Ireland, being particularly hardy and able to bear any amount of wet, cold, and hardship without showing the slightest symptoms of fatigue. Their coat also being a hard and wiry one, they can hunt the thickest gorse or furze covert without the slightest inconvenience.

No doubt this breed has of late years been allowed to degenerate sadly, from want of proper interest having been taken in it, but, notwithstanding this, we can still bring forward specimens of our Irish terriers, such as have been seen at several of our leading Irish shows, which for usefulness, intelligence and gameness as well as general appearance, are second to no breed of terrier in the kingdom.

As to their capabilities for taking the water, and hunting in it, as well as on land, I may mention as one instance, that a gentleman in the adjoining county of Tipperary has kept a pack of these terriers for years with which he will hunt an otter as well as any pack of pure otter hounds can.   Within the last few years and since the introduction of dog shows into Ireland, a far greater interest than heretofore has been taken in this dog, and consequently a greater amount of care is evinced now in selecting the proper specimens to breed from, so that in a short time we may look forward to see the *Irish terrier* just as fashionable and as much sought for in England as the English fox terrier is at present.

The following code of points represents the correct type, and such points are now agreed to by the several breeders, fanciers, and exhibitors who have given their signatures at the foot:—

Head.—Long and rather narrow across skull, flat and perfectly free from stop or wrinkle.

Muzzle.—Long and rather pointed, but strong in make, with good black nose and free from loose flesh and chop.

Teeth.—Perfectly level, and evenly set in good strong jaws.

Ears.—When uncut, small and filbert shaped and lying close to head, colour of which is sometimes darker than rest of body, hair on ears short and free from fringe.

Neck.—Tolerably long and well arched.

Legs.—Moderately long, well set from the shoulders, with plenty of bone and muscle, must be perfectly straight, and covered like the ears and head with a similar texture of coat as the body, but not quite so long.

Eyes.—Small, keen, and hazel colour.

Feet.—Strong, tolerably round, with toes well split up, most pure specimens have black toe nails.

Chest.—Muscular, and rather deep, but should not be either full or wide.

Body.—Moderately long, with ribs well sprung, loin and back should show great strength, and all well knit together.

Coat.—Must be hard, rough, and wiry, in decided contradistinction to softness, shagginess, and silkiness, and all parts perfectly free from lock or curl. Hair on head and legs is not quite so long as rest of body.

Colour most desired is red, and the brighter the colour the better, next in order, wheaten or yellow, and grey, but brindle is to be objected to, thereby showing intermixture of the bull breed.

Tail if uncut, carried gaily without a ring, and showing absence of feather and bushiness.

Weight of good working Irish terriers, varies from 17lb. to 25lb., in olden times I understand that they ran up to 30lb. and 35lb., but it is better to fix the standard weight as mentioned, viz. 17lb. to 25lb.

The following table shows the value of the points :—

	Value.		Value.		Value
Head	20	Muzzle and jaw	10	Back and loin (and general make of body)	15
Ears and eyes	5	Teeth	5	Legs and feet	10
Nose	5	Neck and chest	10	Colour and coat	20
	30		**25**		**45**

Grand Total 100.

Here follows the signatures and addresses of the exhibitors, fanciers, and breeders of the Irish terrier who have agreed that the foregoing code of points represents correctly the pure and true specimen :—

Signature.	Address.	If an Exhibitor, state Number of Prizes Taken.
R. G. Ridgway	Waterford	Breeder.
Geo. Jamison	Movilla, Newtownards, Co. Down	Breeder and Exhibitor ; 54 prizes.
Thomas Erwin	Ballymena, Ireland	,, ,, 1 ,,
David Wilson	Ballymena	Breeder.
Nathl. Morton	Brookville, Ballymena	Winner of Champion and other Prizes. One of the earliest (if not *the* earliest) Exhibitors, and Breeder for about 17 years.
Micke Dooly	Ballymena	Breeder for about 40 years ; Breeder of Mr. Morton's Champion "Fly."
William Moore	Ballymena	Breeder for many years, and Owner of many that have since won Champion and other Prizes.
Robert A. Simms	Newtownards, Co. Down	Breeder and Exhibitor ; 2 prizes.
T. Hutchinson Smyth	17, Trinity-street, Dublin	Breeder and Exhibitor.
Peter Tyrrell	4, Lennox-place, Dublin	Breeder and Exhibitor ; 1 prize.
T. M. Hilliard	Laburnum Cottage, North Strand, Dublin	Breeder.
C. E. Clibborn	Anner Park, Clonmel	Breeder and Fancier.
J. Crosbie Smith	Upper Park, Queenstown	Breeder and Exhibitor of several Prize Winners.
George J. Adams	Cork	Owner and Fancier.
John Frame	Comber, Belfast	Breeder and Exhibitor ; 7 prizes.
James Shane	Comber, Belfast	,, ,, 1 ,,
Thos. Jas. Andrews	Comber, Belfast	,, ,, ,,
James M'Entee	Newtownards	,, ,, 4 ,,
Edward F. Despard		,, ,, 6 ,,
George F. Richardson	Springfield, Lisburn	,, ,, 1 ,,
Robert Erskine	74, North-street, Belfast	,, ,, 1 ,,
William Graham	Newtownbreda	,, ,, 6 ,,
J. J. Pim	Lismagarvey, Lisburn	,, ,, 2 ,,
Geo. Glover	Sydenham, Belfast	,, ,, 3 ,,
W. Desmond O'Connell	Mount Vernon, Cork	,, ,, 1 ,,

The subject of our illustration is Spuds (K.C.S.B. 6846), lately the property of Mr. J. J. Pim, Lisburn, Ireland ; but we understand she has gone back to her original owner, Mr. George Jamison, Newtownards, Ireland. Spuds has won the following prizes :—Cork, 2nd prize, 1876, Mr. Ridgway, judge ; Newtownards, 1st prize and special cup for best in four Irish terrier classes, Mr. Skidmore, judge ; Brighton, 2nd prize, Mr. Sam Handley, judge ; Lisburn, 1877, 1st prize, Mr. Skidmore, judge ; Newtownards, 1877, 1st prize and special cup for best in two Irish terrier classes, Mr. J. J. Pim, judge ; Agricultural Hall, London, 2nd prize, Colonel Cowen, judge ; Bristol, 1st prize, Mr. Percival, judge ; Alexandra Palace, 1st prize, Mr. Handley, judge.

[The above is inserted at the request of several influential Irish breeders of this strain, the signatures being added in order to comply with the condition insisted on by myself to insure unanimity. I am still, however, of opinion that this dog differs in no respect from the rough Scotch terrier commonly met with throughout England during the early part of the present century.—"STONEHENGE."]

CHAPTER III.

SMOOTH TERRIERS

(OTHER THAN TOYS).

THE BLACK AND TAN TERRIER (OR MANCHESTER)—THE WHITE ENGLISH TERRIER—THE BULL TERRIER.

THE BLACK AND TAN TERRIER

(SOMETIMES CALLED THE MANCHESTER TERRIER).

BY HUGH DALZIEL.

HE Black and Tan Terrier has as good a right to be considered the representative of the old English terrier as any breed in existence, and probably a better one ; but not yet having been blessed with a club to protect his interests and quarrel over his pedigree, he has held his position—a very respectable one—in the canine world on his own intrinsic merits. His history begins long before Dandie Dinmonts or Bedlingtons were thought of, and his most distinguishing features had ere that been noted. Daniel, in his "Rural Sports," describes his "black body

MR. H. LACY'S BLACK-TAN TERRIER "BELCHER."

and tanned legs (thumb marks, bronzed thighs, and kissing spots had not then been invented), smooth coat, beautiful formation, short body, and sprightly appearance." Bewick copied Daniel, as several other writers have done; and since their time, through all the vicissitudes of dog life, and apparently without any special care having been taken of him, he remains essentially true to his prototype, with no doubt a finer and more polished jacket, befitting these days of dog parades. As he cannot speak for himself, I must say for him he has a strong cause of complaint against the Kennel Club; for in the first volume of their stud book, which chronicles the principal shows for fourteen years, he was simply and properly described as the black and tan terrier, "English" of course being understood; but since 1874 they have added to his title, "or *Manchester terrier*." The reason for this change I do not know, as the records of their own stud book do not disclose many names of eminent Manchester breeders or exhibitors besides Mr. Samuel Handley, who bred and exhibited some of the best that have been shown, and who is still generally recognised as one of the best judges of them; and, however great an honour it may be to be "Manchester," it is a greater honour to be English, and, so far as I can see, the change in name was useless and uncalled for, and derogatory to the breed. In addition to Mr. Handley, there were years ago the following celebrated Lancashire breeders: Mr. James Barrow, Mr. Joseph Kay, and Mr. William Pearson, all now dead; but the crack dogs now met with at our shows have generally been bred by unknown people, and brought out by astute judges and spirited exhibitors. In the early days of shows Birmingham took the lead in this breed, and Mr. G. Fitter, of that town, who had a good strain, held the first position for several years with his exceptionally good dog Dandy, which served to illustrate the breed in the previous editions of "Dogs of the British Islands." Of late years the most successful exhibitors have been Mr. George Wilson, Huddersfield; the late Mr. Martin, Manchester; and, more so than either, Mr. Henry Lacy, of Hebden Bridge.

This breed is not such a general favourite with the public as it deserves to be, for it has many excellent qualities to recommend it to those who like a nice pet that does not need nursing, an affectionate, lively, and tractable companion, not given to quarrelling, very active and graceful in his actions, and with pluck enough and a keen zest for hunting and destroying such vermin as rats that infest houses and outbuildings; for with larger vermin, such as the fox, badger, &c. (with exceptional cases), he has not the hardness to cope or stand their bites, nor has he the strength even of other terriers of his own weight, as he is formed more for nimbleness than work requiring power. His most ardent admirers cannot claim for him the courage and obduracy of attack and defence that characterise less pure terriers. As a house dog he is unexcelled, always on the alert, and quick to give alarm.

I am writing of the dog from 10lb. up to 16lb., not the small lap dogs of the same colour and markings, which are generally pampered and peevish, and ornamental rather than useful—which, when they do give tongue at the entrance of a visitor, never know when they have yelped enough, and have to be coaxed into silence. These latter are of two sorts: one with a short face, round skull, and full eye (inclined to weep), called in vulgar parlance "apple-headed 'uns," showing the cross at some time or other with the King Charles spaniel; the other type is the thin, shivering dog, that must be kept clothed, and sleep in a warmly-lined basket, his timid shrinking manner, spindly legs, lean sides, and tucked-up flanks showing the Italian greyhound cross. The weight of these two clearly distinct varieties averages from about 3lb. to 6lb.

The black and tan terrier proper is the most elegantly shaped and graceful in outline of all the terrier tribe; and, improved as he has been since dog shows came in vogue, he more than ever deserves the description Daniel gave him, being of beautiful formation and sprightly appearance. Taking his points *seriatim* they are as follows:

POINTS OF BLACK AND TAN TERRIER.

	Value.		Value.		Value.
Head	5	Neck and shoulders	10	Coat	5
Jaws and teeth	5	Chest	10	Colour	25
Eyes	5	Loin	10	Tail	5
Ears	5	Legs and feet	10	Symmetry	5
	20		**40**		**40**

Grand Total 100.

1. The *head* (value 5) must be long and narrow, clean cut, tight skinned, with no bulging out at the cheeks; the skull flat and narrow.

2. The *jaws and teeth* (value 5).—The muzzle should be long, lean, and tapering, with the teeth level, or the incisors of the upper jaw just closing over the under ones. The nose must be quite black.

3. The *eyes* (value 5) are black, bright, and small, neither sunk in the skull nor protruding.

4. The *ears* (value 5) are, for exhibition purposes, invariably cut, and much importance is attached to the result of this operation. It is required that the ears correspond exactly in shape and position with each other. They must be tapered to a point, stand quite erect, or slightly lean towards each other at the tip. This is a practice I strongly deprecate, and never miss an opportunity of protesting against; and I believe there is a general feeling arising against it; and among others who strongly condemn it is the best judge of the breed living, Mr. S. Handley. The supporters of the practice cannot offer a single valid argument in its favour, whilst there are many strong reasons against it. It is sheer nonsense to say the dogs look better cropped. It is not many years since people thought pugs looked better with their ears shorn off by the roots, but nobody thinks so now; and the practice as regards terriers could be effectually stopped by a resolution of the Kennel Club to the effect that no dog with cut ears would be eligible to compete at any of their shows after 1879. There is this practical evil too in cropping, that it places the dog with naturally defective ears

on an equality in competition with the dog born with perfect ears if they have been equally skilfully manipulated. The natural ear is of three kinds—the button or drop ear, like the fox terrier; the rose ear, that is half folded back, so that the interior of the ear can be partially seen; and the prick or tulip ear. But I have never seen the last-named kind, except in coarse specimens. The leather of the ear is thin, and generally finest in the best bred dogs.

5. *Neck and shoulders* (value 10).—The neck must be light and airy, well proportioned to the head, and gradually swelling towards the shoulders; there should be no loose skin or throatiness. The shoulders are not so muscular as in some breeds; but nicely sloping.

6. The *chest* (value 10) must be deep, but not wide; the latter would indicate a bull cross, which would also be shown in the head and other points. The body is short, the ribs rather deep than round, the back ones pretty well let down.

7. The *loins* (value 10) are strong and muscular, with this formation, there is an absence of the cut-up flank which the Whippet and Italian greyhound crosses give.

8. *Legs and feet* (value 10).—The former are straight, light of bone, clean as a racehorse, and the feet round, with the toes well arched, and the claws jet black.

9. The *coat* (value 5) must be short and close; it should look fine and glossy, but not soft in texture.

10. The *colour and markings* (value 25) are in this breed—which is now essentially a fancy dog—important. No other colour than black and tan or red is permissible; the least speck of white is fatal to winning chances, and it is in the richness, contrast, and correct distribution of these that excellence consists. The black should be intense and jet-like; the tan, a rich warm mahogany; the two colours, in all points where they meet, being abruptly separated—not running into each other. On the head the tan runs along each jaw, on the lower running down almost to the throat; a bright spot on the cheek, and another above the eye, each clearly surrounded with black, and well defined; the inside of the ears slightly tanned, spots of tan on each side of the breast, the forelegs tanned up to the knee; feet tanned, but the knuckles have a clear black line, called the "pencil mark," up their ridge; and in the centre of the tan, midway between the foot and the knee, there must be a black spot called the "thumb mark," and the denser the black, and the clearer in its outline, the more it is valued. The insides of the hind legs are tanned, and also the under side of tail; but tan on the thighs and outside, where it often appears in a straggling way, producing the appearance called "bronzed," is very objectionable. The vent has also a tan spot, but it should be no larger than can be well covered by the tail when pressed down on it.

11. The *tail* (value 5) must be long, straight, thin, and tapering to a point. Its carriage should be low, and any curl over the back is a fatal defect.

12. The *symmetry* (value 5) of this dog is of great importance, as this point is developed to as great an extent as in any other breed, not even excepting the greyhound.

Belcher, the subject of the illustration, is a three-year-old dog, bred and up to the present time exhibited by Mr. Henry Lacy, Lacy House, Hebden Bridge. He is considered the most perfect specimen of the breed extant.   First exhibited at Hull in October, 1875, he took first and special prizes, and has ever since kept at the head of his class, having been first at Birmingham, Alexandra Palace, Crystal Palace, Brighton, Darlington, Islington, Manchester, and a number of smaller shows. Belcher is remarkably well bred, being by Mr. Lacy's General out of his Saff II., both sire and dam going back to Handley's celebrated Saff by Gas out of Limie, and is therefore essentially a "Manchester" terrier. Mr. Lacy's dogs having been recently distributed, we understand Belcher is now the property of Mr. Tom B. Swinburne, Darlington.

THE WHITE ENGLISH TERRIER.

Although a separate class is made in the programmes of most of our large dog shows for this breed, under the title "terriers except black and tan," the difference between it and the black and tan is only one of colour.   In size, shape, and mental characteristics the two are identical, and consequently it is needless to repeat the description given in the article on the black and tan terrier, which will serve equally well for the subject of the present one.

In the early exhibitions of dogs, and notably at those held at Islington and Cremorne in 1862-3, the chief prizes were carried off by Mr. White, of Clapham, both in the small (or toy) and large classes.   His dogs, however, were very bare of hair, and in other respects showed signs of in-breeding, from which cause, probably, he did not continue to hold the premiership, Mr. Tupper and Mr. Hinks being first and second at Islington in 1864.   Mr. P. Swindells, of Stockport; the late Mr. J. Martin, of Salford ; Mr. J. Roocroft, of Bolton ; Mr. G. Stables, of Manchester ; and Mr. Skidmore, of Nantwich, have latterly been the most prominent breeders—those dogs exhibited by Mr. Shirley, M.P., the Rev. J. Mellor, and Mr. Murchison having been bred by one or other of the above-named gentlemen.

The originals of the portraits accompanying this article now belong to Mr. Vero Shaw, having recently been purchased by him. Sylph, by Mr. Stables's Viper out of Vic, is well known to fame, having taken first prize at Hull, the Alexandra Palace, Crystal Palace, Belfast, Fakenham, Darlington, and Wolverhampton. Sylvio (late Chance) is by Mr. P. Swindell's Joe, out of Sylph, and has won three first prizes, namely, at Bath, Darlington, and the Agricultural Hall.   He is a very promising young dog, and, with another year to thicken, will, I think, be superior even to his celebrated mother.

THE BULL TERRIER.

The Bull Terrier, like his chief progenitor, the bulldog, is now without a vocation, dog fights being prohibited by law, and rat pits being equally out of the question.   But, unlike the bulldog, he is an excellent companion for the male sex, being a little too violent in his quarrels to make him desirable as a ladies' pet. Careful crossing—said to be with the terrier, but also alleged to be with the

MR. VERO SHAW'S WHITE ENGLISH TERRIERS "SYLVIO" AND "SYLPH."

greyhound or foxhound, or both—has produced a handsome, symmetrical animal, without a vestige of the repugnant and brutal expression of the bulldog, and with the elegant lines of the greyhound, though considerably thickened in their proportions. From fifteen to twenty years' ago, Mr. Hinks, of Birmingham, held undisputed sway in this breed with a kennel of white dogs, in which a " Madman " always existed; but the identical animal varied almost every year, as he was enticed away by the high bids of the lovers of this breed. At that time there was still a slight reminder of the bull in the comparatively full lip; but in 1868 Old Victor suddenly appeared from the Black Country without this appendage, and with such a fine form of head and frame that he succeeded in gaining the fiats of the judges in his favour; and his type has since then been installed as that which is to be considered the proper one for the breed. Nothing is known of his pedigree, and all the guesses made at his greyhound parentage are purely hypothetical. He was, like all the " Madmen " of Mr. Hinks' breeding, a pure white; but when put to an equally all-white bitch, one of the produce was the celebrated " mark-eyed " dog Young Victor, who won nearly every prize open to him till his career was cut short by poison at the Hull Show of 1875. His son Tarquin, whose portrait is appended to this article, is, however, a worthy representative of the breed; and Mr. Vero Shaw also possesses a still more promising puppy, but too young as yet to show the true form of head so characteristic of it.

The bull terrier is still judged by the fighting standard—that is to say, he must have all the points, mental as well as bodily, which are necessary to the fighting dog. If of pure bull parentage or nearly so, he is unfitted for the office; for, instead of laying hold and shaking his adversary for a time with great force, and then changing to a fresh place of attack, as the fighting dog should do, he keeps his hold tenaciously, and never changes it but on compulsion. The infusion of terrier, greyhound, or foxhound, or whatever may be the cross, gives activity of body in addition to the above mental peculiarity, and thus is created an animal calculated to take his own part in any combat, whether with one of his own kind or with any of our native larger vermin, or even with the smaller *felidæ* of other lands. His temper is sufficiently under control to prevent his intentionally injuring his master, under the severest provocation, and he is admitted to be, of all dogs, the most efficient protector against attack in proportion to his size and muscular powers. He is a very cleanly animal in the house, and many years ago I had one which, being by accident confined in my bedroom surreptitiously for four days, under the care of a person who fed him, but neglected to let him out as directed, for fear of discovery, never once relieved himself of any of his secretions, by which he very nearly lost his life. Show dogs of this breed accustomed to the house, if left on their benches, are peculiarly liable to injury from this cause, which is indeed a fertile source of mischief to all dogs, and the higher their courage the worse for their health. The bull terrier is a capital vermin dog, and, if small enough, " goes to ground " well at fox or badger; but is too severe in his attack, his tendency being to kill rather than bolt his fox. For this reason the slightest visible cross of bull with the fox terrier is objected to ; but for all vermin work above ground the bull terrier of the present day is admirably suited.

Nothing reliable is known of the pedigrees of any of the best specimens of the bull terrier in these days ; and in former years, while the dog pits of Birmingham, Walsall, Stafford, Westminster, &c., still existed, the best strains were equally without recognised paternity beyond the first generation, breeders selecting a well-known fighting dog to mate with an equally famous bitch, whose prowess had been proved on more than one occasion. It is true that certain strains were famous among the "fancy ;" but they seldom existed long, subsequent victories bringing out fresh favourites, and these being again displaced by the fortune of war, as fickle in the pit as elsewhere. At present breeders go back to Old Victor as the origin of all the best dogs, and improving upon Mr. Hinks's strain—which had probably been too much in-bred—in size, symmetry, and notably in face and lip.

The points are as follows :—

POINTS OF THE BULL TERRIER.

	Value.		Value.		Value.
Skull	15	Shoulder and chest	15	Coat	5
Face and teeth	10	Back	10	Colour	5
Ears	5	Legs	10	Tail	5
Neck	5	Feet	5	Symmetry	10
	35		40		25

Grand Total 100.

1. The *skull* (value 15) should be long and flat, wedge-shaped, i.e., wide behind with the smaller end at the place of the brow, which should not be at all prominent. The line from the occiput to the end of the nose should be as straight as possible, without either brow or hollow in front of the eyes. This line is never absolutely straight, but the nearer it approaches to a straight line the better. The skull should, however, be "broken up," but not to anything like the same extent as in the bulldog.

2. *Face, eyes, lips, and teeth* (value 10).—The jaws must be long and powerful, nose large and black (though many otherwise first-rate dogs have had spotted or "butterfly" noses, notably Mr. Godfree's Old Puss). *Eyes* small, black, and sparkling. The upper *lip* should be as tight over the jaw as possible, any superfluous skin or approach to chop being undesirable. The under *lip* also should be small. The *teeth* should be regular in shape, meeting exactly, without any deviation from the straight line. A pig jaw is as great a fault as being underhung.

3. The *ears* (value 5) are always cropped for show purposes, and the degree of perfection with which this has been accomplished is generally taken into consideration. They should be brought to a fine point and exactly match. In their uncropped state they vary a good deal in shape, and seldom reach their full proportion till after teething.

4. The *neck* (value 5) should be rather long, and gracefully set into the

Mr. V......shaw's Bull Terriers "Ta......" and "N......"

shoulders, from which it should taper to the head, without any throatiness or approach to dewlap, as in the bulldog.

5. *Shoulders and chest* (value 15).—The shoulders should be strong and slanting with a wide and deep chest; but the last ribs are not very deep, though brought well back towards the hips.

6. The *back* (value 10) should be short and well furnished with muscle, running forward between the shoulder blades in a firm bundle on each side.

7. The *legs* (value 10).—The forelegs should be long and perfectly straight, the elbows lying in the same plane as the shoulder points, and not outside them, as in the bulldog. The hind legs should also be long and muscular, with straight hocks placed low down, i.e., near the ground.

8. The *feet* (value 5) are rather long than cat-like; but the toes should be well arched and close together.

9. The *coat* (value 5) must be short and close, but hard rather than silky, though when in show condition it should shine from constant friction.

10. The *colour* (value 5) for show purposes must be pure white, though there are many well-shaped dogs of other colours. This is, however, purely a fancy breed, and as such there is not the slightest reason why an arbitrary rule should not be made, as it was without doubt in this case, and it is useless to show a dog of any other colour.

11. The *tail* (value 5) or stern should be set on low, fine in bone, and carried straight out without any curl over the back.

12. Of *symmetry* (value 10) this dog shows a considerable amount, all his points being agreeable to the eye of the artist. Any deviation from a due proportion should therefore be punished accordingly.

The dogs I have selected for illustration are, first, Mr. Vero Shaw's celebrated Tarquin, to represent the class above 20lb., he being 44lb. in weight, and having won at Birmingham, Darlington, Wolverhampton, Northampton, Maidstone, Cork, Alexandra Palace, Crystal Palace, and other shows. Tarquin is by Young Victor out of a bitch called Puss, and was bred by Mr. C. L. Boyce, of Birmingham. Secondly, for the small class under 20lb., I have chosen Napper, belonging to the same gentleman. He weighs 18lb., and is by Bardle's Napper (a son of Mr. Shirley's celebrated Nelson, who was admitted to be the best dog of his day) out of Minnie. He has been successful at the Crystal Palace, Cork, and other shows.

Since the last edition of the "Dogs of the British Islands" appeared, one of the great Birmingham breeders has ceased to exist for show purposes; for Mr. J. F. Godfree has disposed of his entire kennels of bull terriers to Mr. Vero Shaw, of London, thereby finally withdrawing from the fancy, as I understand he has agreed to abstain from showing for a long term of years. The name of Mr. Hinks of Birmingham, too, has recently disappeared from the list of exhibitors, most of his stud having passed into the hands of Mr. Hartley, of Altrincham, who has, however, lately disposed of the best to Mr. G. A. Dawes, of Leamington. Messrs. Battersby, of Bolton; Chorley, of Kendal; Tredennick; Parkin, of Sheffield; and

Miller, of Walsall, frequently show first-rate specimens of this breed, which appears to have recently taken a new lease in public favour; for its unusual docility, if properly managed, and its intelligence, enable a bull terrier to learn almost anything that a dog can be taught; whilst its pluck is indisputable, and its mute system of attack renders it on many occasions superior to a fox terrier, who, when working, is apt to give tongue too loudly.

TOY SPANIELS.—MR. J. W. BERRIE'S MODERN BLENHEIM "THE EARL," MR. JULIUS'S OLD BLENHEIM "SPOT," MR. FORDER'S KING CHARLES "YOUNG JUMBO."

BOOK IV.
TOY DOGS.

CHAPTER I.
ROUGH-COATED TOY DOGS.

The King Charles and the Blenheim Spaniels—The Maltese Dog—The Rough Toy Terrier.

THE KING CHARLES AND BLENHEIM SPANIELS.

THE King Charles and Blenheim Spaniels have respectively received their names, the former from the patronage afforded to them by the "Merry Monarch," and the latter from that of the Marlborough family, among whom at Blenheim they have been pets for many generations. In each case, however, the modern prize winner is of a very different type from the original breed.

In considering the several points of the dogs hitherto described, I have been guided to a considerable extent by the uses to which they are usually put; but in the toy dog no such line can be drawn, nor is it possible to compare the modern Blenheim or King Charles and their original breeds with any pretension to arrive at their respective values, except by an appeal to the fashion of the day, which at present settles the question in favour of modern "show form." According to Vandyke the pets of King Charles II. were liver and white in colour, and of a shape varying greatly from that of Mr. Forder's Young Jumbo, who represents the modern type extremely well. According to the authority of the great painter, who is no doubt thoroughly dependable, their noses were comparatively long and sharp, and their ears no larger than those of the Chinese dog now commonly imported into England, which are more like those of a fox terrier than of a modern prize King Charles or Blenheim spaniel. Until the early part of the present century these little spaniels, not exceeding 5lb. or 6lb. in weight, were the fashionable pet dogs; but about fifty years ago the taste of the day changed in favour either of the Oxfordshire Blenheim—a little red and white dog resembling the Cocker spaniel in miniature—or of the then existing King Charles, which was usually of a black tan and white colour, and might be regarded as the Gordon setter reduced in scale, being like that dog not only in colour, which was, as in that breed, black and tan with or without white, but also in shape of body and head; and in this form both breeds have been placed on canvas by Sir Edwin Landseer. But soon after this date the London "fancy" seem to have become discontented with the beautiful natural shapes of their pets, and set to work to import the short faces and upturned noses of the Chinese spaniel, while at the same time they selected puppies with still greater length of feather on ears, feet, and legs than before. It is said that the bulldog, pug, and Chinese spaniel crosses have been used for this purpose; but this is not admitted by the breeders, who declare that the alterations have been effected by selection alone. The *modus operandi* is, however, of little consequence; all that we have to do with is the result, which is embodied in the following description of the points of the modern pet spaniel. The strongest argument in support of the adoption of some cross such as those mentioned above, is that nearly all of the modern breed have lost the low carriage of the tail, which is a peculiar feature in all true spaniels, and which was formerly insisted on as a point of great importance in the toy spaniel, but is now abandoned by modern judges, simply because it is rarely met with among those specimens that come up to their standard in other respects. In order to show the difference between the two types, I have obtained a sketch of Mr. Julius's Blenheim " Spot," which is, I believe, descended from the Woodstock strain, and exhibits the old fashioned shape of head and face in perfection. Contrasting him with Mrs. J. W. Berrie's prize winner, "The Earl," my readers can judge for themselves whether the latter could have descended from ancestors like the former, without any cross with extraneous blood. Knowing full well what extraordinary things can be done in this way by judicious selection, I am still sceptical on this point, and must regard the "stop," upturned nose, short face, and round skull as fresh importations, not developments. Still I must beg Mrs. Berrie, Mr. Forder, and other successful modern breeders to understand that I do not deny the merits of their pets, since I believe that in all fancy dogs Fashion has an undisputed right to be heard; and, as this omnipotent authority chooses to decide that an artifically short, upturned nose is more beautiful than that form of the organ which nature originally gave to the English spaniel, I am quite ready to accept the fiat. The following is the

SCALE OF POINTS GENERALLY ACCEPTED.

	Value.		Value.		Value.
Head	10	Ears	10	Colour	10
Stop	10	Eyes	5	Coat	10
Nose	10	Compactness of shape	10	Feather	10
Lower jaw	5	Symmetry	5	Size	5
	35		30		35

*Grand Total—*100.

1. The *head* (value 10) should be well domed, and in good specimens is absolutely semi-globular, sometimes even extending beyond the half-circle, and

absolutely projecting over the eyes, so as nearly to meet the upturned nose. This globular shape of skull is well shown by Mr. Baker in Young Jumbo.

2. The "*stop*" (value 10), or hollow between the eyes, is as well marked as in the bulldog, or even more so; some good specimens exhibiting a hollow deep enough to bury a small marble.

3. The *nose* (value 10) must be short, and well turned up between the eyes, without any indication of artificial displacement afforded by a deviation to either side. The colour of the end should be black; and it should be both deep and wide, with large open nostrils.

4. The *lower jaw* (value 5) must be wide between its branches, leaving plenty of space for the tongue and for the attachment of the lower lips, which should completely conceal the teeth. It should also be turned up or "finished," so as to allow of its meeting the end of the upper-jaw, turned up in a similar way as above described.

5. The *ears* (value 10) must be long, so as to approach the ground. In an average sized dog they measure 20in. from tip to tip, and some reach to 22in., or even a trifle more. They should be set low on the head, and be heavily feathered. In this respect the King Charles is expected to exceed the Blenheim, and his ears occasionally extended to 24in.

6. The *eyes* (value 5) are set wide apart, with the eyelids square to the line of face, not oblique or fox-like. The eyes themselves are large, lustrous, and very dark in colour, so as to be generally considered black, their enormous pupils, which are absolutely of that colour, increasing the deception. From their large size, there is almost always a certain amount of weeping shown at the inner angles.

7. In *compactness of shape* (value 10) these spaniels almost rival the pug, but the length of coat adds greatly to the apparent bulk, as the body, when the coat is wetted, looks small in comparison with that dog. Still, it ought to be decidedly "cobby," with strong stout legs, broad back, and wide chest.

8. The *symmetry* (value 5) of the toy spaniel is of some importance, but it is seldom that there is any defect in this respect.

9. The *colour* (value 10) varies with the breed. In the King Charles a rich black and tan is demanded without white, the black tan and white variety being discarded, though, in the best bred litters, occasionally a puppy of this colour appears. Tan spots over the eyes and on the cheeks, as well as the usual marking on the legs, are also required. The Blenheim, on the other hand, must on no account be whole-coloured, but should have a ground of pure pearly white, with bright rich chesnut red markings, evenly distributed in large patches. The ears and cheeks should be red, and there should be a blaze of white extending from the nose up the forehead, and ending between the ears in a crescentic curve. In the centre of this blaze there should be a clear "spot" of red, of the size of a sixpence.

10. The *coat* (value 10) in both varieties should be long, silky, soft, and wavy, but not curly. In the Blenheim there should be a profuse mane, extending well down in front of the chest.

11. The *feather* (value 10) should be well displayed on the ears and feet, where

it is so long as to give the appearance of their being webbed. It is also carried well up the backs of the legs. In the King Charles the feather on the ears is very long and profuse, exceeding that of the Blenheim by an inch or more. The feather on the tail, which is cut to a length of about three and a half or four inches, should be silky, and from five to six inches in length, constituting a marked "flag" of a square shape.

12. In *size* (value 5) both breeds vary from 5lb. to 10lb. in weight; the smaller the better, if otherwise well proportioned.

The chief breeders of these beautiful little dogs are the following ladies and gentlemen:

BLENHEIMS.—Mr. J. Barnett, late of Congleton; Mrs. J. W. Berrie, Wood Green, N.; Mrs. Popham, Alresford, Hants; Mr. E. Short, Spitalfields; Mr. J. Garwood, Gray's-inn-road; Mr. V. A. Julius, Abergavenny; Mr. S. A. Julius, Hastings.

KING CHARLES.—Miss E. Dawson, Denmark Hill; Mr. Thorling, Clerkenwell; Mr. J. Garwood, Gray's-inn-road; Mr. Forder, Bow; Mr. Hibberd, Spitalfields.

The specimens I have selected for illustration are—first, Mrs. J. W. Berrie's "The Earl," a very beautiful little dog, and perfect at all points, which took the first prize at the show recently held at the Aquarium in London, in a good class; secondly, Mr. Julius's "Spot," an excellent specimen of the old-fashioned Woodstock strain; and thirdly, Mr. Forder's "Young Jumbo," successful at the last Kennel Club show, and, as Mr. Baker's portrait will testify, a very splendid specimen of his breed.

THE MALTESE DOG,

A pure white silky coated little dog with long hair, has been a ladies' pet from the earliest ages of which we have any record. From some cause or other, a breed of these dogs introduced into the London market within the last thirty years, has received the name of Maltese terrier, but as it has neither been traced to Malta, nor has it any of the properties of the terrier tribe, I am utterly at a loss to know the origin of the name, and as it approaches very closely to the spaniel, I shall include it under that head. Mr. Lukey, the celebrated mastiff breeder, was one of the earliest possessors of the strain, but he obtained it from the Manilla Islands, almost the antipodes to Malta, and altogether unconnected with that Island. The parents of Mr. Lukey's dogs were imported in 1841 by his brother, who was then a Captain in the East India Company's Service, and from them he bred several small litters, which were readily disposed of at high prices. None of Mr. Lukey's breed have ever been exhibited as far as I know, and I believe they have long been extinct. They were however, remarkably beautiful, and quite came up to the level of Mr. Mandeville's strain, which has kept possession of the show bench since 1862, when the first class of this kind of toy dog was established at the Agricultural Hall Show, in which Mr. Mandeville's Mick and Fido were first and second. In the following year at Ashburnham, the same kennel again produced the first and second

Mr. H. Mandeville's Maltese Dog "Fido."

prize holders, Fido being at the head of his class, and a dog called Prince second. Since then Mr. Mandeville's strain has held undisputed possession of the prize list, whether the dogs exhibited belonged to him, Mrs. Bligh Monk of Coley Park, Reading, Lady Giffard, or Mr. Macdonald, who have been the chief exhibitors. At Birmingham the Maltese dog has not been so well represented as in London, and it was not until 1864 that a class was established for it, owing partly to the fact that the breed was almost confined to London and its neighbourhood, and partly to the greater premiums given to sporting over toy dogs at the Midland Metropolis.

The Maltese claims the following merits as a toy dog, but I am not aware, that in any respect they are superior to those of the toy spaniel. In the first place he is said to be very beautiful in shape, colour, and texture of coat, but certainly in these respects he is not more so than the toy spaniel, whether King Charles or Blenheim. Secondly he is said to be more sweet in breath and skin, and here I can give no opinion, never having possessed a specimen, nor have I any good authority to adduce on either side. He is admitted, however, to be a very delicate dog, and more difficult to rear than the toy spaniel, and this is rather an important point to all those who do not depend on the market for their supply. In point of price there is not much difference, so that as far as I can judge, individual taste must as usual settle the matter.

The points of the Maltese are as follows:—

	Value.		Value.		Value.
Coat	30	Ears	5	Size	15
Colour	20	Nose	5	Tail	15
Eyes	5	Symmetry	5		
	55		15		30

Grand Total, 100.

1. The *coat* (value 30) must be long and silky in texture, any approach to wool being specially to be penalised. The little bitch "Psyche" engraved in "The Dog" had a coat measuring 15in. across the shoulder, though only 3¼lb. in weight, and this length when considered in comparison with her small size, I have never seen excelled; it was remarkably silky in texture. There is a slight wave, but no absolute curl to be seen in good specimens.

2. The *colour* (value 20) should be a pure white, rather transparent, like spun glass, than opaque. Many specimens are disfigured by patches of fawn, which are very objectionable.

3. The *eyes* (value 5) must be full and black, and should not show the weeping corner incidental to the King Charles and Blenheim spaniels.

4. The *ears* (value 5) are long, but not so much so as those of the toy spaniel. The ears of Fido were 12in. across from tip to tip.

5. The *nose* (value 5) is short and black, and also the roof of the mouth.

6. In *symmetry* (value 5) there is no great test, as the shape is almost entirely concealed by the long coat, but there ought nevertheless to be a proper

proportion of length, to height, in about the same degree as is exhibited by the toy spaniel.

7. The *size* (value 15) should not exceed 6lb., though many of Mr. Mandeville's best prize winners have somewhat exceeded that weight, his Fido, whose portrait accompanies this article, being 6½lb.

8. The *tail* (value 15) should be short, curled tightly over the back, and clothed with a bunch of glossy silky hair.

Mr. Mandeville's Fido, by Tupper's Fido out of Lilly, won the first prize at Birmingham in 1864 and 1867; also various first prizes at Islington and Cremorne in 1862, 1863, and 1864. Several other dogs of the same name have been also exhibited by Mr. Mandeville.

THE ROUGH TOY TERRIER.

Like the black and tan toy terrier, the rough terrier exactly resembles its larger prototype in all but size. Its description, together with an illustration, is given in the article on the Yorkshire Terrier at page 211.

CHAPTER II.
SMOOTH TOY DOGS.

THE PUG—THE ITALIAN GREYHOUND—THE TOY TERRIER.

THE PUG.

S is the case with most, if not all, of our existing breeds of the dog, the origin of the pug is lost in obscurity. The prevailing opinion is that he is a bulldog modified by a hot climate; but this theory is only founded upon a statement to that effect made by Buffon, "whose word no man relies on," any more than that of the second Charles. According to this story, however, the pug so modified from the bulldog at the Cape of Good Hope was imported into Holland at the time when the Cape was a Dutch settlement, and became the favourite ladies' pet of that country for many years, a few specimens of the breed being scattered throughout Europe, and in this way reaching England, where it became very fashionable in the reign of William III. ("Dutch William"),

THE LATE MR. H. GILBERT'S PUG DOG "PRINCE."

"MOPS" AND "NELL," THE PARENT STOCK OF THE WILLOUGHBY PUGS.

but did not long remain so, and was exceedingly rare in the middle of the present century, even a moderately good one not being procurable for less than 30*l.*, and that at a time when 5*l.* was the average price of a lady's pet, even of the fashionable kinds. During the decade 1840-50, however, several admirers of pugs attempted to breed them from good foreign strains. Foremost among these was the then Lady Willoughby de Eresby, who after a great deal of trouble obtained a dog from Vienna which had belonged to a Hungarian countess, but was of a bad colour, being a mixture of the stone fawn now peculiar to the "Willoughby strain," and black; but the combination of these colours was to a certain extent in the brindled form. From accounts which are to be relied on, this dog was about twelve inches high, and of good shape, both in body and head, but with a face much longer than would now be approved of by pug fanciers. In 1846 he was mated with a fawn bitch imported from Holland, of the desired colour, viz., stone fawn in body, with black mask and trace, but with no indication of brindle. She had a shorter face and heavier jowl than the dog, and was altogether in accordance with the type now recognised as the correct "Willoughby pug." From this pair are descended all the strain named after Lady Willoughby de Eresby, which are marked in colour by their peculiar cold stone fawn, and the excess of black often showing itself, not in brindled stripes, but in entirely or nearly entirely black heads, and large "saddle marks" or wide "traces."

But coincidently with this formation of a new strain was the existence of another, showing a richer and more yellow fawn, and no tendency to excess of black. This strain was possessed by the late Mr. Morrison, of Walham Green; the late Mr. H. Gilbert, of Kensington; Mr. W. Macdonald, now of Winchmore Hill, but at that time residing in London; and some other fanciers of less note. According to Mr. Morrison's statement to me (which, however, he did not wish made public during his life), this strain was lineally descended from a stock possessed by Queen Charlotte, one of which is painted with great care in the well-known portrait of George III. at Hampton Court; but I could never get him to reveal the exact source from which it was obtained. That he himself fully believed in the truth of this story I am quite confident; and I am also of opinion that he never hazarded a statement of which he had the slightest doubt—being in this respect far above the average of "doggy" men. Although he never broadly stated as much, I always inferred that the breed was obtained by "back-stair influence," and on that account a certain amount of reticence was necessary; but, whatever may be the cause of the secrecy maintained, I fully believe the explanation given by Mr. Morrison of the origin of this breed of pugs, which is as commonly known by his name as that of Lady Willoughby de Eresby by hers. His appeal to the Hampton Court portrait, in proof of the purity of his breed from its general resemblance to the dog in that painting, goes for nothing in my mind, because you may breed up to any type by careful selection; but I do not hesitate to endorse his statement as to the Guelph origin of his strain, because I have full confidence in his truthfulness, from having tested it in various other ways. I need scarcely remark that both strains are derived from the Dutch—"the Morrison" coming down to us through the three

Georges from William III., and " the Willoughby " being, as above described, a more recent importation direct from Holland and Vienna. Both strains are equally lively in temperament, moderately tricky and companionable, but their chief advantage as pets is that they are unusually free from smell, both in breath and coat.

Since the decade above mentioned, both strains have been crossed with the bulldog, with a view to enlarge the skull and shorten the face; and the consequence is that many of the best dogs in other respects are underhung, splay-footed, and, what is of more consequence, savage in temper. There is also a tendency in this cross to increase the size; but I confess that the largest prize-winning pug which I have yet seen (namely, Mr. Foster's Comedy, first prize winner at Birmingham, 1877), was perfectly free from all signs of the bull cross in other respects. Though shown in a large and excellent class, Comedy was so perfect in shape, and so full of quality, in spite of his over-size, that the judges (Messrs. Hedley and Peter Eden) at once selected him for premier honours; and I perfectly agreed with the decision. Within the last ten years the two strains have been much crossed *inter se*, and it is difficult to find either a pure Willoughby pug or one in whose pedigree there is no line of that strain. Mrs. Bligh Monk, of Coley Park, Reading; Mr. E. J. Poer, of Limerick; Mr. Annandale, of Edinburgh; Mr. Jolliffe Tuffnell, of Dublin; Captain Digby Boycott, of London; Mr. Sharples, of Manchester; and Mrs. Mayhew, of Twickenham, have been the most successful exhibitors of late years—the last named having introduced a strain of the Chinese pug, but with what view I am at a loss to know, as there is no desirable point shown in excess in the importation from the Celestial Empire.

The following are the

POINTS OF THE MODERN PUG.

	Value.		Value.		Value.
Head	10	Trace	5	Legs and feet	10
Ears	5	Colour	10	Tail	10
Eyes	5	Coat	10	Symmetry and size	5
Moles	5	Neck	5		
Mask, vent and wrinkles	10	Body	10		
	35		**40**		**25**

Grand Total, **100.**

1. The *head* (value 10) should have a round monkey-like skull, and should be of considerable girth, but in proportion not so great as that of the bulldog. The face is short, but, again, not " bully " or retreating, the end being cut off square; and the teeth must be level—if undershot, a cross of the bull is almost always to be relied on. Tongue large, and often hanging out of the mouth ; but this point is not to be accepted for or against the individual. The cheek is very full and muscular.

2. The *ears* (value 5) are small, vine-shaped, and thin, and should lie moderately flat on the face (formerly they were invariably closely cropped, but this practice is now quite out of fashion) ; they are black, with a slight mixture of fawn hair.

3. The *eyes* (value 5) are dark brown and full, with a soft expression. There should be no tendency to weep, as in the toy spaniel.

4. A *black mole* (value 5) is always demanded on each cheek, with two or three hairs springing from it; the regulation number of these is three, but of course it is easy to reduce them to that number.

5. *Mask, vent, and wrinkles* (value 10).—These markings must be taken together, as they all depend mainly on colour. The wrinkles, it is true, are partly in the skin; but over and above these there should be lines of black, corresponding with them, on the face and forehead. The mask should extend over the whole face as a jet black, reaching a little above the eyes, and the vent also should be of the same colour. In the Willoughby strain the black generally extends higher up the skull, and has not the same definite edge as in the Morrison pug, in which this point is well shown, and greatly insisted on by its admirers.

6. A *trace* (value 5) or black line is exhibited along the top of the back by all perfect pugs; and the clearer this is, the better. As with the mask, so with this—the definition is more clear in the Morrison than in the Willoughby pug. When it extends widely over the back it is called a "saddle mark," and this is often displayed in the Willoughby, though seldom met with in the Morrison strain; of course, it is admired in the one, and deprecated in the other, by their several supporters.

7. The *colour* (value 10) of the Morrison pug is a rich yellow fawn, while that of the Willoughby is a cold stone. The salmon fawn is never met with in good specimens of either, and is objected to. In the Willoughby the fawn-coloured hairs are apt to be tipped with black, but in its rival the fawn colour is pure, and unmixed with any darker shade. Of course, in interbred specimens the colour is often intermediate.

8. The *coat* (value 10) is short, soft, and glossy over the whole body, but on the tail it is longer and rougher. A fine tail indicates a bull cross.

9. The *neck* (value 5) is full, stout, and muscular, but without any tendency to dewlap; which again indicates, when present, that the bulldog cross has been resorted to.

10. The *body* (value 10) is very thick and strong, with a wide chest and round ribs; the loin should be very muscular, as well as the quarters, giving a general punchy look, almost peculiar to this dog.

11. *Legs and feet* (value 10.)—The legs should be straight but fine in bone, and should be well clothed with muscle. As to the feet, they must be small, and in any case narrow. In both strains the toes are well split up; but in the Willoughby the shape of the foot is cat like, while the Morrison strain has a hare foot. There should be no white on the toes, and the nails should be dark.

12. The *tail* (value 10) must curve so that it lies flat on the side, not rising above the back to such an extent as to show daylight through it. The curl should extend to a little more than one circle.

13. *Size and symmetry* (value 5).—In size the pug should be from 10in to 12in. high—the smaller the better. A good specimen should be very symmetrical.

As an excellent illustration of the breed, I have retained the portrait of the late Mr. H. Gilbert's Prince, a prize winner in 1863-4. He was of the pure Morrison strain, and the first of it exhibited uncropped. I have also added the very interesting portraits of the parent stock of the Willoughby strain, painted by Alfred Dreux, a French artist of some celebrity, and evidently drawn with great care and apparent fidelity. Nell would take a prize in the present day, barring her throatiness; but the face of Mops is too long for the modern fancy, and has been " bred out " by careful selection. No doubt the cross was a judicious one, as what was absent in Mops was well marked in Nell—the bad colour of the latter being the only adverse point which has been retained.

THE ITALIAN GREYHOUND.

This elegant little pet resembles its English sporting congener in shape and colour, differing mainly in its diminutive size, and in the remarkable " prancing " action which it almost invariably exhibits with its forelegs. No other animal, as far as I know, possesses this action to the same extent. It is true that some horses lift their knees till, as the dealers say, " they are in danger of putting their feet through their curb chains;" but this is done in a comparatively heavy and lumbering style, without the true dance-like " prance " of the Italian greyhound. Occasionally, but very rarely, an English greyhound, or even a deerhound, exhibits the action to some extent, but even then it is exceptional; whereas in the Italian it is the rule, and almost an invariable one.

Owing to the extent to which in-breeding has been carried by the lovers of this dog, he is often extremely delicate, is always difficult to rear, and when attacked by distemper the disease is frequently fatal. To obviate this constitutional defect, recourse has been lately had to a cross with the toy terrier, which has to some extent succeeded in this respect; but unfortunately it has introduced a large round skull and short face, sometimes attended with a falling terrier-like ear, also increased in size. With the exception of these defects, many of these cross-breds have been extremely beautiful, and the practice has enabled breeders to obtain a diminished size without loss of symmetry. In 1859 I published a portrait of Gowan's Billy, whose grandsire, great grandsire, gg grandsire, ggg and gggg grandsire were all the same dog, imported from Italy. At that time he was generally admitted to be the most perfect specimen of his kind in England, and he was possessed of the true greyhound head and ears; but his stock were very delicate, and I believe his strain is now extinct, at all events in a pure state. He was 14¼in. high, and nearly 9lb. in weight, which would now be considered somewhat over the proper size; but his symmetrically elegant shape has been reproduced on a smaller scale since then in the case of Mr. Bourke's Molly, who was absolutely faultless in all respects but her head, which was a trifle " bullety " as compared with Billy and other dogs of the old strain. In nearly all breeds of dogs elegance of form is shown more in the female than in the male; but this is especially to be noted in the various kinds of greyhounds, and in their ally the deerhound. Just as

ITALIAN GREYHOUNDS—MR. PIM'S "BISMARK" AND MR. J. DAY'S "CRUCIFIX."

among bulldogs, mastiffs, St. Bernards, and bloodhounds, in whom the head is the most prominent feature, the male has the advantage in a mixed class, so in the greyhound the reverse holds good; and, on searching the prize lists since the institution of dog shows, it will be seen that nineteen-twentieths of the prizes have been won by bitches in the class for Italian greyhounds, even leaving out of the calculation that wonderfully beautiful animal above mentioned, Mr. Bourke's Molly (afterwards Mr. Macdonald's). With the exception of Billy (alluded to above), I have never yet seen an Italian greyhound *dog* approaching perfection in shape, and I am therefore compelled to fall back upon the nearest approach to it within my reach, namely, Mr. Pim's Bismark, a considerable prize-winner at Bristol and in Ireland, although he has recently been twice unnoticed beyond a high commendation at Birmingham and the Alexandra Park Shows. These defeats were, however, mainly owing to the excellence of the bitches amongst which he was classed; for at Birmingham there were four of that sex only a trifle behind the celebrated Molly in shape and colour, while at the Alexandra Park there were nearly as many. Bismark is, nevertheless, a very neat dog; and, barring his round head and his colour, which has a shade of blue in the fawn, he is very little behind the first-class bitches of his day. His pedigree is unknown, so that it is not possible to trace these defects to their cause; but I have little doubt that,'at some time more or less remote, a terrier cross in his pedigree would creep out. At all events, he is the best dog exhibited of late years, and as such I have selected him for Mr. Baker's pencil. Crucifix, his companion in the engraving, was, like him, passed over at the above shows, obtaining only a second prize at the shows recently held at Birmingham and Alexandra Palace. My own opinion, however, was strongly in her favour at both of these shows; and, in spite of the high authority of Messrs. Hedley and Handley (the respective judges), I have accordingly selected her for portraiture as the most worthy possessor of Molly's mantle. Her beautiful golden-fawn colour is even superior to Molly's dove-colour, and her general shape and symmetry are nearly equal; but no doubt in head Molly has the advantage, and if the two were shown together, both in their prime, the latter would weigh down the scale considerably. Like Bismark, she has had more honour in her own country than at Birmingham and London, having been awarded the first prize at Manchester in 1875 and 1877, and also at Glasgow in 1875 and 1876. She is by Bruce's Prince out of his Beauty; Prince by Old Prince—Speed; Beauty by Chief—Tit.

The Italian greyhound, as now bred to a weight of 5lb. or 6lb., is wholly useless in any kind of chase; but he was formerly sometimes slipped at rabbits, and I have seen a brace, belonging to a lady who was a well-known follower of the chase in Worcestershire thirty years ago, course and kill rabbits in very good style. But, though imported from Italy, they were about 10lb. or 12lb. in weight, and in these days would be classed as "whippets." This last named breed is extensively used at Manchester and in the midland districts for rabbit coursing, and is a cross between the Italian and the English greyhound, or between the latter and the smooth English terrier. All these greyhound breeds are usually considered to be void of intelligence and fidelity; but this is a mistake, and certainly the trick performed by

Mr. Walton's whippet, as shown in the engraving of the poodle published with the article on that dog in the Appendix, marks a high order of mental power, and a like degree of obedience, founded on love for his trainer, since no severity would lead to its execution. These whippets are so quick and clever as to cope with the short turns of the rabbit; but they are not fast enough for the hare, and the sport for which they are bred is confined to the artisan and mining classes of the districts in which it is the fashion.

The points of the Italian greyhound differ only in proportional value from those of its English congener; colour, size, and symmetry being in the former more especially secured than in the latter.

POINTS OF THE ITALIAN GREYHOUND.

	Value.		Value.		Value.
Head	5	Fore quarters	10	Colour	15
Neck	5	Hind quarters	10	Symmetry	15
Ears and eyes	5	Tail	5	Size	15
Legs and feet	10	Coat	5		
	25		30		45

Grand Total, 100.

1. The *head* (value 5) if possible, should be as snakelike as that of the English greyhound, but such formation is now never met with. The nearer it approaches to it, however, the better. In all recent exhibits the skull is more or less round, and the face, though still pointed, too short, with a tendency to turn up.

2. The *neck* (value 5) is long and elegant, resembling closely its larger congener.

3. The *ears and eyes* (value 5).—Many modern prize takers are deficient in the proper shape of the ear; but this should not be overlooked, for it still exists in the breed as an exact counterpart of the English greyhound's corresponding organ, though always somewhat enlarged in comparison with the body. The eye is much larger proportionately, soft and languishing; but it ought never to weep. The colour of the iris is usually a dark brown.

4. *Legs and feet* (value 10).—These should be exactly counterparts of the large breed.

5. *Fore quarters* (value 10).—Here again I must refer my readers to "The Greyhound," in "Dogs of the British Islands," Part 2.

6. *Hind quarters* (value 10).—As with the two last sections, the only difference lies in comparative value, the English dog's points being estimated from the workman-like point of view, whilst the Italian is regarded from the artistic standpoint.

7. The *tail* (value 5) is somewhat shorter than the English dog's; but it must be gently curved in the same tobacco-pipe way, and should be fine in bone except at the root, as well as free from hair.

8. The *coat* (value 5) should be short, soft, and silky.

9. The *colour* (value 15) of the Italian greyhound is largely to be taken into

MR. HOWARD MAPPLEBECK'S TOY TERRIER "BELLE" CONTRASTED WITH HIS MANCHESTER TERRIER "QUEEN III."

consideration, and I have consequently estimated it at a high figure. Fawns are now far in the ascendant, and to no other colour would the full value be accorded. I should place them as follows: 1, whole golden fawn (value 15); 2, whole dove fawn (14); 3, whole blue fawn (13); 4, whole stone fawn (12); 5, whole cream colour, or white with black tips (10); 6, whole red or yellow, with black muzzles (6); 7, whole black or plain red or yellow (5); 8, whole blue (4); 9, parti-coloured (0). A small star on the breast, or a white toe, takes off a point or two, according to the extent of white; but in all cases the toenails should be dark.

10. The *symmetry* (value 15) of this little dog must be carefully estimated, as a want of elegance in detail, or of combination in due proportion, alike lowers the value of these points separately to a very low ebb.

11. The *size* (value 15) of the bitch for modern successful exhibition should be little over 5lb., nor should the dog exceed 7lb. or 7½lb. Beyond these weights a specimen, however good in other respects, has little or no chance of a first prize in anything like a good class.

THE SMOOTH TOY TERRIER.

In the rough and smooth varieties of the terrier, distinctions are made between the larger and the toy classes, but this is chiefly noticeable in the black and tan, though the rough toys are still very numerous at our large shows. As already observed in the chapter on the black and tan terriers, there are two distinct types of this dog, when of the size limited to the toys, namely, not exceeding 6lb., and, to be successful, limited to 3lb. or 3½lb. One of these shows the Italian greyhound cross, the other that with the spaniel, resorted to probably in order to restore the coat, which in these little abortions is often almost entirely absent, owing to in-breeding. In consequence of dwarfing, the points are seldom exhibited in anything like the perfection shown by Mr. Lacy's large strain, but still, the nearer the approach is made to it the better, and it is needless to recapitulate them here.

In addition to the black and tan, and the white toy terrier, there is also the blue fawn, differing only in colour, and seldom noticed by our judges of the present day.

Annexed is a portrait of Mr. Mapplebeck's wonderfully good toy terrier Belle, winner of the first prize at Birmingham and at the late Kennel Club show held at the Alexandra Palace, together with his Queen III., also a first prize winner at the latter show in the class for black and tan or Manchester terriers—the latter serving as a contrast to the former in point of size. In the article on the black and tan terrier, by Mr. Hugh Dalziel, at page 216, the author alludes to the toy terrier as of "two sorts, one with a short face, round skull, and full eye (inclined to weep), called in vulgar parlance 'apple-headed 'uns,' showing the cross at some time or other with the King Charles spaniel; the other type is the thin shivering dog, that must be kept clothed, and sleep in a warmly lined basket; his timid, shrinking manner, spindly legs, lean sides, and tucked-up flanks showing the Italian greyhound cross. The weight of these two clearly distinct varieties averages from 3lb. to 6lb." Such is no doubt a fair description of the ordinary toy terrier; but there is a third variety represented by Belle, which, though extremely rare, still exists in considerable numbers. This little dog is, in fact, the large black and tan terrier reduced in size from 15lb. or 16lb. to 3lb. or 4lb., the little one being exactly a copy of the larger kind except in size, and possessed of equal hardihood and spirit. Mr. Baker has reproduced on paper the two bitches with his usual fidelity, and the exact likeness shown is perfectly justified in nature. The great difficulty is to breed such little dwarfs without loss of symmetry or substance, the general result being a reduction of the size of the body and an enlargement proportionally of the head. The pedigree of Belle is unknown.

As the points of this breed are precisely similar to those of the larger variety fully given in the article above alluded to, it is needless to reproduce them here. All departures from these points in the direction of either the spaniel or Italian greyhound cross are to be penalised according to their degree.

POODLES AND WHIPPET—GROUP OF MR. WALTON'S PERFORMING DOGS.

APPENDIX.

POODLES, FRENCH AND RUSSIAN—THE TRUFFLE DOG—THE CHINESE CRESTED DOG—THE GREAT DANE.

THE POODLE.

BY " WILDFOWLER."

HE POODLE was (and to a certain extent is still) *the* water spaniel *par excellence* of Continental shooters; but the fact that draining is carried on to an unlimited extent has necessarily curtailed considerably the use of water dogs of all species, including that of the poodle; and now the vast majority of poodles one may see are decidedly aptly ranked, in show catalogues, with the non-sporting division. Nevertheless, the poodle was originally, to all intents and purposes, and exclusively, a sporting dog, and to this day in the fenny districts of the Continent he may be seen in all his purity; and he is then a large and grand dog, not to be compared with the specimens which are now being bred to suit the requirements of the toy or companion market.

There are, therefore, two grand classes of modern poodles—one which is still strictly sporting, and one which should include performing, companion, and toy poodles—and each of these two classes comprises several different types. Concerning the first category, it is very rare indeed to see a poodle used as a sporting dog in the British Islands (I have only seen one in the course of my experience); and we have therefore to refer to foreign writers for information on the subject, or go abroad to see the dogs at work. I have done both, and in the course of this paper will beg to submit the fruit of my gleanings in book lore and my own sporting experience concerning the poodle. Dr. Fitzinger, in his book, " Der Hund und seine Racen," states that there are no less than six very distinct varieties of poodles, viz.: der grosse Pudel, der mittlere Pudel, der kleine Pudel, der kleine Pintsch, der schnür Pudel, and der Schaf-Pudel, besides other, but minor, varieties, produced by crossing.

The characteristics of the breeds he names, the eminent doctor states to be as follows :—

Der grosse Pudel, or the great poodle, he says, originated in the north-west of Africa, probably in Morocco or Algeria. He is always larger than the largest-sized spaniel, which, however, he resembles in form. He is robust in build, and has a peculiarly thick and full covering of hair. His *os occipitis* is well pronounced, his head is round, his forehead is strongly arched, his muzzle is short, high, and stumpy, his neck short and thick; his body is compact and cobby, his legs are comparatively short and strong, and he is more web-footed than any other breed. The hair over his body is long, thick, soft, woolly, and entirely curled, even over the face, and especially the mouth, where it forms a decided moustache. On the ears and tail the hair is more knotty and matted. ·Specimens of this breed are white, light liver, liver, light grey, dark grey, dark liver, or black. Sometimes the markings are peculiar, inasmuch that, on a light ground, great irregular dark grey, or black patches occur. When the dogs are liver-coloured or black there are white spots on their muzzles and throats, on the nape of their necks, on their breasts, bellies, feet, and tail. They are seldom cropped, but are almost invariably docked. The Italians call them *can barbone;* the French *barbets, grands barbets, barbetons caniches;* the English denominate them water dogs, water spaniels, finders, and poodles. Neither the Greeks nor the Romans appear to have known these dogs, and the old German authors of the middle ages do not mention them. In the sixteenth century they are, for the first time, mentioned by Conrad Gesner, who, in 1555, gives a description and illustration of these dogs. The great poodle is most easily trained, and his peculiar adaption for marsh work is not found in any such high degree in any other kind of dog.

His liveliness, attachment, and faithfulness, combined with his good temper, trust, and obedience, make of him a thorough good companion. He always looks for his master, likes to please him, and is never tired of doing all he can to further that end. He is a splendid swimmer, and the best of water retrievers. He grasps everything he is taught so readily that he is trained very quickly; hence he is a good performer in whatever pursuit his talents may be called into requisition.

Der mittlere Pudel, or medium-sized poodle, is only a variety of the great poodle. He has the same qualities and properties. Size is the only difference between them; he is sometimes a third, and sometimes only half, the size of his greater congener. There is no difference in their colour or markings, and the mittlere Pudel is also docked.

In Italy, France, or England no difference is made between this variety and the great poodle; they go by the same name. This medium-sized poodle, however, was known to the Romans, although no writing mentions it; but on certain pictures on antiques, from the time of the Emperor Augustus (last century before Christ), his portrait is found. He was not, however, known to the Germans of the middle ages. In many places he is used for finding truffles.

Der kleine Pudel, or little poodle. In this mongrel race the peculiarities of their ancestors are so pronounced that they are called " half bastards of pure crossing" (*sic*). They look like the medium-sized poodles, but are only half their size, and in make they are much lighter. Their heads are not so high, the muzzle is longer, the body slenderer, and the legs are comparatively thinner. The hair covering the body is long, fine, and soft; on body and legs more curled and more woolly ; on head, ears, and tail it is decidedly longer and more knotty, but silky. The tail is carried straight, and sometimes its tip turns slightly upwards. On the face the hair is long, especially about the mouth. The colour is the same as for the previous classes.

The Italians call the kleine Pudel *barbino*, the French *petit barbet*, and the English *little barbet* (?)

Portraits of these dogs are also seen on antique monuments, but they are not mentioned in any German MSS. of the middle ages.

The little poodle is not pure, but a mongrel. He has, however, all the winsome qualities of the larger breeds. He is used as lapdog by ladies, and can also be employed for finding truffles.

Der kleine Pintsch, or the little griffon (Aquaticus gryphus). The peculiarities of this mixed race lead to the supposition that it is a product of a cross between the little poodle and the Pomeranian (?). It has a long head, an arched forehead, a stumpy mouth, and very long hair on its body. In all other respects, and in colour, it is like other poodles. They are called *barbets griffons* and *chiens Anglais* by the French.

Der schnür Pudel (corded hair poodle) is of pure breed, but seems to be some variation of the large poodle, from which, however, he differs in his coat. His size is quite that of the large poodle, the length of his body being sometimes 3ft. (German), and in build, in all cases, he is very much like the large poodle. The characteristic feature of this breed is the peculiar nature of its coat, which is not only of great length, but which grows in a peculiar manner—*i.e.*, the soft woolly hair does not hang down in ringlets or in curls, or in feather, but it comes down regularly in rows of straight cords, from the skull, from the middle line of the neck and of the back ; and it hangs down on both sides of the head, neck, and body, sometimes 2ft. long, dragging on the ground, so that the legs are invisible. From the ears and tail the hair sometimes hangs to the length of 1½ft. Only the face, muzzle, and paws are clothed in shorter hair. Generally these dogs are white ; rarely are black ones to be seen.

The origin of this dog has been a matter of discussion among *savants*, some saying that he came from Spain or Portugal, and others from Greece. His qualities are like those of the great poodle, but he is much more valued, simply because he is very rarely met with.

Der Schaf-Pudel, or woolly-coated poodle. His similarity to the great poodle and the Calabrian (?) dog induces Dr. Fitzinger to think that it is a double bastard, as it is a perfect link between these two breeds. He has the hair of the first ; but his size and general appearance are like those of the second. He has a less arched forehead, and shorter and smaller ears, than the great poodle ; his body is more tucked up, he is higher on legs, and his hair more thinly curled on the neck and belly ; it is longest on the ears and shortest in front of the legs. On other parts of his body and face his coat is very woolly. His colour is generally white, and then sometimes he has a circle of bluish grey round the eyes, and the top of his nose is of a greyish or fleshy colour. Other specimens are light liver or grey, ticked or spotted, sometimes with patches of brown or black. This breed is generally found in the Campana of Rome. In English it is called Calabrian dog (?). They are a very favourite breed, because they are so faithful and companionable.

Besides the afore-mentioned breeds, the professor gives the description of sundry crosses of poodles with sheepdogs, Newfoundlands, &c.; but these lack interest, the crosses being decidedly removed and even doubtful, since in many cases they are purely suppositious. I have, therefore, only given at some length those details which are of interest.

So much, then, for the eminent German professor's opinions on the poodle. And now, what have the French authors to say about him? First of all comes M. Revoil. M. Revoil, who is considered a great authority on sporting matters in France, published, some years ago, a book on dogs, entitled "Historie Physiologique et Anecdotique des Chiens de toutes les Races" (E. Dentu, publisher, Paris), and in this work, page 188, M. Revoil classifies—and justly so, of course—the poodle with spaniels; but he seems to think that on this side of the Channel we cultivate particularly the breed of poodles for sporting purposes; for he mentions them in a breath with water spaniels and cockers, and gives the name "poodle" actually in English! Now, I have done as much wildfowl and other shooting as most men of my age; and I must acknowledge that, for one or two poodles that may be used by British wildfowl shooters, a hundred—nay, thousands perhaps—are used by their Continental *confrères*; and certainly in England the poodle is but little used in connection with that or any other branch of the art of fowling. In fact, one may say, as a very general rule, that the poodle in England is almost universally either a performing dog or a mere pet, or lap or companion dog, according to his size; but he is rarely employed as a sporting dog.

Not so in the vast marshes of the Continent, and especially in those *marais* of the French departments of the Pas-de-Calais, Nord, and Somme; in Belgium, in Holland, in Denmark, in Northern Germany, and in Russia, where night-decoying of ducks to the hut is extensively practised. As late back as January, 1872, an article of mine appeared in *Baily's Magazine*, entitled "Duck-decoying in Abbeville Marshes," wherein I related the performance of a celebrated poodle who accompanied a French *huttier* and myself on our expeditions. Without him half our birds would have been lost; and this will become apparent when I state that at least half the birds fired at are only winged or disabled, and thus, without a dog gifted with sense, nose, and pluck, it would be perfectly impossible for the shooters, in the dead of the night, to collect their game. This the poodle does, with a rapidity and intelligence which are simply unsurpassable. In short, he is so well adapted for that sort of work, that in French his generic name *caniche* is directly derived from duck (*canard*). He is also called *chien canne*, which is quite as much a derivation; and in some districts where the ooze abounds the name *barbet* is applied to him. This word *barbet* is evidently a diminutive for *barbotteur*, i.e., a "mud-lark"—a dog fond of paddling about in the mud.

For summer work the sporting poodle on the Continent is invariably clipped from the middle of his back to his hocks, and the rest of his coat is simply trimmed;

but the French and Dutch fowlers have the strange habit of clipping him also over the face in such a manner as to leave him very distinctly a moustache and an impériale, which " ornaments " give the dogs a very comical and cunning appearance. I do not remember ever having seen a poodle that was not thus " adorned."

In winter time, however, when severe frosts have set in, and long nights are to be spent at the hut or in a *bachol* (*i.e.*, a flat-bottomed wildfowling punt), it would not do to have the dogs' bodies partly bare; and, accordingly, from the end of the summer all the sporting poodles in the fens are allowed to recover their winter coats, so that by the time that their endurance is to be severely tested they are ready for all the inclemencies of the season.

In his winter coat a sporting poodle is perfectly impervious to frost or wet, and will face the greatest hardships without so much as a shiver. This coat resembles to some extent sheep's wool in its texture, and in the smaller variety of the poodle —that used as lapdogs—when the little dogs' coats are clean and bright they look not unlike lambs; hence the French ladies call them *chiens moutons*. The large poodle's coat, however, is coarser in texture, and, if the dog is required as a companion, a great deal of grooming is necessary in order to keep him in presentable order. Revoil does not speak favourably of the poodle's appearance. " He is a short and stumpy dog," he declares, " coarse and ugly; his legs are disproportioned; he is apple headed, and withal carries his head badly; his ears are too long and too large," &c. But he has evidently only seen curs, for this description does not apply to the poodle proper. The French author, however, grows enthusiastic when he speaks of the poodle's qualities: " He has an excellent nose; he is as faithful—as a poodle; he is intelligent enough to play cards or dominoes—and win! He is extremely active, and water seems to be his element." All this is correct enough; but when Revoil states, further on, that the poodle is *probably* descended from the land or the water spaniel, the question arises whether the compliment could not be reversed; and there we lose ourselves in fruitless speculation. Then our author relates that, in the sixteenth century, poodles were used for duck shooting; but now, he says, they are simply transformed into *chiens savants*. Now, French writers are noted for their unconquerable wish to appear witty, and their love of brilliancy is so great that they will even sacrifice truth if it has to give way to a pun. However, in the present case Revoil evidently does not practically know what he writes about. There are certainly *less* poodles employed now for sporting purposes than there used to be, but there are still many so employed; and the difference between the number to be seen now and in past years arises simply from the fact that the majority of marshy lands are being reclaimed and cultivated, and, like Othello's, the poodle's occupation will soon be entirely gone, as well as that of our own breeds of water spaniels, if all marshy lands are to be drained. As regards poodles when considered as *chiens savants*, everybody knows that this breed is almost invariably chosen by tumblers or circus performers whenever they wish to train dogs for any peculiar tricks, and there are but few people who have not witnessed their extraordinary talents in that line. Revoil states that, in his youth, a certain poodle named Munito performed wonderful feats. He also says that in 1829 there were two poodles in London who played a game of *écarté* with all the rapidity and skill of professional players. As regards that sort of thing, General Hutchinson, in his work on dog breaking, sixth edition, page 246, narrates what he himself saw performed by a Russian poodle in Paris. The dog told what o'clock it was, told fortunes, &c. . . . . and there is an illustration, page 245, of a notorious poodle playing a game of dominoes. Several of these dogs have played cards well, and numberless tricks have been taught them. They are, in fact, *the* performing dogs of all public exhibitions.

To return now to foreign authors' opinions about the poodle, I find in a small book entitled "Conseils aux Chasseurs," by Charles Bemelmans, gamekeeper, page 102, a few lines relating to *barbets*. Strange to say, Bemelmans, who really ought to know better than even allude to the exploded idea, says that poodles are but mediocre *setting* dogs! Who ever saw a poodle on point? Evidently this author is all at sea there. He, however, testifies that poodles are extremely good retrievers, and very intelligent.

Another French author, the Viscount de la Neuville, in "La Chasse au Chien d'Arrêt," devotes a paragraph to poodles. He declares that they can be broken easily to do anything one likes, they are so clever and sensible. He says that the "poodle is not, strictly speaking, a setting dog" (which shows a better knowledge of the subject than Bemelmans exhibits), "but that he is excellent for retrieving in marshes or flushing marsh birds. He is, however, slow in his work, and easily put out of wind. The usual colour is liver, but a smaller breed, called *petit barbet*, is black." So he says. But I have seen hard-working poodles of as many varieties in size, form, and colour as one might notice in all our breeds of spaniels, barring Clumbers, put together. As regards colour, I have seen black poodles, liver poodles, white poodles, and varieties of black and white and liver and white *ad libitum*. Concerning size, I have seen a Russian poodle quite as big as a large-sized retriever; and a sporting French or Belgian poodle not much bigger than a Sussex spaniel. In form, again, they vary greatly. Some have almost exactly the lines of the Irish water spaniel, and others were as broad as they were high; but they all had the same head, the same intelligent eye, and the same texture of coat, woolly and thick underneath, and hanging in ringlets outwardly. The length of ear is also a remarkable feature in the poodle. As a rule, it ought, when brought over the nose, to reach at least over the other ear.

As regards utility, personal experience, especially in sporting matters, goes a very long way, and I have myself seen poodles at work in Holland, in Belgium, and in France. In fact, throughout the Continent, wherever marshes are still to be found, the professional duck shooters use poodles. Why? Why, for two very good reasons: the first of which is that there are no other good breeds of water spaniels to be had there, for love or money, except in a few favoured localities where British shooters have imported English and Irish water spaniels. The French and the Dutch have no spaniels proper. What they call *épagneuls de marais* (which expression, naturally enough, we would translate *verbatim* by "marsh spaniels," *i.e.*, water spaniels) are simply setters which have been broken to marsh shooting. The few regular spaniels proper which are, now and then, to be met with on the Continent are of British descent, and, although they are greatly prized by those who own them, they are not placed by the professionals on a par with their native poodles. Now, as a matter of fact, a first-rate poodle, thoroughly experienced in his work, is not easy to beat, and the extraordinary intelligence these dogs display is well-nigh marvellous; but, nevertheless, those who have seen a good English water spaniel or a not-over-stubborn Irish ditto at work, will bear in mind that better work than theirs is not to be witnessed everywhere, and there the matter remains.

It is, however, chiefly in the retrieving part of his business that the poodle distinguishes himself. He is so patient and so indefatigable, and so sensible in his search for wounded or dead game, that, even in the face of the greatest difficulties, he succeeds. In this he is greatly encouraged by his native master, to whom a bird lost is perhaps the day's bread lost; and the dog seems to understand that all-pressing demand on his talents. One will often hear the *huttiers* of the northern coasts of the Continent say of their poodles that they won't come back without the dead or wounded birds; and this is perfectly correct. It is very, very rare indeed that a bird is lost. In this characteristic determination the Irish or the English water spaniel will join issue with the poodle, and, in fact, it seems a distinctive point in all the breeds of water spaniels that, when once they have seen a bird, or heard him, come down, they mean to have him, and will have him too, by hook or by crook; and those marsh shooters who have seen their dogs repeatedly diving after wounded ducks or widgeons will testify that the performance is a treat.

The poodle never "sulks" in his retrieving. The fact is, retrieving seems to be to him quite a second nature. Evidently, he inherits it from a very long list of retrieving ancestors; for, when yet quite a puppy, a poodle will deliberately pick up things and carry them to, or behind, his master. There is, therefore, no need of training him to retrieve. It comes to him as naturally as a duckling takes to water, and he never tires of it. Now, this is of paramount importance for the professional *huttier*, who kills his birds especially in the night, over his decoy ducks, and who therefore must rely implicitly upon his dog to collect the slain and wounded. This the dog does without being spoken to, and he generally concludes his search in the pool by a walk round the shores, in the reeds, for any stray wounded bird; and he is not content with walking there, but paddles in the reeds and grass slowly and carefully, and sniffs and listens now and then, for he knows by experience that some of the birds will dive and hold back under water until he has passed. If, therefore, he hears the slightest splash in the water, he remains perfectly still, and watches for any further signs. Of course, all this shows good breaking—granted; but there is thought in it, too, and I verily believe that some sporting poodles have quite as much sense as their masters.

Respecting poodles for show purposes, I have often wondered why so few have ever made their appearance on the show benches. If beauty and utility combined are really considered a desideratum in show dogs, then I contend that a good, well-bred, working poodle is a most handsome and most useful animal, well worthy of competing, for instance, with the very ugly specimens of retriever proper which nowadays find their way in shows, especially in the curly-coated classes.   And who could say Nay to the judge who should award a prize to a handsome working poodle, entered either with retrievers or with water spaniels (according to the colour of his coat)? for is he not a retriever, and he is not a water spaniel; and, moreover, is he not, in the vast majority of cases, pure bred? Therefore I beg to submit that the exhibition of poodles should be encouraged by all means. There is no more sagacious dog than the poodle, none more persevering in his work, none more affectionate to his master; and the true lines of his body are simply as perfect as can be.   Then, let poodles be rescued from the oblivion into which their breed seems to have fallen of late; and many a true sportsman will say Amen to that from the bottom of his heart, for, morally and physically, the poodle is the very emblem of what a dog, as man's help and companion, should be; and it is a great mistake to allow such a valuable breed to become extinct—as extinct it certainly will soon be, if no effort be made, and that very speedily too, to rescue it from that neglect and indifference which have allowed him almost to disappear from the face of the earth.

The group of dogs selected for illustration, which were exhibited last spring at the Westminster Aquarium by Mr. Walton, consists of two French poodles (white), and a black Russian imported by his present owner; besides which a remarkably clever little rabbit greyhound is introduced, in the act of performing the trick of ascending bar by bar to the top of two ladders, which in the actual exhibition are held for him by assistant dogs.   The large poodle described above is so uncommon in this country that no specimen has been within reach, and he is not, therefore, put on paper by Mr. Baker, who has succeeded admirably with Mr. Walton's pupils.

THE TRUFFLE-DOG.

By "IDSTONE."

We are far behind the Germans, French, and Italians in our knowledge of esculent fungi.   Our Continental neighbours are far more skilled, both in their preservation and production.   They can dry them or preserve them in oil, vinegar, or brine; and in neither case do these conserves lose much of their aroma, flavour, or nutritious quality.   One Italian species is produced by scattering a shallow layer of soil upon a porous slab of stone, and occasionally moistening it with water; another, by slightly burning, and subsequently watering, blocks of hazel-wood; and a third (a species of *Agaricus*) is cultivated by placing the grounds of coffee in places favourable for its growth.   The market returns of Rome show that as much as 4000*l.* a year are expended on those productions; and that the peasantry of France, Germany, and Italy in many places subsist to a great extent upon them, is an established fact.

The truffle—an edible underground fungus—is classed by Berkeley with the *morel*, as one of the *Ascomycetes*, because in these the "spores," or organs of reproduction, are arranged in *asci* (tubular sacs, or vesicles).   The best writers

MRS. MALCOLM'S TRUFFLE DOG "JUDY."

on fungi have arrived at this learned conclusion; but, in spite of all their discoveries, and their elaborate remarks on "spheroidal cells," and "spores," and "fructification taking place in some particular membrane," we believe attempts to cultivate the truffle have failed.

Science has ascertained that they form an intermediate link between the animal and vegetable kingdom, for they do not absorb carbonic acid from the air and give out oxygen; but, like animals, they absorb oxygen and give out carbonic acid.

The truffle is found in many districts of France, Spain, and Italy; and in other parts of these countries, doubtless (as in England), it exists, though it has not been discovered.

In this country it may be found on almost every chalky down, especially where plantations of beech flourish, and in many gentlemen's parks, and on lawns. Hampshire, Wilts, Dorset, and Kent, all these counties produce truffles of rich quality and in great abundance. Beneath the beech, the cedar, the lime, the oak, the hazel, the Scotch fir, it is frequently to be found in clusters, one, two, or three feet apart. It is known to be at Tedworth (the seat of the late Mr. T. Assheton Smith); at Charbro' Park, Dorset (the seat of Mr. Drax); at Olantigh Towers, in Kent; and at Holnest House, in Dorset (both seats belonging to the same gentleman); whilst Kingston Lacey, in Dorset (the property of the Bankeses), produces both morels and truffles. Truffles are also found at Eastwell Park, Kent; at Sir J. Sebright's, in Beechwood Park; at Lord Barrington's; at Lord Jersey's; at Longleat, Wilts; at the Countess of Bridgwater's; at Lord Winchilsea's; and, we believe, at the Earl of Abingdon's seat, near Oxford.

In some of these localities they are found in beds of twenty, thirty, or more. Sometimes they are discovered singly, in most unpromising situations and of extraordinary size; occasionally they are on the surface of the earth, half eaten by hares, squirrels, rats, mice, or rooks—their natural enemies. Sometimes they are raked up with the dead leaves by the gardener; and one of the finest we ever dug was found by a truffle dog close to an old gate post; whilst within a fortnight of the writing of this article a keeper picked up a large truffle dropped from a fir tree by a squirrel.

They are in season from November until March, and when fit for the table are nearly black. Cut open, they are of a close texture, marbled or spotted, with a grey tint. In the summer they are white inside, and give but little smell, and are unsavoury. They vary in size. Occasionally they are so minute as to be scarcely visible, frequently as large as a walnut, and they are commonly as large as a moderate-sized potato.

We have questioned two experienced truffle diggers, and gather from them the following information:

Truffle digging gives employment to many hands during winter, and in the early months of spring 100lb. a week is not an uncommon amount when a man has a good dog, and works hard; and instances have been known of a man digging 35lb. or even 40lb. in a day, where truffles were unsuspected, and the ground had not been "worked."

The truffle with a rough scaly coat, much resembling the fir cone, these men call a "bud truffle;" the smooth-coated variety they call a "garlic truffle." Both are equally good for the table; but there is a *red-skinned truffle* found deeper in the ground, which they assert to be poisonous.

Our informant stated that, some years ago, a specimen was found weighing 3¼lb., and "nearly as large as a half-gallon loaf." This assertion we doubt; but we *do* believe they are frequently met with weighing 1¾lb. or 2lb., though inferior in flavour to the smaller specimens.

In Italy this fungus is hunted with a pig (a fact confirmed by Youatt); in France (as with us) the truffle-hunter depends upon his dog. The breed is rare, and the men dislike to sell them. It is said that about two hundred years ago an old Spaniard brought two dogs into Wiltshire, and made a great deal of money by the sale of truffles which his dogs found for him; and at his death he left his money and his dogs to a farmer from whom he had received some kindness, and that the present dogs are derived from those he left that farmer.

The truffle-dog is a small poodle (nearly a pure poodle), and weighing about 15lb. He is white, or black-and-white, or black, with the black mouth and under-lip of his race. He is a sharp, intelligent, quaint companion, and has the "homeing" faculty of a pigeon. When sold to a new master he has been known to find his way home for sixty miles, and to have travelled the greater part of the way by night.

He is mute in his quest, and should be thoroughly broken from all game. These are essential qualities in a dog whose owner frequently hunts truffles at night—in the shrubberies of mansions protected by keepers and watchmen, who regard him with suspicion. In order to distinguish a *black* dog on these occasions, the hunter furnishes his animal with a white shirt, and occasionally also hunts him in a line.

These dogs are rather longer on the leg than the true poodle, but have exquisite noses, and hunt close to the ground. On the scent of a truffle (especially in the morning or evening, when it gives out most smell), they show all the keenness of a spaniel, working their short-cropped tails, and feathering along the surface of the ground for from twenty to fifty yards. Arrived at the spot where the fungus lies buried, some two or three inches beneath the surface, they dig like a terrier at a rat's hole, and the best of them, if let alone, will disinter the fungus and carry it to his master. It is not usual, however, to allow the dog to exhaust himself in this way, and the owner forks up the truffle and gives the dog his usual reward, a piece of bread or cheese; for this he looks, from long habit, with the keen glance of a Spanish gipsy.

The truffle-hunter is set up in business when he possesses a good dog; all he requires besides will be a short staff, about 2ft. 5in. long, shod with a strong iron point, and at the other end furnished with a two-fanged iron hook. With this implement he can dig the largest truffle, or draw aside the briers or boughs in copse-wood to give his dog free scope to use his nose. He travels frequently thirty or forty miles on his hunting expeditions; and with this (to use a business

The Chinese Crested Dog.

term) inexpensive "plant" keeps a wife and children easily. We know personally one blue grizzled dog of the old truffle breed which supports a family of ten children.

The truffle dog is a delicate animal to rear, and a choice feeder. Being continually propagated from one stock, he has become peculiarly susceptible of all dog diseases, and when that fatal year comes round which desolates the kennel in his quarter, many truffle hunters are left destitute of dogs, and consequently short of bread; for they will not believe (as we believe) that any dog with a keen nose and lively temper can be taught to hunt and find truffles.

The education of the dog commences when he is about three months old. At first he is taught to fetch a truffle, and when he does this well and cheerfully his master places it on the ground, and slightly covers it with earth, selecting one of peculiar fragrance for the purpose. As the dog becomes more expert and keen for the amusement, he buries the truffle deeper, and rewards him in proportion to his progress. He then takes him where he knows truffles to be abundant, or where they have been previously found by a well-broken animal, and marked. Thus he gradually learns his trade, and becomes (as his forefathers have been for many generations) the bread-winner for his master and his master's family; unless he is so fortunate as to become *attaché* to some lordly mansion, or possibly to a royal palace, in which case he is a fortunate dog indeed.

The supply of truffles is uncertain, and the price varies from tenpence to thirty shillings a pound.

In the summer months we have found them, not with a dog, for at this season they have little smell, but from a peculiar cracking of the ground. We have more than once marked the place with a stick, and examined the specimen from time to time. On one occasion we left a truffle from July to November, and could discover no perceptible alteration in its size. Frost destroys those exposed to its influence, and the very old, or very large, or frosted truffles are frequently infested by small brown insects. We have given the result of our inquiries and experience. We must refer our readers for further information to a work of which we have heard, although we have not been able to procure it, "Badham's Esculent Fungi."

THE CHINESE CRESTED DOG.

The Chinese edible dog has been long well known in this country as a curiosity, but the variety furnished with a crest and tufted tail is by no means common. Like the ordinary breed, it is quite hairless on the body and limbs, save only a few scattered and isolated hairs (about a dozen or eighteen on the whole surface); hence the thick tufts on the two extremities are the more remarkable. The skin is spotted, as shown in the engraving.

The individual from which our illustration was taken is the only one remaining of a litter of six, born from parents imported direct from China, both of which are now dead. She is (1866) two years old, but has never bred in consequence of the difficulty experienced in finding a mate of the same strain. As would be expected from her greyhound shape, she is fast and active, and is very affectionate in disposition, so that if the breed could be naturalised it would be acceptable to many as a novelty in the pet department.

THE GREAT DANE.

BY FRANK ADCOCK, Esq.

"The dog has so frequently been represented on canvas that it would be idle to refuse a description of it in a work professing to treat of the dog in all his varieties." So commences the paragraph on this breed in the second edition of "Stonehenge," and so far, it appears to me, such paragraph is strictly accurate. There are only thirteen additional lines in the work alluded to in which to describe the appearance and give the history of this most ancient race of dogs, and I think you will confess that the information therein contained fairly merits the term "meagre."

It is useless to speculate upon the origin of this breed, beyond submitting that it must have come into existence after the Flood at any rate; for otherwise certain long-nosed, loose, and limber animals yclept mastiffs by a Devonian gentleman not unknown to fame would clearly never have maintained their existence. That the Great Dane is sufficiently ancient to "boast the claims of long descent" all the books that I have found bear ample testimony, whilst old paintings, both English and foreign, but more especially the latter, show beyond all dispute that he has remained true to type for a thousand years, more or less; and not only in outward form is this so, for a personal knowledge of these dogs, commencing on the Continent in 1856, has demonstrated the fact that they retain the marvellous courage and power which warranted their use in the arena and as war dogs by the ancients. These dogs have been for some hundreds of years in the possession of the nobility of this country, and are so still. A splendid painting (date fifteenth century, I think) of the head of a dog of this breed can be seen in the Spencer collection at South Kensington, and helps to prove the assertions I make; and there can be no doubt a class for these dogs will shortly be made at our own large shows, as is the case in Paris and other large Continental shows, for the qualities of this breed only require to be known to be valued. Enormous in size, sensitive in nose, of great speed, unyielding in tenacity and courage, and full of intelligence, there is no dog that can so well sustain the part of the dog of the hunter of large game, the guardian of the camp, the keeper's night dog, the companion of long and lonely journeys on horse or on foot; and, when judiciously used as a cross, the result for some of the purposes named is even more useful. Surely such a dog deserves more than the sixteen lines "Stonehenge" favours him with. The following, which I copy from the Monograph of the Mastiffs by H. D. Richardson, will to a great extent bear out the statements I make. Richardson (writing in about 1846 or 1847) says:

This is, I think, the largest dog in existence, and it is likewise decidedly the most serviceable as a destroyer of the wolf and the boar. In this country he is but seldom seen in a state of purity; and is, in any case, seldom recognised as what he really is. The Dane rarely stands less than 30in. in height at the shoulder, and usually more. His head is broad at the temples, and the parietal bones diverge much, thus marking him to be a true mastiff; but, by a singular discrepancy, his muzzle is lengthened more than even that of an ordinary hound, and the lips are not pendulous, or at least very slightly so; his coat, when thoroughbred, is rather short and fine; the tail is fine and tapering; the neck long; the ears small and carried back, but these are invariably taken off when the dog is a whelp. The finest dog of this breed I ever saw was the celebrated Hector, the property of his Grace the Duke of Buccleuch. Hector stood 32in. at the shoulder, and when I saw him was about eighteen years old, and his legs had begun to give way, and his back to fall in; so that, I should say, when a young dog, he stood at least an inch and a half higher, or 33½in., a height equal to that of many Shetland ponies. As many persons contradicted my assertion as to Hector's being the true Saxon boar dog, the same that used to be kept in the royal establishments of that country, I took the liberty of writing to his Grace on the subject, and was kindly favoured with the following reply: "Sir,—I received your letter of the 31st (yesterday). The dog Hector mentioned by you was bought by my brother from a student at Dresden. Of his pedigree I know nothing, but understand the breed is used to hunt the wild boar. His height I do not recollect, but he was the tallest dog I ever saw. He must have been upwards of twenty years of age when he died, as he was supposed to be eight years old when my brother bought him.—Your obedient servant, BUCCLEUCH."

I had likewise the honour of a letter from his Grace's secretary, who very kindly took the pains to have the stuffed remains of poor Hector measured for me. In that state he measured but 29in. to the shoulder; this is, however, by no means much for a dog to shrink, especially when death takes place at so advanced an age.

His Royal Highness Prince Albert has a very fine dog of this description, named Vulcan; and Mr. Maynard kindly furnished me with a description of him, from which I should be disposed to regard him as being of a mixed race—between the great rough boar dog mentioned in last chapter, and the dog at present under consideration. His height is 30in. The colour of the Duke of Buccleuch's dog was a light slate ground, with large brown blotches distributed here and there; that of his Royal Highness's dog is a mixture of smoky grey and black, pretty equally distributed. The hair is close, and inclined to be wiry, judging from a specimen sent me by Mr. Maynard. Mr. Hague, distiller, of Bonnington, near Edinburgh, had a very beautiful dog of this description, colour a light fawn, with markings of a deeper tint. The muzzle of these dogs presents a remarkable peculiarity, appearing as if suddenly brought to a termination by a chop of a hatchet, so abruptly does it become blunt. There are few dogs possessed of such determination as this. Shortly after Hector was brought to Scotland, he selected and pursued a stag, singled him from the herd, and ran him through the domains until he overtook him in the middle of the river Esk, where he killed him.

In further proof of the gigantic size of this dog, a writer in a sporting magazine —Capt. Medwin—says, speaking of a tremendous wolf which fell before his rifle: " Monster as he was, there are dogs in the town of Heidelberg who would have proved more than a match for him or any wolf. This part of Germany possesses a breed much in esteem among the students of the University, larger, more muscular, and fiercer than any with which I am acquainted; and in saying this I do not forget the dogs of the Pyrenees, St. Bernard, Greece, or Lapland. Our mastiffs, now becoming rarer every day, are to them what a cat is to a tiger." I have taken considerable interest in these dogs, ever since I first saw one at Heidelberg some twenty years ago, and have ever been on the watch to find and secure a really good specimen. In 1863 there were, I think, five exhibited at the Cremorne show, and amongst them a magnificent specimen shown by Capt. Palmer, and called Sam, a print of whom, cut from one of the illustrated papers, I had until quite recently. His fault was his colour, being brindle and white. There was also at that time in London a very handsome brindled dog of this breed, but he did not appear to have that amount of "go" in him that distinguishes it. There have been a great many shown since then, but all of them deficient in size, or in some other vital point ; of these Nero was a remarkably good dog but for that defect. At the last Kennel Club Show there were, I think, five, including my own dog, and some of them were exceedingly good, particularly the almost too beautiful blue bitch shown by Lady Charles Innes Ker. At the Cremorne show there were no dachshunds exhibited, and five Danes. Now the former form large and interesting classes. At the last Paris show the class for Grand Danois contained, I think, twenty-two entries, and a splendid class it was. Surely it is time we English amateurs took this splendid and useful breed in hand, and do for it what we have done for many another which was never half so well worth the trouble.

There is to me considerable pleasure to be derived from a belief that I am in possession of a dog who is capable of doing something more than hold his own with any dog of any other breed ; and I doubt not a desire to be in a similar position operates upon the minds of other Englishmen, and that it can be gratified at the sacrifice of some little trouble and expense, and will, I have no doubt. Should "Stonehenge" deem it necessary that this breed should meet with some considera-tion at his hands in the new edition of his work on dogs, I shall, in the interests of those who admire them, be very happy to give him further information, illustrations, and extracts ; or, should he be unable to find a better, and is desirous of personally studying the physical and mental attributes of a dog of this breed, my dog Satan is at his disposal for as long as he thinks proper to keep him.

[In spite of Mr. Adcock's urgent pleading for this breed, I cannot consider it as one of " The Dogs of the British Islands."—" STONEHENGE."]

In Royal 4to., bevelled boards, gilt edges, price 12s.,

PHEASANTS

FOR

COVERTS AND AVIARIES:

THEIR

NATURAL HISTORY AND PRACTICAL MANAGEMENT.

BY W. B. TEGETMEIER, F.Z.S.

Illustrated with numerous full-page Engravings drawn from life by T. W. Wood.

"No one will regret that Mr. Tegetmeier's skill in bringing to bear upon any department of the history of gallinaceous birds the stores of research which he has amassed has been directed into this channel. With him for guide and Mentor we may fairly hope to be spared absurd exaggerations, and to find reasonable explanations of statements about which doubt might suggest itself."—*Saturday Review*, Oct. 18, 1873.

London: ' THE FIELD ' OFFICE, 346, Strand, W.C.

THE FIELD
THE FARM · THE GARDEN
THE COUNTRY GENTLEMAN'S NEWSPAPER

| No.] | SATURDAY. | [Price 6d. |

LEADERS
ON interesting Sporting subjects are given every week in THE FIELD.

"SHOOTING."
CONTAINS: Original Articles and Correspondence on Shooting Adventures, Game Preservation, New and Old Shooting Grounds, New Guns, Cartridges, and all the paraphernalia of a sportsman.

"ANGLING."
ARTICLES and Correspondence on Fishing, Reports from the Rivers, Oyster and Salmon Culture, and everything connected with river, lake, or sea fishing are given.

"YACHTING."
REPORTS of Matches, Accounts of Cruises, Correspondence, &c., will be found here in the season.

"THE FARM."
GIVES practical advice for the proper management of Farms (both arable and pasture) and Farm Stock.

"ARCHERY."
ALL the principal Matches of the week throughout the United Kingdom are reported during the season.

"DOGS AND HORSES."
ARTICLES and Correspondence on the above subjects appear constantly from the pens of well-known authors.

"HUNTING."
FULL and accurate reports of the Runs, with the various Packs of Hounds, Hunting Appointments, Visits to the Kennels, Notes from the Shires, &c., are given during the season.

"HUNTING APPOINTMENTS."
AN Alphabetical List of the Appointments for the ensuing week are given during the season.

"THE NATURALIST"
CONTAINS Observations, Articles, and Correspondence from Naturalists of note.

"THE COUNTRY HOUSE."
UNDER this heading will be found Articles, Notes, Queries, &c., on all Subjects and Inventions that concern the Country House.

EVERY SATURDAY
PRICE 6d.; Stamped 6½d.

"ROWING."
THE Reports of Matches, Articles on Training, and Letters from men well versed in the subject, are given every week.

"THE VETERINARIAN."
GIVES full and practical instruction for the management of Cattle in health and disease.

"COURSING."
REPORTS of all Meetings are given weekly for the duration of the season.

"CROQUET."
IS thoroughly discussed, and the pros and cons of disputed points are carefully weighed.

"FOOTBALL"
IS thoroughly reported by competent authorities.

"ATHLETIC SPORTS"
ARE fully reported every week during the season.

"POULTRY AND PIGEONS"
ARE given of all Shows.

"NOTES AND QUESTIONS."
WITH their Answers, on every subject interesting to Country Gentlemen, will be found in their respective departments.

"CRICKET."
FULL and accurate Reports of all Matches of interest are given during the season.

"THE TURF."
REPORTS of all Race Meetings, except those of only local interest, are always given.

A CHESS PROBLEM
IS given constantly.

"TRAVEL."
CONTAINS graphic and trustworthy Articles upon Explorations in new or little known parts of the world, with accounts of their flora, fauna, and geological formations, &c., and the manners and customs of the natives.

"THE GARDEN."
THOROUGHLY practical instruction for laying out and managing Flower and Kitchen Gardens, Grape Houses, Orchard Houses, Forcing Beds, &c., are given.

"THE LIBRARY TABLE."
CONTAINS Reviews of Books on Sports, Hunting, Cards, Natural History, and in fact all those that treat of subjects that come within the scheme of THE FIELD.

"SKATING."
ARTICLES and Diagrams on the above are given during the season.

"FOREIGN FIELD SPORTS."
ARTICLES descriptive of Sport in all parts of the world.

"CARDS."
WHIST Hands illustrated by "Cavendish," with Notes on other Games.

"RACQUETS."
THE University and other great Matches of the season are given.

"BILLIARDS."
THE University and other great Matches of the season are given.

"STEEPLECHASING."
ALL Steeplechases of general interest are fully reported.

"THE MARKETS."
IN this department will be found the Current Prices of Farm Produce, including Hay, Straw, Manure, Cattle, Corn, Poultry, Butter, Fruit, Vegetables, &c.

SPECIMEN COPY
FOR six postage stamps.

REGISTERED
FOR transmission abroad.

POST-OFFICE ORDERS
SHOULD be drawn on the Somerset House Order Office, payable to Horace Cox, 346, Strand, London.

SUBSCRIPTIONS
MUST be paid in advance.

SUBSCRIPTION:
QUARTERLY, 7s.; Half-yearly, 14s.; Yearly, £1 8s.

OFFICE:
346, STRAND, LONDON, W.C.

FORM OF ORDER.

To MR. HORACE COX, 346, Strand, London, W.C.

Please send me THE FIELD, *commencing with last Saturday's number, and continue sending it until countermanded. I enclose £   :   :   for* _____

Subscription in advance.

Date _____   Name _____

                                  Address _____